# Organization, Crime – Organisation, Management und Kriminalität

**Series Editors**
Markus Pohlmann, Heidelberg, Germany
Stefan Bär, Heidelberg, Germany
Friederike Elias, Heidelberg, Germany
Julian Klinkhammer, Heidelberg, Germany
Elizangela Valarini, Heidelberg, Germany

Die Reihe ist im Bereich der *Organization Studies* angesiedelt und hat ihren Schwerpunkt im Schnittfeld von Wirtschafts- und Organisationssoziologie. Sie widmet sich dem Zusammenhang von verschiedenen institutionellen Feldern (Wirtschaft, Medizin, Staat etc.) mit den Organisations- und Managementformen, die in diesen vorherrschen. Neben organisationssoziologischen Studien werden managementsoziologische Analysen sowie Studien zur organisationalen Kriminalität in die Reihe aufgenommen. Darüber hinaus beschäftigt sich die Reihe mit aktuellen Themen (z.B. Liberalisierung der Wirtschaft, Subjektivierung der Arbeitswelt, Ökonomisierung der Medizin oder der Politik) und sie hinterfragt gängige Erklärungen öffentlicher Skandale, die von Manipulation, Korruption oder Betrug in Organisationen handeln.

This book series establishes itself in the field of *organization studies* and focuses on the intersection between economic and organizational sociology. It is dedicated to the context of various institutional fields (economy, medicine, state, etc.) with the predominant organizational and management forms therein. In addition to studies on organizational sociology, management-related sociological analyses as well as studies on organizational crimes are included in the series. Also enclosed are current developments, such as Neoliberalism in the economy, the economization of medicine as well as the state of and the explanation for current scandals of manipulation, corruption and fraud.

More information about this series at http://www.springer.com/series/15792

Markus Pohlmann · Gerhard Dannecker · Elizangela Valarini
Editors

# Bribery, Fraud, Cheating

## How to Explain and to Avoid Organizational Wrongdoing

With a foreword by the editors

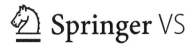

*Editors*
Markus Pohlmann
Max-Weber-Institut für Soziologie
Universität Heidelberg
Heidelberg, Germany

Elizangela Valarini
Max-Weber-Institut für Soziologie
Universität Heidelberg
Heidelberg, Germany

Gerhard Dannecker
Institut für deutsches, europäisches
und internationales Strafrecht
und Strafprozessrecht
Universität Heidelberg
Heidelberg, Germany

With support of the Volkswagen Foundation

Organization, Management and Crime – Organisation, Management und Kriminalität
ISBN 978-3-658-29061-0      ISBN 978-3-658-29062-7  (eBook)
https://doi.org/10.1007/978-3-658-29062-7

© Springer Fachmedien Wiesbaden GmbH, part of Springer Nature 2020
This work is subject to copyright. All rights are reserved by the Publisher, whether the whole or part of the material is concerned, specifically the rights of translation, reprinting, reuse of illustrations, recitation, broadcasting, reproduction on microfilms or in any other physical way, and transmission or information storage and retrieval, electronic adaptation, computer software, or by similar or dissimilar methodology now known or hereafter developed.
The use of general descriptive names, registered names, trademarks, service marks, etc. in this publication does not imply, even in the absence of a specific statement, that such names are exempt from the relevant protective laws and regulations and therefore free for general use.
The publisher, the authors and the editors are safe to assume that the advice and information in this book are believed to be true and accurate at the date of publication. Neither the publisher nor the authors or the editors give a warranty, expressed or implied, with respect to the material contained herein or for any errors or omissions that may have been made. The publisher remains neutral with regard to jurisdictional claims in published maps and institutional affiliations.

This Springer VS imprint is published by the registered company Springer Fachmedien Wiesbaden GmbH part of Springer Nature.
The registered company address is: Abraham-Lincoln-Str. 46, 65189 Wiesbaden, Germany

# Preface

The fight against corruption, organizational wrongdoing, malpractice and organized crime has entered a new era. The regulation and combat of public and private corruption as well as organized crime has become an international standard of anti-corruption legislation and law enforcement, which has been adopted by many countries. The global diffusion of regulatory agencies, which began in the 1990s, took place mainly in countries with long lasting tradition of a regulatory state and regulatory capitalism such as Brazil and China. In a joint effort to fight corruption, new international cooperation agreements were signed; international guidelines and governmental regulations were tightened and sanctions and penalties have become more severe. The boom in the regulatory state was accompanied by a boom of compliance measures in the private sector, in companies, hospitals, football associations, etc. However, the trend of more stringent regulations at international, national and organizational level does not seem to have produced the expected results. Illegal behavior could not be prevented and new white-collar crime was exposed. This has happened not only through the transformation of established habits and customs of giving and taking into illegal acts or through more thorough monitoring, but also through the inability of globally operating companies to comply with all—often contradictory—new rules and laws in the different countries where they do business. New scandals at Volkswagen, Petrobras and Glencore raise the question whether they stem from the fact that the new regulations boom exerts an excessive burden on companies or simply from some individuals' determination to commit illicit acts such as deliberate profit-seeking at any price.

This book is the result of an intensive debate that aims to explain the emergence and persistence of organizational and individual malpractice in the light of the new regulation boom, but also to come up with effective measures to combat and prevent such illegal practices. This dialog began in 2015 with the international research project "The Fight against Corruption and Manipulation—Regulation and Self-Regulation in Medicine and the Economy", at Heidelberg University. This international research project was coordinated by Professor Markus Pohlmann of the Max-Weber-Institute for Sociology, Professor Gerhard Dannecker of the Institute for German, European and International Criminal Law and Law of Criminal Procedure; Professor Dieter Dölling and Professor Dieter Hermann of the Institute for Criminology. It is based on a research grant from the Volkswagen Foundation. The Heidelberg research team investigated the contradiction between better law enforcement and more comprehensive measures to combat corporate crime, corruption, malpractice and the limited preventive effect they have. The study began with a comparison between two sectors: industry and medicine (organ transplantation) in two countries, USA and Germany. In recent years, the research network has expanded to include other countries such as Brazil and China, integrating additional areas such as funding of political parties.

Within this research project, numerous publications, lecture series and conferences have been presented. This book is the result of the latest international and interdisciplinary scientific contributions in the field of organizational deviation and organized crime, which were presented at the Herrenhausen Symposium "Bribery, Fraud, Cheating—How to Explain and to Avoid Organizational Wrongdoing?" in October 2017 in Hanover. Many people have contributed to the success of this edited volume. Our gratitude goes to all authors of this book and referents at the Herrenhausen Symposium who contributed to a broader understanding of organized crime, corporate crime, corruption and malpractice in organ transplantation. Many thanks to the Heidelberg research team for their firm commitment to achieving the expected research goals, especially for their meticulous organization of the Herrenhausen Symposium and the time and energy spent on preparing for this book: Yuanyuan Liu, Alexander Fürstenberg, Dr. Elizangela Valarini, Dr. Julian Klinkhammer, Dr. Sebastian Starystach, Dr. Friederilke Elias, Jiawei Mao, Dr. Christian Mayer, Christin Schultze, Ludmila Hustus, Felizia Rein and Sonja Linder. We thank Jiawei Mao and Laura Hauck for proof-reading the texts line by line. Last but not least, we thank the sponsor of the Herrenhausen Symposium, the Volkswagen Foundation, in particular Dr. Vera Szoelloesi-Brenig, who has always supported our Herrenhausen Symposium with great commitment and enthusiasm.

*Markus Pohlmann, Gerhard Dannecker, Elizangela Valarini*

Heidelberg, September 2019

# Content

Introduction – Money is only half of the story ........................................................ 1
*Markus Pohlmann*

Organizational wrongdoing: Bribery, fraud, cheating – Insights into the
Herrenhausen Symposium, October 5-7, 2017 ..................................................... 25
*Ludmila Hustus and Christin Schultze*

## Organized crime, money laundering and corruption in Europe

The fight against the mafia in Italy and Europe ................................................... 43
*Roberto Scarpinato*

The mafia in the media ......................................................................................... 57
*Petra Reski*

The fight against organized crime ........................................................................ 67
*David Ryan Kirkpatrick*

## Corporate crime and political corruption in South America

Anti-corruption in Brazil – Criticisms and developments ................................... 77
*Fausto De Sanctis*

Operation Car Wash – The new paradigm to fight corruption .......................... 105
*João Pedro Gebran Neto*

The incomplete transition. A review of the recent changes in Brazil's electoral financing model .................................................................................. 121
*Wagner Pralon Mancuso*

'Do not try to outsource dirty business into your Value Chain'. An interview with Matthias Kleinhempel............................................................................ 145
*Julian Klinkhammer*

The FIFA's case and corruption in Brazil. An expert dialogue with Markus Asner and Fausto De Sanctis ............................................................................ 151
*Elizangela Valarini and Wagner Pralon Mancuso*

## Corruption in China

Corporate compliance and industrial sophistication ......................................... 167
*Xiuyin Shi*

Corruption issues in China. An interview with Jianyuan Yang ........................ 187
*Anja Senz*

## Fraud in medicine

Manipulation of medical patient data in organ transplantation as attempted homicide?........................................................................................................... 207
*Torsten Verrel*

## How to explain and to prevent corporate crime?

Esprit de corps as a source of deviant behavior in organizations. Applying an old concept with a new livery .............................................................................. 219
*Peter Graeff and Julia Kleinewiese*

Corporate non-compliance and corporate identity building – A management dilemma. Early indicators of organizationally driven deviance traps .............. 247
*Christiane Gebhardt*

Overcoming the current system of corporate criminal law – sanctioning corporate citizens. Crime prevention within the limits of the rule of law ........................ 285
*Gerhard Dannecker and Thomas Schröder*

Does illegality become natural? Systemic and preventive effects of the market economy .................................................................................................... 321
*Kai-D. Bussmann*

About the authors ...................................................................................... 349

# Introduction – Money is only half of the story

*Markus Pohlmann*

Scandals never stop. From Siemens to VW and Petrobras, from FIFA to the DFB—in Germany as well as in other countries—it is the large, renowned companies, clinics, associations and parties that come into the limelight because of their illegal activities with sometimes severe consequences. It is striking that a wide range of areas from economy to politics, from medicine to sports have been affected. Not only countries rife with graft, but also those considered less prone to corruption have been ensnared. Therefore, the question arises as to whether these cases of corruption and cheating have anything in common. Is there a specific pattern of crime at work and has it increased in importance?

At the same time, we cannot complain about too little regulation, laws, or preventive measures. On the contrary, we can speak of a regulatory boom over the last two decades. Although this has brought a lot of cheating and corruption to light, the preventive effect was obviously not strong enough. The explanation of this phenomenon as well as the alternatives to conventional forms of prevention are the topics of this volume.

So far, we still know too little about the common pattern behind these scandals. They usually revolve around organizations as well as their high-ranking executives in representational functions. Still, the circumstances under which organizations stray from and return to legal paths are largely uncharted territory. While many authors deal with criminal organizations that are systematically pursuing illegal goals, organizations that try to achieve their legal goals with (partially) illegal means remain under researched. However, it is only when one knows the conditions under which organizations tend to use illegal means that effective prevention can be devised.

While the media rushes to target individuals and the so called "bad apples", the scientific contribution is to uncover the system behind these cases and to seek ways to effectively prevent it. The affected organizations often have a history, e.g., in the case of cheating at VW, and operate within an environment in which cheating is not a rare phenomenon. The hierarchies and incentive systems of organizations also play a role. They can—unintentionally—imply that they resort to illegal means. After all, the use of these illegal means is usually beneficial for the organization. Only if the cheating is detected, harm to the organization is the consequence. Therefore, we are dealing here with a different form of crime than e.g., fraud to the detriment of the organization, which requires other means of control.

Against this background, this volume has emerged out of a forum for discussions that aim to explain the recent cases of corruption and cheating and to find ways to reduce them. It therefore puts the cases of corruption and cheating on the agenda in various countries (Germany, Brazil, China, and USA) and sectors (medicine, business, sports, and politics). Its goal is to discuss the similarities and differences of these cases and to gather knowledge about the conditions that lead organizations and their senior staff to leave the path of legality at a very high risk to the organization and their careers. It deals with the way in which current perpetrators have internalized the unwritten rules of the respective organization.

This approach has already been tested and further developed in the research project "The Fight against Corruption and Manipulation—Regulation and Self-Regulation in Medicine and the Economy" funded by the Volkswagen Foundation. The volume emerged from the contributions of many experts at the Herrenhausen Symposium on October $5^{th}$–$7^{th}$, 2017 at Herrenhausen Palace. Around one hundred participants from academia, law enforcement agencies, law firms and corporations participated in the international event.

## The return of the regulatory state

In times of globalization, economic activities not only produce more profits, but also a greater number of scandals, and the suspicion is omnipresent that what has been revealed is just the tip of the iceberg. Organized crime, corruption and organizational misconduct seem to be pervasive all around the globe; however, the power of the judiciary and law enforcement agencies often ends at the state border. At the same time, a race has already begun whose rules shall be applied to control the global economy.

Corruption and corporate crime as well as the regulatory fight against them are transcultural, global phenomena. Fraud schemes, laws, and compliance measures are not only crossing national borders, but are very often transcultural by origin. Most of the violations of the Foreign Corrupt Practices Act (FCPA) documented by the United States Department of Justice (DOJ) were carried out across various nations, promoted by cross-cultural networks of firms, agencies, and actors. Moreover, the emergence of international anti-corruption regimes, and the converging modes of law enforcement—inspired by the role model of the US legislation—in East Asian, Latin American and European countries provide evidence for isomorphic changes towards far stricter and more specialized regulations.

The fight against corruption has entered a new phase in the last two decades. On the one hand, the regulatory state has made an impressive comeback and new anti-corruption laws have sprung up almost everywhere in the world. On the other hand, the rapid rise of NGOs worldwide with almost exponential growth in terms of the number of civil society actors has placed companies, administrations, and governments under constant observation. The fact that the world map of perceived corruption is dark red in most countries also indicates that the everyday give and take at the expense of third parties is now also perceived as corruption. Even though corruption is part of everyday life, it is beginning to be widely recognized that corruption should not go unpunished. The many civil society actors who have set the countries on the track of no longer treating corruption as a trivial offense have also contributed to this.

During the 1990s, the global diffusion of regulatory agencies (Braithwaite 2008; Jordana et al. 2011; Rugy and Warren 2009) took place in many countries (Braithwaite 2008). Despite large differences across legal spheres and the persistence of legal loopholes, the convergence towards international anti-corruption regimes have channeled the recent development of national legislation against corruption. The FCPA also served as a model for the OECD Convention on Combating the Bribery of Foreign Public Officials in International Business Transactions, which came into force in 1999. Similarly, the United Nations adopted a Convention against Corruption (UNCAC) in 2003 and added anti-corruption to the original nine principles of its Global Compact (Barkemeyer et al. 2015, p. 351). Latin American, and East Asian countries, where corruption is part of everyday life, joined the global "anti-corruption campaign", and moved into the direction of fighting corruption with new legislations and new law enforcement. Latin Americans, as Castaneda puts it, are denouncing corruption as never before (Castañeda 2016, p. 145).

How do global players react to this new regulatory thrust and to the new sets of norms that emerge on the organizational, the national, and even the global level? This is one of the questions our volume is giving answers to.

## The blooming of organized crime and the difficulties to fight against it

We begin our volume with the Italian Mafia: The Mafia is seen as a very successful and persistent criminal organization. It is not without reason that the police and judiciary speak of "organized" crime in their case. Are we dealing with an organization and where does it come from? To answer these questions, we highlight the social forms of the Italian Mafia. Above all, we place the form and type of membership at the center, in order to differentiate between organized and organizational crime.

A first understanding of the Italian Mafia relates the phenomenon to the idea of an organization. We do have hierarchies—from the supreme position of the so-called godfather or "capo dei capi" to the "consiglieri" (counselor) down to the simple members (Arlacchi 1995; Paoli 1999)—and the police speaks of an organization as well. Organizations also imply clear instruction structures, over- and under-subordinate relationships, and joint objectives. Everything is true for the Italian Mafia.

At second sight, the Italian Mafia reminds more of an archaic fraternity with no organizational kind of membership. The Italian Mafia usually recruits its members by cooptation. One cannot apply. Very often, family and clan members are proposed and accepted after consultation with the other Mafia heads of families. In this type of recruiting and the associated initiation rituals one recognizes a peculiarity already: The oath of obedience and silence to death does not resemble organizational recruiting but reminds rather of secret societies. Thus, the entry does not take the form of a labor contract, as is customary in organizations. There are no contracts and no termination of membership. Mafia membership takes the form of a "fraternity agreement". It presupposes the inclusion of the whole person, of body and soul—far beyond what an organization usually demands of its staff (see also Hessinger 2002). What is even more intriguing, there is no exit option once you became a member. The mafia is not an "organization" from which one can exit alive. In most cases, the exit takes place through death, specifically through the murder of those willing to leave. Even if you go to jail, you cannot escape their influence. Only a witness protection program of the state may be able to offer protection, but still the witnesses do not feel safe. According to the membership rules, the mafia is not an organization. It is an "archaic fraternity" that is devoted to criminal offenses determined by profit and/or power aspirations. Murder and manslaughter, the endangering of life and limb are constitutive for the business model of the mafia, blood revenge on family and clan is part of their tradition.

On the other hand, the police and judiciary are modern forms of organizations for which the total inclusion of life and limb are the exception rather than the rule. It is true that "in certain situations, even officials of the police, the penal system and the fire brigade [...] may even have the duty to put their life and health in danger". However, we expect, e.g., a police officer in Germany to commit his or her life only if it is necessary to defend the interests of the state or the well-being of the citizens and if the risk to be taken into account is calculable. Difficulties in fighting the Italian Mafia result from the fact that for the staff of the modern organizations in charge of the task, total commitment or inclusion is the exception, not the rule. Who will risk the physical well-being of himself, spouse, children, and relatives in exchange for a small salary, a shady reputation and bureaucratic disregard? No organization, neither the police nor the judiciary, can generate such commitment and dedication on a regular basis. Falcone and Borsellino were among the few exceptions that confirmed this rule. In any case, this structural disadvantage of the modern organizations in combating the mafia results from the fact that the Mafia is not an organization. It can be contained by the rule of law, prosecuted by the police and the judiciary, but not completely eliminated (Paoli 2008). Thus, the Italian Mafia always remains one step ahead because of its "backwardness" as an archaic fraternity. It's a social structure from an old world, which protrudes into the new world of organizations that is not able to fight against this kind of ancient association with the modern means of law enforcement (Baecker 2000). But also the use of global means and global infrastructures to organize global crimes of these archaic fraternities is hard to combat by administrative organizations that are bound to the nation states or even federal states. Because and as long as the mafia succeeds in strategically linking up with modern global organizations and systematically exploiting or corrupting their positions (Luhmann 2000, p. 385ff.), it could continue to thrive. Also because of the global footprint in their criminal activities, the archaic fraternities are one step ahead of the mainly regional and national operating police and judicial organizations.

In his paper, senior attorney general of Sicily and probably the most experienced mafia hunter *Roberto Scarpinato* explains that today, the mafia no longer corresponds to the picture that coined the book "The Godfather". The Italian Mafia is not confined to southern Italy, doesn't draw attention to itself with murder and manslaughter and cannot be separated from the legal economy clearly anymore. Scarpinato describes them as a "silent mafia" operating internationally, profiting from the growing global demand for illegal goods such as prostitution, drugs, garbage trafficking, and money laundering and gambling. The Italian Mafia is a global player. Reports in the media about violence would only disturb the legal market in their flourishing business and their "hidden partnership." For example, in 2007, when six people were bullied by a mafia killer squad, Duisburg mafia orders were recognized by the mafia as a tactical error. However, the national security authorities have their hands tied when investigating "transnational mafia capitalism": The proposal to set up a European investigative authority was shelved because of national political interests. The journalist *Petra Reski*, who has been researching and publishing on the Italian Mafia for years, describes Germany not only as a place of refuge, but as a sanctuary for their activities. Anyone who, like the media, draws attention to their ploys, will be prosecuted with all legal means. This year she lost a civil lawsuit against an Italian restaurateur living in Germany whom she had described as a member of the "Ndrangheta" in a report. Reski was sentenced by court to stop naming him. The research of critical journalists is not protected in Germany. She wants to point out the great responsibility of the media. Senior Public Prosecutor *David Ryan Kirkpatrick* turns another spotlight on the subject of the Italian Mafia in Germany in this volume. According to kirkpatrick, the Italian Mafia helps the legal economy to save social security contributions in an amount, that the German state loses estimated € 300 billion in social fraud each year. The mafia runs a parallel economy in Germany that the official statistics of the police (2017: 562 Mafia members) hardly can figure out. They need a new investigation strategy: "Follow the money trail!" recommends Kirkpatrick. Rather than individual national investigators, however, they would need significantly more international personnel—Kirkpatrick cites the figure of 20,000 additional civil servants—to prosecute cross-border money laundering, and he is especially concerned that organized crime was not only a consequence of insufficient law enforcement but also a sign of weakness of the political system.

**Corruption in Brazil, Argentina, Latin America: Going haywire?**

The Brazilian federal judge Sérgio Moro, responsible for the criminal processes of Operation Car Wash at the Federal Court of Paraná, detonated a political tinderbox when he lashed out against the former President Luiz Inácio Lula da Silva and political corruption in his political party, the Workers' Party (PT). Not only have the accusations against the two-term ex-President Lula, the impeachment against his successor Dilma Roussef, the arrest of the President of the Parliament, Eduardo Cunha (PMDB) and current proceedings against roughly 279 politicians robbed the Brazilians of their sleep, the sheer multitude of corruption scandals in the economy also keeps them in suspense. Since the start of Operation Car Wash (Operação Lava Jato) in March 2014, politicians, senior executives and the judiciary have been in great turmoil. Having ensnared the construction industry and Petrobrás, the state-run oil company, the spectrum of corruption is now threatening to envelop other state-owned enterprises, such as the nuclear energy industry, with the construction of nuclear power plants as well as other federal entities, such as the Brazilian Development Bank (BNDES), a federal savings bank (Caixa Econômica Federal), etc. The Operation Car Wash became the largest ever corruption case exposed and investigated in Brazilian history.

What was going on in Brazil? And what was behind these scandals? Whereas criminal processes and sentences, if ever occurred, were half-hearted and only pronounced with the exclusion of the general public, they now come fast and furious, hit hard and are well publicized. With the enacting of the Freedom of Information Act[1] (N. 12.527/2011), anyone who is curious enough and has a bit of free time can easily follow the trials on official sites of the judicial system, but also in the media, for example on YouTube. Punishment is substantial. For example, Marcello Odebrecht, the president of one of the biggest business groups in Brazil, and a descendant from a German immigrant family, was sentenced to 19.4 years in prison by the Federal Court of Paraná for bribery, participation in organized crime (cartel), and money laundering.

In this section of the volume, we will investigate the unlawful practices of the Brazilian companies involved in the Petrobras's plot and their relationship with the public sector. We attempt to demonstrate the institutionalized patterns in a deviant environment and the competitive pressure, which enterprises are embedded in and exposed to. Furthermore, we examine the political corruption and its prosecution in Brazil.

Section 2 addresses "Corporate Crime and Political Corruption in South America." *Fausto De Sanctis*, Federal Appeals Judge at the Federal Court of the 3rd Region, São Paulo, reported on corruption and anti-corruption measures in Brazil. While the public opinion favors transparency and integrity and shows increasingly less tolerance for corruption and money laundering, the judicial system is lagging behind. De Sanctis therefore calls for better measures in order to tackle corruption effectively. The fact that De Sanctis is a symbol of the Brazilian anti-corruption struggle was highlighted by the Federal Appeals Judge at the Federal Court of the 4th Region, Porto Alegre, *João Pedro Gebran Neto* at

---

[1] According to the Freedom of Information Act, enacted in November 2011, all public agencies, members of the direct administration of the Executive, Legislature, including the Audit Courts and Judiciary and Public Prosecution as well as all municipalities, public foundations, state-owned enterprises, mixed-capital-companies, and other entities directly or indirectly controlled by the Federal Government, States, Federal District and Municipalities must to divulge all information related to their administration. This includes income and expenses as well as information that are of collective interest (http://www.planalto.gov.br/ccivil_03/_ato2011-2014/2011/lei/l12527.htm).

the beginning of his speech at the Symposium. Currently 760 cases are pending, 67 criminal cases, 18 appeals have been decided, 107 people have been convicted and 80 illegal arrangements have been discovered. Central to the success of the anti-corruption authorities was the fact that in Brazil no direct evidence of corruption must be present to open a procedure. The papers of the two judges were supplemented by the political scientist *Wagner Pralon Mancuso*. He focused on electoral financing in Brazil. In view of the situation that has arisen, however, efforts must be made to ensure no donor enjoys bigger political influence than others. Nevertheless, the answers to the question of how framework conditions for a fair election campaign should be designed are still unclear. In Brazil, at any rate, there was for many years no cap on donations to political campaigns. Hence, the dependence of the candidates on individual donors was particularly high.

What are the special challenges of combatting corruption in transnational companies? This question was pursued by *Matthias Kleinhempel*, who used to be a manager at Siemens, in an interview with *Julian Klinkhammer*. Corruption can no longer be fought only by compliance, i.e. rather procedural, technical rule compliance, as all major corporations also work in countries fested with corruption. Instead, companies would have to run risk management and, above all, strengthen the corporate culture at senior management level. It is also important that they take responsibility for their subcontractors. The main focus of compliance programs with "dilemma-based training" was on employees who basically wanted to act correctly but who face difficult decision-making situations. The goal must be prevention.

*Elizangela Valarini* and *Wagner Pralon Mancuso* discussed the FIFA case and corruption in Brazil with *Markus Asner* and *Fausto De Sanctis*. In particular, they talked about FIFA's role in the regulation of football and the slow onset of public and institutional support for investigations concerning illicit activities in football in Brazil as well as emotional connections, organized crime, and the role of politics in hosting the World Cup in 2014.

## Tigers and flies must be beaten: Corruption in China

"Both tigers and flies must be beaten" is now the catchphrase in the official discourse of China's anti-graft campaign and claims to be targeting both high-ranking and low-ranking corrupt officials in the Chinese state apparatus.

In today's China, this is not just a catchphrase, it is serious politics. The measures taken three years ago by President Xi Jinping have drastic effects. For example, ex-Minister of Railways Liu Zhijun was sentenced to death with reprieve in 2013, and former security chief Zhou Yongkang, a member of the Politburo Standing Committee, was sentenced to life imprisonment in 2015. Within the state apparatus, about 300,000 civil servants were charged with bribery.

By mid-2015, 93 officers had been arrested at ministerial level alone. 29 top managers from among the top 100 enterprises (2014 ranking) were charged. The background of President Xi Jinping's anti-corruption campaign is difficult to assess: Are they part of political selections or are they a step towards more rule of law? What is really behind the corruption proceedings in China? The people consider them to be more of a political selection, as the speech of a "selective anti-corruption" illustrates.

The anti-corruption campaign has many facets. For example, the government has set up online platforms so that the population can report corruption cases at any time. Well-known cases included, among other things, the so-called "house uncle", who possessed 22 real estates whilst earning a monthly salary of merely 10,000 RMB (approximately 1.200 euro) and the "clock uncle", which adorned himself with a dozen luxury watches. Such anti-graft efforts are popular among the population. At the same time, the Communist Party has published a new prohibition catalog for party members. According to this, party members may for example not do anything extravagant like holding sprawling state banquets or engaging in inappropriate sexual relations, at the risk of disciplinary sanctions.

Measures to combat corruption have also targeted active corruption i.e., bribes paid by individuals or companies. Except for the case of British pharmaceutical company GlaxoSmithKline (GSK), which was a bribe-giver, all the defendants were the recipients of bribes—primarily party officials. Ex-Premier Wen Jiabao summarized the matter as follows: The bribery stems from the abuse of power by the officials. That is why the officials who take bribes must be monitored and punished. This is illustrated by the prominent case of former Vice Chairman of the National Development and Reform Commission Liu Tienan. According to the court ruling, he has received around 36 million yuan (about 4.5 million euros) in bribes and was subsequently sentenced to life imprisonment. Others, however, were not charged. For example, Song Zuowen, chairman of Nanshan Group, and Qiu Jianlin, chief executive of Zhejiang Hengyi Group Co. Ltd, had over the years bribed Liu with cash and valuable gifts worth 7.54 million RMB and 16.49 million RMB respectively, according to court files. This one-sided approach has been heavily criticized as providing incentives for companies to bribe officials.

The prominent case of the pharmaceutical company GSK has shown the other side of the corruption fight. On October 27, the draft for the Ninth Amendment to the Criminal Law of the PRC was issued. In it, the legislature enforces penalties against persons who pay bribes. The risk of penalty therefore increases significantly for the bribe-payers. This is another reason why both foreign and Chinese companies attach greater importance to compliance. By 2015, 60.6 percent of state-owned enterprises and 23.8 percent of privately-owned Chinese companies have established internal compliance programs.

The question of whether the compliance measures in Chinese companies will be taken seriously or languish in obscurity remains open. At any rate, the "storm of anti-corruption" continues. However how long will these measures last is unclear. China has persistently refused to introduce rule of law modelled after western democracies and the cultural tradition of giving and receiving gifts is still firmly anchored. Up to now, the Communist Party has not been able to change that; rather, the Party itself is embedded in this culture.

A theoretical approach to understanding corporate compliance was presented by *Xiuyin Shi* from the Chinese Academy of Social Sciences. Chinese and foreign companies have engaged in corrupt behaviors in China on a massive scale in recent years. He draws on current legitimacy belief, rational choice, indigenous culture, and institutional environment theories to illustrate the meaning of (non-) compliance in Chinese context. Shi concludes that corporate as well as structural sophistication and complication are results of innovation and—at the same time—a response to the structure of the industry as well as the environment.

In a talk with Professor *Anja Senz*, *Jianyuan Yang* from Fangda Partners, a Beijing law firm, presents various measures used by the Chinese authorities to tackle corruption and graft. For state-owned enterprises, compliance rules are a relatively new topic. Nevertheless, many already have defined a policy. In 2015, a new law had been amended that raises penalties against bribe-givers. However, enforcement still lags behind, because the central as well as local governments are no less concerned with the performances of these enterprises and are hence reluctant to disrupt their business operations. Yang also pointed to some silver-linings, such as the "Anti-Bribery Management System", a pilot project launched in 2017 in Shenzhen.

The "storm of anti-corruption" is certainly not a storm in a glass of water, but a nationwide political campaign, the effects of which cannot be fully estimated yet. New rules have only changed the scale and types of corruption in China so far but have not fundamentally transformed the culture.

**The transplant scandal in Germany: Cheating of the waiting lists**

Crime in transplantation medicine is discussed in Germany with reference to the recent (liver) transplant scandals (2012) and the associated waiting list cheating by doctors. Due to the topicality of the events, however, there are no reliable empirical studies on this topic with the exception of the non-representative results of the Examination and Supervision Commission, which was used by the German Medical Association, the German Hospital Association and the GKV-Spitzenverband, to evaluate the Transplantation Act and the compliance with the guidelines of the German Medical Association in Germany's transplant centers.

What happened exactly in Munich, Leipzig, Göttingen, and Heidelberg and at other university hospitals? In 2012, the supervisory board of the German Medical Association (Bundesärztekammer, BAK) received an anonymous tip about irregularities in the liver transplantation section of the Göttingen University Hospital. The BAK started an investigation and discovered various violations of the BAK's directives concerning the order of priority of patients waiting for an organ transplantation. The number of violations was surprisingly high. Most of these consisted in, among others, false statements of medical facts and medical data, which served to determine the ranking position on the waiting list of Eurotransplant, the agency responsible for the allocation of organs. The cheating helped the culprit's own patients to move up the waiting list at the expense of others. The BAK informed the press, which flashed up the issue by relating it to organ trafficking and illegal personal enrichment of vicious surgeons. Again, it was the basic idea of a few rotten apples among a basketful of fresh ones. Public prosecutors stepped in and the indictment shocked all other surgeons: attempted manslaughter. According to the allegations, the defendant should have known about the lethal consequences of his act for the displaced patients.

In fact, the story is not about a few rotten apples. The whole system, which is based on a choice between Scylla and Charybdis, is put in the dock. No matter what directives are issued, the scarcity of organs makes it inevitable that some patients will die due to these rules. This is exactly what is happening. In sociology, we call this a situation of tragic choice (Calabresi and Bobbitt 1978). If you put the survival rate first, patients in urgent conditions will die; if you put patients in urgent conditions first, patients with a slightly better survival rate will die while waiting for an organ. In whichever way one acts, it is the wrong way. That's why politicians are trying not to get their fingers burnt and delegate the responsibility to the German Medical Association, which finds itself in a difficult situation with regard to its own directives on organ donation, for it too struggles to find a solution to overriding the tragic choices. While there were no complaints about kidney and pancreas transplantations, those about liver, heart and lung transplantations accounted for 19 percent, 15 percent and 14 percent of the inspected cases, respectively. Of the 2,120 examined transplantations, 354 were manipulated according to the BAK's Investigative Commission. This is very significant when one compares it with the occurrence, for example, of fraud and counterfeiting in Germany (3.4 cases per 100,000 inhabitants). According to the Commission's reports, not all, but rather 12 out of 52 transplantation centers were involved. Of these 12, Göttingen was at the top with directive violations in 75 percent of the examined cases, followed by Jena with 63 percent and Heidelberg with 56 percent. On average, directive violations were listed in 38 percent of cases at the 12 centers. As always, it turns out that we are not dealing with individual deeds, but with policy violations by the entire system.

*Torsten Verrel* reported on the Göttingen transplant scandal and the consequences of the court ruling. A physician working at the Göttingen liver transplant center had tampered with the order of priority of patients waiting for transplantable organs in the so-called MELD score and had been charged with attempted manslaughter and assault with fatalities. In June, however, the Federal Court of Justice had the previous decision by a court in Göttingen *that declared the surgeon not guilty* on the grounds that it had not been possible to prove the direct cause of death by his actions and the BAK's guidelines are not legally binding. The consequence is that organ transplantations are a legal gray area in Germany.

## How to explain and to prevent corporate crime?

It is not only on the societal and cultural levels that we have to consider rules that legitimize "give and take" arrangements. These rules exist as well at the level of organizations. As Luhmann (1964 [1995]) already pointed out in his early writings, we know that organizational deviance is a prerequisite for organizations to function. No organization will survive just by sticking to formal rules alone. Proof for this assumption is provided by cases, in which workers have decided to go on strike by "work-to-rule" activities. Just take the case of the British Rail as an example, where this kind of work-to-rule strikes produced disastrous results. According to Morgan, hardly any train left the station on time. The whole railway system quickly slowed down to snail's pace, if it did not come to a halt. As the example shows, not all organizational deviance from formal rules is unlawful. Once organizations have become used to specific kinds of deviance, unwritten rules emerge that streamline activities as well. Some of these unwritten rules thrive in the legal gray area of organizational activities, others are utterly illegal. If we ask how to explain the deviations from the rules and laws in organizations, then we will find two very different phenomena.

Research on corruption usually grapples with the idea of "bad apples" and the complementary role of "rotten barrels". Corrupt behavior is often attributed to individual characteristics, such as greed for personal gain, lack of self-control, and deviant personality traits. For example, some scholars have argued that psychopathic traits and Machiavellianism mark the personalities of corrupt actors (Knecht 2009; Nerdinger 2008; Rabl and Kühlmann 2008; Zettler and Blickle 2011). The basic assumption of such approaches, which are located within the psychology of corrupt actors and the broader rational choice framework, is that organizations become corrupt through individual deviance—the longing for individual benefit or personal gain (Becker 1968; Gottfredson and Hirschi 1990; Shover and Hochstetler 2002, p. 13). In the case of managers, this means that the very personality traits that help managers advance in the corporate hierarchy also make them more prone to individual deviance. Thus, stricter laws and consistent compliance measures would serve as credible deterrents against corruption; they raise both the likelihood of detection and the costs that the deviant actor faces if caught. "Good barrels", as opposed to bad ones, are institutional and organizational settings that provide the right incentives and penalties to flag corrupt behavior as the irrational choice of a few "bad apples". In this way, corruption is commonly perceived as being adverse to the organization's objectives. Structural corruption is then mostly a matter of "bad barrels", the negligent or willful blindness of the principal, who either fails to provide the right incentives or to guarantee the necessary managerial control (Ashforth et al. 2008, p. 672f.).

However, if we take the basic supply-and-demand model of corruption as a starting point, the explanations for individual deviance hardly apply to the "active corruption" of the bribe-giver, as opposed to the bribe-taker. In cases of international bribery, most of the bribe-givers are high-ranking, well-educated, and well-paid managers. They commit crime at high personal risks and without being primarily interested in lining their own pockets. Until the crime is revealed, the illegal actions could be understood as useful to the organization. This is what Luhmann (1964 [1995], p. 304) called "useful illegality"; a behavior that violates the terms of membership, but is conceivable as a useful action in light of the organization's purpose. This concept has been known in German sociology for a long time, but until very recently it has never been used for empirical research (Bergmann et al. 2014; Klinkhammer 2013; Kühl 2007; 2010; Ortmann 1999; 2010, p. 20; Pohlmann 2008, 2016; Tacke 2015, p. 70). We have investigated empirically whether it is possible to explain high-profile cases of structural corruption as instances of this particular kind of organizational deviance and have further developed an institutional approach to corruption (Pohlmann et al. 2016).

The purpose of this approach is not to exonerate those who perpetuate such organizational actions—especially where an actual crime has been committed—but rather to explain how it takes place and why it may be difficult for organizations to prevent this type of deviance. This is where the criminological concept of organizational deviance and the sociological concept of useful illegality merge and create a new paradigm.

In contrast to "organizational crime"—which can be read as a legitimate limitation of our object of study in western democracies (Braithwaite 1985, p. 17ff.)—we use the term "organizational deviance" to mark the fact that analyzing the legal regulations is not sufficient to understand organizational wrongdoing. Organizational deviance takes the self-regulation of the social actors as a starting point to understand the trespass in its interplay with legal rules. Thus, we define this type of deviance from formal organizational rules as the use of illegitimate or illegal means in and by organizations in the pursuit of socially legitimate purposes and goals that comply with the law. The rule violations are primarily oriented towards the benefit of the organization. The gains for individual members are not pursued in an illegitimate or illegal way. Instead, they are based on the legitimate incentive systems of the organization. In contrast to the broader definition by Vaughan (1999, p. 273), we exclude rule violations that merely represent isolated, inadvertent or negligent events. Instead, when we use the term organizational deviance, the rule violations occur repeatedly and are in line with the goals of the organization. They are based on unwritten, informal interpretations and action rules of the organization, which justify and normalize the deviation from formal rules, guidelines, and laws. This understanding of organizational deviance has a long tradition in the Anglo-American debate and has been conceptually developed further, especially in the past decade (Brief et al. 2001; Campbell and Göritz 2014; Palmer 2012; Pinto et al. 2008; Vaughan 1999). Though the dominant approach is still preoccupied with the individual calculus or the preferences of the perpetrators, this debate also features an alternative approach that accounts for various deviant practices that are rooted in the socialization of individuals and thus often carried out mindlessly (Palmer 2012, p. 12). From the latter perspective, individual deviations from the rules are thus deciphered as an institutionalized expression of collective practices in a particular organization.

Individual deviance, on the other hand, refers to occasional violations, by which individual actors inadvertently, negligently or purposefully deviate from the internal rules of the organization, regulations or laws. Such occupational crimes may even entail the fraudulent harm to the organization and might be carried out for the purpose of illegitimate or illegal personal enrichment (Braithwaite 1985; Green 1990). They are not covered by any collectively acknowledged, unwritten rules within the organization. Individual and organizational deviances are not mutually exclusive; instead, the relationship between the two is a relevant empirical question. We will exemplify the added value of this perspective mainly with regard to corruption offences, but we will also show that it applies beyond this specific crime.

It is usually assumed that high morale in a (work)group leads to higher work performance and while the extent to which this is accompanied by negative effects has been tentatively indicated, it has not been discussed to a sufficient extent. Since high morale leading to higher work performance is effected through higher social cohesion within the group, conflicts with general rules or laws may arise (cf. Waytz et al. 2013; Portes and Vickstrom 2011; Pfarrer et al. 2008). As the normative ambivalence between group and generally applicable rules and norms, in which team or group members can be situated, indicates, cohesion in groups (such as in the specific form of team spirit or morale) can potentially also have negative effects. *Peter Graeff* and *Julia Kleinewiese* (Kiel) are pointing to an intricate connection between work efficiency and non-compliance, especially in small organizational units. Based on an investigation into volunteer fire brigades in Schleswig-Holstein and North Rhine-Westphalia they concluded that the higher the respective morale, the more effective the working unit was, but also the stronger the tendency to a "code of silence" became—rule violations would be concealed from the outside.

*Christiane Gebhardt* spoke less about morale and more about corporate identity building and making difficult decisions in the context of non-compliance. She focused on the role of the manager and managerial behavior as an element of governance. She differentiated between organizational accountability and leadership responsibility, which includes refusing "killer jobs" and decisions against social pressure in favor of the integrity of character.

In the last decade, the term "integrity" has come into fashion in the corporate world. In the boardroom of both Daimler and Volkswagen, there have been chairs established for Integrity and Legal Affairs. Compliance seems to be the slogan of yesterday. Now, search "integrity management" on Google Scholar and you get over 14,000 entries, of which over 13,000 have been published since 2000. Most of them are not addressing the homonymic IT-solution. It is mirroring a newly emerging consulting business and fashion of management. It looks like corporations are not only striving for compliance with rules, but also for moral perfection.

A distinction has been made between "compliance", which is achieved through controls and penalties, and the management of "integrity", which is realized through the internalization of values and norms. At the same time, according to Paine's seminal article in 1994, the moral competences of the employees would be expanded. Employees should be able to make ethically correct decisions based on their independent value judgements in tricky and questionable situations that are not covered by the code of conduct. Integrity management has thus succeeded value management in the corporate world, without reacting to the problems already associated with this management mode.

The Latin word "integritas" alludes to honesty, purity, integrity, which means to stand by one's values and norms in words and deeds, so that one does not allow oneself to be corrupted. For companies, it is about producing an internally guided employee who completes the rules and regulations by internalizing the underlying values and norms. This pious wish of the companies packs a punch. From a sociological perspective, the new reference to the ethically demanding concept of integrity as well as the recurrent reference to values surprises us for several reasons:

(1) The assumption behind the concept of integrity that internal psychological conditions of employees can be deliberately induced seems immune to refutation. Practice shows repeatedly that downright value-related educational efforts are often ignored or trigger reactance, thus leading to opposite effects. The intervention of a good intention is always to be distinguished from what is learned unintentionally through socialization in the companies, e.g., how formal rules and educational efforts can be successfully circumvented. Therefore, the problem

is not one of "education" by the management, but one of socialization within the organization.

(2) And yet, it is forgotten that access to employees has its limits and it is likewise assumed that employees are obviously not able to develop integrity themselves. As with the notion that is repeatedly expressed in management literature, the attempt at "leading the staff to happiness" seeks to co-opt employees in their personal value references without seeing a transgression of limits. However, this eliminates a separation that is often important to the staff: The separation of a limited inclusion of the person through the instrumental use of his labor from other aspects of their lives, which also leaves room for other values and moral attitudes.

(3) With the topic of integrity, the preventive measures focus on educating employees once more. Here too, with simultaneous addressing of culture, priority is again given to behavioral prevention—and not situational prevention: The idea of forestalling deviations by making the staff morally perfect. The rather disappointing experiences of the church, socialism, and humanism are persistently ignored. The constellations within the companies themselves, such as the insider-dominated career systems, the endless working hours of the executives, the output-oriented performance indicators, etc., which are more often the reason for deviations from the rules, are therefore largely off the radar.

(4) Last but not least, anyone who works for companies, hospitals, universities, and the like knows that integrity is a scarce resource, because organizations are often unable to use them at all. Rather, they are constantly working to ensure the conformity of their staff with changing goals, values and standards, because even the social moral standards and laws change with the zeitgeist. To deal with this, adaptability and opportunism are an important resource. Morality is fickle, integrity is not. And which moral standards should be applied? Business models of companies that fully comply with the sometimes contradictory, culturally diverse and inconsistent social moral standards will barely exist. So, as an honest employee, can one still work for VW, Audi and others, which keep failing to abide by environmental regulations? Can we work for chocolate, tobacco or leather producers if we know that child labor is still being used? Taking integrity seriously would lead to moral obstacles that organizations would trip over.

Nevertheless, orientation to social norms and laws is important. The more they are cultivated by the democratic state with its regulations and are under scrutiny by civil society actors as well as included in the calculations of the economy, the better. No one could want the moralizing company. Who wants, for example, companies to choose their employees based on the currently prevailing rules of social respect or disrespect that would stop hiring smokers, drivers of cars with serious exhaust emissions, bad fathers, and so forth? Maybe companies should stick to compliance more closely, gear them to prevention, and not burn their fingers on "good morals". The fast exchange of the newly hired, ambitious board members responsible for Integrity and Law at Volkswagen indicates for many observers as well that the company was not really interested in enforcing integrity and transparency.

*Thomas Schröder* and *Gerhard Dannecker* focused on the specific situation in Germany. They explained in their double lecture why corruption and organizational misconduct must be adequately addressed: Globally operating companies are the protagonists of the $21^{st}$ century – and have to live up to their responsibilities. The double standard—an individual can be prosecuted, but not a company—has to be corrected, and a corresponding bill is in the drawer; but a procedure such as in the US, where the companies and employees play against each other, should not be adopted in Germany. At the same time, the legal system in Germany must now be reformed without delay and the inaction with regard to violations of the law must end.

*Kai-D. Bussmann* asked the question if illegality actually becomes natural and discussed the significance of the market economy in regard to different types of crime focusing on the role of deception which he points out to be intrinsic to the capitalist system. Furthermore, he explained that the criminals' greed cannot easily be distinguished from regular profit-maximizing behavior with the attribution of illegality being the only difference. In this context, he viewed the crime-promoting as well as crime-inhibiting effects of the market economy as a socialization agency fostering ruthlessness and imparting values.

## References

Arlacchi, Pino (1995): Mafia von innen. Das Leben des Don Antonio Calderone. Frankfurt am Main: Fischer.

Ashforth, Blake E.; Gioia, Dennis A.; Robinson, Sandra L.; Treviño, Linda K. (2008): Re-Viewing Organizational Corruption. In *Academy of Management Review* 33 (3), pp. 670–684.

Baecker, Dirk (2000): Korruption, empirisch. In *Die Tageszeitung*, 1/24/2000 (6049).

Barkemeyer, Ralf; Preuss, Lutz; Lee, Lindsay (2015): Corporate reporting on corruption: An international comparison. In *Accounting Forum* 39 (4), pp. 349–365.

Becker, Gary S. (1968): Crime and Punishment: An Economic Approach. In *Journal of Political Economy* 76 (2), pp. 169–217.

Bergmann, Jens; Hahn, Matthias; Langhof, Antonia; Wagner, Gabriele (2014): Scheitern - Organisations- und wirtschaftssoziologische Analysen. Wiesbaden: Springer VS (SpringerLink).

Braithwaite, John (1985): White Collar Crime. In *Annual Review of Sociology* 11 (1), pp. 1–25.

Braithwaite, John (2008): Regulatory Capitalism: How it Works, Ideas for Making it Work Better by John Braithwaite. Cheltenham/Northampton: Edward Elgar.

Brief, Arthur P.; Buttram, Robert T.; Dukerich, Janet M. (2001): Collective Corruption in the corporate world. Toward a process model. In Marlene E. Turner (Ed.): Groups at work. Theory and research. Mahwah, NJ: Erlbaum (Applied social research), pp. 471–499.

Calabresi, Guido; Bobbitt, Philip (1978): Tragic choices. [the conflicts society confronts in the allocation of tragically scarce resources]. New York: Norton (The Fels lectures on public policy analysis).

Campbell, Jamie-Lee; Göritz, Anja S. (2014): Culture Corrupts! A Qualitative Study of Organizational Culture in Corrupt Organizations. In *Journal of Business Ethics* 120 (3), pp. 291–311.

Castañeda, Jorge G. (2016): Latin Americans Stand Up To Corruption. The Silver Lining in a Spate of Scandals. In *Foreign Affairs*, 2016. Available online at https://www.foreignaffairs.com/articles/central-america-caribbean/2015-12-14/latin-americans-stand-corruption, checked on 8/15/2019.

Gottfredson, Michael R.; Hirschi, Travis (1990): A general theory of crime. Stanford, Calif.: Stanford Univ. Pr.

Green, Gary S. (1990): Occupational crime. Reprint. Chicago: Nelson-Hall (Nelson-Hall series in law, crime, and justice).

Hessinger, Philipp (2002): Mafia und Mafiakapitalismus als totales soziales Phänomen. Eine vergleichende Perspektive auf die Entwicklung in Italien und Russland. In *Leviathan* 30 (4), pp. 482–508.

Jordana, Jacint; Levi-Faur, David; i Marín, Xavier Fernández (2011): The Global Diffusion of Regulatory Agencies. In *Comparative Political Studies* 44 (10), pp. 1343–1369.

Klinkhammer, Julian (2013): On the dark side of the code: organizational challenges to an effective anti-corruption strategy. In *Crime, Law and Social Change* 60 (2), pp. 191–208.

Knecht, Thomas (2009): Persönlichkeit von Wirtschaftskriminellen. In *Psychiatrie* 25, pp. 25–29.

Kühl, Stefan (2007): Formalität, Informalität und Illegalität in der Organisationsberatung. Systemtheoretische Überlegungen eines Beratungsprozesses. In *Soziale Welt* 58 (3), pp. 271–293.

Kühl, Stefan (2010): Informalität und Organisationskultur. Ein Systematisierungsversuch. Universität Bielefeld (Working Paper, 3).

Luhmann, Niklas (1964 [1995]): Funktionen und Folgen formaler Organisation. Berlin: Duncker & Humblot.

Luhmann, Niklas (2000): Organisation und Entscheidung. Opladen/Wiesbaden: WDV.

Nerdinger, Friedemann (2008): Unternehmensschädigendes Verhalten erkennen und verhindern. Göttingen: Hogrefe Verlag.

Ortmann, Günther (1999): Organisation und Dekonstruktion. In Georg Schreyögg (Ed.): Organisation und Postmoderne. Grundfragen - Analysen - Perspektiven ; Verhandlungen der Wissenschaftlichen Kommission "Organisation" im Verband der Hochschullehrer für Betriebswirtschaft e.V. Wiesbaden: Gabler, pp. 157–196.

Ortmann, Günther (2010): Organisation und Moral. Die dunkle Seite. 1. Aufl. Weilerswist: Velbrück Wissenschaft.

Palmer, Donald (2012): Normal organizational wrongdoing. A critical analysis of theories of misconduct in and by organizations. Oxford: Oxford Univ. Press.

Paoli, Letizia (1999): Die italienische Mafia. Paradigma oder Spezialfall organisierter Kriminalität? In *Monatszeitschrift für Kriminologie und Strafrechtsreform* 82 (6), pp. 425–440.

Paoli, Letizia (2008): The Decline of the Italien Mafia. In Dina Siegel, Hans Nelen (Eds.): Organized Crime. Culture, Markets and Policies. New York: Springer-Verlag.

Pfarrer, Michael D.; Decelles, Katherine A.; Smith, Ken G.; Taylor, M. Susan (2008): After the Fall: Reintegrating the Corrupt Organization. In *Academy of Management Review* 33 (3), pp. 730–749.

Pinto, Jonathan; Leana, Carrie R.; Pil, Frits K. (2008): Corrupt Organizations or Organizations of Corrupt Individuals? Two Types of Organization-Level Corruption. In *Academy of Management Review* 33 (3), pp. 685–709.

Pohlmann, Markus (2008): Management und Moral. In Tanja Münch, Tobias Blank, Sita Schanne, Christiane Staffhorst (Eds.): Integrierte Soziologie. Perspektiven zwischen Ökonomie und Soziologie, Praxis und Wissenschaft ; Festschrift zum 70. Geburtstag von Hansjörg Weitbrecht. With assistance of Hansjörg Weitbrecht. 1. Auflage. Mering: Rainer Hampp Verlag, pp. 161–175.

Pohlmann, Markus (2016): Soziologie der Organisation. Eine Einführung. 2., überarbeitete Auflage. Konstanz, München: UVK Verlagsgesellschaft mbH; UVK/Lucius (UTB Soziologie, 3573).

Pohlmann, Markus; Bitsch, Kristina; Klinkhammer, Julian (2016): Personal Gain or Organizational Benefits? How to Explain Active Corruption. In *German Law Journal* 17 (1), pp. 73–99.

Portes, Alejandro; Vickstrom, Erik (2011): Diversity, Social Capital, and Cohesion. In *Annual Review of Sociology* 37 (1), pp. 461–479.

Rabl, Tanja; Kühlmann, Torsten M. (2008): Understanding Corruption in Organizations – Development and Empirical Assessment of an Action Model. In *Journal of Business Ethics* 82 (2), pp. 477–495.

Rugy, Veronique de; Warren, Melinda (2009): Expansion of Regulatory Budgets and Staffing Continues in the New Administration. An Analysis of the U.S. Budget for Fiscal Years 2009 and 2010. Mercatus Center & Murray Weidenbaum Center on the Economy, Government, and Public Policy. Arlington/St. Louis. Available online at https://www.mercatus.org/system/files/Regulators-Budget-Report-Final-Version-October-29.pdf, checked on 8/15/2019.

Shover, Neal; Hochstetler, Andy (2002): Cultural explanation and organizational crime. In *Crime, Law and Social Change* 37, pp. 1–18.

Tacke, Veronika (2015): Formalität und Informalität. In Victoria von Groddeck, Sylvia Marlene Wilz (Eds.): Formalität und Informalität in Organisationen. Wiesbaden: Springer VS (Organisationssoziologie), pp. 37–92.

Vaughan, Diane (1999): The dark side of organizations: Mistake, Misconduct, and Disaster. In *Annual Review of Sociology* 25 (1), pp. 271–305.

Waytz, Adam; Dungan, James; Young, Liane (2013): The whistleblower's dilemma and the fairness–loyalty tradeoff. In *Journal of Experimental Social Psychology* 49 (6), pp. 1027–1033.

Zettler, Ingo; Blickle, Gerhard (2011): Zum Zusammenspiel von "wer?" und "wo?". Eine psychologische Betrachtungsweise personaler und situationaler Determinanten kontraproduktiven Verhaltens am Arbeitsplatz. In *Zeitschrift für internationale Strafrechtsdogmatik* 6, pp. 143–147.

# Organizational wrongdoing: Bribery, fraud, cheating – Insights into the Herrenhausen Symposium, October 5-7, 2017

Ludmila Hustus and Christin Schultze

The Herrenhausen Symposium, which took place at the Herrenhausen Palace in Hanover, Germany, on October 5–7, 2017, was a major platform for academic exchange about the phenomenon of organizational wrongdoing for scientists and practitioners from all over the world. As a complement to the project "The Fight against Corruption and Manipulation—Regulation and Self-Regulation in Medicine and the Economy", organized by the research group for "Organizational Deviance Studies" from Heidelberg University and generously funded by the Volkswagen Foundation—the largest German private non-profit organization promoting research and education in sciences, social sciences and humanities, which is independent from the car manufacturer of the same name—, this symposium offered an excellent opportunity to shed light on bribery, fraud and cheating in various sectors as well as considering the different theoretical and practical perspectives while focusing on the key issues of these manifestations of organizational wrongdoing.

To inspire an interdisciplinary and intercultural discussion about patterns of destructive behavior based on the latest large-scale corruption and manipulation cases, the professors *Markus Pohlmann* of the Max-Weber-Institute of Sociology, *Gerhard Dannecker* of the Institute for German, European and International Criminal Law and Law of Criminal Procedure, *Dieter Dölling* and *Dieter Hermann*, both of the Institute of Criminology, invited leading experts and internationally renowned scientists from Argentina, Brazil, China, Germany, Italy, Slovenia, Switzerland and the USA. Surrounded by the Herrenhausen Gardens— one of the most beautiful parks in Europe—they analyzed the cir-cumstances leading organizations and their high-ranking members to choose the path of illegality in order to develop new prevention models.

© Springer Fachmedien Wiesbaden GmbH, part of Springer Nature 2020
M. Pohlmann et al. (eds.), *Bribery, Fraud, Cheating*, Organization, Management and Crime – Organisation, Management und Kriminalität,
https://doi.org/10.1007/978-3-658-29062-7_2

According to the objectives of the project, the symposium consisted of eight sessions dealing with "Organized crime, money laundering and corruption" (session 1), "Operation Car Wash—Corporate crime in Brazil" (session 2), "China's anti-corruption campaign" (session 3), "Corporate crime in the West" (session 4), "Unfair play in sports" (session 5), "Fraud in medicine" (session 6), "How to deal with corporate crime—Fines, deterrence and prevention" (session 7) and "The dark side of compliance" (session 8). The wide range of topics presented corresponded with the diverse professional and personal backgrounds of the participants: Public prosecutors, university professors, a journalist, federal appeals judges, the president of the transplantation society, lawyers and many others entered into a lively debate. Different aspects, which were addressed in the individual sessions, were later taken up in the discussions of young scientists from Argentina, Brazil, China, France, Germany, Ghana, Poland, Switzerland, United Kingdom and the USA.

The introduction to the symposium, delivered by *Wilhelm Krull*, Secretary General of the Volkswagen Foundation, Germany, and *Markus Pohlmann*, Professor at Heidelberg University, Germany, already confronted the audience with the first major topic of the symposium: the mafia and organized crime as global phenomena.

### Session 1: Organized crime, money laundering and corruption

*Roberto Scarpinato*, Attorney General of the Republic at the Court of Appeal of Palermo, Italy, opened the scientific part of the symposium with an introduction to the world of the modern mafia and the fight against it. As the slogan "From Violence to Consensus" illustrates, the contemporary mafia—partly mentioned as "mafia silente" or "marketist mafia"—is characterized by a silent, "new" form of shady behavior—a fact not always depicted realistically in the media, which spread a certain image of the mafia. The cultural perception of the mafiosi as rude and violent characters from the "cities of evil" in Italy, Turkey and the Balkan countries, which emerged in the $20^{th}$ century, no longer reflects the new reality of the mafias in the $21^{st}$ century. *Scarpinato* saw the socio-economic innovative transformations in the mafia's way of being and operating compared to the past as a result of the growing global demand for goods and services of the illegal economy. The progressive components of the mafia have become agencies on the free market that profitably satisfy these demands for drugs, counterfeit branded products, gambling or prostitutes. If we look at the mafia's activities regarding the latter services, the need to recruit, to transfer and find a destination for the prostitutes has led to an international division of criminal labor between the mafias in different countries. Corruption is an excellent tool for the hidden intrusion of the "silent" mafias: *Scarpinato* explicitly pointed out their effectiveness in comparison to violence.

According to *Scarpinato*, there is a gap between the complex reality of the mafias and public knowledge of this criminal phenomenon.

For this reason, journalist and writer *Petra Reski*, Italy, considered it to be her task to report on the mafia, raise society's awareness of the dangers posed by the mafia and to communicate facts supported by numerous reliable sources—unhindered and without censorship. *Reski* wrote about turncoats and state witnesses, about mafia women and about the abolition of the anti-mafia laws under the orders of the anti-mafia prosecutors *Giovanni Falcone* and *Paolo Borsellino*. She also came to the conclusion that the mafia owes its worldwide success not only to violence, but above all to money and friendly words.

Threats and legal actions against *Reski* have changed her way of writing. From a literary point of view at least, *Reski* is still interested in the so-called grey area, which is more diverse than the mafia itself. As part of society, the mafia is a criminal organization whose existence would be inconceivable without the active support of the entire society and its subsystems.

During the symposium, *Scarpinato* did not want to hide his fear of organized crime gradually becoming a stable and dominant criminal form of the third millennium. As *David Ryan Kirkpatrick*, Senior Public Prosecutor in the Public Prosecutor's Office Darmstadt, Germany, interpreted organized crime as the production and sale of illegal products or as the illegal sale of legal products, it becomes clear that this phenomenon is a reflection of the legal economic system and has a strong impact on daily life: There is—so *Kirkpatrick*—no special crime committed by criminal gangs and individuals. Against this background, it is not surprising that there is no internationally recognized definition of this type of crime. According to *Kirkpatrick*, a uniform terminology of organized crime is necessary for statistics, for the harmonization of legislation and for special arrangements in multilateral treaties for mutual assistance. In order to fight organized crime effectively, which appears in many different ways, *Kirkpatrick* pleaded for a change in the methods of fighting it, whereby the penal law including prosecution measures must not be the only means against organized crime. He called for better technical support and more staff for law enforcement: Without a political interest and a change in most traditional opinions and methods in the fight against organized crime, it will hardly be possible to combat this type of crime successfully in the future.

### Session 2: Operation Car Wash – Corporate crime in Brazil

Numerous corruption and money laundering scandals involving high-ranking politicians and businessmen, such as the high-profile corruption scandal involving the well-known Brazilian Oil company Petrobras or the famous Mensalão case, brought Brazil into the focus of international attention. The former case was an outcome of the famous "Car Wash" investigation, which led to other cases being uncovered as well. The latter was the first emblematic case against politicians in power. It marked a starting point of the fight against corruption in Brazil, which is an ongoing process.

*Fausto Martin De Sanctis*, Federal Appellate Judge of the Regional Federal Court of the $3^{rd}$ Region, São Paulo, Brazil, reported on the progress and the changes in the Brazilian legal system in connection with money laundering and financial crime. In his overview of the political dimension of economic corruption in Brazil, *De Sanctis* described that the Brazilian population reacted with street protests and unrest to the many scandals in Brazil, which involved corruption and money laundering in the political environment. The judiciary had been unsuitable for fighting corruption and had discouraged law enforcement agencies from fighting corruption: a statement, which *De Sanctis* documented with numerous "examples of misrepresentation of the purpose of the rule of law". Ultimately, the National Anti-Corruption and Money Laundering Strategy (Estratégia Nacional de Combate à Corrupção e à Lavagem de Dinheiro—ENCCLA) launched an initiative to combat organized crime. *De Sanctis* presented a series of measures which, in his opinion, could contribute to improving the legal system, such as a law supporting whistleblowers or recognition of lobbying as a particular form of legally accepted corruption.

Law enforcement and corruption in Brazil is a well-known terrain for *João Pedro Gebran Neto*, Federal Appellate Judge of the Regional Federal Court of the 4$^{th}$ Region, Porto Alegre, Brazil. He reported on the far-reaching dimensions of "Operation Car Wash" ("Operação Lava Jato") and on some significant changes in the Brazilian judicial system with regard to law enforcement. Among the changes is the creation of task forces of the Federal Police and the General Federal Ministry, which are composed of experts who have gained experience from previous operations. Most importantly, the deviant behavior has to be prevented at first. The process of change in the Brazilian legal system has also not yet been completed. Laws such as the False Claims Act (FCA), the Foreign Corrupt Practices Act (FCPA), or the Bribery Act 2010 may serve as models for the Brazilian legal system.

The focus of the presentation given by *Bruno Wilhelm Speck*, Professor at the University of São Paulo, Brazil, was on the normative background of regulations on money in politics that frames the debate on this matter and guides regulatory reforms but often has not been taken into account sufficiently. *Speck* pointed out that there is hardly any democratic country in which no questionable money flows have been uncovered in politics. He explained that many countries reformed their legislation in reaction to this awareness and achieved some kind of balance. However, the question remains what exactly the purpose of such regulation is. There is an intrinsic contradiction in campaign funding: While parties are expected to be closely connected to the parts of society and interest groups they represent, the funding regulations apply only to individual citizens. *Speck* then proceeded to elaborate, whether there should be an absolute limit to campaign financing, which poses the question if large donations cause political competition to be unfair or if they express the candidates' acceptance. He concluded that there are multiple issues concerning the funding of political parties, however, most of them can be resolved by a fair and coherent system of legislation—an aim, that Brazil does not achieve in all cases.

## Session 3: China's anti-corruption campaign

In China, efforts have been made in recent years to adapt the fight against corruption according to international standards. Here, specific peculiarities must be taken into account that are rooted in China's culture and economic development and, therefore, present a particular challenge.

*Thomas Heberer*, Senior Professor at the University of Duisburg-Essen, Germany, has set himself the task of deciphering the mystery of rapid economic growth and social development despite high levels of corruption in China. He familiarized the listener with the importance, the concept and the causes of corruption in China in order to pave the way for his own attempt of an explanation: the existence of developmental corruption in a developing country—a statement that revises the widespread notion of the harmfulness of corruption for economic growth in political and economic literature. According to *Heberer's* thesis, even if in a strong developmental state, the prevalence of "developmental corruption" is higher than "predatory corruption" and a temporary and relative acceptance of the corrupt practices of leading local cadres' by the Chinese leadership contributed to a high level of economic development in China, this development does not question the necessity of combating corruption.

Since preventing corruption is more important than fighting corruption, *Jianyuan Yang* of Fangda Partners, China, looked into the question of giving companies the right incentives. As a lawyer and partner at a recognized leading PRC law firm in the commercial field with the largest team dedicated in providing full-scale regulatory compliance services, she cannot escape the current trend towards increasing punishment for bribes, which is accompanied by significant changes in corruption law. Based on the results of empirical research, the health, TMT and manufacturing industries, automotive, real estate and financial sectors are considered to be particularly susceptible to anti-competitive corruption, with state-owned enterprises and their employees at a higher risk of punishment. In her search for ways to provide companies with the right incentives to prevent corruption in China, *Yang* stressed the need for the development of effective compliance programs that also take into account the specifics of Chinese anti-competitive practices laws. If one considers the consequences of corruption in China in the form of various types of administrative sanctions, including the termination of the business license of the company concerned, criminal sanctions up to the death penalty and the long-term reputation-damaging punishment through the social credit system, giving companies the right incentives to prevent corruption is no less effective than the creation of bilateral and multilateral frameworks for combating corruption worldwide and China's participation in international cooperative efforts.

Embedded in the scenario of a case study from China, the subject of which was the bribery of the officials of the China Food and Drug Administration (CFDA) by Chinese and foreign pharmaceutical companies, the presentation of *Xiuyin Shi*, Professor at the Chinese Academy of Social Sciences (CASS), Beijing, China, focused on the phenomenon of bribery on a "guanxi" basis. A distinctive feature of bribery in oriental societies is that it differs from Western problem-based bribery in the social significance that characterizes the transfer of money or valuables: Guanxi-based bribes are gifts expressing friendship or emotions based on blood ties, marriage, brotherhood or comradeship. In other words, these payments are a mixture of emotions and interest in money, valuables and social resources. As an instrument for circumventing administrative vetting and approval procedures in an authoritarian state, guanxi-based bribery can be conducted in different ways and comprises two different processes that do not have to occur simultaneously: The emotional exchange could continue where transactional activities stop. According to *Shi*, guanxi-based bribery is subject to generally recognized and respected rules—ethics and code of conduct—and proves resistant to traditional anti-bribery methods due to its strong roots in Chinese history and tradition. *Shi* saw a strategy for combating guanxi-based bribery based on the roots, characteristics and mechanisms in a compelling separation between public affairs and private connections on the one hand and an urgent rationalization of institutions on the other: an institutional structure that can contribute to the emergence of a regulatory regime according to *Max Weber's* ideal.

### Session 4: Corporate crime in the West

In recent decades, criminal penalties against legal entities have been introduced worldwide in order to meet the international requirements of the United Nations, the OECD and the Council of Europe. This has resulted in an adaptation to US criminal law, which traditionally provides for corporate penalties. For states that have taken this step, this means a paradigm shift. In this context, corporate culture, especially integrity, and compliance play just as important a role as the legal incentives and the possibilities of consensual termination of the procedure.

In the discussion about compliance and anti-corruption measures in transnational corporations *Matthias Kleinhempel*, Professor at IAE Business School and the Center for Governance and Transparency, Buenos Aires, Argentina, drew the attention to the importance of corporate culture, which is more revealing than national culture in the context of misconduct. He stressed that only a strong culture of integrity will succeed in the fight against corruption: "Compliance is dead, at least almost!" However, changing the corporate culture, which is expressed through aspects like tone at the top, incentive systems, promotions and firings etc., is not an easy task, since it can be strongly rooted. This ambitious goal can be achieved by changing the incentive systems to systems rewarding long-term results and company results as well as by establishing Ethics & Compliance (E&C) programs. As the results of a survey conducted in July 2017 among E&C Officers of international companies in southern South America show, boards of directors are more committed to anti-corruption programs than ever and recognize their increasing importance. Furthermore, the survey proves that staff training and a better awareness and understanding for corporate culture enhance these anti-corruption programs. *Kleinhempel* summarized the trends in the development of compliance programs for transnational corporations based on the results of the survey: a shift of emphasis from monitoring to strengthening the corporate culture, a reduction in incentives for corruption while increasing penalties and strengthening the focus on legal obligations.

Preventing and combating corporate crime as an important concern of compliance programs is not very promising without a deeper understanding of social integration instruments like the means of corporate identity or team building. The concept of esprit de corps can be employed to properly ascertain the qualities of a team concerning attitude and conduct.

The assumption that esprit de corps as a particular form of team spirit is a social mechanism, in the sense of analytical sociology, which regularly brings about a social outcome, is the underlying concept of the study conducted by *Peter Graeff*, Professor, and *Julia Kleinewiese*, Research Associate, both from Kiel University, Germany. Instigated by several new studies which suggest a beneficial relationship between higher degrees of social integration and some forms of deviant behavior, the researchers examined esprit de corps in the context of a mechanism of threats in its possible positive and negative effects on the basis of an online vignette-based factorial survey involving the volunteer fire departments as a specific group. These departments differ from professional economic organizations in the voluntary nature of their work, their deep rootedness in local communities, the breadth of their work assignments and the degree of danger of their activity. In any case, the results of the study presented for discussion prove the probability of the adherence to particularistic group-specific norms in the case of activation of esprit de corps as well as prevalence of a deviance norm in the form of a "code of silence" as a mechanism of in-group protection.

For *Thomas R. L. Best*, lawyer and partner at Steptoe & Johnson LLP, USA, the central question was whether a US-style anti-corruption enforcement system based on settlements is suited to prevent corruption. Given his professional background as a lawyer primarily working on international cases concerning the FCPA, *Best* stressed that compliance is not dead. He explained to the participants of the symposium that the FCPA covers bribery worldwide. However, the US authorities largely forfeit the resolution of the proceedings by trial in favor of settlements, where the companies forfeit any ill-gotten gains and cooperate with the authorities, disclosing any information on the incidents in question. The companies and individuals gladly make use of this option in exchange for leniency. While *Best* admitted that this approach may reduce the deterrent value of law enforcement, it is preferable to the traditional trial-based systems. The advantage of such a settlement-based system is that the internal investigations, the restructuring and the impact on corporate culture increase corporate and individual compliance with FCPA to a significantly higher extent.

Through the contribution of *Amy Jeffress*, lawyer and partner at Arnold & Porter Kaye Scholer LLP, USA, the symposium participants delved into the world of corporate investigations. For her as a lawyer, who also works on criminal defense cases, it is an important decision both in the defense of individuals and companies whether and how to cooperate with law enforcement agencies in corporate investigations. She pointed out the significant incentives provided by the US system to reward timely and full individual and corporate cooperation. These incentives lead to—in the words of *Jeffress*—a "race" to the government. In addition to providing an overview of the development and formalization of incentives for individual cooperation in the US sentencing regime, *Jeffress* explained that the US Department of Justice (DOJ) evaluates corporate crime concerning these factors, focusing on a corporation's willingness to cooperate in the investigation, the timely and voluntary disclosure of wrongdoing, the corporation's remedial actions and the role of the responsible individuals. She introduced the audience to the observations on the "Yates memorandum", issued in 2015, and included in her presentation the incentives for corporations to provide information about other corporations.

**Session 5: Unfair play in sports**

As sports have expanded into the global economic sector with powerful impact, they became structurally susceptible to bribery, fraud and cheating. Some of these developments have been discovered in recent years.

*Marcus A. Asner*, lawyer and partner at Arnold & Porter Kaye Scholer LLP, USA, who works on corruption matters within the Fédération Internationale de Football Association (FIFA), discussed the topic of investigations into corruption. In light of numerous arrests throughout the world and a significant number of convicts, the FIFA case is a dramatic one, which charges general crimes such as fraud, money laundering and racketeering, which are not really covered by the FCPA. It was not without justification that *Asner* raised the question why Brooklyn, New York, became the center of the FIFA investigation for the most part if—as *Asner* says—football is hardly a US sport and many of the issues at the center of the investigation have little to do with the US or their citizens: a fact that serves as proof of the long reach of US criminal law.

On the subject of "Football, Sports Bets and Money Laundering", *Fausto Martin De Sanctis*, Federal Appellate Judge of the Regional Federal Court of the 3$^{rd}$ Region, São Paulo, Brazil, gave an insight into the problems in the fight against financial crimes in the sports world. He argued that large sums of money and the lack of transparency that characterize the sports industry make it so vulnerable to crimes such as corruption, money laundering, tax evasion and fraud. Furthermore, he emphasized that the uncertainty of the origin of funds makes it hard to find evidence for prosecuting individual perpetrators. Although national law enforcement agencies already improved their efforts in the fight against corruption and financial crimes in the sports world, it is necessary—according to *De Sanctis*—that national football associations comply with international regulations. He also addressed the need for stricter controls of the sports industry in general. With this, *De Sanctis* hopes for creating a more transparent and honest atmosphere in the sports industry, since sports are a vessel for the transmission of cultural and universal values.

**Session 6: Fraud in medicine**

Even if sports as a popular activity clearly differ from medicine, they have something in common: susceptibility to manipulation. As routine checks carried out in Germany have revealed, most of the doctors involved in the organ transplantation process do comply with legal requirements. Nonetheless, there are always exceptions, especially concerning transplantations of organs such as liver, lung and heart—for example the German "Göttingen Transplant Scandal" (Göttinger Transplantationsskandal). However, in the USA there have also been problems with the distribution of organs in the past.

Lawfully donated organs require a highly differentiated system for each step of the process while adhering to ethical and professional standards. *Nancy L. Ascher*, Professor at the University of California, San Francisco (UCSF) and President of The Transplantation Society (TTS), USA, emphasized the outstanding importance of organ transplantation as a major advance in medicine. Due to the medical success of solid organ transplants, the disparity between the potential donors and the patients waiting for an organ transplant has increased. This results in a higher need for organ transplantations. As *Ascher* outlined the possible limitations to donations, which is the potential for exploitation though commercial transaction with the donor, she stressed the need for combatting organ trafficking through governmental regulation. With the example of Iran being the only country in the world where regulated paid donation is legal, *Ascher* criticized the way governmental donation schemes are regulated. According to her, the entire organ transplantation process needs compliance with certain standards. These include treatment procedures for end stage organ disease, clear methods to ascertain cerebral and cardiac death, admission procedures for transplantation centers and their staff, organ procurement systems and registrations for donors as well as patients, and a method for organ distribution.

*Torsten Verrel*, Professor at the University of Bonn, Germany, dealt with the problems of criminal evaluation of waiting list manipulations. Based on the acquittal of the Federal Court of Justice in the case known as the "Göttingen Transplant Scandal" (Göttinger Transplantationsskandal), whose criminal relevance was based on the manipulation of the place on the waiting list for the allocation of livers through false statements on the patient's health status by the head of the liver transplantation program of the University Medical Center Göttingen in the years 2010 to 2012, *Verrel* investigated the fundamental question whether the manipulation of medical patient data in organ transplantation can be regarded as attempted manslaughter. Even if the exceeding of the rules of organ distribution is not an injustice equaling a killing offence from his point of view and he agrees with the conclusion of the Federal Court of Justice, *Verrel* subjec-ted the court's justification for the acquittal to a critical appraisal. Not only did *Verrel* draw the symposium participants' attention to the inadequacies of the court decision, he also urgently warned of the consequences for transplantation medicine resulting from the acquittal in the Göttingen case: the transplantation surgeons' uncertainty of the binding effect of the organ allocation guidelines, which comply with international rules for the distribution of organs, and the discontinuation of current investigation proceedings in the other organ manipulation cases implemented before August 1, 2013, are only a few examples.

**Session 7: How to deal with corporate crime – Fines, deterrence and prevention**

The current debate in Germany on plans to establish a corporate criminal law regime provided the participants of the symposium with the opportunity to discuss whether the sanctioning of corporations is indispensable and, based on that, whether corporations need to be recognized as corporate citizens, having all guaranties provided by law.

*Gerhard Dannecker*, Professor, and *Thomas Schröder*, Postdoctoral Researcher, both from Heidelberg University, Germany, introduced the participants to the problem of corporate criminal liability on the basis of a detailed catalogue of theses. They pointed to the serious effects of corruption in the public and private sector. From an economic point of view, corruption leads to overpriced services and the displacement of more efficient competitors, which ultimately entail inadequate quality of goods and services and higher expenditures for the public budget. Ultimately, corruption is an obstacle to economic growth, especially for underdeveloped countries. Corruption affects not only the economy but also causes macrosocial damage. As confidence in the incorruptibility of persons acting for institutions decreased, so did the willingness of the general public to accept the offers, services and decisions of these institutions. As a result, the functionality of important subsystems of society is diminishing. The fundamental question arises as to how infringements of the law within companies can be explained. *Dannecker* and *Schröder* emphasized the importance of the efforts in criminology as a vital prerequisite for shaping a future corporate criminal law. Criminology is paramount in order to understand the motivation and situation of individual members of companies as well as the reality of these organizations and to be able to take it into account in law. They pointed out that organizations are key protagonists of the $21^{st}$ century and must, therefore, assume responsibility. *Dannecker* and *Schröder* continued by discussing the thesis that citizens abiding to law in their private lives behave quite differently than in their role as employees. This brings them to the concept of "useful illegality" which, according to present interpretations of a concept originally devised by *Niklas Luhmann*, is providing a possible explanatory approach. This concept, *Dannecker* and *Schröder* continued, possesses some explanatory power in that it highlights a contemptuous attitude within corporations towards the law and calls for new legal concepts. Compliance efforts are not effective if the corporate culture is oriented towards "useful illegality".

*Dannecker* and *Schröder* advocated the criminal responsibility of companies as independent actors of modernity with the status of corporate citizens and recommended the introduction of corporate criminal law based on moderate penalties supplemented by compliance measures. Here, compliance should maintain a balance between trust and control socialization. Therefore, compliance rules should not feature a very high level of detail and bureaucracy that—in the long term—may play a part in strangling creativity and innovation. Since, in their view, corporate criminal law ought to supplement individual criminal law, *Dannecker* and *Schröder* pointed out the necessity for cumulative and proportionate punishment of employees and companies, especially as this does not infringe the constitutional prohibition of double jeopardy under German and European law. They also recommended the introduction of a leniency program or—depending on the crime committed—of a program for voluntary self-disclosure. Introducing these possibilities of mitigation would facilitate the otherwise very difficult detection of corruption and enable the prosecution of all corporate and individual culprits involved in the wrongdoing.

As a result, *Dannecker* and *Schröder* proposed that corporate criminal responsibility be reconciled with the responsibility of individuals, both in accordance with national constitutional and European law and in an economically compatible manner. Further, sanctions ought to be distributed in a balanced manner and the areas of influence, thus, be conveyed appropriately. This leads to the fact that the German law maker is facing a major challenge: His task is to establish a corporate criminal law regime that is dogmatically sound, in line with European law, constitutional and at the same time consistent with social reality.

**Session 8: The dark side of compliance**

At the end, *Drago Kos*, Chair of the OECD Working Group on Bribery, France/Slovenia, *Gerhard Dannecker*, *Matthias Kleinhempel*, *Christiane Gebhardt*, Vice President at Malik Management Institute, Switzerland, and *Nancy L. Ascher* touched on the question of corporate culture and the possibility of changing the law system—trust, education, communication, prevention, the role of the public and enhancing integrity were only a few key approaches in this context. Furthermore, the panel discussion summed up the results of the symposium, outlining the new challenges associated with bribery, fraud and cheating which give new impetus for research in the field of preventative measures against organizational wrongdoing. The interdisciplinary discourse between sociology, economy and law, including the intradisciplinary discourse of legal disciplines, such as criminal law, criminology and constitutional law, involving science and practice, proved to be a viable approach to understand and explain the phenomena of manipulation and corruption. On this basis, the possibilities and legal limitations of the national and international fight against these phenomena of deviant behavior could be displayed.

In the first seven sessions, the theoretical, empirical and practical foundations were laid to explain the phenomenon of organizational wrongdoing with its manifestations in the form of bribery, fraud, cheating and deviant behavior. As "a stable and dominant criminal form of the third millennium" organized crime can at any time turn a perpetrator into a victim, it occurs across borders and there is no area of life that is spared—medicine, sports and politics are just a few examples. In view of this breadth of manifestations and the high social harmfulness on the one hand and the diversity of causes of organizational wrongdoing on the other, a promising control approach can only exist in the interdisciplinary development of control strategies. While phenomenology and explanatory approaches fall within the remit of criminology and sociology, it is the task of criminal law studies to counter this divergent behavior and to develop preventive possibilities for combating crime.

Starting point of criminal law prevention is the thesis that modern criminal law derives its legitimacy from the consequences it has for society and its subsystems. Criminal law is intended to document the inviolability of norms and to have deterrent effects, but it should also enable rehabilitation and reintegration of the offenders. In other words, modern prevention by criminal law should contribute to system control. Criminal law as a means of system control competes with the norms of civil and administrative law, which are attributed a controlling effect, too. Therefore, criminal law rules are in competition for functionality. In particular, business criminal law is indispensable to support confidence in the functioning of economic systems. In this context, it requires an in-depth discussion of the relationship between individual and administrative penalties.

If the use of criminal law is expanded internationally in order to combat cross-border economic crime, in particular with regard to the fight against public and private corruption, this approach always entails the removal of power. It is, therefore, necessary to develop effective counterweights, principles of criminal law and effective fundamental rights in order to develop a proportionate and constitutionally balanced system of sanctions. Until now, only the principle of proportionality has certain outlines: Sanctions must be appropriate and a last resort to be used as a legitimate means of stabilizing the norm. Here, demands such as the criminal liability of legal persons raise specific problems, even if this requirement belongs to the usual repertoire of European and international criminal policy. The criminal law in this context requires special legitimacy. Wide and contourless criminal offenses open control and investigative powers for regulatory authorities, which involve the uncontrolled risk to be subject to broad sanction rules.

Risk analysis and risk assessment are the core business of corporate compliance departments and specialized law firms. The blending of criminal law with items of general control and coerce leads to a risk-taking policy that is characterized by whistleblowers and informal persecution and the elucidation of breaches of the rule. Compliance must not be equated with economic criminal law. Rather, compliance is about a new type of sanctioning procedure, split between public and private actors that transforms rights of control into a mingling of private and public actors between prevention, intervention and repression. Compliance rules give rise to condensed social control, through general risk-specific data and information collection and through individual risk control. The fact that internal investigations must also withdraw principles of criminal procedure, such as freedom from self-incrimination, because they are private actors, is a further step backwards in terms of criminal procedural legal protection, which should not be accepted without resistance.

This range of problems raises fundamental questions: Is the preventive criminal law at the end of its control capacity, at the end of its limiting function, at the end of its legitimacy? Or is the right associated with the power of coercion a consequence of the violation of the freedom of others? Should criminal law protect freedom and oppose the ruining of an economic system with freedom-damaging consequences for the citizens and emphasize the gravity of injustice? These issues have been studied in various areas in order to develop solutions and to discuss them further between scientists and practitioners.

# Organized crime, money laundering and corruption in Europe

# The fight against the mafia in Italy and Europe

*Roberto Scarpinato*

One of the main hurdles to building an effective European anti-mafia strategy is the cultural gap that exists between the complex reality of such criminal phenomena and knowledge thereof held by public opinion. The belief is still widespread that the mafias are criminal phenomena that are only present in certain countries—Italy, Turkey and the Balkan countries—where they originate from the particular cultures and national histories of those peoples. The media have also contributed to instilling in the collective imagination the idea that *mafiosi* are rude and violent characters, animated by an insatiable thirst for wealth, exactly as they are featured in highly successful films and television series. On the basis of this simplified representation of reality, the opinion has been strengthened that there is a well-defined border line between the "city of good" populated by multitudes of citizens respectful of the laws and the "city of evil" inhabited by criminal minorities responsible for the "evil of the mafia". Therefore, this is an evil that comes from outside and whose diffusion can be neutralized in those countries that have remained immune to this day, thanks to the counter-activity of the judiciary and of the police.

In view of such cultural paradigms, in Germany, for example, for a long time, it was considered that the mafia problem could be reduced to a few hundred foreign *mafiosi* who practiced extortion to the detriment of their fellow immigrant countrymen and recycled their proceeds in restaurants and pizzerias. The Duisburg massacre of 2007 shook the German public, revealing the fiercest and violent face of the mafia, but it was an isolated episode that was soon forgotten. The same heads of the *"Ndrangheta"* realized that carrying out that massacre on German territory had been a serious mistake and that for the future it was necessary to return to work, as in the past, avoiding any act of violence that could draw the attention of the media and alarm the public opinion.

The cultural perception of the mafia took shape in the historic season of the 20th century and, to a great extent, no longer reflects the new reality of the 21st century mafias. In the transition from the 20th to the 21st century there have been a series of macro events of historic proportions and international reach that have not only deeply altered the geopolitical and global geo-economic balances but have also altered the pre-existing traditional social and economic structures in countries where the mafias had developed and operated until the end of the 20th century. This sudden acceleration in history is causing the "selection of the species" within the criminal world, condemning to obsolescence traditional criminal organizations which are incapable of evolving, adapting to the new habitat, therefore favoring the extraordinary development of other criminal forms more capable of adapting to the ongoing transformations, exploiting new opportunities for illicit enrichment. These transformations of the way of being and operating mafias compared to the past are so innovative that in recent years in Italy, the magistrates and researchers have been forced to create new denominations and classifications to define new types of organized crime that can no longer be placed in the categories of the past. Therefore—to name just a few examples— the definitions of *"mafia silente"*, "marketist mafia", "criminal systems", "criminal-business committees" have been created.

This is not just a terminological problem, but a delicate problem of criminal policy. In spite of Italian legislation being among the most advanced in the world in terms of fighting the mafias, the legal instruments of criminal repression developed against traditional mafias in the twentieth century begin to become ineffective with the new criminal mutants originating from the selection of the species. To suggest an analogy with the world of medicine, it is as if antibiotics effective against certain bacteria have become ineffective against new bacteria evolved from the original strains.

The Italian observation is extremely interesting because it does not only reflect a national matter, but also highlights an international transformation and evolution of the criminal economy that is creating an increasingly finer border line with the legal economy. Being a concise description, it is not possible to provide a detailed illustration of the complex socio-economic processes that have led to the ongoing evolution. I will therefore limit myself to some rapid notes. In the 20th century, the existing geopolitical and geo-economical balances restricted the illegal activity of mafias especially within the nations of origin, thus restricting the expansion of the criminal market abroad. In that historical phase, the Cold War and international bi-polarism divided the world into two spheres of influence, respectively subjected to the hegemony of the United States and of the Soviet Union. In this context, Western traditional mafias especially practiced their violent predation in their native territories where they were rooted, and engaged in corrupt complicity and exchanges with members of the national political class who managed tenders and public spending. Outside the national borders, mafias were mainly concerned with drug trafficking, but–due to the previously mentioned geopolitical factors–were limited only to the Western countries where the per capita income was high enough to allow the purchase of illegal goods by a significant section of the population. All countries of the former Soviet empire and China were excluded from the illegal foreign market, as well as all third world countries where the per capita income was so low that it was only sufficient to survive, therefore it was not possible to purchase luxury goods.

The collapse of the Soviet empire and the resulting end of the international bipolarity season, economic globalization, the creation of a single world market for goods and the free movement of capital have completely changed the socio-economic framework in which the mafias had developed and operated until the end of the 20th century. Following the afore mentioned phenomena and other factors, over the last twenty years, a massive demand for illegal goods and services marketed by mafias has increased worldwide. Hundreds of millions of newly rich and wealthy people in the former Soviet bloc countries, in China, India and in emerging countries have gained the opportunity to share the lifestyle and its vices of the rich West, whose cultural models have an extraordinary capacity for propagation and cultural homologation. This huge part of the world's population not only consumes luxury goods and disposable goods produced by the legal economy, but also increasingly goods and services produced by the illegal economy: old- and new-generation drugs, human beings for prostitution, gambling, perfectly counterfeit brand products, etc. Growth in aggregate global demand for illegal goods has resulted in a growth in supply and an exponential growth in illegal business volumes.

The most advanced components of the mafia have therefore turned into agencies that offer on the free market the goods and services demanded by millions of people around the world. Therefore, the most significant part of criminal activity is now classifiable as a market phenomenon governed by the laws of supply and demand. Criminals exist and thrive because millions of "ordinary" citizens seek to buy illegal goods and services. They are the mirror that reflects the secret vices of so many common people in the most diverse countries in the world. Paraphrasing Hannah Arendt, we could say that the cause of the proliferation of the mafias throughout the world is not the particular wickedness of some minorities of criminals but the "banality of evil".

Following the globalization of the world economy that has disproportionately increased the amount of final consumers and goods offered, the demand for goods and services offered by the mafia has taken on macroeconomic dimensions that can no longer be governed solely by the tools of criminal law. With regard to the existing structural relationships between global market dynamics and the growth of transnational crime, I will limit myself only to two examples of drugs and prostitution. By the end of the 1980s, the world market for cocaine was limited to Western countries and was already saturated, so that the prices of drugs had dropped to become accessible to new consumers among the less well-off population. The situation changed completely when globalization opened up huge markets for new potential consumers. The emergence of a newly wealthy world bourgeoisie and the per capita income growth in emerging countries have laid the foundations for the growth of a new global drug market, which is expected to include a very high share of the world population over the next 20 years. The rapid global expansion of the drug market to engulf the entire world would render the criminal repression apparatus impotent despite all the international cooperation efforts, bearing in mind that every year only 10% of the total drug turnover is confiscated and that all the plantation eradication policies tried until now have been a failure. Revenues from the new global drug market would experience such a growth that they would give a share of wealth to transnational criminal organizations, and therefore of global power, higher than that of many states and the largest multinationals. The subsequent transformation in political terms of such economic power would entail the construction of a new hierarchy among the powers of the world. For this reason, some expect that the drug-liberalization policy may soon become an inevitable solution imposed by the disproportion of the forces involved. This first example helps to understand how the strategies to tackle transnational crime are structured on various levels, based on the evolution of macroeconomic and macro-political dynamics, realistically taking into account that transnational crime has become one of the players in the great web of powers in the world.

A second example is the prostitution market. Until the end of the 1980s, the offer of women for prostitution was limited to domestic markets and drawn from local resources, so this sector was not managed by organized crime, but predominantly by individual criminals or smaller organizations that operated in small areas of the territory. In the 1990s, the sudden entry of hundreds of thousands of women from Russia, Eastern Europe, Africa and South America into the illegal market of the prostitution led to a revolution of that market segment, causing a radical change in criminal actors and in the illegal production cycle. The increase in the supply corresponds to an ever more impressive growth in the demand by Western countries, including countries such as Israel, where prostitution was restricted and only local prostitutes are available. The need to manage industrial-scale traffic involving a number of countries—as countries of recruitment, transit and final destination of women—has led to an international division of criminal work between the mafias of various countries that corresponds to the various phases of the value-adding production process. As such, Russian, Bulgarian and Romanian *mafiosi* organizations have engaged in recruiting women in Eastern European countries. Crime in the Balkans focuses on the transit and transportation throughout various Western countries. In countries such as Italy where there are local mafias controlling the territory, economic and exchange agreements between foreign mafias and local mafia are reached. The Calabrian *"Ndrangheta"* specializes in offering foreign mafias a service consisting of the recycling of proceeds from prostitution through a deduction from recycled money. Following this extraordinary reorganization of the prostitution market, common criminal organizations that formerly managed local prostitution with artisan methods were replaced by powerful international mafias and used solely as a criminal labor force.

This phenomenon is interesting because it shows how the illegal market is dominated by the same hard Darwinian selection that characterizes competition in the legal market today. As is well-known, in the most profitable sectors of the legal economy, the market has been conquered and thus dominated by increasingly powerful economic oligopolies that have absorbed and incorporated smaller businesses. In the same way in the illegal market, transnational mafias—which can be compared to large criminal oligopolies—are progressively absorbing and incorporating common crime that is expelled with military force from the most profitable sectors. Such evolutionary selection of the "species" leads to the belief that organized crime is destined to gradually become the stable and dominant criminal form of the third millennium in all countries of the world.

The basic examples provided here show how far away from reality the cultural prejudices I mentioned at the beginning of my report are, which reduce the mafias to mere localistic phenomena arising from particular socio-cultural conditions existing only in their countries of origin. Although the socio-economic processes mentioned are causing exponential growth in the illegal activity of mafias, the perception of their danger in this historic phase is diminishing due to two factors. The first factor–immediately understandable–comes from the explosion of international Islamic terrorism that has led the most exposed states to focus their police force resources on fighting this criminal phenomenon. The second, more complicated factor derives from the fact that the mafias, following evolution in the above-mentioned marketist sense, are progressively changing both their relationship with newly established territories, reducing the use of violence, and their relationship with the legal economy which is no longer parasitic and predatory but more of a partnership and exchange. This progressive transition of mafias from violence to consensus has once again socio-economic motivations that need to be briefly mentioned. The traditional 20th century mafias were parasitic organizations that used the abuse of power to impose their domination on the territories in which they were forcing legal firms to pay bribes to colluding companies in order to secure oligopoly positions in certain market sectors. Because of their violence, their actions were visible in the territories and was considered a handicap for economic growth because it subtracted resources from the production cycle and discouraged free competition. Unlike the violent and predatory mafias of the past, the new marketist mafias are instead gaining wealth from the marketing of goods and services subject to free economic bargaining on the international market. When violence becomes necessary for the production of the illegal goods and services required, it is relocated to territories other than those of the outlet markets where the goods and services are sold.

In this respect, it is interesting to observe what has happened in Italy in recent years. Until a few years ago, in Italy the belief was widespread that the mafias existed and operated only in the three poorest and culturally underdeveloped regions of the South, namely Sicily with Cosa Nostra, Calabria being the place of origin of the *"Ndrangheta"* and Campania with the *"Camorra"*. In the northern regions, characterized by an industrial economy and a culture that is more similar to that of the countries of Central Europe, local political authorities had repeatedly claimed that the mafia did not exist in their territories because it was incompatible with the cultural traditions of those places that are more evolved than the culture of the South. To prove the absence of the mafia in the northern regions, local authorities pointed out that indeed, in those territories, no apparent forms of abuse of power and violence existed that were typical of the southern mafias. Recent investigations by the Italian judiciary have brought to light a very different and disturbing reality, proving that the southern mafias in recent decades have also silently spread into the northern regions, adopting a strategy of penetration that is different from the one practiced in the South.

In the northern regions, mafias have in fact minimized the use of violence by making targeted and careful use of it and limiting themselves to marketing illegal goods and services required by local populations (drugs, prostitutes, gambling, smuggling products), or to providing capital to local investors to be invested and services that reduce production costs or increase profit margins in an increasingly competitive market. One of the most requested services of manufacturing companies is the disposal of industrial waste at prices reduced by up to 50% compared to the market, because it is carried out with illegal methods in illegal landfills resulting in environmental damage. Another service is the supply of cheap skilled labor at minimal cost and without trade union protection. And yet, businesses are turning to mafia organizations for debt collection from debtors against whom ordinary legal proceedings are ineffective, or to request the issue of invoices attesting to non-existent costs for the purpose of tax evasion. The most advanced components of the mafia (especially the *Ndrangheta*) also invest in local economies in a forward-looking approach in order to colonize the territories in a hidden way and to integrate peacefully within the social pattern. In this way, the marketist mafias are changing their relationship with the northern territories of the new settlements. There is no longer a relationship based on aggression and predation that can give rise to alarm and rejection reactions, but a free trade relationship aligning each other's interests that generates indifference in most companies and acceptance in its most unscrupulous elements enticed by the opportunity to increase their earnings. There is thus a progressive degeneration of large parts of the social fabric that spreads from entrepreneurs to other sectors of civil society and the ruling class.

One of the most serious effects of the spread of the marketist mafia is the exponential growth of bribery of political groups and administrative personnel. Corruption has become the main channel for the penetration of the mafia into newly-established territories. Today in Italy, the term "mafia-corruption" is increasingly used to indicate the structural interpenetration between silent mafia and corruption. In order to obtain licenses, permissions, contracts, and other favors, it is not necessary to use violent methods that cause alarm. It is sufficient to use the corruptive power of money or to build up hidden partnerships with the public administrators and with the politicians who receive a share of the profits. Corruption is more effective than violence. The use of violence creates visibility in the territory and entails the risk of the threatened person finding the courage to go to the police. Corruption instead turns the corrupted subject into a partner who also has an interest in remaining silent and creates a stable and invisible network of hidden complicity, which will be useful in the future.

In recent years, criminal proceedings in the northern regions of Italy have led to the arrest of several hundreds of *mafiosi* operating in those regions where they had established subsidiaries of mafia organizations operating in the south. Together with the *mafiosi*, dozens of entrepreneurs, professionals, public administrators and politicians in business with the mafias were tried and sentenced. In some cities of the north, mafia infiltration has become so deep that the national government has had to adopt extraordinary measures set forth by Italian law, which allow ordering the dissolution of town councils elected by the populations as well as the entrustment of municipal administration to special commissioners appointed by the government. The Italian Court of Cassation, dealing with various processes involving marketist mafias operating in the north of the country, has called them the "silent mafias" simply to point out that they are entering territories invisibly.

The development of marketist and silent mafia is not an Italian phenomenon but the international paradigm of the new *modus operandi* of the most evolved mafias of the 21st century. These are mafias that, thanks to globalization, relocate the use of violence only in the territories of origin where they extract the capital and raw materials used for the production of goods and services that are then marketed on the international market. To name a few examples, Mexican mafias only use violence in their territories to control the trading of cocaine, which is then marketed in the United States and Europe in thousands of squares and places of trafficking where free market bargaining takes place. The same is true for violence in some African countries and former Soviet republics. They used to "export" thousands of women to the countries of the center of Europe. These women are condemned to be sex slaves by criminal organizations who then sell them on the free market to thousands of citizens. The Russian mafia practices violence in the areas of origin, but then invests the capital in Italy. The Italian mafia, in turn, invests capital in Russia and in the countries of the former Soviet Union. All the mafias then invest their capital in the rich countries of the center of Europe whose populations are convinced–as I said at the beginning–that the mafias do not exist in their territories because no violence is visible in the streets and neither are those *mafiosi* shoot-outs and drug lords like the protagonists of successful films and television series.

The spread of mafia-corruption is not only an Italian phenomenon but an international paradigm. It is well known that measures to combat Mexican, Russian, Balkan, and African mafias in their territories of origin are practically inexistent or extremely difficult because of the extremely dense network of complicity and protection created by corruption in the institutional bodies of those countries. Some investigations then show how corruption is a formidable tool for the hidden penetration of silent mafias even in the most advanced countries in the center of Europe. The total dissociation between basic criminal activity and capitals thanks to the marketing of illegal goods and services causes the phenomenon of silent mafias. They silently integrate into the end markets of the goods, deactivating the social reaction and response of the police force that only targets the forms of criminality that endanger public order and disturb the security of citizens.

The choice of the mafias to invest capital from illegal activities in different states and away from those of origin or from the markets where they market illegal goods and services is the result of a far-sighted strategy. It aims to neutralize the risk of criminal investigations and confiscation of capital, exploiting the opportunities for free movement of capital in the globalized world. To return to the first examples, it is extremely difficult for Italian magistrates to prove the illegal origin of the capital invested in Italy by the Russian mafia and coming from criminal activity which has taken place in that country, and for the Russian judiciary it is equally difficult to prove the illegal origin of capitals invested in Russia by Italian mafias coming from illegal activities carried out in Italy. The same difficulties exist for the mafia's investments in all countries in the center of Europe, where there are no adequate anti-money laundering laws, special criminal confiscations and specialized police forces. For this reason, for many years much of the investments of the *"Ndrangheta"* has no longer been made in Italy, but in Germany, Spain and in other countries where less effective laws and institutional mechanisms exist for the detection of illegal capital. The European Commission has pointed out that 98.9% of criminal proceeds within the European Union are not confiscated and remain accessible to criminals. In all relevant studies and conferences (e.g., in the Hague Conference on Asset Recovery-Eurojust of December 11, 2014), it clearly emerges that the existing instruments for reciprocal recognition of confiscation measures are only used in a very small number of cases. Moreover, in a historic phase such as the present one, characterized by a severe economic crisis, many countries are not interested in determining the origin of foreign capital invested in local businesses.

As I have repeatedly stressed in my report, the Italian observation is extremely interesting because it highlights a transnational historical phenomenon. The historical trend I have described is driving a revolution in the world of crime that is less focused on the individual and increasingly focused on the organizations, which are insensitive to the criminal fate of their members and to the confiscation of small parts of their illegal global turnover. The old criminal law of the criminal individuals seems destined to become an artefact of the pre-modern era, good only for the traditional forms of crime in the various states, whereas the development of a new European criminal law for criminal organizations adapted to the complex evolution of reality is still slow due to cultural resistance within the member states of the European Union. You only need to consider, to name just one example, that it has not yet been possible to establish the European Public Prosecutor set forth by Art. 86 of the Treaty on the Functioning of the European Union. Neither do the projects underway for such an establishment appear to be adequate for effectively addressing the challenges of the evolution of the organized crime in the third millennium. In an article published in a national newspaper on March 28, 2017, the Italian Minister of Justice Andrea Orlando expressed his concern that the European Commission's proposal for the creation of the European Public Prosecutor's Office in 2013 in large part lacked its innovative content after more than three and a half years of negotiations between member states' delegations within the European Council. He publicly criticized many states' resistance to the creation of a European Public Prosecutor able to effectively carry out its duties, and expressed Italy's objection to the project of creating a weak, bureaucratic structure linked to the influence of individual member states, neither suitable for its immediate purpose of protecting the Union's budget from fraud, nor with respect to possible future developments in its field of action. The latter should be extended to the repression of terrorist offenses and organized crime. While the criminal economy is already fully projected for the future in the new globalized world of the 21st century, the policies against crime still remain linked to cultural conceptions of the 20th century in many states. Although the setting up of a new European criminal order is an essential aim, it is necessary to realize that the criminal law response, albeit relevant, does not resolve the problem. In contrast, it must be seen as only one of the levers of a more complex multilevel global strategy. In order to face the complex criminal phenomena described, such a strategy must operate simultaneously on different levels, including the macro-political and macro-institutional level. A response strategy uses solely the tools of criminal repression. It is, in fact, increasingly inadequate for a criminal economy that appears to be in unstoppable expansion and silently converts the acquired economic power into social power.

Transnational mafia capitalism has assumed macroeconomic dimensions. Thus, it can become a hidden structural component of that financial capitalism now aspiring to become a hegemonic power, and aiming to renegotiate to its own advantage the leadership relationships with democratic political power on the global chessboard. The recurring phrase, which has almost become a mantra in the public discourse of politicians, that certain choices and reforms have to be made, because that is what the "markets" require, is a linguistic warning light of the hidden passage of the scepter from politics to economy, or rather to the big oligopolies capable of directing the markets by shifting enormous masses of capital from one state to another in order to influence the political choices of the states. Adequate to the "Zeitgeist", the mafias have converted to the neoliberal belief in the lawfulness and productivity of each exchange as if it were a result of free self-determination of contractors. According to this economy-centric view of social life, what counts is not the object of exchange but the freedom of exchange: the criterion for negative behavior is not legal-ethical but exclusively that of their cost-effectiveness or non cost-effectiveness. In a world in which markets and capital can dictate terms, in a society where money has become the symbolic generator of all values, in a society that has "growth" as its sole horizon, no matter how the growth was obtained, marketist mafias have ample opportunities to camouflage themselves and to integrate into the system as members of the global economic game. Capital deriving from illicit trade in the global market in fact flows as subterranean rivers into a single large sea where all the waters merge: financial capital is the driving force of the legal economy.

In this context, it is appropriate to recall that in December 1998 the prestigious American weekly "Time" drew up a list of the most influential men of the twentieth century. Among some of the top ranking men, alongside a number of giants of American capitalism such as Henry Ford, Bill Gates and others, Time introduced the famous boss of the Italian-American mafia, Lucky Luciano, of Sicilian origins. Sometime later, when I was in the United States for business, I asked them to explain the reasons for the choice to elevate Lucky Luciano to the same level as other giants of US capitalism. Luciano, I was told, had set up a historical watershed in the history of mafia-organized crime as he was the forerunner and the founder of the mafia's marketist turning point. Before Luciano, the mafia in the United States was in fact only a parasitic organization that drew resources from the productive cycle through extortion and other predatory activities, and was therefore a passive cost to the economic system. Lucky Luciano said that he could become rich without violence, transforming the mafia into an agency that provided, on the free market, illegal goods and services for which there was a massive demand from American citizens. He therefore started with the production and marketing of alcohol during Prohibition, to which he added the marketing of drugs, and then the management of prostitution on an industrial scale, gambling and so on, listing all the goods and services required by a vast market of millions of people. In this way, a market dynamic was created in which supply and demand met on a consensual basis. The enormous cash flow from this free trade activity was then invested in the legal economy, thus giving the impetus for the development of American capitalism. That's why, I was told, Luciano could be considered one of the giants of US capitalism alongside Henry Ford and Bill Gates.

For similar macroeconomic evaluations that do not include ethical and legal assessments, the EU has established that from 2014, the turnover from drug trafficking, prostitution and smuggling should be accounted for in the calculation of the GDP of the European Union countries. The marketing of drugs, sex and contraband is, in fact, considered to be a free economic transaction, unlike other illegal activities, such as extortion, characterized by the use of violence and harmful to the economy. Lucky Luciano's story is therefore not just a criminal story of the past, but the best key to understanding the success of modern markestist mafias, heirs and imitators of Luciano. I hope that the summarized considerations I have presented can help to challenge the simplified and obsolete cultural visions of mafias and raise awareness of the complexity of the challenges that await us for an effective fight against the criminals of the third millennium.

# The mafia in the media

*Petra Reski*

The media are largely responsible for the portrayal of the mafia. Articles, movies, music and even literature: They spread a certain image of the mafia. Mario Puzo did the bosses a great favor when he turned the mafia into a myth.

I must confess that I also became one of the victims of this kind of mafia folklore. I was a student, 20 years old, when I saw and loved The Godfather. I was impressed by his deeply amoral family values. So I decided that summer to drive from my hometown in the Ruhr area to Corleone, the Sicilian Mafia stronghold. I drove in a rusty Renault 4, together with my fiancé. We've never been to Italy before, ignored Venice, Rome, Florence and drove directly to Corleone within four days—just because I wanted to know how the fictional hometown of The Godfather really was. Arrived in Corleone, we saw nothing but a dusty, inconspicuous city, which looked like a boulder thrown by a giant into a rocky landscape: No indication of Mario Puzo. No resemblance to Coppola's masterpiece. So we decided to go to the beach instead.

I came back in 1989 as a journalist during the so-called "Palermo Spring"—which was not just any spring. It was the "Palermo Spring". It was a moment of hope; the world was finally stirring. Concrete crumbled in the east and even in Sicily, the foundation on which the Mafia had built its power for more than a century seemed to shift: two anti-mafia prosecutors—Giovanni Falcone and Paolo Borsellino—were seen as a ray of light, besieged by journalists from all over the world. Only three years later, there was no more hope: Falcone and Borsellino were killed.

Since then, I have never stopped writing about the Mafia in Italy. I wrote about turncoats and state witnesses, about mafia women, and how, in the years following the killings, the anti- mafia laws were gradually phased out.

One of the most important things I learned was that if there is no blood, if there is no dead body in your article, you cannot sell it. That's why I stopped writing about the mafia when on August 15th in 2007 six Italians from Calabria were executed - in the middle of Duisburg, one of the cities in the Ruhr area, the old industrial centre of West Germany. I grew up near the city.

In fact, the crime scene in Duisburg reminded me perfectly of "Goodfellas": In the hours before their death, the Italians participated in a very special mafia event—in the pocket of the eighteen-year-old Francesco Tommaso Venturi was a burnt-out prayer card of the Archangel Gabriel. That evening, the six Italians had celebrated the admission of the youngest member to the clan.

All victims came from San Luca, the stronghold of 'Ndrangheta, the Calabrian Mafia organization. Germany's most powerful Ndrangheta clan, Pelle-Romeo, has been linked to the killings.

The 'Ndrangheta is not only the richest mafia organization in Italy, but also the most mobile and largest multinational one; and the first to take root in Germany, where they found a second home in the early 1960s, ahead of the Sicilian Cosa Nostra and the Campanian Camorra. Nevertheless, German journalists barely knew of their existence.

The village of San Luca is known among Italian investigators as "the mother of crime" because it is characterized by its—even for Calabria—high density of thirty-nine clans to only four thousand inhabitants. The mafia families from San Luca are among the most powerful clans of the 'Ndrangheta—and they have a lot of members in Germany who are involved in all sorts of crimes. Whether in the international drug or arms trade, in shakedowns, abductions, car theft or money laundering, the clans of San Luca look back on decades of experience. In order not to attract attention in Germany, "fresh" young men from San Luca, who have no criminal records but are blood relatives with the bosses, are sent regularly.

The morning after the night of the Duisburg murders, Germany was in shock. The mafia only exists if there are bodies on the streets. The Germans knew the mafia from The Godfather films, maybe from The Sopranos—but hardly anyone had ever heard of the Italian mafia organization with the unspeakable name 'Ndrangheta, who had brought their war to Germany.

For decades, two clans from San Luca, the Pelle-Romeo and the Nirta-Strangio, have fought for supremacy in the drug and arms trade in Germany. Until the Duisburg massacre, the Germans saw the mafia only as an Italian problem.

The argument had always been: The German constitutional state was well prepared against all dangers; Germany was at most a "retreat" for the mafia, as if the *mafiosi* were only using Germany as a holiday destination. But as more and more research on mafia activity in Germany came to light, the situation became increasingly worrying. Suddenly Germany began to suspect that the mafia had by no means moved across their country like a summer storm, but had been firmly established in the heart of Germany for more than forty years.

The fact that the mafia had been there since the 1960s did not bother anyone—in those places where southern Italian guest workers once found work on the assembly line, in the steelworks and in the mines. The classic mafia bases in Germany are the industrial centers in the west, south and southwest: in North Rhine-Westphalia, Bavaria, Hesse and Baden-Württemberg, in cities such as Duisburg, Bochum, Oberhausen, Stuttgart and Munich; and since the fall of the Berlin Wall also in East Germany, especially in Erfurt and Leipzig.

The families of the Campanian Camorra and the Sicilian Cosa Nostra are also active in Germany. There is no competition between the individual Italian mafia organizations. There are enough pieces of "German cake" for all.

And it's not just Germany. The clans of the 'Ndrangheta are big fans of European travel freedom. They are also active in the Netherlands and Belgium, where they control the ports; in France they have invested in villas on the Côte d'Azur; in the Balkans, they control drug smuggling routes. In Portugal, Greece and Bulgaria, they invest in tourism. They do all this in harmony with the clans of the Sicilian Cosa Nostra and the Neapolitan Camorra, who have learned from the mobility of the 'Ndrangheta and also do business throughout Europe. A considerable part of the Spanish Costa del Sol belongs not only to the Neapolitan Camorra. They are also active in England and Scotland, where its members invest in real estate and cover their tracks through import-export companies. The European economic crisis is boosting the mafia's business enormously. As long as there is money, people are not interested in where it comes from.

Because the Duisburg mafia massacre initially belied the myth of Germany as a "retreat" for mafiosi, the bloody night in Duisburg was a mishap at least from the perspective of the mafia.

It was certainly not in the interests of the clan to make it clear that the mafia is not a purely Italian, but a global problem. Following the shooting in Duisburg, the Italian intelligence service from the Calabrian San Luca reported, the two enemy clans Pelle-Romeo and Nirta-Strangio had proclaimed a truce. This was also in the interest of German politics, which had as little desire as the bosses to discuss the issue of "mafia in Germany".

There was reluctance not only to alarm the citizens, but also to endanger the investments of the 'Ndrangheta. Entire East German city centers were rebuilt with 'Ndrangheta money after the fall of the wall.

Immediately after the mafia killings, a German editor asked me to write about the mafia in Germany. My book Honored Society was published a year after the massacre in Duisburg—at a time when the bosses tried with all their strength to convince the Germans: "Do not worry, the mafia exists only in backward Italian villages!"

The mafiosi devoted themselves intensively to image management: Giovanni Strangio, one of the Duisburg murderers, has already given interviews on the run in which he portrayed himself as an Italian unjustly persecuted by the criminal justice system, who alone was guilty of being born in San Luca.

The worldwide triumph of the mafia is not only based on violence; it is based primarily on money and friendly words.

As long as people believe in the myths of the mafia, the mafia is not in danger. That's why journalists in the mafia's service are so valuable: the bosses do not hide from journalists, but want to use them as megaphones for their messages. Therefore, it does not raise the question of whether a journalist manages to talk to a boss; but rather, whether one is prepared to be used by him for his propaganda.

In Germany, too, many naive journalists became servants of mafia propaganda. German defenders of the mafia spread press reports of innocent, persecuted pizza bakers, and many German journalists recorded heart-breaking immigrant stories on their notepads. There was talk of "clinging to the clan" and racism—but not of the 229 clans and over 1800 members of the 'Ndrangheta on the list in the report of the Bundeskriminalamt (the German Federal Criminal Police Office).

When my book came out, forgetfulness had already set in again. The mafia was once again a "cult": As computer games, TV series, as party music, veiled in folkloristic garb successfully sold their propaganda—like the belief that members do not murder women and children, that they are God-fearing and victims of the Italian state, and that they do not want to do anything other than to make a good Pizza Romana in Germany.

One of 'Ndrangheta's most successful public relations agents is Francesco Sbano, a well-known Calabrian producer of mafia music CDs. Based in Hamburg, he launched a successful media campaign designed to convince people that the Mafia is a special folkloric brigade, a vulnerable group that sings, dances and occasionally kills somewhere in the Aspromonte gorges. There was almost no German media outlet that had not written about it. Sbano promotes songs about the murder of the prefect of the Palermo police, Dalla Chiesa: "The General was killed / He had no time for one last prayer / He was sent directly to Paradise." Almost every year, Sbano shows up in Germany with a new PR campaign in favor of 'Ndrangheta. He could even add an illustrated book to his mafia music with lyrics by respected anti-mafia writers such as Roberto Saviano, Nicola Gratteri or Rita Borsellino—without the authors knowing.

Indeed, one year after the Duisburg murders, Sbano was lauded in an editorial by Der Spiegel magazine as "the man who enjoys the trust of many bosses" and was therefore selected to accompany two reporters from the magazine on their trip to Calabria to conduct a mafia reportage.

Together with a reporter from Der Spiegel the mafia music producer presented the alleged confessions of the alleged mafia boss "Giuliano Belfiore", which were published in Germany as "The honor of silence—The true confession of a mafia boss". The Confessions were given under a false name and certifiable documents have either been left out completely and/or changed. In the preface, Sbano explains that he wants to keep the identity of the boss secret in order not to harm his professional reputation.

The title of the book itself is nonsense: A mafia boss who tells the truth about his life and the Mafia is about as realistic as a flying cow. And yet, such stories are apparently easy to sell in Germany; just like this fairy tale from the chatterbox boss.

In Germany, people are also unaware that the bosses never hide from journalists, but eagerly chase after those who can spread their mafia messages in the language of the media. The question here is not whether a journalist manages to talk to a boss; it depends on how journalists can be used as propaganda tools.

How much my book has disturbed the mafia's tour of benevolence in Germany, I soon found out. It was necessary to make an example: Punish a person to teach hundreds to a lesson. Shortly after the publication, I was threatened at a reading in Erfurt. Five lawsuits and two complaints were filed against me and my book.

When I came to Palermo for the first time as a journalist in 1989 and saw Giovanni Falcone and Paolo Borsellino, I could not have imagined that one day I would stand trial for a book on the mafia and my readings in Germany require police protection. Soon after, my book was censored at the behest of German judges.

When I held my book with its judicially arranged, darkened parts for the first time, these pages seemed strangely unreal to me. As if the book had emerged from the underground—as if it were a book that could be dangerous to read. I expected my fingers to turn black when I ran them over these sections. The Italian media reported extensively on the peculiarity that an Italian restaurant owner and a Duisburg-based hotelier born in San Luca had darkened some parts in my book—per disposal. Even the rigorously tested Italian mafia journalists never had to blacken pages in a book about the mafia but I had to blacken parts that I had thoroughly backed up with the files of German and Italian mafia investigators.

How few German judges know about the mafia, I learned first-hand in various German courtrooms. You may be forgiven for not being able to pronounce the word "Ndrangheta", but not for underestimating what lies behind the mafia's strategy—trying to prevent journalists from reporting on the mafia. I do not see a journalist's job in reporting on a mafioso already sitting behind bars. As a journalist, I am much more concerned with raising awareness of the dangers of the mafia and providing information that is supported by numerous reliable sources (this is better known in the German legal language as "Verdachtsberichterstattung" or "press coverage of suspicions"). Ultimately, it's about whether the names of suspected parties are kept secret by the authorities or may be publicly disclosed by journalists like me.

It is no merit to show that the mafia is made up of violent, bad guys. It is not very difficult to show problems of mafia bosses as a kind of outlaw story. But the mafia is not an outlaw story. It is the story of a criminal organization that has survived only through the active support of entire societies—policemen, politicians, prosecutors, lawyers, business people—of the entire white collar community.

If your portrayal on the mafia only shows the bad guys, it is like writing about fascism and talking only about Hitler and Goebbels. All this was possible only because of the moral support of a whole country. The same goes for the mafia. The mafia is not a foreign body, not an alien element in a society. Wherever they are, they are part of society.

After The Honored Society with its blackened sentences, I wrote another book in which I illustrated the journey that I had made to Corleone from my hometown in Kamen, Germany, all those years ago. It is a kind of "Grand Tour of Mafialand". Just to show them: Okay, if you're trying to threaten me, this new book is my answer.

Still, I felt some kind of self-censorship as I was writing, and even afterwards, sitting down at the table with the attorney to check what I can write and what not.

A legal way to silence journalists is the personal rights, which German courts consider more important than public interest. Today, the influence of the mafia on the media is much more sophisticated and not just based on fear. You can write as much as you like about mafia violence, but journalists are in trouble if they discover the mafia's business or relationships with politicians and business people.

Even though it is common knowledge today that the mafia's business in Germany is worth billions due to drug and arms trafficking deals, and money laundering by cover-up companies, the legal framework is not keen. Unlike Italy, membership in the mafia is not a criminal offense per se in Germany. While the authorities in Germany have to prove that the millions invested in real estate have been acquired illegally, the opposite is true for Italy: if a suspect cannot prove how he acquired the money, the money is confiscated.

Compared to the damage caused to the economy and civil society, the mafia's business goes unnoticed. Publishers fear legal actions: According to my book, two more books on the mafia in Germany have been blacked out. This is how it works for the "Godfathers", they became a kind of guardian of freedom of speech in Germany.

The publishers may not want to pay for the lawsuit, so you as a writer become a problem for them. And if you are personally sued and you cannot afford long court cases, they can eventually ruin you economically. I experienced it this year: I wrote an article about the oddity that not a single journalist, brought to justice in Germany by "successful Italian businessmen", has won the lawsuits.

In my article in the weekly newspaper Freitag I mentioned the name of a "successful Italian businessman" who operates in Erfurt and puts German television on trial. The verdict already drew attention to his name in public—two newspapers and a news agency had already cited his name in their articles before me. So I did nothing but "court reporting". It was a public ruling I referred to—but I lost the case. And not only that: The owner and editor-in-chief of Freitag—the son of the Der Spiegel founder—refused to help me and deleted the article from his website without even discussing it with me. I have been told that the "legal fee for a publisher as small as ours is quite a burden."

It does not seem to have occurred to anyone working on Freitag that the legal and attorney fees may be even more burdensome for someone like me who wrote the article for 321 Euros. That's why I went public—and started crowdfunding my attorney fees: I am pleased to say that I have raised 25,000 Euros. But the trial is not over yet: The Italian businessman wanted compensation: 25,000 Euros, as much as my crowdfunding. Only in April 2018, the court dismissed the action.

My response to threats and legal action was to change my way of writing. It was also a way to turn a very humiliating experience into something positive. To avoid further complaints, I have translated my experience into three fictional novels: In 2017, my third novel, Despite Love [Bei aller Liebe], was published. It is about Serena Vitale, a Sicilian anti-mafia prosecutor.

But as we see with Mario Puzo, there are also risks in literature. Many authors of mafia novels turned out to be victims of their own fascination. Andrea Camilleri even accused his friend, the Sicilian writer Leonardo Sciascia, of portraying the mafia too sympathetically and too intriguing, for example when he lets Don Mariano talk on the division of humanity into "human, half human, ass kissers and chatterboxes" in The Day of the Owl.

Roberto Saviano also seems to be as blinded by mafia spells as many guys in Naples—without noticing that he does the mafia a favor by describing them as invincible characters.

The mafia is powerful only by its followers who can be used as service providers for their purposes. Without them, the mafia would not exist for a long time.

For me, the really exciting thing about writing about the mafia is the so-called "gray area": It is infinitely productive literary—more interesting and multifaceted than the mafia itself. Without this "gray area", the mafia would have never existed. Without the support of the supposedly good, without the cowardice of many and the closed mouths of all those who can realize personal advantage from the mafia, without their sympathizers—entrepreneurs, politicians, wives, lawyers, notaries, bishops, mayors, policemen and journalists—The mafia would have been defeated for a long time.

All those who only pretend that they are on the right side are extremely rewarding—at least from a literary point of view.

# The fight against organized crime

*David Ryan Kirkpatrick*

Our traditional understanding of organized crime is influenced by Italian criminal gangs. Much better known as Mafia they represent a national phenomenon divided by regional roots and developments. Those groups have been established in the 19<sup>th</sup> century and started with black mailing and other crimes which have been realized on local or regional fields only. Even today they are trying to enforce their own interests in controversy to political authorities and administration. Corruption may play an important role when asking why the Italian law enforcement authorities are not able to disband those groups. Active and passive bribery makes it possible to influence political decisions and violence is one of their ways to keep noncriminal entrepreneurs out of their territory. It seems like a virus which has infiltrated Italian society.

Today, for most of the people, drug trafficking is the centerpiece of organized crime. It is true that there are more than only a few aspects to focus on in order to realize how this phenomenon is characterized. In history, we have had a very liberal handling until the consumption of drugs did become a serious problem for society. The modern legislation was following the significant change in drug use by different social classes. In the decades before, selling drugs was not illegal; all kinds of products were easy to buy in any pharmacy. Obviously, the so called "hardline-approach" was to reduce the number of customers for sanitary reasons and became a success story. For a very long period, drug consumption was no problem in the Western world until the need for drugs did change as a result of the Vietnam War. It started with cannabis sales and was followed by heroin and cocaine in the early 80`s of the last century. It is not a surprise that German law enforcement authorities did change their organizational structure and methods of investigation at the same time. It was simply a reaction to a new kind of criminality using typical characteristics of legal economy.

The production of the raw material occurs in South America or southern Asia by planting and harvesting coca plants or opium poppy. The further processing of these natural products either takes place close to the farmers in South America,

© Springer Fachmedien Wiesbaden GmbH, part of Springer Nature 2020
M. Pohlmann et al. (eds.), *Bribery, Fraud, Cheating*, Organization,
Management and Crime – Organisation, Management und Kriminalität,
https://doi.org/10.1007/978-3-658-29062-7_5

Colombia for example, or outside of Afghanistan and some other opium producing countries. There is a complex system of production in the background beginning with the cultivation of plants and ending with the final sale to the customer. By the time, offenders living in other regions were inventing new forms of Methamphetamine which demands acquisition of some basic chemical elements only.

All kinds of those illegal goods are transported and distributed by freelance professionals. We cannot notice a variety of internationally operating criminal gangs as significant character of organized crime but a system of division of labor. Different tasks involve risks such as prosecution but also profit. Based on analysis we must realize that organized crime means nothing else but the production and sale of illegal goods or the illegal sale of legal goods. There is no special crime realized by criminal gangs or individual offenders. They are all taking part in a system of merchandising illegal products. Any discussion about the organized crime must realize that we are confronted with a mirror image of legal economic system.

Another kind of typical modern crime is the still growing market of illegal employment which should remind society of slavery in the past. Social standards of the labor market are suspended for low costs and maximum profit. And it is especially alarming that former drug dealers are entering this growing market.

Due to the many different forms of appearance of organized crime there is no simple solution for fighting this kind of criminality. But most of the essential manifestations of organized crime could be prevented without legislation and criminal proceedings because it is a question of supply and demand. If there were no customers for illegal products the criminals would be forced to search for alternative professions. Without drug abuse or the desire for (faked) luxury items for low prices there would be no illegal market for these goods. Insourcing of different services would end illegal employment and allow for fair competition between legal operating companies, income taxes could be reduced and social security contribution as well. This shows how much daily life is affected by organized crime.

Organized crime is an endless story of misunderstanding caused by several deficits. There is no international agreement on a definition of this special kind of criminality. More than 50 different explanations are known all over the world, all trying to express an individual approach. It would be valuable to develop a common terminology which could then be used for statistics and harmonization of legislation. It would also allow for special arrangements for mutual assistance in multilateral treaties.

This lack of valid statistics hinders a solid political discussion about our legislation and staffing levels of law enforcement authorities in the future also. Whenever discussing current or new methods of law enforcement, protesters resort to civil rights to protect innocent citizens from the theoretical risk of prosecution. By the way, they always do forget that a serious suspect is necessary to start an investigation. Another reason for the deficit may be implemented in our criminal code because there are only a few articles demanding economic damage as an element of the offense. As a result, we don't have a valid overview of the economic consequences for society. The United Nations Office on Drugs and Crime has been reporting on the international drug market for 20 years in its World Drug Report. Most of the facts about the economic damage either to the national economy or individual victims can only be obtained by analyzing public databases of private sources like assurance companies. As a result, we cannot provide any legitimate information about the extent of illegal activities. However, without a valid overview, there will be no political reason to optimize legislation.

Any evaluation of criminal gangs shows that there are always different reasons responsible for their creation and development. However, one common reason is an institutional weakness and deficits in the social welfare system.

Cases of bribery are typically not identical with organized crime. Corruption may be used by groups of organized crime as a tool to enforce their own interests in a specific matter, but it is not a criterion. The story behind the FIFA investigation, for example, is interpreted by the press as a mafia case due to the hush money and the money paid for decisions. But is there any indication for distribution of illegal goods or illegal employment? It's a simple case of corrupt officials wanting to participate when a city or state wants to organize a soccer championship.

For a very long period of time, organized crime did appear in a lot of different types of organizations. However, technical revolution and new forms of communication make it possible to create international cooperation without having to be a member of the same or even any organization. Car theft and theft of vehicle parts like navigation systems primarily realized by Lithuanian offenders for Eastern European market and customers in China is representative of the actual situation. The search for the location of an automobile requested by a client takes place via the internet, using the manufacturers' databases. Vehicle parts are stolen for a global market and distributed via internet shops. It only takes about two weeks from the theft of a navigation system is in Germany and its installation in an automobile in China. Until the product is identified as a stolen good, the internet shop will be closed down and there will be no further chance to prosecute the offenders. Most of the involved persons want to remain anonymous and prefer online communication. There is no need for personal contact. The anonymity of the internet is giving organized crime opportunity to make its business with very low risks of prosecution outside the dark net as well. Therefore, any investigation must fail if it is not possible to get electronic communication under surveillance.

This example shows that it is not necessary to form an organization with a large number of members. You need an agent for acquisition and a close contact to a corrupt employee of the manufacturer who has access to the databases. Only a few members with technical skills are necessary and the capital of 30.000,00 Euros to finance a scanner for the keyless entry system of modern cars. Every criminal act is carried out within five minutes which provides the opportunity to get several items in just one night.

In spite of technical invention, receiving stolen goods for gain has become a prospering illegal market. Theft of automobile parts causes damages of more than 300 million Euros each year paid by innocent individual victims and the community of policyholders. Actually, law enforcement authorities are not able to protect society against these forms of organized crime. It is alarming how the abolishment of the border controls in the EU is exploited for criminal purposes without risk of punishment. The investigation of such crimes demands a close co-operation between law enforcement agencies in the affected states.

Organized forms of burglary are another version of modern criminality. Both variants of theft are caused by different groups of offenders which may give us opportunity to recognize that there must be an annual international agreement about the division of crime scenes and criminal activities. Whenever investigating cases of drug trafficking, we have to realize that there is a special relation between the type of drug and the nationality of the (foreign) offender. And there is no gang war to report when focusing either management of cross border transports or those dealers who are selling the drugs to the final customer. In cases of burglary, there is serious information that foreign criminal groups make territorial arrangements and the period of time for the execution of their criminal operations. Only the existence of an annual conference with leading representatives of organized crime could give a satisfying explanation for the peaceful partnership between several organizations.

The constitutional state is actually endangered as a result of a constant negative process. There is a variety of factors responsible for the weakness of law enforcement. In principle, the constitution is the foundation of the rule of law and democracy and establishes the institutional and material core elements of the legal system of each state. However, these abstract rules have to be guaranteed in practice. The general agreement to the constitutional state will disappear if law enforcement authorities are not able to protect society.

Today, organized crime is visible for everyone. Product piracy gives opportunity for everyone to get in contact with illegal products. No product is safe from unauthorized production in Asia and hence from being sold for less. Once again, the interests of the offenders match those of the buyers. The interest of customers in saving money and the offenders in profit maximization gives organized crime a platform for economic growth without the risk of prosecution. Most of the customers know about the illegal aspect, but it is more important to them to get an item from their favorite brand.

Organized crime is still a job machine in several countries all over the world. Farmers in South America and Afghanistan are strongly dependent on cultivating coca plants and opium poppy. As long as there is no alternative the legislation in the western hemisphere will not be able to reduce the annual drug production. And if Western societies are unable to integrate all members into general economic growth, there will be a constant demand for drugs, as the current situation in the USA shows. There are a lot of participants in those chains from production to final sale. That makes it easy to replace any drug dealer immediately.

Law enforcement cannot be the only reaction and criminal law only the last resort. Every nation has a portfolio of strategies. Nevertheless, there is no cooperation between several institutions and disciplines even yet. Foreign offenders, drug dealers for example, don´t have to fear deportation as a consequence of conviction. For most of them, imprisonment is nothing but an accident and a "nice" time to recover.

Germany has become a perfect crime scene. After the Duisburg shooting, mafia operations became known in Germany. But did anything change? Not one single article in our code of criminal procedure has been evaluated and nothing has changed. There is not even any political interest in starting the fight against organized crime. Law makers are not taking care of the protection of individual rights and citizens have to protect themselves supported only by tax benefits. There's no lobby for the idea of a state under rule of law. In order to execute national law, personnel must be able to carry out long term investigations. But for more than 25 years, the number of employees of law enforcement authorities has been reduced for fiscal reasons.

Today, the challenge of terrorism may influence political interests for law enforcement authorities and their requirements to prevent terror attacks. However, there is no interest in getting organized crime under control, because there is no understanding for the evident linkage between both kinds of criminality. The funding of terrorist organizations requires organized forms of criminality like drug trafficking in Europe. Street sale of cocaine in the Netherlands followed by money laundering in Germany is only one example of how Arabian terrorist groups are financing their activities. Sales tax fraud in Europe is a further example of how terrorism is financing its different organizations. The annual profit may reach more than 100 billion Euros when focusing on criminal actions in Europe. This situation should give reason for changing political decisions referring to essential national interests.

The political discussion about interception and recording of private conversations on private premises and getting information on telecommunication connections expresses that there is no understanding for the measures that law enforcement authorities need for successful investigations. In spite of the public opinion, the constitution is not only taken care about privacy. As an essential aspect of civil rights, it also demands that the political institutions have to respect for and protect the individual interest in staying free and save without becoming a victim of serious criminal offenses. Today, offenders are using any kind of telecommunication in order to operate in an international setting. Cross-border businesses are part of criminal activities daily. Without technical surveillance, no network will be identified and no evidence will be collected. Private economy is supporting offenders as well. Cellphone manufacturers are trying to provide interception or analysis of phone calls and internet communication, messenger systems are designed for secret communication.

The state under rule of law is an indispensable achievement and an essential part of any democracy. Actually, lawmakers are responsible for creating the legal and regulatory framework for any kind of investigation. Most of them are not able to realize that we are talking about a profession and a second kind of economy. Our traditional understanding of criminal law explains it as a legislation made for a subculture only. That makes it hard to realize that our legal system gives organized crime opportunity to save their profits. Bank accounts as crime scenes and financial advisors as assistants of unlawful acts are hard to imagine.

Following the money trail could be an important practical asset to get to the center of criminal networks. Successful operations of Drug Enforcement Administrations in are proof of the importance of new forms of proceedings. To focus only on one single offender is old fashioned and does have any positive effect. Nonetheless, any investigation into money laundering requires detailed knowledge of the financial market and available methods of anonymization. Only specialists of global financial markets are able to carry out successful investigations.

For the economy, there is no difference between legally earned money and illegal profits. Political decisions depend on the interests of economy only. In both cases, we are talking about an investment which creates jobs and therefore reduces unemployment. Russian organized crime shows that it is possible to become a very successful businessman respected by politicians and the public.

By the time any high class offender changes into the role of a manager of a legit company nobody is cares about their criminal career before.

The history of the Financial Intelligence Unit (FIU) in Germany shows that political interest does not focus on the clear up of serious crime. July 1$^{st}$ 2017 the FIU became a fig leaf which doesn't support prosecutor offices and tax investigation. Information about suspicious transactions reported by the finance sector does not reach prosecution offices any longer. It's a political decision of the government to support the sector of illegal employment influenced by powerful lobby groups. Without the instrument of financial investigations as a result of suspicious financial transactions and investments, law enforcement loses an important source for starting criminal proceedings in cases of organized crime. Obviously, it doesn't matter that this handling of money laundering is not in conformity with the recommendations of the Financial Action Task Force and its international standards for combating money laundering, terrorist financing and proliferation of weapons of mass destruction. It is one further piece of evidence that the idea of the state under rule of law has no political advocate any longer.

In the near future, lawmakers will have to notice that there are several challenges and threats to be identified for serious political reaction. Therefore, legislation has to be evaluated for implementing modern technical methods.

Law enforcement authorities need constant technical support and more employees for being able to act powerful. Data protection belongs to our civil rights. But if legislation prefers it as a guideline for any reform of criminal proceeding acts, there will be no chance to get efficient tools for efficient investigations. Personal freedom is guaranteed by the constitution and the rules of law. But that doesn't mean that a professionally operating offender must not fear criminal prosecution. Without efficient law enforcement, the political system will lose its reputation and its general acceptance in society. Any criminal prosecution is under control of the legal system and prevents capriciousness of prosecution offices. There is no reason for mistrust and a kind of legislation which does not follow technical requirements.

Most traditional opinions and methods need to change so that organized crime can be successfully combated in the future.

# Corporate crime and
political corruption in South America

# Anti-corruption in Brazil – Criticisms and developments

*Fausto De Sanctis*

## 1 Introduction

Brazil is well known for courtesy, but courtesy has become a synonym of corruption. Brazilians feel that our moral reached the bottom of the well. On the other side, even lay people are aware of the meaning of money laundering. They know the names of the Justices of the Brazilian Supreme Court, including the way they decide, because it is possible to watch judicial sessions live on TV.

Also on TV, in the 70s, in an advertisement with a famous Brazilian football player, Gérson de Oliveira Nunes, a sentence became the symbol of our culture: "we must take advantages in all situations", which was taken as a good orientation in that time; but, today it has been taken as a symbol of corruption.

In Brazil, public institutions historically have been used for a great variety of private interests, allowing all sorts of schemes to obtain illegal gains, in a constant exchange of favors, excesses, and neglect of public resources. During the last few decades, Brazil has experienced moments of deep uneasiness with the many scandals involving corruption and money laundering in the political environment which culminated in street protests. The overwhelming demonstrations that occurred were fueled by discontent with inadequate public services and recurring corruption scandals. The demands from demonstrators were many and they made their voices heard.

People went to the streets (in 2014, 2015, and 2016), tiring of so much corruption and high levels of taxation, but deficient public services. They started a cognitive liberation when the public collectively came to realize that they have power and they have a voice. Little by little, they became aware that corruption is a co-production work and a part of human rights issues. In fact, there is no corruption without affecting people at the same time (education, food, environmental, healthcare). For many people, especially some politicians, it seems not to matter if there is no clean water, a sewer system etc.

© Springer Fachmedien Wiesbaden GmbH, part of Springer Nature 2020
M. Pohlmann et al. (eds.), *Bribery, Fraud, Cheating*, Organization, Management and Crime – Organisation, Management und Kriminalität, https://doi.org/10.1007/978-3-658-29062-7_6

Most people, being part of a so called informal democracy, are more vigilant, denouncer and qualifier or disqualifier against rulers. These are protected by themselves and the population remains unprotected. Thereby, on the one hand, there are the rulers and their protégés and, on the other hand, the governed and the unprotected. They ask for clear answers that are not the result of cynicism, egocentrism, corporatism and self-protection.

Internet has helped a lot to combat this unfair situation: It turns out to be an uncensored source of opinion and the place of origin of a lot of criticism of the authorities' decisions.

A large number of Brazilians are looking forward to the jail term of Luís Inácio Lula da Silva, our former president. The current one, Michel Temer (indicted twice for racketeering, acting in favor of private interests), had one of his right-hand ministers being caught with 51 million reais (17 million dollars) in cash. The Lower House rejected both indictments on President Michel Temer, not allowing the criminal procedure to take its course at the Brazilian Supreme Court. In short, what Brazilians expect today is to apply the rule of law, equally.

## 2    Brazilian criminal doctrine and jurisprudence

In Brazil, there is a devaluation of the law and of the importance of respecting the law. This is due to a long period of dictatorship (from 1937 to 1946 and from 1964 to 1985) which usually misrepresented the purpose of the law. That is why the fundamental principles, given the abuses committed at the time of the dictatorship, have gained enormous strength and the Constitution has been praised as a diploma that should have as many principles and rules as possible. The current Constitution (of 1988) has 250 articles, not counting the 114 articles of the Acts and Transitory Provisions. It has been amended for more than a hundred times. Brazil has had eight federal Constitutions (1824, 1891, 1934, 1937, 1946, 1964, 1967, and 1988).

"Brazilian Criminal Doctrine and Jurisprudence" was always developed with the justification of the criminal guarantee, the right to a fair trial. The criminal procedure has a guarantor role. All the rights provided for in the Constitution will be guaranteed to the citizen; there is no point in, for example, assuring the right of ample defense with all means and resources inherent therein (article 5, LV) if the criminal sanction was applied without a person being able to defend himself against the facts that he was charged with.

This has led to an ineffective judicial system. Many times, the interpretation of law is done in an absolute way. But absolutism goes against the idea of democracy. Democracy is a form of government in which one establishes who has the power of decision, in what form, and on behalf of whom, the majority or the minority. The "defenders" of democracy usually attack some judicial positions either because they represent their potential actions or internal temptations, or their sources of getting easy money. Most of them try to combat their rebellious desires or third party interests.

In fact, the "Brazilian Criminal Doctrine and Jurisprudence" was designed, conceived and applied mainly to wealthy or politically influential people. Impunity is the rule. This has contaminated the whole system, even when dealing with soft targets like drug traffickers and common street crimes. So far, Judiciary has been meager to combat corruption, thus discouraging all enforcement bodies to tackle corruption accurately.

In the following, a few examples of misrepresentation of the purpose of the rule of law shall be outlined:

i. *Habeas Corpus*: Any single decision can be challenged by a *Habeas Corpus*, even if there is an appeal to manage or the defendant is not in jail. For example, a refusal to hear a witness who does not know the facts may take place. This constitutional measure can become a way to dismiss any case by a single judicial decision in higher courts and can become a way to defraud the due process of law;
ii. Detention after being convicted: It is possible only in case of a final decision; in 2016, however, the Supreme Court in two different decisions allowed for people also to be arrested if the decision is upheld by a court of appeals because higher instances of Justice only interpret the law. The Supreme Court decided to review this last legal position, after heavy pressure from lawyers, notably those who work for defendants in high-profile cases;
iii. Handcuffs: They are prohibited unless there is a proven risk to the life of others. The binding decision of the Brazilian Supreme Court (no. 11/S.T.F.)

states in this regard: "It is only lawful to use handcuffs in cases of resistance and a well-founded fear of flight or danger to the physical integrity of the prisoner or others, justifying the exceptionality in writing, under penalty of disciplinary, civil and criminal liability for the policeman or authority and of the nullity of the arrest or of the procedural act to which it refers, without prejudice to the civil liability of the State". The decision was made when a well-connected banker went to jail;

iv. Access to investigation: Binding decision no. 14/S.T.F.: "It is the right of the defender, in the interests of the defendant, to have ample access to evidence that, already documented in an investigative procedure, concerns the exercise of the right of defense". There is a risk of ineffectiveness of the investigation if it investigates the participation of accomplices;

v. Tax crime configuration: Binding decision no. 24/S.T.F.: "There is no material crime against the tax order, provided for in art. 1°, items I to IV[1], of Law no. 8.137/90, before the definitive taxation by the tax administration" has taken place. Criminal Judicial decisions depend on administrative authorities, whose decisions usually take a long time for the verification of tax disorders. Many cases are being dismissed due to the Statute of Limitations;

vi. *Plea Bargaining*: Law n. ° 12,850, Aug 2, 2013, articles 4 to 6, allows plea bargaining after the trial even if the case is being decided by Superior Courts. There is a trend (justices debate at the Supreme Court) to bind judges to the prosecution agreement reg. the penalty what represents a risk of Check and Balances policy. It is possible to observe a non-respect to the legal principle of legality: penalties without criteria being dealt with defendants (any fine or execution of sentence different from the criminal law; several pleaders in the same case etc.). This constitutes clear evidence of

---

[1] Art. 1° - It is a crime against the tax order to suppress or reduce tax, or social contribution and any accessory, through the following conducts: I – omitting information, or give a false declaration to tax authorities; II – Cheating tax inspection, inserting inaccurate elements, or omitting operation of any nature, in a document or book required by the tax law; III – Falsify or alter invoice, invoice, duplicate, sales note, or any other document related to the taxable transaction; IV – To elaborate, distribute, supply, issue or use document that knows or should know false or inaccurate; V – Deny or fail to provide, when required, invoice or equivalent document, relating to the sale of goods or rendering of service, effectively carried out, or to provide it in disagreement with the legislation. Penalty - imprisonment of two (2) to five (5) years, and fine.

impunity for pleaders too. Judicial pardons have been granted by prosecutors without strict criteria;

vii. Abuse of power crime bill (PLS 85/2017): If a court of appeals reverses the decision it will constitute a crime ("hermeneutic crime"). This represents a threat to the independence of judges and prosecutors;

viii. Repatriation law: Any investigation from the Federal Reserve, Internal Revenue Service and any other body is prohibited under law when there is a simple statement that the funds have no origin in corruption (Law no. 13,254, Jan. 13, 2016);[2]

ix. **Soft penalties:** High risk of the dismissal of case due to the Statute of Limitations (it can be counted retroactively)[3];

---

[2] Article 5 – The adhesion to the program will be given by means of delivery of the declaration of the resources, goods and rights subject to the regularization provided for in the caput of art. 4 and full payment of the tax provided for in art. 6 and of the fine provided for in art. 8 of this Law (15% + 15%). Paragraph 1. The fulfillment of the conditions set forth in the caput before a criminal decision will extinguish, in relation to resources, assets and rights to be settled under the terms of this Law, the punishability of the following crimes, practiced up to the date of joining the Repatriation Law (RERCT): (Given by Law no. 13,428 of 2017). **I** – In art. 1 and in items I, II and V of art. 2 of Law no. 8,137, of December 27, 1990; **II** – In Law no. 4,729, of July 14, 1965; **III** – In art. 337-A of Decree-Law no. 2,848, of December 7, 1940 (Penal Code); **IV** – In the following articles of Decree-Law no. 2,848, of December 7, 1940 (Penal Code), when its harmful potentiality is exhausted with the practice of the crimes foreseen in items I to III: A) 297; B) 298; C) 299; D) 304; **V** – (Vetoed); **VI** – In the caput and in the sole paragraph of art. 22 of Law no. 7,492 of June 16, 1986; **VII** – In art. 1 of Law 9,613 of March 3, 1998, when the object of the crime is a good, right or value derived, directly or indirectly, from the crimes provided for in items I to VI; **VIII** – (Vetoed). Paragraph 2. The extinction of the punishment referred to in § 1o: I – (Vetoed); II – Will only occur if the fulfillment of the conditions precedes the final decision of the condemnatory criminal decision; III – Will produce, in relation to the public administration, the extinction of all obligations of a foreign exchange or financial nature, principal or accessory, including those of a merely formal nature, that could be payable in relation to declared assets and rights, except those provided for in this Law. § 3o (Vetoed). § 4o (Vetoed). Paragraph 5 In the hypothesis of items V and VI of § 1o, the extinction of punishability shall be restricted to cases in which the resources used in the unauthorized exchange transaction, currencies or currencies leaving the country without legal authorization or deposits held abroad and not declared to the competent federal office, have a lawful origin or come directly or indirectly from any of the crimes provided for in items I, II, III, VII or VIII of § 1. Article 6 For the purposes of the provisions of this Law, the amount of assets subject to regularization shall be considered as a capital increase acquired on December 31, 2014, although on that date there is no balance or title of ownership, pursuant to item II of the caput and § 1 of art. 43 of Law 5,172 of October 25, 1966 (National Tax Code), subject to a physical or legal person to pay income tax thereon, as a capital gain, at the rate of 15% (Fifteen percent), effective as of December 31, 2014. **Article 7** – The adhesion of RERCT may be made within 210 (two hundred and ten) days, counted from the date of entry into force of the Brazilian IRS (RFB) act referred to in art. 10, with a declaration of the equity situation on December 31, 2014 and the consequent payment of the tax and the fine. **Paragraph 1.** The *disclosure or publicity* of the information present in the RERCT shall imply *an equivalent effect to the breach of tax confidentiality*, subjecting the person responsible to the penalties provided for in Complementary Law no. 105, of January 10, 2001, and in art. 325 of Decree-Law no. 2,848, of December 7, 1940 (Penal Code), and, in the case of a public official, to the penalty of dismissal. **Paragraph 2.** *Without prejudice to the provisions of paragraph 6 of art. 4, the Brazilian IRS (RFB), the National Monetary Council (CMN), the Central Bank of Brazil and other public agencies intervening in the RERCT are prohibited from disclosing or sharing information provided by the declarants who have joined RERCT with the States, the Federal District and Municipalities, including for tax credit constitution purposes.*

x. Pardon: In 2016, even in case of penalties up to 12 years it is possible to get this benefit, unless there is threat or violence (art.3). If there is threat or violence, up to 4 years' imprisonment, the defendant can benefit from a pardon

---

[3] *Passive corruption.* Art. 317 - Request or receive, for himself or for another, directly or indirectly, even if out of the function or before assuming it, but on account of it, improper advantage, or accept promise of such an advantage: Penalty - *imprisonment, from two (2) to twelve (12) years, and fine.* (Drafting provided by Law 10,763, dated 12.11.2003). Paragraph 1 – The penalty is *increased by one third* if, as a result of the advantage or promise, the civil servant delays or stops practicing any act of office or practices it in violation of functional duty. Paragraph 2 – If the civil servant practices, fails to practice or delay an official act, with violation of functional duty, yielding at the request or influence of others: Penalty - detention, from three months to one year, or fine. *Active corruption.* Art. 333 – To offer or promise an undue advantage to a public official, to determine him to practice, omit or delay act of office: Penalty – *imprisonment, from two (2) to twelve (12) years, and fine.* (Drafting provided by Law 10,763, dated 12.11.2003). Sole paragraph – The penalty shall be increased by one third if, due to the advantage or promise, the official delays or omits an act of office, or practices it in violation of functional duty. *Money laundering* (Law no. 9,613, March 3, 1998). Article 1 – Hide or disguise the nature, origin, location, disposition, movement or ownership of property, rights or values arising, directly or indirectly, from a criminal offense. (Drafting provided by Law no. 12,683, of 2012). Penalty: *imprisonment, from 3 (three) to 10 (ten) years, and fine.*

(art. 5)[4]. By the decree of 2017, there is no more limit of penalties for the granting of pardon, that is, regardless of the penalty applied, and provided that it is not a heinous crime (homicide practiced in extermination, qualified

---

[4] Decree no. 8,940, Dec 22, 2016. Art. 1 The pardon will be granted to national and foreign persons sentenced to deprivation of liberty, not substituted by restrictive rights or by fine, who have, by December 25, 2016, fulfilled the conditions set forth in this Decree. § 1 *The requirements for the granting of pardon will be differentiated in the hypothesis of persons:* I – pregnant women; II – over 70 years of age; III – who have a son or daughter under 12 years of age or with a serious chronic illness or a disability who needs their direct care; IV – who are serving a sentence in the semi-open or open regime or are in conditional release and have attended or are attending a course of elementary, middle, senior, vocational or professional qualification, in the form of art. 126, caput, of Law no. 7,210, of July 11, 1984, or exercised, for at least twelve months in the three years counted retroactively to December 25, 2016; V – with paraplegia, tetraplegia or blindness, provided that such conditions are not prior to the commission of the offense and are evidenced by an official medical report or, failing that, by a physician appointed by the court of enforcement; or VI – serious and permanent illnesses that present a severe limitation of activity and restriction of participation or require continuous care that cannot be provided in the penal institution, provided that the hypothesis is proven by an official medical report or, failing this, by a physician designated by the Judgment of the execution, stating the history of the disease, if there is no opposition of the condemned person. § 2 The hypothesis provided for in paragraph III of paragraph 1, does not reach people convicted of crime committed with violence or serious threat against the son or daughter or for crimes of sexual abuse against children, adolescents or persons with disabilities. Art. 2 *The hypotheses of pardon granted by this Decree do not cover penalties imposed for crimes:* I – of torture or terrorism; II – typified in the caput and paragraph 1 of art. 33, as well as in arts. 34, 36 and 37 of Law 11,343, of August 23, 2006, except for the hypothesis provided in art. 4 of this Decree; III – considered to be heinous or to those treated as such after the publication of Law no. 8,072, of July 25, 1990, with its subsequent amendments; IV – provided for in the Military Penal Code and corresponding to those mentioned in this article; or V – typified in arts. 240 and paragraphs 241 and 241-A and paragraph 1 of Law no. 8,069 of July 13, 1990. *Article 3 In crimes committed without serious threat or violence to the person, the pardon shall be granted when the custodial sentence does not exceed twelve years, provided that it has been fulfilled: I – a quarter of the penalty, if not repeat offenders (non-relapsing defendants), or a third, if recidivists; or II – one-sixth of the sentence, if not recidivists, or a quarter, if recidivists, in the hypotheses of § 1°, of art. 1. Article 4 In the case of the crimes foreseen in the caput and paragraph 1, combined with paragraph 4, of art. 33 of Law no. 11,343 of 2006,* when the conviction has acknowledged the agent's primacy, good background and lack of dedication to criminal activities or lack of participation in a criminal organization, pardon will only be granted in the hypotheses of §1, Art. 1 of this Decree and provided that a quarter of the penalty has been served. *Article 5 In the crimes committed with serious threat or violence to the person, the pardon will be granted, in the following hypotheses: I – when the custodial sentence does not exceed four years, provided that he has:* A) one third of the sentence, if not recidivists, or half, if recidivists; B) a quarter of the sentence, if not recidivist, or a third, if recidivists, in the hypotheses of § 1°, of art. 1st; II – when the custodial sentence is more than four years and equal to or less than eight years, provided that: A) half of the sentence, if not recidivist, or two-thirds, if recidivists; B) one third of the sentence, if not recidivists, and half, if recidivists, in the hypotheses of § 1 of art. 1.

homicide, serious bodily injury, robbery, rape, genocide), terrorism and or drug trafficking (except in the case of mere drug carriers), it will suffice to have fulfilled one fifth of the sentence (if not recidivist) and one third (if recidivist) or one third (if not recidivist) and half of the sentence (if recidivist) in cases of crimes including serious threats or violence. The decree also provides for ways to reduce sentences in crimes without violence and serious threat. It may also be granted in the event of an appeal by the prosecution or if the convicted person responds to another case without conviction by the second instance. Cases of corruption that have had repercussions in the country, especially involving politicians, were covered by the pardon and the Supreme Court decided, in a preliminary decision (on Dec. 28, 2017), alleging deviations of purposes, to suspend the effects of the concession in crimes without violence and serious threat (article 1, item I), of the reduction of the penalty (article 2, paragraph 1, item I) and of the extinction of the fine (article 8 and 10), in addition to the concession even in the case of appeal and conviction at first instance[5] (article 11).

---

[5] Pardon. **Decree** no. 9246 of December 21, 2017. He grants Christmas pardon and commutation of penalties and gives other measures. *The President of the Republic,* in the exercise of the exclusive competence conferred by art. 84, caput, item XII, of the Constitution, and considering the tradition, on the occasion of the commemorative festivities of Christmas, to grant pardon to persons convicted or subjected to security measures and to commute sentences of convicted persons, **Decrees**: Art. 1 The collective Christmas pardon will be granted to national and foreign persons who, by December 25, 2017, have fulfilled: I – a fifth of the penalty, if not repeat offenders, and a third of the penalty, if recidivists, in crimes committed without serious threat or violence the person; II – one third of the sentence, if not recidivist, and half of the sentence, if recidivist, in crimes committed with serious threat or violence to the person, when the custodial sentence does not exceed four years; III – half of the sentence, if not recidivist, and two thirds of the sentence, if recidivist, in crimes committed with serious threat or violence to the person, when the custodial sentence is more than four years and equal to or less than eight years; IV – a quarter of the sentence, if men, and one-sixth of the sentence, if women, in the hypothesis provided in § 4 of art. 33 of Law 11,343 of August 23, 2006, when the custodial sentence does not exceed eight years; V – a quarter of the period of conditional release, if not recidivist, or a third, if recidivist, provided that the remaining sentence, on December 25, 2017, does not exceed eight years, if not recidivist, and six years, if recidivists; VI – one sixth of the penalty, if not recidivist, or one fourth, if in case of crime against property, committed without serious threat or violence, provided that the damage is repaid by December 25, 2017, unless there is no harm or economic incapacity to repair it; or VII – three months of deprivation of liberty, if the deposit in court of the amount corresponding to the loss caused to the victim has been proven, unless there is an economic incapacity to do so, in the case of a sentence of deprivation of liberty of more than eighteen months and not more than four years, for

crimes against property, committed without serious threat or violence the person, with prejudice to the offended in an estimated value not exceeding a minimum wage. Sole paragraph. Christmas pardon shall be granted to persons sentenced to a custodial sentence who, in the course of the execution of their sentence, have been victims of torture, pursuant to Law no. 9455 of April 7, 1997, recognized by a collegial decision of the second degree jurisdiction. Art. 2 The time of compliance with the penalties provided for in art. 1st shall be reduced to the person: I – pregnant; II – aged seventy or over; III – who has a child up to fourteen years of age or of any age, if a person with severe chronic illness or with a disability, who needs his/her care; IV – who has a grandson of up to fourteen years of age or of any age, if a person with a disability, who needs his/her care and is under his/her responsibility; V – who is serving a sentence or conditional release and has attended, or is attending, a course of elementary, middle, advanced, vocational or professional qualification, recognized by the Ministry of Education, or who has worked for at least twelve months , in the three years counted retroactively to December 25, 2017; VI – with paraplegia, tetraplegia or blindness acquired after the commission of the offense, evidenced by an official medical report, or, in the absence of the award, by a physician appointed by the execution court; VII – with paraplegia, tetraplegia, blindness or malignant neoplasm, even if in remission, even if such conditions are prior to the commission of the offense, evidenced by official medical report or, in the absence of the award, by a physician appointed by the execution court, and in serious limitation of activity or require continuous care that cannot be provided in the penal establishment; VIII – a serious and permanent illness that presents a severe limitation of activity or that requires continuous care that cannot be provided in the penal establishment, provided that it is proved by an official medical report or, in the absence of the award, by a physician appointed by the execution; or IX – Indigenous, who has an Indigenous Birth Registration or other equivalent supporting document. Paragraph 1 – The reduction referred to in the caput will be: I – one sixth of the sentence, if not recidivist, and one fourth of the penalty, if recidivist, in the cases provided for in item I of the caput of art. 1st; II – a quarter of the sentence, if not repeated, and a third of the penalty, if it is a repeat offense, in the cases provided for in item II of the caput of art. 1st; and III – one-third of the sentence, if not recidivist, and half of the penalty, if recidivist, in the cases provided for in item III of the caput of art. 1st. Paragraph 2. The hypotheses provided for in items III and IV of the caput do not include persons convicted of a crime committed with violence or serious threat against the child or grandchild or for a crime of sexual abuse committed against a child, adolescent or disabled person. Article 3. Christmas pardon or commutation of sentence shall not be granted to persons convicted of a crime: I – of torture or terrorism; II – typified in art. 33, caput and § 1°, art. 34, art. 36 and art. 37 of Law 11,343, of 2006, except in the case provided for in art. 1°, caput, item IV, of this Decree; III – considered heinous or similar, even if practiced without serious threat or violence to the person, under the terms of Law no. 8,072, of July 25, 1990; IV – committed with violence or serious threat against the military and public security agents, which deal with art. 142 and art. 144 of the Constitution, in the exercise of the function or as a result thereof; V – referred to art. 240, art. 241 and art. 241-A, caput and paragraph 1 of Law no. 8,069 of July 13, 1990; or VI – referred to art. 215, art. 216-A, art. 218 and art. 218-A of Decree-Law no. 2,848, of December 7, 1940 - Penal Code. Art. 4 Christmas pardon or commutation shall not be granted to persons who: I – have been sanctioned by the competent court in a hearing of justification, guaranteeing the right to the principles of adversary and ample defense, due to the practice of serious disciplinary infraction, in the twelve months prior to the date of publication of this Decree; II – have been included in the Differentiated Disciplinary System, at any time of fulfillment of the sentence; III – have been included in the Federal Penitentiary System, at any time of the sentence, except in the event that the collection is justified by the interest of the prisoner himself, pursuant to art. 3 of Law 11,671, of May 8, 2008; or IV – have failed to comply with the conditions established for the prison house, with or without electronic monitoring, or for conditional release, guaranteed the right to the principles of adversary and ample defense. § 1 In the event that the determination of the disciplinary infraction has not been completed and sent to the competent court, the process of declaration of the Christmas pardon or commutation shall be suspended until the conclusion of the investigation or administrative procedure, which shall occur within thirty days, under penalty of continuation of the process and execution of the declaration. § 2 Once the period referred to in paragraph 1 has expired without the conclusion of the determination of the disciplinary infraction, the process of declaration of the Christmas pardon or commutation shall continue. Art. 5 The special Christmas pardon will be granted to women prisoners, national and foreign, who, until December 25, 2017, meet the following requirements, cumulatively: I – are not responding or have been convicted of another crime committed by violence or serious threat; II – have not been punished with the practice of serious misconduct, in the twelve months prior to the date of publication of this Decree; and III – fall within one of the following assumptions, as a minimum: (a) women convicted of deprivation of liberty for crimes committed without serious threat or violence against the person, who have reached the age of sixty or are not twenty-one years of age; b) women convicted of a crime committed without serious threat or violence against the person, who are considered persons with disabilities, under the terms of art. 2nd Law 13,146, of July 6, 2015; or c) pregnant women whose pregnancy is considered to be at high risk, sentenced to a custodial sentence, provided that the condition is proved by medical report issued by a professional appointed by the competent court. Art. 6 – Christmas pardon will be granted to persons subject to a security measure that, irrespective of the termination of dangerousness, have suffered deprivation of liberty, hospitalization or outpatient treatment: I – for a period equal to or greater than the maximum penalty commenced for the criminal offense corresponding to the conduct practiced; or II – in the cases of substitution contemplated in art. 183 of Law no. 7,210 of July 11, 1984, for a period equal to the remainder of the sentenced conviction. Sole paragraph. The decision that extinguishes the security measure, with the purpose of psychosocial reinsertion, will determine: I – referral to a Psychosocial Care Center or another equivalent service in the locality where the person with mental disorders in conflict with the law is previously indicated in the Unique Therapeutic Project, in accordance with the principles of the Psychosocial Attention Network established by Ordinance no. 3,088, of December 23, 2011, of the Ministry of Health; II – the reception in therapeutic residential service, pursuant to Ministerial Order no. 3,088, of 2011, of the Ministry of Health, previously indicated in the Unique Therapeutic Project, a hypothesis in which the Health Department of the Municipality in which the person with mental disorders in conflict with the law will be summoned to give effect to the Unique Therapeutic Project or, in the alternative, the State Department of Health; III – the fulfillment of the singular therapeutic project for planned discharge and assisted psychosocial rehabilitation, when there is an indication of hospital admission, by medical criteria or by the absence of deinstitutionalization process, under the terms established in art. 5 of Law 10.216 of April 6, 2001; and IV – the science to the state prosecutor's office or the Federal District and Territories of the locality in which the person with mental disorders in conflict with the law is, to follow the inclusion of the patient in health treatment and to evaluate their civil situation, in the terms established in Law no. 13,146, of 2015. Art. 7 The commutation of the remaining custodial sentence, measured on December 25, 2017, shall be granted in the following proportions: I – to the person sentenced to deprivation of liberty: a) in a third, if not recidivist, and that, by December 25, 2017, he has served a quarter of the sentence; and b) in a quarter, if a recidivist, and that, by December 25, 2017, he has served a third of the sentence; II – in two thirds, if not recidivist, in the case of a woman convicted of a crime committed without serious threat or violence, a person who has a child or grandchild under the age of fourteen or of any age if he or she is considered to be a person with a disability or a person with a disability. serious chronic illness requiring his or her care, and who, by December 25, 2017, has completed one-fifth of the sentence; and III – in half, if recidivist, in the case of a woman convicted of a crime committed without a serious threat or violence, a person who has a child or grandchild under the age of fourteen or of any age if he or she is considered to be a person with a disability or a person with a chronic illness grave and in need of his or her care, and that, by December 25, 2017, he has completed one-fifth of the sentence. Sole paragraph. The commutation referred to in the caput shall be granted to persons sentenced to deprivation of liberty who do not have, by December 25, 2017, obtained the commutations deriving from previous Decrees, regardless of previous request. Art. 8 The requirements for the granting of the Christmas pardon and commutation of sentence dealt with in this Decree apply to the person who: I – had the deprivation of liberty replaced by restrictive rights; II - is serving the sentence in open regime; III – has been granted a conditional suspension of the proceedings; or IV – is in conditional release. Art. 9 The Christmas pardon and the commutation dealt with in this Decree do not extend: I – to the accessory penalties provided for in Decree-Law no. 1,001, of October 21, 1969 - Military Penal Code; and II – the effects of the conviction. Art. 10. The pardon or commutation of penalty reaches the penalty of a cumulative applied penalty, even if there is a default or registration of debts in the Active Debt of the Federal Government, observing the values established in an act of the Minister of State of Finance. Sole paragraph. The pardon will be granted regardless of the payment: I – of the fine, applied in isolation or cumulatively; or II – of the value of pecuniary conviction of any nature. Art. 11. The Christmas pardon and the commutation of sentence referred to in this Decree are applicable, although: I – the judgment has become final and non-appealable for the prosecution, without prejudice to the judgment of appeal of the defense in higher instance; II – there is appeal of the charge of any nature after the appraisal at second instance; III – the convicted person responds to another criminal proceeding without a conviction in a second instance, even if it concerns the crimes referred to in art. 3rd; or IV – the collection guide has not been issued. Art. 12. The penalties corresponding to various infractions will be unified or added for the purpose of the declaration of Christmas pardon or commutation, in the form of art. 111 of Law no. 7,210 of 1984. Sole paragraph. In the event of contest with infraction described in art. 3, the Christmas pardon or commutation shall not be granted corresponding to the non-impeding crime as long as the sentenced person does not fulfill two-thirds of the penalty corresponding to the preventive crime. Art. 13. The authority that holds the custody of the prisoners and the executive organs provided for in art. 61 of Law no. 7,210 of 1984, shall submit to the competent court, the Public Prosecutor's Office and the Office of the Public Defender, including by digital means, as established by item "f" of item I of the caput of art. 4 of Law no. 12.714, of September 14, 2012, the list of persons who meet the requirements necessary for the granting of the Christmas pardon and commutation of sentence dealt with in this Decree. Paragraph 1 – The procedure set forth in the caput shall be initiated ex officio or at the request of the interested party, the Public Defender or his/her representative, spouse or companion, ascendant or descendant. § 2 – The competent court shall pronounce the decision after hearing the Public Prosecutor and the defense of the beneficiary. Paragraph 3. In order to comply with the provisions of this Decree, the Courts may organize joint efforts. Paragraph 4 – The granting of the Christmas pardon and the commutation referred to in this Decree shall be applied by the judge of the knowledge process in the event of primary convicts, provided that there is a final and non-appealable decision on the conviction for the prosecution. Art. 14. The

xi. Exit permits from prison: Law no. 7,210, July 11, 1984[6], up to 7 days if temporary. In São Paulo State, during the Father's Day (Aug 5, 2017), almost 18,000 convicts (convicted defendants) had the right to be out of pris-prison for 7 days even though the holiday is celebrated on a single Sunday;

xii. Right of a second appeal (infringement embargoes) only for defendants: In case of non-majority decisions in a panel of court of appeals or Superior Courts (in Brazil, there are two: Superior Court of Justice and Supreme Court)[7];

xiii. The judge of guarantees bill: It is an attempt to create a judge specialized in urgent decisions (called "Guarantee Judge") in investigations in case of jail request, breach of secrecy of data, tap monitoring etc. The following trial

---

declaration of Christmas pardon and commutation of sentences shall have preference over the decision of any other incident in the course of criminal execution, except for urgent measures. Art. 15. This Decree shall enter into force on the date of its publication. Brasília, December 21, 2017; 196th of Independence and 129th of the Republic. MICHEL TEMER Torquato Jardim.

[6] Exit permit. Art. 120. Convicts who serve a sentence in a closed or semi-open regime and provisional prisoners may obtain permission to leave the establishment, by escort, when one of the following events occurs: I - death or serious illness of the spouse, partner, ascendant, descendant or sibling; II - need for medical treatment (sole paragraph of article 14). Single paragraph. The permission of exit will be granted by the director of the establishment where the prisoner is located. Article 121. The stay of the prisoner outside the establishment shall have the necessary duration for the purpose of the departure. *Temporary output. Art. 122. Convicts who serve a sentence in semi-open regime may obtain authorization for temporary departure from the establishment, without direct supervision, in the following cases: I – family visit; II – attendance to a vocational training course, as well as instruction in the 2nd or higher degree, in the Judicial District of the Execution; III – participation in activities that contribute to the return to social life. Single paragraph. The absence of direct supervision does not prevent the use of electronic monitoring equipment by the convicted person, when it is determines the execution judge.* (Included by Law no. 12,258, of 2010). Art. 123. The authorization will be granted by a reasoned act of the Judge of the execution, after hearing the Prosecutor and the penitentiary administration and will depend on the satisfaction of the following requirements: I – *adequate behavior;* II – *minimum compliance of 1/6 (one sixth) of the penalty,* if the convicted person is a primary, and 1/4 (one fourth) if he/she is a repeat offender; III – compatibility of the benefit with the objectives of the penalty. Art. 124. The authorization shall be granted for a period *not exceeding 7 (seven) days,* and may be renewed for another 4 (four) times during the year.

[7] Code of criminal procedure. Art. 609. Appeals are judged by Courts of Justice, chambers or criminal groups, according to a specialized jurisdiction in the laws of judicial organization. (Redaction given by Law no. 1,720-B, dated 3.11.1952). *Single paragraph. When the decision of second instance, unfavorable to the defendant, is not unanimous, infringements and nullity are admitted within 10 (ten) days from the publication of the judgment, in the form of art. 613. If the disagreement for partial, the embargoes are restricted to the subject matter of divergence.*

judge will be able to reverse the previous decisions of the original judge. That will represent, in practice, another judicial instance, the fifth one;

xiv. Jail requirements and criminal politics: Arrest warrants must be registered in the Registry at the National Council of Justice (CNJ) prior to its enforcement. Also, Alternative Measures to jail, after custody hearings, are being encouraged by the CNJ in order to avoid overcrowding of prisons. Letters are being issued to hear witnesses before a different judge in a term[8];

xv. Special courts for high authorities: Under the Constitution, the Supreme Court has the authority to put on trial federal authorities, Congressmen, the President, the Vice-President, the General Prosecutor, Federal Account Court Members, and Ministers for common crimes (art. 102, I, "c"); the Superior Court is able to put on trial Governors, Vice-Governors, State Ac-

---

[8] Code of Criminal Procedure. Art. 289-A. The competent judge shall arrange for the immediate registration of the warrant of arrest in a database held by the National Council of Justice for this purpose. (Included by Law no. 12,403, of 2011). Paragraph 1. Any police officer may carry out the arrest determined in the arrest warrant registered with the National Council of Justice, even if outside the territorial jurisdiction of the judge who issued it. *Precautionary measures to jail.* Art. 319. The following are precautionary measures different from the prison: (Redaction given by Law no. 12,403, of 2011). I – periodic attendance at court, within the period and under the conditions set by the judge, to inform and justify activities; (Redaction given by Law no. 12,403, of 2011). II – prohibition of access or frequency to certain places when, due to circumstances related to the fact, the accused or defendant should stay away from these places to avoid the risk of new infractions; (Redaction given by Law no. 12,403, of 2011). III – prohibition of maintaining contact with determined person when, due to circumstances related to the fact, the accused or accused of staying distant must be held; (Redaction given by Law no. 12,403, of 2011). IV – prohibition to leave the Shire when the stay is convenient or necessary for the investigation or instruction; (Included by Law no. 12,403, of 2011). V – home collection at night and on days off when the investigated or accused person has fixed residence and work; (Included by Law no. 12,403, of 2011). VI – suspension of the exercise of public function or activity of an economic or financial nature when there is a fair fear of its use for the practice of criminal offenses; (Included by Law no. 12,403, of 2011). VII – temporary admission (hospitalization) of the accused in cases of crimes committed with violence or serious threat, when the experts conclude that they are unimpeachable or semi-imputable (article 26 of the Penal Code) and there is a risk of repetition; (Included by Law no. 12,403, of 2011). VIII – bail, in crimes that admit it, to assure the attendance to acts of the process, to avoid the obstruction of its progress or in case of unjustified resistance to the judicial order; (Included by Law no. 12,403, of 2011). IX – electronic monitoring. *Custody hearings.* The procedure adopted is for a period of 24 hours for the judges to hear the persons who were arrested in the act (fragrant delicto). With this, judges can assess whether it is necessary to keep the person in custody, whether they can be released on bail, whether there is a punitive measure of an educational nature – such as electronic anklets – or whether they should be released for not having his imprisonment justified.

count Court Members, and Appeals Judges. It takes excessive time to get a final decision. Also, this can lead to a risk of having contradictory decisions. There is a draft amendment trying to modify this issue. On December 26, 2017, the senators made the reduction of the jurisdiction of Special Courts through constitutional amendment conditional on the approval of the law on abuse of power.[9] This is the newest attempt to promulgate the law of abuse of power.

## 3  ENCCLA – The National Anti-Corruption and Money Laundering Strategy

The National Anti-Corruption and Money Laundering Strategy (ENCCLA— Estratégia Nacional de Combate à Corrupção e Lavagem de Dinheiro) is a good and important initiative to combat organized crime due to the concentration of knowledge of enforcement bodies. Several annual strategy meetings with more than 60 enforcement bodies since 2003[10] (the date of the creation of Specialized Courts in financial crimes and money laundering (basically on the capitals, 24 Criminal Courts), have been held after a large number of preceding workshops with small groups during each year had taken place.

It represented the beginning of task forces (IRS, Police, Prosecutors, Federal Court of Accounts, and Federal General Controller) and the attempt to make effective and rational the judicial system related to the combat of economic and financial crimes. It broke the prejudice among bodies and the vanity of their members. Before, there was the following perception: "What I don't do is wrong, illegal and has to be annulled. I am honest, but I don't believe you are" or "Us against others".

Some results have been achieved with the support of ENCCLA and a great feature of independent Prosecution:

---

[9] The Amendement 10/2013 maintains the special courts only for the President of the Republic and for the presidents of the Supreme Court (STF), the Chamber of Deputies and the Senate Senado Notícias (2017).

[10] In Sao Paulo, it was created in 2004.

i. Criminal Clean Record Act/LC n° 135, 04.06.2010: A politician cannot be elected if he or she has been convicted by a final decision of any Court of Appeals;
ii. Administrative Misconduct Act (Law n° 8,429, June 2, 1992) in case of illicit self-enrichment: Against civil servant for loss of property, full compensation, loss of function, suspension of political rights (5-8 years), ineligibility for public power, fine; this procedure needs further adjustment and support;
iii. Anti-Corruption Act (Law n° 12,846, August 1, 2013): Strict administrative liability for legal entities and subjective liability for natural persons; leniency programs;
iv. Free Public Information Access Act (Law n° 12,257, November 11, 2011): Access to expenses; public procurements or bids; salaries;
v. Criminal Procedure Code: If alternative measure to imprisonment (removal from the position) are applied, the civil servant cannot remain in jail (art. 282, § 6°, and 319, VI - Law 12,403, May 4, 2011);
vi. Money-Laundering Act (Law n° 9,613, March 3, 1998, and Law n° 12,683, July 9, 2012): No list of precedent crimes; plea bargaining (no more seen as act of vengeance); extension of gatekeepers (art and sport sectors, real estate registry, accountant and audit service). Acquittal of a precedent crime (drug trafficking), but money laundering in Brazil recognized by STJ ("soft targets");
vii. Organized Crime Act (Law n° 12,850, Aug 18, 2013): Drug Act/Law 11,343, August 23, 2006, requires a minimum of two persons; Criminal Code/three; Collective Judgment Act/Law 12,694, July 24, 2012/three; Organized Crime Act/Law 12,850, August 2, 2013/four) – law regulated plea bargaining, controlled action (to avoid flagrant arrest), undercover operation regulation. Wiretappings are regulated by Law 9,296, July 24, 1996;
viii. Beneficial Ownership registration to get the Brazilian IRS number: Normative Instruction no. 1,634, May 6, 2016.

## 4 Emblematic cases involving corruption

i. Satiagraha in 2008: Conviction of a banker who allegedly paid a Federal Police Chief to exempt him and his sister of a financial crime investigation: Dismissal by nullity due to the participation of the Brazilian Intelligence Unit – ABIN – just to transcribe the wiretapping records;
ii. Sand Castle (Castelo de Areia) in 2009: Alleged collusion among corporation, politicians and bureaucracy – involving bribes. A new bill was proposed at Congress: "Abuse of Power Crime Act". This case was dismissed by nullity because of an anonymous report that could not have started a wiretapping procedure, but it had also the support of preliminary investigations, a plea bargaining and evidence from another investigation;
iii. Monthly kickbacks (Mensalão) in 2012-2013: Major scandal that hit Lula's Government, monthly kickbacks were paid with the main objective to guarantee the continuity of the power; Facts: 2002-2003; indictment: August 22-29, 2007; trial: August 2-December 17, 2012 (25 convicted); decision published: April 22, 2013; appeals accepted for review for 12 defendants: September 18, 2013; decision for imprisonment in a closed and semi-open system for 11 defendants: Nov 14, 2013 by the Supreme Court. This was the first emblematic case against politicians in power;
iv. Car Wash (Lava Jato) since 2014 and still ongoing: Involvement of Petrobrás, a mixed-capital company, Odebrecht, a big private contractor, and JBS, a large rural producer and cattle processor. A big corruption scheme was revealed that also allows illicit campaign financing and the distortion of the most important bidding principles, such as equality, transparency and administrative probity. Arrests of those convicted demonstrated that actions were properly being undertaken by federal police, public prosecution, and the Judiciary, showing that the country was acting to correct its course. The conclusion that public funds had been misappropriated to supply a plot, with spurious payments to many congressmen, made it clear how bold, voluptuous, and neglectful the actions of these groups were, in order to achieve their objectives. Money Laundering of R$20billion, including R$10 billion of kickbacks Huge self-enrichments. So far, there has only been convictions by trial Courts. High Authorities are still being under investigation. In the original case, a Search Warrant in 2014 was issued of

the headquarters of Mossacka Fonseca Firm, mentioned in "Panama Papers". It was the first judicial order against it. Until November 30, 2017: 158 Plea Bargaining; 177 convictions (1$^{st}$ instance); 6,4 billion reais in bribes; 800 million of repatriation; 3,2 billion reais of seized assets from defendants. In the Brazilian Supreme Court: 6 cases (without convictions) in 185 investigations of politicians (). Also, from Operation Car Wash, other criminal activities were discovered with the involvement of state and local politicians (like in Rio de Janeiro State) such as, for instance, the misure of funds of 2014 FIFA World Cup and 2016 Olympic Game organizations.

These cases have something in common with the use of remittances, "doleiros" (foreign exchange dealers), offshore vehicles, corruption, illegal payments, cash, money laundering and International Cooperation.

## 5 Transforming the transformation

The big demonstrations that occurred in June 2013, April 2015, and March 2016, were the initial sparks of the impeachment process, originally due to bus fare increases, but in fact because corruption appeared to be endemic.

It generated an ongoing crisis of governability in the Brazilian political system due to weak institutions and the fact that political power is concentrated and personalized in the president. Although elected democratically, the president is able to govern autocratically.

Former presidents Fernando Collor (1990-1992) and Dilma Rousseff (2010-2014; 2015-2016) fell thanks to personal foibles (unable to govern effectively), and accusations of corruption (especially in Petrobrás, Brazilian Oil Company, and big private companies like Odebrecht, contractor, and JBS, meat producer and distributor) and budget law fraud (impeachable offence).

There is a sense that corruption is being fought in Brazil, but this fight is still far from the final victory. Although it has been accepted in everyday life, it is not possible to deny a new social conformation and reflection.

The current mistrust of authorities has arisen from the lack of a reasonable explanation since many decisions that are born of authority are not explained to the citizens or, if they are, carry a certain cynicism, egocentricity, self-glorification and self-protection.

The form of expression of popular dissatisfaction outside the formal channels of political action, the informal democracy, can be summed up in a state of vigilance, denunciations and (de)qualification of public actions. The realization of the absence of what people expect as appropriate public governance and transparency in time and space has generated repudiation and segregation.

In consequence, various forms of manifestations that question formal power are generalized, especially on the Internet. What citizens desire is seeing powerful authorities to descend from their pedestal. Democracy is defined by what is constructed and not only by its forms or the life of its structures.

In fact, the current government does not provide for a real plan of progressive transformation of society, that is, a firm decision that sends the message that Brazil, through political authorities, really wants to improve the appropriate perception of corruption: a perennial and effective change in the mentality of all. There are no strategic areas of action that seek this goal.

For example, there are very restricted (or no) debates of:

- achieving higher levels of success in investigations and prosecutions of corruption,
- speed up investigations so that they do not linger for more than a year or two;
- improving the judgment rate of cases of corruption;
- the reinforcement of educational programs of our schools that contemplate in elementary and secondary education the anticorruption discipline, also valid for the training of our teachers;
- better regulating the lobbying activity, whose holder is between the businessman/client and the politicians and acts for obtaining public contracts;
- a reformation of political finance so as to minimize opportunities for misappropriation of public money by removing the human element from the flow of money;

- a mandatory implementation of compliance for parties that have signed contracts with the Government (except some States initiatives), and their real social responsibility.

Is it right that a company convicted of corruption can continue to be hired by the government? Why is there no "professional death" of a public official or a politician convicted of corruption so that he or she will never return to a public or political service? Why is there no reward for all those who report corruption and not just the informant/defendant? Why do convicted companies continue to remit profits from the country without fulfilling their obligations?

It is important to expect from those who think of the law as an intellectual honesty, a harmony with the critical moment, in which the conscious citizen can, together with the press, fulfill the monitoring role that corresponds to it, especially when the formal channels of control seem inoperative.

## 6   Challenges

Operation Car Wash has been deemed a paradigmatic Brazilian case due to some new and important outcomes in the judicial system, notably regarding defendants without special jurisdiction. In general terms, the efficiency of the Judiciary is recognized because the work done by the first and second instances of the Federal Courts and Circuits. It seems certain that this outcome was made possible by several improvements implemented as a result of ENCCLA initiatives.

In order to further improve the system, there are some challenges to be met. These are specifically:

i. Improvement of the public's corruption perception index that makes the country occupy the $79^{th}$ position in 2016 according to Transparency International ;
ii. Freedom of Press and support of civil society are two sides of the same coin and must be preserved from any attempt of changes;
iii. There should be a government transformation program in which the government should set National Key Result Areas, specific areas that have been identified as priorities to be addressed by the public and private sec-

tors, especially by setting the tone. In order words, providing a clear message of cultural integrity enforced;
iv. Whistleblower Protection through a law which protects whistleblowers who work with the government and report an agency's misconduct. Confidentiality and immunity from criminal and civil charges must be guaranteed;
v. Procurement Law and Criminal Law Reviewed, empowering compliance units and public disclosure of the details in contracts; increase of penalties;
vi. Insurance contracts as a viable solution that could end the direct dialogue between government and contractors (type of guarantee insurance). They guarantee public administration against any risk of default of the contract signed with the hired contractor, with respect to price, quality and timelines. It is not mandatory (it can raise the prices);
vii. A Corruption Court System should allow a complete prosecution within one or two years, particularly for cases generating intense public interest. Special courts for Politicians and high authorities must be ended or sharply reduced. Also penalties and statutes of limitations must be reviewed;
viii. Public and Private Education Programs and Corporate Integrity Program, incorporating anti-corruption elements in primary and secondary schools, and signing a pledge to adhere to anti-corruption principles;
ix. Political funding reform must be performed considering a strict way to measure accountability and transparency inside parties. The simple prohibition of corporate funds for political campaigns can be replaced by the corporate crime organization;
x. Instilling transparency and professionalism in positions of free appointment, which should be avoided in public service, to ensure a clear path for the future;
xi. Upholding principles of independence (not the opposite) for the Police, Prosecution, Judges by avoiding the (further) reduction of budgets and wages, and/or high oppression, social security rights reductions and attacks on these civil servants;
xii. Lobbying can be considered a particular kind of corruption that is legally accepted. It is a delicate issue that must be well-established under law

|       | since only natural persons (individuals), without any limit in Brazil, can donate to political campaigns; |
|-------|---|
| xiii. | Code of Ethics should be effectively applied to lawyers since they must adhere to the truth as any other important partner of the Judiciary Branch; |
| xiv.  | International Cooperation improvement must be ensured; what is not acceptable, for instance, is the refusal of extradition due to alleged "bad conditions of prisons" or summon of someone just because he or she is a national defendant; |
| xv.   | Strengthening Intelligence acts to be able to seize "big fish criminals" and establish unjust enrichment as a crime. |

## 7 Conclusions

The clash between the emergence of modern democracy and human rights on the one hand and the entrenched cultural traits on the other hand has left Brazil at a crossroads.

However, the judgment of Criminal Case no. 470 ("Mensalão" case) in 2014 by the Brazilian Supreme Court represented a landmark in Brazilian investigation and adjudication of corruption and money-laundering cases, although it took a long time to make any difference. The Supreme Federal Court found that there was a scheme of illegal funding that had the goal of distributing money to congressmen of the governing coalition during the government of former President Lula. This money was supposedly used to generate a slush fund used in electoral campaigns and in bribes to congressmen for their support of the federal government's agenda.

The same illegal use was figured out, more recently, by mixed-capital companies, public companies and private ones. The major Brazilian corruption and high profile scandal involves, as has been mentioned before, Petrobrás, the Brazilian Oil company, which is one of the most popular companies in Brazil, besides big private companies, such as Odebrecht (contractor), and JBS (meat producer and distributor). This ongoing case, an outcome of the "Operation Car Wash", is revealing a big scheme of corruption that also allows campaign financing and the distortion of the most important bidding principles, such as equality, transparency and administrative probity. The use of shell companies, some of them set up in Panama through assistance of the law firm "Mossack & Fonseca" (a prolific generator of offshore companies and questionable accounting advisory services), revealed that they belonged to political figures and business moguls as it was shown by the "Panama Papers". The first search and seizure warrant involving Mossack & Fonseca took place in Brazil, at its Brazilian subsidiary. The arrest of those convicted and some defendants demonstrated that actions were properly being undertaken by federal police, public prosecution, and the Judiciary, showing that the country is acting to correct its course. The conclusion that public funds had been misappropriated to supply a plot, with spurious payments to many congressmen, left clear how dare, voluptuous, and neglectful these groups were in order to achieve their goals.

The Brazilian judicial criminal system's sluggishness is recognized by the population and, therefore, needs to be reviewed in order to better enforce penalties in crimes practiced against Public Administration—including corruption—a nd, notably, criminalize government employees' unjust enrichment obtained through distorted public procurements. Also, the Brazilian Criminal Doctrine and Jurisprudence must be reviewed since it has represented a source of impunity making the Judiciary largely incapable of combating corruption, and, consequently, discouraging all enforcement bodies to accurately tackle this serious and endemic crime.

The popular reaction that was observed recently can be deemed as a breakdown of the culture of tolerance towards corruption. The Internet turned out to be an uncensored and important source of opinion.

Due to the ineffectiveness of the judicial system for politicians, it seems that defendants are not feeling guilt, regret or shame (negative conception of others) regarding their demeanors, entailing a serious risk for the greater social and moral behavior.

The Congress did not realize that some recent law reforms certainly improved part of the institutions in a good manner, but that these measures were and are not enough. It is necessary to deepen the improvement of the legal system in other areas to render the ever-present impunity.

Corruption is like cancer and must be put under continuous surveillance with constant vigilance. We will never be sure that there will be no more metastases. It is a permanent fight, especially in an environment of banality of evil and irrational feelings.

Most politicians in Brazil see the current situation as part of the game. They failed to repeal some anti-corruptions laws. On the other side, people can barely contemplate good options for their vote in the next general elections. Despite institutional and legislative advances and popular support for the fight against corruption and money laundering, there is a clear movement to destroy what has been working with the revision of legislation, initiated in 2018 and led by investigated politicians, and those linked to them including from other branches.

Finally, Brazilians today request a genuine public policy against corruption that ensures transparency and integrity, and gives a certain direction to the country, showing to every citizen that our courtesy should be safeguarded as long as it does not mean mixing public with private interests. This message has to be clear and will depend, of course, on the constant rejection of the lethargy and the alienation of Brazilian politicians.

## References

Andrioli, A. I. (2006) 'Structural causes for corruption in Brazil. [Causas estruturais da corrupção no Brasil]', *Espaço Acadêmico Review*, IV, no. 64.

Araújo, J. (2015) *Support paper of her presentation in the panel "Doing business globally: The challenges of corruption": New York State Bar Association*, Sao Paulo Seasonal Meeting.

Avritzer, L. (June 6, 2011) 'The Brazilian political reality [A realidade política brasileira]', *Carta Capital Review*, 6 June [Online]. Available at http://www.cartacapital.com.br/sociedade/a-realidade-politica-brasileira.

Benevides, M. M. (May 13, 2012) 'It is the ethic of the market! What ethic? There are huge challenges to be faced for Brazil to overcome in the combat of corruption. [É a ética do mercado! Que ética?" Há enormes desafios a serem enfrentados até que o Brasil avance no combate à corrupção]', 13 May [Online]. Available at http://www.logweb.com.br/artigo/e-a-etica-do-mercado-que-etica/ (Accessed 1 December 2017).

Bonne-Blanc, A. (Sept 11, 2015) 'Ethical corporation', 11 September [Online]. Available at http://www.ethicalcorp.com/business-strategy/globalethicist-new-era-governance-latinamerica (Accessed 10 November 2017).

Brazilian Department of Justice *ENCCLA 10 anos* [Online]. Available at https://www.justica.gov.br/sua-protecao/cooperacao-internacional/arquivos/enccla-10-anos.pdf/view (Accessed 1 December 2017).

Brazilian Justice Department (2013) *Reinvicações sociais pautam metas para a Enccla combater a corrupção* [Online]. Available at http://www.justica.gov.br/noticias/reivindicacoes-sociais-pautam-metas-para-a-enccla-no-combate-a-corrupcao (Accessed 30 November 2017).

Calmon, E. (2013) 'Justice of the Superior Court of Justice. The Brazilian way of being [O jeitinho brasileiro]', *ETCO - Instituto Brasileiro de Ética Concorrencial Review*, vol. 10, no. 20, pp. 23–25.

Carvalhosa, M. (2015) 'Aspectos relevantes da Lei Anticorrupção e o caso Petrobrás', *Interesse Nacional Magazine*, 2015 [Online]. Available at http://interessenacional.com.br/2015/04/11/aspectos-relevantes-da-lei-anticorrupcao-e-o-caso-petrobras/ (Accessed 1 December 2017).

Chizzotti, A., Chizzotti, J., Ianhez, J. A., Trevisan, A. M. and Verillo, J. *Combating corruption in Brazilian municipalities [O combate à corrupção nas prefeituras do Brasil]* [Online], Transparencia.org. [S.l.]. Available at http://www.transparencia.org.br/docs/Cartilha.html (Accessed 1 December 2017).

Controladoria Geral da União *Prevenção da Corrupção* [Online]. Available at http://www.cgu.gov.br/PrevencaodaCorrupcao/CompromissosInternacionais/index.asp (Accessed 1 December 2017).

Diário do Nordeste (2017) *Congresso quer votação casada para fim do foro e abuso de autoridade* [Online] (Accessed 1 December 2017).

European Commission - *Home affairs corruption. Boosting anti-corruption policy at EU level* [Online]. Available at http://ec.europa.eu/dgs/home-affairs/what-we-do/policies/organized-crime-and-human-trafficking/corruption/index-eu (Accessed 30 November 2017).

Federal Prosecution - *Caso Lava Jato* [Online]. Available at http://www.mpf.mp.br/para-o-cidadao/caso-lava-jato (Accessed 1 December 2017).

Godinho, J. A. F. (2001) *About the crime of capital 'laundering': Introduction and definition [Do crime de 'branqueamento' de capitais: introdução e tipicidade]*, Coimbra, Almedina Ed.

Grayley, M. V. (2013) *UN Says that corruption worsens poverty and inequality situations in the world [ONU diz que corrupção piora situação de pobreza e desigualdade no mundo]* [Online], Notícias e Mídia Rádio ONU. New York. Available at http://www.unmultimedia.org/radio/portuguese/2013/12/onu-diz-que-corrupcao-piora-situacao-de-pobreza-e-desigualdade-no-mundo/ (Accessed 1 December 2017).

Greco, L. (2004) 'Which behaviors can the state prohibit with criminal sanctions? A study about the legitimacy of criminal punishments. [Que comportamentos pode o Estado proibir sob ameaça de pena? Sobre a legitimação das proibições penais]: Study translated by Luiz Greco for the Financial Criminal Law Seminar', *in Porto Alegre*, March 18-20, p. 2.

Gurovitz, H. 'Long live Gérson's law. [Viva a Lei de Gérson!]', *Superinteressante. [S.l.]* [Online]. Available at http://super.abril.com.br/superarquivo/2004/conteudo_313516.shtml (Accessed 30 November 2017).

Hage, J. (2013) 'A força da Transparência', *Revista ETCO - Instituto Brasileiro de Ética Concorrencial*, vol. 10, no. 20, pp. 22–23.

Junior, J. T. P. and Dotti, M. R. (2012) 'Liability for price research in bidding and direct contracting: Theory and practice of tenders and contracts', *Tenders and Contracts Bulletin*, Mar., pp. 181–197.

Ki-Moon, B. (2013) *Message from the UN Secretary-General [Mensagem do Secretário-Geral da ONU]* [Online], Rio de Janeiro. [S.l.], Centro de Informações das Nações Unidas. Available at http://www.unicrio.org.br/dia-internacional-contra-a-corrupcao-%E2%80%93-9-de-dezembro-de-2010-2/ (Accessed 1 December 2017).

Limongi, Mário de Magalhões Papaterra 'Change of attitude [Mudança de postura]', *O Estado de S. Paulo.*

Martin De Sanctis, F. (2015) 'Voice and accountability: Improving the delivery of anticorruption and anti-Money laundering strategies in Brazil', in Wouters, J., Ninio, A., Doherty, T. and Cisse', H. (eds) *The World Bank Legal Review Volume 6: Improving Delivery in Development*, Washington, D.C., The World Bank, pp. 391–414.

Monassa, C. C. S. and Leonelli, O. A. (2013) 'It is interesting to Brazil to join the WTO agreement on government procurement?', *Brazilian Journal of International Law*, vol. 10, no. 1, pp. 72–84.

Pacelli, M. (2013) *Greater International Cooperation Helps Brazil face corruption crimes, Counselor States [Maior cooperação internacional ajuda Brasil a combater crimes de corrupção, afirma conselheiro]* [Online], Portal CNJ. [S.l.]. Available at http://cnj.jus.br/noticias/cnj/25375-maior-cooperacao-internaciona-ajuda-brasil-a (Accessed 30 November 2017).

Pedra, A. A. (2013) 'International competitive bidding: National standards x foreign standards: A constitutional vision', *Theory and Practice of Tenders and Contracts*, Bulletin Jul. 2003, pp. 461–472.

Pietro, Sylvia Maria Zanella Di (2011) *Direito administrativo [Administrative Law]*, 24th edn, Sao Paulo, Atlas.

Portal da Transparência. [S.l.] *Federal office of the inspector general. About the portal [Sobre o Portal]* [Online]. Available at http://www.portaltransparencia.gov.br/sobre/ (Accessed 1 December 2017).

Possamai, G. B. (Mar. 2014) 'State enterprises and the regulatory function of administrative contracts Doutrina: Reflections from bidding PETROBRAS', *Doutrina, Pareceres e Atualidades*, pp. 231–238.

Rondinelli, D. A. *In partnering for development: Government-private sector cooperation in service provision* [Online]. Available at http://unpan1.un.org/intradoc/groups/public/documents/un/unpan00231.pdf (Accessed 1 December 2017).

Senado Notícias (2017) *Fim do foro privilegiado e mudanças da Lei de Abuso de Autoridade são os destaques da semana* [Online]. Available at https://www12.senado.leg.br/noticias/materias/2017/04/28/fim-do-foro-privilegiado-e-mudancas-da-lei-de-abuso-de-autoridade-sao-os-destaques-da-semana (Accessed 1 December 2017).

Soares, E. *Government procurement law and policy: Brazil* [Online], In Library of Congress electronic. Available at http://www.loc.gov/law/help/govt-procurement-law/brazil.php (Accessed 30 November 2017).

Takahashi, A. 'Black Bloc and the Response to Social Violence [O black bloc e a resposta à violência social]', *Carta Capital* [Online]. Available at http://www.cartacapital.com.br/sociedade/o-black-bloc-e-a-resposta-a-violencia-policial-1690.html (Accessed 1 December 2017).

Transparency International *Corruption Perceptions Index 2016* [Online]. Available at https://www.transparency.org/news/feature/corruption_perceptions_index_2016 (Accessed 1 December 2017).

Un-BR – United Nations in Brazil (2012) *Corruption takes away US$40 Billion from developing countries, UN states [Corrupção tira 40 bilhões de dólares de países em* *desenvolvimento, afirma ONU]* [Online], Nações Unidas no Brasil. [S.l.]. Available at available at http://www.onu.org.br/corrupcao-tira-40-bilhoes-de-dolares-de-paises-em-desenvolvimento-todo-ano-afirma-onu/ (Accessed 1 December 2017).

Vasconcellos, J. and Euzébio, G. L. *Judiciary convicts 205 for corruption, laundering and improbity in 2012 [Justiça condena 205 por corrupção, lavagem e improbidade em 2012]* [Online]. Available at http://www.cnj.jus.br/noticias/cnj/24270:justica-condena-205-por-corrupcao-lavagem-e-improbidade-em-2012 (Accessed 30 November 2017).

Young, R. (2013) 'The occult magic [A mágica oculta]', *ETCO - Instituto Brasileiro de Ética Concorrencial Review*, vol. 10, no. 20, pp. 28–29.

# Operation Car Wash – The new paradigm to fight corruption

*João Pedro Gebran Neto*

## 1  The beginning

In December 2013, I received, in the Federal Regional Court of Appeals for the 4th region (TRF4), an unpretentious *writ of mandamus*[1] lodged against a judicial decision that froze the assets of a company that was required to report on a breach of data secrecy.

The subject matter of the *writ of mandamus* was the still heated debate about the possibility of impositioninga daily fine as a way of enforcing a judicial order. However, this constitutional procedure had another unique role: to bond me with procedures that in a few months would have an impact. In March of the following year, the first preventive detentions were ordered: black market dealers and a drug dealer.

Obviously, at that moment, nobody was aware of what the facts under investigation would reveal. However, the 8th Panel of the Court of Appeals, which was to judge all the following procedures, obtained jurisdiction by prevention.

The initial investigations sought to unravel crimes of money smuggling, money laundering and drug trafficking. It happens that while performing legal wiretaps, not only intense activities in the black markets for currency were discovered, but also ties between these and corruption crimes perpetrated at the heart of Petrobras were found. The *Operation Car Wash* was born.

---

[1] *Writ of mandamus file* N. 5030054-55.2013.4.04.0000.

© Springer Fachmedien Wiesbaden GmbH, part of Springer Nature 2020
M. Pohlmann et al. (eds.), *Bribery, Fraud, Cheating*, Organization, Management and Crime – Organisation, Management und Kriminalität, https://doi.org/10.1007/978-3-658-29062-7_7

## 2 The context

The *Operation Car Wash* has unprecedented dimensions with respect to the value of financial flows volume of financial resources involved and the number of ongoing lawsuits. For example, in TRF4 alone, in a little more than 3,5 years 750 actions were tried, among them *habeas corpus* actions, pleas requesting the restoration of seized items, *writ of mandamus*, motions to recuse, jurisdictional pleas and no-merit appeals. Almost a hundred defendants were prosecuted, tried and convicted. Many appeals against these decisions are waiting to be tried.

It is not very difficult to summarize the facts in a general fashion, without going into details about specific lawsuits[2].

Some political parties and politicians started to sponsor appointments of persons, civil and public servants (with long careers in service or not), to high ranks in the Direct or Indirect Public Administration.

It follows that those who have been appointed endeavor to flow illicit payments into the accounts of those parties and the pockets of some of its leaders. Nervertheless, they also received parts of the misappropriated funds.

The misappropriation was usually committed by means of bidding processes or administrative procedures that appear to be legal but are illegal in its essence, or by forming cartels, with the guilty consent of wrongdoing by public administrators. This resulted in the overbilling of contracts worth billions that were rewarded to some of the largest national companies by the government agency bidder.

A certain percentage of the contract value was transferred, by means of money laundering, illegal transfer of funds abroad or cash payment to political parties, their leaders and people that have been sponsored for an appointment to public offices.

---

[2] The narrative here laid down is extremely generic, and does not derive from any ongoing suit in the first or second jurisdictional degrees, but exclusively from what was tried in the TRF4 and the matters of confessions by some of those under investigation.

What started in the singular became plural. According to a quote attributed to different Supreme Court Justices: "One feather was pulled and the entire hen came with it". I believe that today it is possible to say that "one feather was pulled and the entire hennery came with it."

Although this summary may erroneously lead to the conclusion that examining the evidence was an easy task, the situation is much more complex when the facts are thoroughly examined. This is because the wrongdoings are based on contracts and amendments, successive payments and bank transfers, all of which appear to be legal.

In any case, the sad facts unraveled by the *Operation Car Wash* paradoxically ended up representing a window of opportunity for a paradigm change.

Many national ills came to light, such as the failure of the party-political system as it is. However, the sunlight allows sanitizing a moldy electoral system, where parties raise fund for their campaigns and to keep themselves in power. A small step was taken when, in the 2016 municipal elections, legal entities were forbidden to donate to political campaigns.

It was also shown how ungovernable a country is with over 30 political parties, almost all of which represented in the National Congress. In such a system, any majority is obtained with a very high cost for the rulers.

All of this contributed to deviant, unethical and illicit behaviors committed by public and civil servants, businesspersons and many other people wishing to enrich at the expense of the treasury.

The knowledge of such endogenous and endemic vices represents the opportunity for reacting to this state of affairs.

## 3     New paradigms

If much can be said about facts and specific circumstances, I want to believe that one of the most relevant points involving the *Operation Car Wash* together with revealling the ills of the Brazilian state- lies in the change of the Brazilian judicial system. This change stems from a new standard of criminal prosecution, in which context the performance of the federal police, public prosecutor's office, and the federal courts are worthy of praise.

The facts under investigation and the matters of the criminal procedures are extremely complex, in a chain of successive conducts, with many players and of hard examination.

To cope with this, it is essential to remove the veil that obscures the illegality of the acts of corruption whit a paradigm change. That means, the creation of a new landmark to interpret the evidences, because the context of the investigated crimes might not find aswers under the traditional interpretation of the criminal prosecution.

1. The first change resides in the creation of task forces by the federal police and by the federal public prosecutor's office, with professionals who gained broad experience in former cases, such as Banestado, Castelo de Areia, Satiagraha, illegal international transfer of funds from CC5 accounts and Mensalão. Enough knowledge had been gathered in order to know exactly what path to follow for an adequate investigation. The formation of task forces with experienced professionals shows that the fight against crime demands determination, experience and wisdom in the decision-making process.

2. Another behavior change happened in the judicial bodies that were able to understand, in all jurisdictional degrees, the complexity of the facts and the importance of a systematic answer, different of the answers ordinarily given to those cases. Notoriously, the understanding on the requesites for the preventive detention are not fulfilled only when there is a vionlent crime or drug traffic, but also when we are facing systemic and impregnated criminality. The TRF4 has already decided that in cases of large and complex criminal gangs preventive detention should be restricted to those under investigation that have mens rea, such as the representatives of the companies involved in the formation of cartels or those that had important roles in the criminal mechanism[3].

---

[3] *Habeas Corpus* (HC) N. 5045442-90.2016.404.0000/PR, 8ª Panel, Federal Judge-Rapporteur João Pedro Gebran Neto, unanimous decision, on 15/12/2016.

The many phases of the Operation Car Wash (there has been over 40) have already revealed a disturbing picture of systemic corruption. Managers of the largest state-owned company (Petrobras), persons in their terms of office and dummy corporations and contracts are involved. This scheme was in its essence organized to pay bribes. In face of the involvement of hundreds of suspects and defendants in this gargantuan corruption scheme, certainly, the absolute number of measures that restrict freedom may impress. However, it shows to be very proportionate to the context under investigation. Thusly an authentic change of paradigm in the national precedents was made. It is very well analyzed by many legal practitioners, as the papers published by Vladimir Passos de Freitas[4] and Joaquim Falcão[5] allude to.

3. The institute of turning state's evidence as provided in the law n° 12.850/2013 brought a third and sensible parameter. It makes available to the bodies responsible for criminal prosecution instruments that are essential for the assessment of criminal offenses, especially those committed by criminal organizations. Also because this instrument showed to be an effective and important defense instrument, a side of it that seems to often go unnoticed. Criticised by many criminal lawyers and being called by the vile nickname of *delação premiada*[6], this tool demonstrated that reality imposed over academic criticism. Those who previously have fervently opposed to this institution now advise their clients to take the deals that benefit them[7]. At a certain moment, the number of defendants that took a deal was over a hundred, while only a bit more than a dozen were actually in custody when they took the deal. It is important to make it clear that no prejudgement of specific cases is made here, only a reiteration of what the criminals have already confessed to in their testimonies. Among the defendants that plead guilty are players that made viable money laundering, people that

---

[4] http://www.conjur.com.br/2014-nov-30/crimes-operacao-lava-jato-mudam-justica-penal-brasil
[5] http://www1.folha.uol.com.br/opiniao/2015/07/1662597-lava-jato-muda-a-justica-e-a-advocacia.shtml
[6] Translator's note: „delação premiada" is a colloquialism for „colaboração premiada", and means „turn state's evidence".
[7] The change in the behavior of some lawyers became clear in recent trials, while closing their arguments, when the behavior of the public prosecutor's office was criticised for not showing interest in making a deal with some defendant. The plea deal was no longer criticised, but the lack thereof.

solicited bribes, people that gave bribes to public officers, dollar smugglers, middlemen, among others.

4.   The adoption of adequate standards of proof to ground the establishment of the facts is a meaningful change. In complex cases with disseminated actions of many players, introducing evidence is really hard, sometimes even impossible. However, accurate examination of the evidence, may that be circumstantial or direct, allows adopting the standard of evidence beyond all reasonable doubt as the limit to be verified by the parts. Both direct and circumstantial evidence have legal value, because circumstantial evidence is not less valuable, in the scope of freedom of judgment (…) but it should be admitted more cautiously, notably when it comes to the model of applicable finding, as Danilo Knijnik (2007) explains. The jurist adds in a precise lesson, reproducing Ignazio Manzoni's lesson:

> [...] "It is not enough for the unknown fact to appear to be a possible or a more or less likely consequence of the known fact for it to be taken as proved by presumptio hominis. The simple possibility that a fact can occur cannot be considered sufficient for the fact to be regarded as factual [...]. *Something extra is necessary for the presumption to become relevant evidence. It requires that the ignored fact is within the scope of possible consequences, but in such a degree of probability that induces the rational persuasion that the unknown fact has effectively occurred. It is in the degree of inference between the known and unknown fact that lies the demonstrative power of this probative mean.* The higher the chances that the unknown fact is a consequence of the known fact, the bigger the probative relevance of the presumption" (op. cit. 2007, p. 49) (emphasis added)

The issue of proof is key because crimes are complex and hard to investigate. It often depends on a set of circumstantial evidence to establish the facts, because it will not always be possible to have direct evidence. Thus "the activity of using evidence to establish the facts developed aiming the verification of the historical facts serves as grounds for the pretension. When it is successful, it will allow the conclusion that there is a "very high likelihood" that such facts occur" according to Gustavo Badaró (2003, p. 62).

This standard of proof is adopted by many legislations, including the Brazilian one, as of decree no. 4.388/2002, embodying the Rome Statute of the International Criminal Court that establishes in the article 66 that "in order to convict the accused, the Court must be convinced of the guilt of the accused beyond reasonable doubt". Also, the Federal Supreme Court has been adopting the orientation of using evidence beyond reasonable doubt as the standard of proof that is able to ground a guilt verdict[8].

This attitude implies ending the naivety that surrounds complex cases where direct evidence is hard to obtain, but circumstantial evidence can be powerfully strong.

5. In this context, a change in interpretation of the norms that happened in February 2016 was received as an effectiveness tool for jurisdiction. That was when the Federal Supreme Court, in a decision worthy of praise, reviewed its stand on the moment at which the beginning of the execution of the sentence should start. The hermeneutics in which the sentence should be executed after trial in the second instance was recast, closing the door through which those convicted use to scape through or delayed indefinitely serving their sentences. This in fact only benefited those that had the means to appeal in higher degrees of jurisdiction, almost always with the best, most qualified and best paid lawyers. The presumption of innocence worked in favor of the wealthy.

The resistance coming from the Academia and the Brazilian Bar Association against this decision is based on fragile and demagogic arguments. These arguments usually take the less fortunate part of the population as the starting point, even though any person with the slightest awareness knows that almost always instances are accessed by those with financial means to hire the most qualified professionals. And even so, the rate of revision of the lower degrees of jurisdiction rulings are very low.

Maybe Brazil is the only country, or one of the very few countries, that have adopted the presumption of innocence to such a large extent, as is pointed out by

---

[8] AP 521 (Justice Rapporteur Rosa Weber, 1ª Panel, p. 06.02.2015 and Inquiry 2968, Justice Rapporteur Dias Tóffoli, Full Court, p. 17.08.2011.

justice Teori Zavascki[9], referring to an in-depth study made by Luiza Cristina Fonseca Frischeisen, Mônica Nicida Garcia and Fábio Gusman (2015). This study indicates that similar rules were adopted by England, Canada, United States of America, France, Spain, Portugal, Germany, Argentine, among others[10].

By the way, few voices are heard in favor of thousands of defendants in unappealable judgments still at the first instance who have no access to appeal and are often underrepresented. Neither do we hear strong outcries against the presumption of innocence for convictions in cases of violent crimes or drug trafficking, which do not have the same right to wait for the end of the proceedings in liberty.

6. Finally, another thought-provoking point that is still unsolved in the precedents regards the statements made by the collaborator and the necessary evidence. One can't stress enough that a body of circumstantial evidence allows arriving at a conclusion about the defendant's criminal responsibility. Conclusive proof of participation in the crimes that the defendant is charged with is not demanded. Evidence beyond all reasonable doubt is sufficient for a conviction. It is known, in corruption offences hardly exist receipts; let alone criminal organizations have a statute filed with the Secretay of State. Thereby, circumstantial evidences such as transfer of funds made by dubious enterprises—used mainly for the re-integration (the last stage of money laundering) of the obtained values by corruption—is that make possible to confirm, or not, the crime occurrence.

---

[9] „The execution of a criminal conviction appeal does not compromise the principle of presumption of innocence provided by the article 5 item LVII of the Federal Constitution even if it is subject to appeal to the Superior Court of Justice or to the Federal Supreme Court." (Habeas Corpus N. 126292/SP, Justice Rapporteur. Teori Zavaski, published in 17.02.2016)

[10] Lee Jae Yong, the heir of Samsung (one of the biggest companies in the world and the biggest in South Korea), was taken into custody right after his conviction in court. He was sentenced to five years for the crime of corruption. Moreover, Park Geun, the ex-premier of the same country is in custody for the same reason. This fact got a lot of coverage in the international media, as can be seen here: http://g1.globo.com/jornal-nacional/noticia/2017/08/herdeiro-da-samsung-e-condenado-prisao-por-corrupcao-na-coreia-do-sul.html.

Such contexts guide the analysis of the evidence, at the risk of an isolated examination leading to a different conclusion. One can not have in mind a static image, as if it were a picture, but a bundling of frames that make a movie made of the facts, confirmed, in the worst-case scenario, by a compelling body of evidence. This doesn't belittle the probative framework, to the contrary, reveals it.

The collaborator, certainly interested in the benefits obtained in the deals made with the public prosecutor's office and ratified by the competent judicial authority, will probably turn evidence in her testimony. However, nothing disallows that the statements about the facts during the testimonies be discredited when subjected to adversary testing. Furthermore, the identification of untruth in the testimonies would only hurt the collaborator, since it opens up the possibility that the deal, and therefore all the benefits that come with it, be invalidated. The rule in Paragraph 16, Article 4, of the law 12.850/2013 sets forth restrictions on the usage of the word of a collaborator to sign a guilt verdict, in verbis: *§16. No guilt verdict will be rendered solely on the basis of the statements of the collaborators.*

It happens that the words of a collaborator should be garnered with double caution, also in comparison to witness testimonies.

However, the rule above is no longer imperative when there are multiple collaborators whose statements lead to the same direction since one statement is ratified by another. Frederico Valdez Pereira highlights regarding the topic of corroboration:

> "There are no restrictions on the nature of the confirmative data: they can be other statements and documents, or even objective data or confirmed facts that attribute reliability to the narrative provided by the collaborator. These external elements do not need to provide thema probandum, but only confirm the credibility of the declaration made by the collaborators. And perchance the narrative is complex, involving the attribution of many facts and participants, it can be the case that only a part of the revelations will be corroborated by external elements. From that it will not be possible to ratify the whole set of collaborations, neither can one disregard the entirety of it. Two important logical conclusions can be drawn from the ideas above: logical support derived from the evidential inference can be admitted as corroborative elements. This

> data must confirm the veracity of the state's evidence and not necessarily of the facts attributed to the defendant. The same can be said about documents or witnesses that may corroborate the informer's information: it is demanded that what this evidence reveals concerns what was said in the state's evidence, it does not matter for this purpose that it concerns the crime itself." (2016, p. 207)

Acknowledging the complexity of the topic, Valdez recognizes the possibility of mutual corroboration, that is, a later state's evidence may be used as a corroborative element of a previous state's evidence:

> "It could be hypothetically admitted, as long as the evidence became known by the prosecutor's office independently and in different procedures, under circumstances that exclude the risk of fake deals or reciprocal inferences between the informers. But, as a general rule, it should be demanded that at least one of the state's evidence be corroborated by external data other than the state's evidence. This seems to have been the intention of the Italian lawmaker when demanding that the valuation of the state's evidence should occur with other elements that vouch for its veracity, understanding that the other elements are distinct. The demand for external corroboration of the cooperation after the crime has at least two very important consequences that deserve special attention. The first is that the judge must present the fundaments of her findings concerning the credibility of the state's evidence; and, secondly, this justification cannot be limited to internal aspects of the state's evidence. It must be accompanied by mention to objective elements that are exterior to the state's evidence." (2016, p. 210)

The judge should obviously be guided by free and informed assessment, without considering to apply any veto, when there is mutual corroboration, surrounded by elements that make it internally and externally credible. That is, repeating Knijnik's lesson, that the many evidence of the fact that one wishes to prove should be analyzed in two stages: first individually and then as a whole. *Thereby, if every piece in a set of circumstantial evidence is certain and precise, a conclusion can be met from analyzing the whole of it* (Knijnik, 2007, p. 51). However when there is only one piece of circumstantial evidence, even if certain and serious, it may still lead to the exclusion of a judgment on the certainty about the fact that is to be proved.

In the same direction, Patrícia Silva Pereira states that...

"[...] this imposition that the circumstantial evidence is conjugated to each other, 'as to produce a coherent and natural whole' is applicable not only to the evidence but also to the inferences that result from them. It is elementary that if the fundamental facts (factos base) converge, they cannot lead to different conclusions, or in other words, it is not possible to arrive at one knowledge of presumption that is incompatible with one other. Similiar to the Italian case, the compatibility among the pieces of circumstantial evidence can be used as an evaluation criterion." (Pereira, 2017, p. 139)

Ultimately, if there is enough evidence of the functioning of the criminal scheme, revealed by a strong set of circumstantial evidence, all of which leading to the same direction, it is possible to arrive at a conclusion *beyond all reasonable doubt*. This surmounts the allegations regarding the utilization of hearsay evidence, as long as it is coherent with the whole of the evidence.

As Ana Lara Camargo de Castro explains,

"[...] the evidence does not have preestablished value and, as it is known, the appreciation system is that of freedom of judgment. There is no hierarchy among the evidence, any form can be admitted even though it might not be expressly provided by the criminal procedure legislation, as long as it is legal. She goes on: testimonial evidence is admitted in this parole system every time the witness knows something that is of interest to the ruling of the lawsuit and the reason of her knowledge allows the evaluation of her credibility." (2017, p. 243).

Obviously one cannot make the mistake of importing the institute existing in the North-American law without observing the necessary safeguards.

Drawing a parallel with the American hearsay and emphasizing the danger of a unweise import of the institute, Ana Lara Camargo de Castro says:

"[...] finally, if in the United States the rule can be made flexible by notions of justice, relevance and reliability, in Brazil the law determines that any person whose testimony can be of interest to the ruling of the lawsuit can be a witness and whose credibility can be drawn out from the circumstances or from the reasons of her knowledge." (Castro, 2017, p. 256)

Effectively, the necessary appraisal on the statement should be made, seeking to extract the necessary reliability for it to be used in the criminal procedure. However, as a rule, a witness' testimony (especially of the colaborator) can be used to recite the grounds for the conviction if it is reliable enough. This is the essence of Article 203 of the Code of Criminal Procedure, according to which the witness should report what she knows, always explaining the reasons of her knowledge or the circumstance from which her credibility can be evaluated.

On the other hand, it must be verified whether there is rebuttal evidence that is enough to debunk the rest of the evidence. As explained by Patrícia Silva Pereira, the absence of evidence to the contrary is equally a requisite of the proof. "The inference is rejected if the rules of experience[11] cannot be applied in the light of other facts. If there is circumstantial evidence that repels the application of this rule, the presumed fact shall have no probative value." (Pereira, 2017, 147f.)

In addition, emphasis can be put on something circumstantial but very important. If it is true that turning state's evidence has emerged as an effective investigative way, especially of organized crime, it is no less true that the ordinary lawmaker never expected it would have so much importance in the investigation of multiple crimes, on multiple investigation fronts and in autonomous criminal groups with many players.

It is not possible to attribute a tight and unique interpretative rule to this perspective. It is very important to keep in mind that the emergence of many informants at independent moments of the investigation and facing different courts brings more credibility to the same conclusions, minimizing the possibility of adjustments to the testimonies.

Moreover, the adequate examination of the evidence, whether direct or circumstantial, is the building block to build a solid conclusion. The state's evidence of many informers may be used to support such conclusion if they are convergent and surrounded by caution.

---

[11] Translator's note: Article 375 defines "regra de experiência" (experience rule) as "rules of common experience provided by the observation of what ordinarily happens"

## 4 Final considerations: A time of vigilance

It is evident that this is no exhaustive picture of the change in paradigm that the *Operation Car Wash* represents, let alone the causes of its occurrence. What we show here are just some of the changes in institutional behavior that enabled progress in knowledge, investigation and the accountability of criminal agents.

However, the fundamental role played by social participation and media coverage must be recognized. The Brazilian society should not be demobilized, nor should it believe that not all is or will be solves.

As Modesto Carvalhosa warned[12], if there is great action on a corruptedsystem of public contracts, it will try to rebuild itself and all agents should be vigilant for the morality of these agreements.

If the political system is also placed under pressure, then it will as well react with the mechanisms that it has at hand.

The history of the *Operation Clean Hands* indicates that legislative changes will be attempted. It also shows that criminal procedures are not the best instrument to resolve these ills, since it operates related to acts in the past, suiting only for punishing those who deviate for punishing.

Public opinion, freedom of press and transparency in the public administration are essential to arriving at a good state of moral order that has been attempted to be installed in Brazil. This was the weakness of the *Operation Clean Hands*. It lost popular support and saw a campaign be orchestrated by the new people possessed power against judges, especially those that were symbols of combat.

As Modesto Carvalhosa warned[13]...

---

[12] http://www.estadao.com.br/noticias/geral,a-medida-provisoria-do-escarnio,10000005856
[13] http://opiniao.estadao.com.br/noticias/geral,os-acordos-de-leniencia-perpetuam-a-corrupcao,10000055184

"In Brazil, despite the extraordinary work made by the Operation Car Wash, the same phenomenon that happened in Italy after the Operation Clean Hands will take place. [...] If ample amnesty is provided to all corrupt contractors, the current and future effects of our exemplary Operation Car Wash will be null. Corruption will persist in the government's projects and services."

Thus, strong and serious reactions can take place. It is imperative that the Brazilian society stays vigilant, not to make the same mistakes as the Italians did.

Successful international cases should also be analyzed for the improvement of national institutions. We live with an absurd level of corruption, lack of transparency, diversion of resources, and waste. Certainly, countries that flaunt minimally acceptable rates have a lot to tell us.

Perhaps laws similar to the FCA (False Claim Act), the FCPA (Foreign Corrupt Practices Act) and the Whistleblower in the US (Whistleblower Protection Act) or the Bribery Act in the UK should be subject of in-depth study and be later introduced in the Brazilian legal system. Not to mention the imperative maintenance of the precedents over the beginning of the enforcement after the judgment in the second degree of jurisdiction.

The fight against corruption is not only one of the goals of the National Council of Justice[14], it is also one of the goals of the United Nations in the criminal[15] and non-criminal[16] perspectives.

This window of opportunity should be used and social participation is essential for it to happen.

Some opportunities might have been wasted, as the newspaper Folha de São Paulo[17] points out. In the light of spectacular scandals, the Decree no. 2.475/98, which allows Petrobras not to be bound by the Brazilian Federal Acquisition

---

[14] The goal 4 of the National Council of Justice establishes: „*To prioritize the trials of lawsuits regarding corruption and misconduct in office (Federal Supreme Court, State Courts, Federal Courts and Military Courts)*".

[15] http://legislacao.planalto.gov.br/legisla/legislacao.nsf/Viw_Identificacao/DEC%205.687-2006?OpenDocument

[16] 6ª Conference of the States Parties to the United Nations Convention against Corruption, in 2015.

[17] "Before and after the *Operation Car Wash*", published on 20/03/2017.

Law (Law no. 8.666/93), could be changed or revoked. Public contracts, especially those signed by Petrobras, could be more transparent, specifically forcing companies hired by, for example, Petrobras to reveal their accounting records regarding their expenses with the work. The calendar of Petrobras' managers should be transparent and published on the state-owned company's website. Those are a few examples of what could have already been corrected.

However, criminal jurisdiction is neither the one responsible for the social, political and economic problems faced by the Brazilian society nor the one in charge of resolving them. To the contrary, criminal intervention emerges exactly when other institutions have failed. The Supreme Court Justice Luís Roberto Barroso, during the Mensalão trials, warned that "the political system represses virtue and potentializes evil" and that "if the electoral and partisan systems are not modified, this logic of buying and selling will go on as torrential water that runs down". The criminal procedure does not adjudicate people and their histories, but facts, unfortunate facts.

However, I do not intend with this speech to alarm or dishearten. My goal is to stir a debate over important points, because the moment is not for optimism, but for hope, along the lines of Rubem Alves' (1998) chronicle:

> "Today there are no reasons for optimism. Today only hope is possible. Hope is the opposite of optimism.
> Optimism is when, while there is spring outside, spring grows inside.
> Hope is when, while there is absolute drought outside, the springs keep on bubbling inside the heart.
> Camus knew what hope was. His words: and in the middle of winter I found out that inside me there was an invincible summer (…)"

# References

Alves, R. A. (1998). *Concerto para corpo e alma* (11. ed.). Campinas, SP: Papirus.

Alves, R. (1998). *Concerto para corpo e alma [About optimism and hope in Repair for the Body and Soul]*. São Paulo: Papirus.

Badaró, G. H. R. I. (2003). *Ônus da prova no processo penal*. São Paulo: Ed. Revista dos Tribunais.

Castro, Ana Lara Camargo de. (2017). Hearsay tropicalizado: A dita prova por ouvir dizer. *Revista Da Escola Da Magistratura TRF Da 4ª Região*, *6*, 241–256.

Frischeisen, L. C. F., Garcia, M. N., & Gusman, F. (2015). Execução provisória da pena um contra ponto à decisão do supremo tribunal federal no *Habea Corpus* N. 84.078. In B. Calabrich, D. Fischer, & E. Palella (Eds.), *Garantismo penal integral: Questões penais e processuais, criminalidade moderna e aplicação do modelo garantista no Brasil* (3rd ed., pp. 411–430). São Paulo: Editora Atlas.

Knijnik, D. (2007). *A prova nos juízos cível, penal e tributário* (1. ed.). Rio de Janeiro: Forense.

Pereira, F. V. (2016). *Delação premiada: Legitimidade e procedimento : aspectos controvertidos do instituto da colaboração premiada de coautor de delitos como instrumento de enfrentamento do crime organizado* (3a edição - revista e atualizada de acordo com a Lei 12.850/2013). Curitiba: Juruá Editora.

Pereira, P. S. (2017). *Prova indiciária no âmbito do processo penal: Admissibilidade e valoração*. Monografias. Coimbra: Almedina.

# The incomplete transition. A review of the recent changes in Brazil's electoral financing model

*Wagner Pralon Mancuso*

## 1 Introduction

Competitive elections are the major element of contemporary representative democracy (Schumpeter, 1942) and they come at a cost. Hence, the importance of electoral financing is an issue that has attracted increasing attention from political scientists (Mutch, 2016; Norris and van Es, 2016; Stratmann, 2005). With regard to electoral financing sources, the key question is to define the types of resources allowed (private resources, public resources or both) and the relative weight assigned to each (Bourdoukan, 2009). This issue is crucial to the very functioning of democracy as the prevalence of private resources may result in the seizure of politics by wealthy interests (Przeworski, 2011), while the preponderance of public resources may result in the disconnection between parties and society (Katz and Mair, 1995, 1996, 2009, 2012).

Brazil has recently witnessed an intense debate on the issue of political financing (Mancuso, 2015a; Speck, 2016). Thus far, the debate has focused on the three main sources of private electoral financing allowed in the country until the last national elections in 2014, namely: corporate, individual, and the candidate's own resources. The widespread impression is that the existing legislation led to the predominance of major corporations, as well as wealthy voters and candidates, within the electoral financing game (Mancuso, 2015b). The Direct Action of Unconstitutionality (ADI in Portuguese), proposed in 2011 to the Supreme Federal Court (STF in Portuguese) by the Order of Attorneys of Brazil's Federal Council (Conselho Federal da OAB in Portuguese), represented an important chapter in this debate by soliciting the Supreme Court to ban corporate contributions and limit voter and candidate donations to an equal and adequately low level (Mancuso and Speck, 2014).

Several changes came after the 2014 elections, albeit not exactly as OAB intended. Corporate contributions have been banned, but wealthy voters and candidates continue to influence electoral funding to an extent commensurate to their economic power. Moreover, the role of public resources has increased significantly, reinstating relevant and still unanswered questions at Brazilian society, regarding (i) the desired level of public investment in electoral competition, (ii) the criteria for dividing this investment among political parties and (iii) how to use such investment to promote democratic values, such as increasing the political presence of historically underrepresented social segments (e.g., women, black people, and people with disabilities).

The objective of this paper is to identify the main recent changes in Brazil's electoral financing legislation—with a focus on the electoral financing sources—and explore the meaning, scope, and limitations of such changes for Brazilian democracy.

My central argument is that since 2014 national elections Brazil has undergone an incomplete transition with regard to political financing sources, which was predominated by private resources (and, within these, the undeniable prevalence of corporate resources) towards a new situation where public resources prevail, but in which the influence of voters and wealthy candidates remains substantial. This transition paralleled the period where three major corruption scandals broke out—*Mensalão*, *Lava Jato*, and *JBS*—at the center of which was the issue of corporate electoral financing. The main challenge of the transition was how to hamper corrupt interactions among politicians who sought resources for themselves and their campaigns, and business people who pursued benefits for their companies. However, the new context brought by the transition also poses its own challenges.

To support my argument, I divided the article in two parts in addition to this introduction. The first part presents the prevailing electoral financing model in Brazil until the 2014 elections, underlining the main private and public sources of electoral campaign financing and comparing the relative importance of each source. The second part addresses the changes that took place from 2015 onwards, which altered crucial features of the previous order—namely, the balance between public and private electoral resources—but preserved other dimensions such as the potentially disproportionate political influence that economically powerful agents (voters and candidates) possess. In the concluding remarks thoughts on possible developments triggered by the identified changes are carried out.

## 2 The Brazilian electoral financing model until 2014

### 2.1 Private resources

Private resources were clearly the main source of electoral funding in Brazil until the 2014 elections. Among the private resources, donations from legal entities stood out. Practically all donations from legal entities came from private companies, which is why the expressions "donations from legal entities" and "donations from companies" appear interchangeably in this article. Data from the first and second rows in tables 1 (above), 2 and 3 (below) clearly show the predominance of corporate donations.

**Table 1: Electoral donations from legal entities, 2002-2014**

|  | 2002 | 2006 | 2010 | 2014 |
|---|---|---|---|---|
| BRL | 477,730,315.74 | 900,508,009.30 | 2,297,349,981.50 | 3,031,864,138.09 |
| % private resources | 67.2 | 67.0 | 75.2 | 76.5 |
| % increase in BRL | -- | 88.5 | 155.1 | 32.0 |
| Cumulative inflation | -- | 35.5 | 21.8 | 28.8 |
| N | 12,501 | 17,497 | 19,442 | 16,647 |
| Gini | 0.871 | 0.887 | 0.918 | 0.925 |
| 1% largest | 48.2 | 49.5 | 60.0 | 62.6 |
| 5% largest | 71.8 | 74.7 | 80.6 | 81.9 |
| 10% largest | 81.7 | 84.1 | 88.6 | 89.3 |

Source: Data from the Superior Electoral Court (TSE) organized by the author

Over the period for which official data is available (2002-2014)[1], the total number of corporate electoral donations increased from 477.7 million to 3 billion reais. Taking into account the three main sources of private funding of Brazilian elections (legal entities, individuals, and the candidates themselves), we find that, in the first two analyzed elections, companies were already responsible for just over two thirds of the total donations, and this amount further increased in the last two elections of the period, to just over three quarters of the total contributions.

The third and fourth rows in table 1 indicate that, in every subsequent election, the increase in corporate donations has always been higher than the cumulative inflation in the same period. For example, between October 2002 and October 2006 the inflation measured by the National Consumer Price Index, calculated by the Brazilian Institute of Geography and Statistics (IPCA-IBGE), was 35.5%, while the leap in corporate contributions was 88.5%. We find an even greater discrepancy between October 2006 and October 2010, when inflation rose by 21.8% and corporate financing grew by 155.1%. Even between October 2010 and October 2014, when corporate donations were already soaring to billions, the increase in donations surpassed inflation: 32.0% against 28.8%.

Although the vast majority of private companies were apt to make electoral contributions[2], relatively few were willing to enter the political game as shown

---

[1] All data referring to electoral financing in Brazil comes from the Superior Electoral Court (TSE) and is available at the following website: http://www.tse.jus.br/eleitor-e-eleicoes/estatisticas/repositorio-de-dados-eleitorais-1/repositorio-de-dados-eleitorais. To analyze the information for 2002 and 2006, I used the databases organized by Bruno Carazza dos Santos, kindly made available at: http://leisenumeros.com.br. The data presented in this paper only refers to official electoral financing, i.e., formally declared to the Electoral Court. Very difficult to measure is the amount of resources that may have flowed unofficially into campaigns—the famous "slush fund" ("caixa dois" in Portuguese). Information on "slush funds" usually comes to light by way of police or legal investigations.

[2] The legal entities prohibited from donating, according to article 24 of Law no. 9,504/97, were the following: foreign governments or entities; direct and indirect public administration bodies or publicly funded foundations; public service concessionaires or licensees; entities under private law receiving, as beneficiaries, compulsory contributions due to legal provisions; entities of public utility; class or trade union entities; non-profit legal entities receiving foreign funding; charity and religious entities; sports organizations; non-governmental organizations receiving public funds; and civil society organizations of public interest.

in the fifth row of table 1. In fact, corporate electoral financing has always involved no more than a few thousand Brazilian companies[3].

In turn, the data in the last four rows in table 1 suggest that a select group of major companies has always dominated the game. This dominance was facilitated by the Elections Law (no. 9,504/97, article 81, §1°), which allowed companies to donate up to 2% of the gross revenue obtained in the year prior to that election. Since the legal threshold for donations was not in absolute terms, but rather a percentage of the company's revenue, the highest-grossing companies were able to donate the most.

The vast and growing concentration of corporate political donations between 2002 and 2014 may be revealed, for example, by the Gini coefficient, which ranges from 0 to 1 and larger values indicate more concentration. The coefficient for the set of donating companies starts at a very high level in 2002 (0.871) and increases successively until reaching an impressive 0.925 in 2014.

Another way to show the increasingly high level of concentration of electoral contributions made by a few major companies is to indicate the proportion of contributions made by 1%, 5%, and 10% of the largest donor corporations. While the values obtained in 2002 reached 48.2%, 71.8%, and 81.7% of total corporate electoral contributions, respectively, these figures continued to grow, reaching 62.6%, 81.9%, and 89.3% of the total in 2014.

In the 2002-2014 period, donations by individuals stood out as the second most important source of private electoral financing in Brazil (see table 2). The amount donated by individuals increased from approximately R$122.3 million at the beginning of the period to approximately R$556.8 million in 2014.

In comparative terms, individual donations were at 17% in the first two elections, and dropped to circa 14% in the following two elections. In absolute terms, the volume of individual donations grew above the cumulative inflation for each

---

[3] The number of companies that were qualified to make electoral donations during each of the four elections is not available. That being said, this number is certainly in the millions.

electoral cycle, especially in the 2006 and 2010 elections, as well as in the 2014 elections, albeit at a lower rate.

Table 2: Electoral donations from individuals, 2002-2014

|  | 2002 | 2006 | 2010 | 2014 |
| --- | --- | --- | --- | --- |
| BRL | 122,323,980.44 | 238,327,611.26 | 426,344,762.48 | 556,860,093.90 |
| % private resources | 17.2 | 17.7 | 13.9 | 14.0 |
| % increase in BRL | -- | 94.8 | 78.9 | 30.6 |
| Cumulative inflation | -- | 35.5 | 21.8 | 28.8 |
| N | 59,822 | 105,186 | 183,153 | 138,113 |
| Gini | 0.709 | 0.784 | 0.818 | 0.743 |
| 1% largest | 26.9 | 37.0 | 42.0 | 35.2 |
| 5% largest | 45.8 | 55.9 | 61.0 | 53.3 |
| 10% largest | 58.2 | 67.6 | 72.1 | 64.4 |

Source: Data from the TSE and organized by the author

The proportion of Brazilians who have made electoral contributions has always been very small. In 2002, 59,822 individuals donated to campaigns, while there were 115,254,113 registered voters, resulting in a rate of approximately 0.5% of voter-donors.[4] The following two elections had a small increase in the rate of voter-donors: circa 0.8% in 2006 (105,186 donors and 125,913,479 voters) and circa 1.3% in 2010 (183,153 donors and 135,804,433 voters). However, in the last analyzed election, the rate dropped to approximately 1% (138,113 donors and 142,822,046 voters).

---

[4] Information regarding the size of the Brazilian electorate in the four analyzed elections was compiled from the Superior Electoral Court website <http://www.tse.jus.br>.

Within the relatively small group of individuals who have contributed to electoral campaigns in Brazil, very few people made up a large part of these donations. Once again, this concentration was made possible by Law no. 9,504/97, which, throughout the period, did not set a low threshold for individual donations in absolute values. Conversely, the limit for this type of donation was connected to the agent's economic capacity—10% of the gross income obtained in the year prior to the elections (article 23, §1°, Section I). Once again, those who earned more could also donate more.

Between 2002 and 2010, the concentration of individual donations grew steadily. The Gini coefficient for individuals who donated started at the high level of 0.709, increased to 0.784, and reached 0.818. The share of donations made by 1%, 5%, and 10% of the largest donors also increased in every election. In 2014, the degree of concentration suffered a slight decrease, albeit remaining at very high levels and well above those observed in 2002.

Candidates were the third most significant source of private financing for political campaigns, contributing circa R$110.6 million in 2002 and an amount 3.4 times greater—circa R$377 million—12 years later (see table 3). Over time, therefore, there has been a considerable increase in the volume of their own resources contributed to electoral campaigns in absolute terms, an increase that greatly surpassed inflation in the 2006 and 2010 elections, even though it was well below inflation in the 2014 elections. Nevertheless, the relative importance of this source declined over the period of investigation from 15% in 2002 and 2006 to circa 10% in 2010 and 2014.

A significant share of the candidates used their own resources in their election campaigns. In 2002, the electoral courts approved 17,208 candidacies for all vacant offices[5] and 6,700 candidates (38.9% of the total) invested a certain amount of their own resources in the pursuit of votes. In the following elections, the ratio grew in comparison to 2002: 46.5% in 2006 (18,039 candidates and

---

[5] These offices in the Brazilian national elections include: president, vice president, governor, vice governor, senator, first surrogate senator, second surrogate senator, federal deputy, and state deputy. Information on the number of candidacies was obtained from the TSE website.

8,390 self-donors), 52.3% in 2010 (18,415 candidates and 9,639 self-donors), and 45.7% in 2014 (21,922 candidates and 10,023 self-donors).

**Table 3: Electoral donations from the candidates' own resources, 2002-2014**

|  | 2002 | 2006 | 2010 | 2014 |
|---|---|---|---|---|
| BRL | 110,686,835.88 | 204,338,234.15 | 331,097,489.84 | 377,006,656.10 |
| % private resources | 15.6 | 15.2 | 10.8 | 9.5 |
| % increase in BRL | -- | 84.6 | 62.0 | 13.9 |
| Cumulative inflation | -- | 35.5 | 21.8 | 28.8 |
| N | 6,700 | 8,390 | 9,639 | 10,023 |
| Gini | 0.775 | 0.809 | 0.839 | 0.837 |
| 1% largest | 25.8 | 27.3 | 34.6 | 33.8 |
| 5% largest | 50.2 | 54.5 | 61.8 | 60.6 |
| 10% largest | 64.7 | 70.1 | 75.6 | 74.7 |

Source: Data from the TSE and organized by the author

The concentration of electoral donations within a certain group—already mentioned for corporations and individuals—also applies to candidates. Once again, it was made possible by the legal system. In fact, with regard to self-donations, Law no. 9,504/97 was even more permissive. In this specific case, in addition to the lack of a monetary threshold in absolute values, the electoral law allowed candidates to donate their own resources to their campaigns up to the maximum amount of expenses set by their own parties (article 23, §1°, Section II). In other words, candidates could entirely self-finance their own campaign, spending their own resources up to the threshold defined by the party for the particular office in question. The advantages provided by law for wealthier candidates were blatant.

In such a scenario, the high concentration levels throughout the analyzed period come as no surprise. The Gini coefficient for candidates who made self-donations started at 0.775 in 2002, increased to 0.809 in 2006, rose even further to 0.839 in 2010, and remained practically at the same level in 2014 with 0.837. The share of self-donations from 1%, 5%, and 10% of the candidates who made the largest contributions of this type also increased significantly between 2002 and 2014.

* * *

From the data above, we find that until the 2014 elections the existing rules associated the agents' capacity to contribute to electoral campaigns with their economic power. The greater the gross revenue of a company, or the greater the gross income of an individual, the greater the ability to invest resources into political competition. For rich candidates, the only limit to self-donations was the spending ceiling set by their party for the disputed office. In practice, only a very small number of companies and individuals made electoral donations. With regard to candidates, the ratio of self-donors was significantly higher. In all cases, however, donations were heavily concentrated by companies, individuals, and candidates who commanded a large volume of economic resources and who were willing to finance the political competition.

## 2. 2 Public resources

In addition to private resources, national elections during the 2002-2014 period were also supported by public resources. One of the sources for public funding of electoral campaigns in Brazil is the "Special Fund for Financial Assistance to Political Parties", better known as the "party fund". According to the Law no. 9,096 of 1995 (Law on Political Parties), the party fund mainly consists of an annual allocation of the federal budget[6], but it also receives money from other sources, such as electoral fines, donations from individuals and companies, or budget allocations defined by law on a permanent or occasional basis (Article

---

[6] The minimum amount for this allocation is determined by the following calculation: the number of registered voters on December 31 in the year prior to the budget proposal multiplied by R$0.35, in August 1995 values adjusted for inflation.

38). The party fund is distributed as follows: 5% goes to all parties in equal parts and 95% is spread proportionally to obtained votes in the last election for the Chamber of Deputies (article 41-A).

Table 4 shows the volume of resources made available to the party fund by the federal budget in the last four national elections[7]. There is a steady increase over the period investigated, far beyond the cumulative inflation – with exception of the cicle between 2002 and 2006[8]. Parties may spend party fund on running election campaigns as well as other expenses, such as maintenance, advertising, payments to international party institutions, and food. From the party fund resources received, parties are required to use at least 20% for their own research institutes and 5% for programs promoting the political participation of women (Article 44). Therefore, party fund resources are not only for electoral expenditures, although parties have increasingly received funds from this source, which may be used for electoral purposes.

**Table 4: Party fund, 2002-2014**

|  | 2002 | 2006 | 2010 | 2014 |
|---|---|---|---|---|
| BRL | 83,527,578.64 | 117,875,438.74 | 160,375,147.57 | 308,201,016.21 |
| % increase in BRL | -- | 41.1 | 36.1 | 92.2 |
| Cumulative inflation | -- | 44.3 | 26.1 | 34.5 |

Source: Data from the TSE and organized by the author

Another type of public resource is the free electoral advertising time on radio and TV. Regulated by Law no. 9,504/97, electoral advertising time on radio and TV during national elections was as follows until the 2014 elections:

---

[7] Resources from other sources—such as electoral fines—are not included in the table.
[8] Since the transfer of the party fund to political parties is performed in twelfths—that is, in 12 monthly installments—I calculated, for this case, the inflation between January 1st of the previous election year and the 31st of December of the next election year.

i. from 45 days to two days before the first election round, two 50-minute blocks, from Monday to Saturday, plus 30 minutes of daily insertion[9];
ii. in case of a second round of elections, from 48 hours after the announcement of the results of the first round until two days before the elections, two daily blocks of 20 minutes for each vacant office in addition to 30 minutes of daily insertion[10].

From 2002 to 2010, the criterion for dividing advertising time among parties prior to the first round of elections was as follows: one-third was divided equally among all parties and two-thirds in proportion to the number of federal deputies from each party. Law no. 12,875/13 made the distribution of time more unequal in the 2014 elections: A ninth was divided equally among all parties and eight-ninths in proportion to the number of federal deputies. In the second round, the distribution of time among candidates has always been distributed evenly.

In compensation for the time slots dedicated to electoral advertising, radio and TV stations received tax relief. The estimated value for this tax compensation is shown in table 5.

Table 5: Tax Compensation for free electoral advertising time, 2002-2014

|  | 2002 | 2006 | 2010 | 2014 |
|---|---|---|---|---|
| BRL | 121,539,800.00 | 191,603,574.00 | 851,119,427.00 | 839,534,999.00 |
| % increase in BRL | -- | 57.6 | 344.2 | -1.4 |
| Cumulative inflation | -- | 35.5 | 21.8 | 28.8 |

Source: Brasil, 2002, 2006, 2010, 2014

---

[9] Before the first round, political advertisement was divided among the majority elections (president, governor, and senator) and proportional elections (federal and state deputies).
[10] A second round may take place for two offices: the presidency and the governorship.

The estimated tax benefit from free electoral advertising increased significantly from 2002 to 2006, with a significantly greater increment from 2006 to 2010. It fell slightly between 2010 and 2014, but tax exemption in the last national election was 6.9 times higher compared to 2002.

\* \* \*

The data presented above shows that national elections from 2002 to 2014 received a significant and increasing amount of public resources, whether via party fund or via free electoral advertising. The distribution of such resources privileged the larger parties. An even greater upsurge of public investment in Brazilian electoral campaigns will mark the next period, as shown in the next section.

## 3  The Brazilian electoral financing model after the 2014 elections

### 3.1  Private resources

#### 3.1.1  Corporate donations

Without a doubt, the most significant change in Brazil's electoral financing model took place on September 17, 2015, when the STF decided, by 8 votes to 3, to ban electoral donations from business corporations, thus abolishing the main private source of campaign financing in the country. The Supreme Court decision complied with a request by the OAB Federal Council, which, four years earlier, submitted ADI no. 4,650, which proposed a ban on corporate electoral contributions.

A few days after the decision by the STF, the Brazilian Congress approved a bill that, in flagrant disagreement with the Supreme Court's decision, reinstituted corporate electoral financing at least for political parties.

However, in what became Law no. 13,165/15, President Dilma Rousseff vetoed sections of the bill allowing the return of corporate donations. Congress did not overturn the presidential veto.

## 3.1.2 Individual donations

ADI no. 4,650/11 signed by the Order of Attorneys of Brazil (OAB) also recommended the Supreme Court to repeal the aforementioned rule that allowed individuals to donate up to 10% of their gross income obtained in the year prior to the election. The proposal, however, was not accepted by the STF.

In October 2017, the Brazilian Congress approved a bill that continued to allow individual donations of up to 10% of the gross income in the year prior to the election, but also imposed an absolute limit on these donations, corresponding to 10 times' the monthly minimum wage for each office or ticket disputing majority elections, including all donations. This rule sought to restrict the influence of wealthy individuals on the odds of electoral success[11]. Since the monthly minimum wage in 2018 in Brazil was R$954.00, the limit for individual donations would be R$9,540.00 for each office or ticket disputing majority elections.

President Michel Temer vetoed this provision before endorsing the bill that became Law no. 13,488/17 and, once again, Congress did not overturn the presidential veto.

## 3.1.3 Self-donations

ADI no. 4,650/11 signed by the OAB recommended to the STF the repeal of the rule that favored wealthy candidates by allowing self-donations up to a maximum amount defined by the parties. Once again, however, the STF did not accept the appeal.

Law no. 13,165/15 stripped parties of the prerogative of setting the limit for their candidates' campaign spending. Instead, the law established a maximum value in an attempt to decelerate the increase in the costs of electoral campaigns[12]. How-

---

[11] The literature suggests a positive and significant correlation between financing and electoral success in Brazil (Samuels (2001, 2002), Figueiredo Filho (2009); Peixoto (2010); Lemos et al. (2010), Speck and Mancuso (2013, 2014), Heiler et al. (2016)).

[12] According to articles 5-8 of Law no. 13,165/15, in the 2018 elections for the presidency and the governorship the spending limit for the first round should be as follows: 70% of the highest declared expenditure for the same office, in the 2014 elections, in electoral districts with a single electoral round and 50% of the highest declared expenditure for the same office in the 2014 elec-

ever, a candidate was still able to make self-donations to the extent defined by law. Thus, the bias favoring wealthy candidates persisted.

The same bill approved by Congress two years later, which set a limit for individual donations in absolute values, also revoked the provision allowing self-financing up to the spending limit defined by law. The intention behind the bill was to treat candidates like any other individual, limiting their donations (self-donations and donations to third parties) to 10% of the gross income in the year prior to the election as well as imposing a limit of ten times' minimum wages for each office or majority ticket.

In an attempt to maintain the *status quo ante*, president Michel Temer also vetoed this section of the bill approved by Congress. However, parliamentarians rejected the presidential veto in this case, thus limiting donations of candidates to 10% of the gross income in the year prior to the election. Thus, after the approval of Law no. 13.488/17, candidates began to receive the same treatment as any other individual. This law also established new spending limits for the 2018 elections[13].

\* \* \*

Recent changes regarding the role of private resources in Brazil's electoral financing have had different effects on different sources of funding. Private

---

tions in electoral districts with two electoral rounds. The spending limit for the second round would be 30% of the amount predicted for the first round. In the elections for senator, federal deputy, and state deputy, the limit would be 70% of the highest declared expenditure for the same position in each electoral district, in the 2014 elections. Such values were to be updated every election according to the IBGE's National Consumer Price Index (INPC).

[13] In the presidential elections, the limit for the first round was 70 million reais, and 50% of this amount for the second round. In gubernatorial elections, the limit for the first round was established in six groups that vary according to the number of voters in each state, ranging from a minimum of 2.8 million reais (in states with up to one million voters) to a maximum of 21 million reais (for states with more than 20 million voters). For the second round, the limit was 50% of this value. In senatorial elections, the limit was set in five groups that vary according to the number of voters in each state, ranging from a minimum of 2.5 million reais (for states with up to two million voters) to a maximum of 5.6 million reais (for states with more than 20 million voters). In elections for federal deputy, the limit was 2.5 million reais, and 1 million reais for state deputy elections.

companies, which dominated the entire picture between 2002 and 2014, were forbidden to donate by court order.

Despite the parliament's initiative to set a relatively low threshold for individual donations in absolute values, a presidential veto overturned this measure. Thus, the voters' ability to fund political campaigns continues to be proportional to their income. In the future, therefore, individual donations will continue to mainly come from wealthier voters more willing to act politically through this route. The parliament also sought to limit self-financing by treating candidates just like any other voter. In this circumstance, change was only partial. If, on the one hand, the presidential veto barred a threshold in absolute values for self-donations, on the other hand candidates were bound to the 10% limit like any other individual. The capacity for self-financing remains proportional to the candidate's economic capacity, and wealthier candidates are likely to remain the main source of self-financing. However, we may see a decrease in the number of candidates capable of managing competitive campaigns mostly or fully with their own resources.

## 3.2 Public resources

Along with the ban on corporate donations, another notable recent change in the Brazilian electoral financing model was the increase in the flow of public resources. This increase is noticeable when we look at the party fund.

Table 6: Party fund, 2014-2018

|  | 2014 | 2018 |
| --- | --- | --- |
| BRL | 308,201,016.21 | 780,357,504.96 |
| % increase in BRL | -- | 153.2 |
| Cumulative inflation | -- | 29.8 |

Source: Data from the TSE and organized by the author

Table 6 shows the increase in public funding to political parties from 2014 to 2018[14]. The increase was 153.2%, while the cumulative inflation between 01/01/2014 and 03/31/2018 was 29.8%[15]. This significant increase is all the more remarkable as the period between 2015 and 2018 was marked by deep cuts in federal public spending across almost all areas in an attempt to tackle the economic crisis through austerity. As previously stated, parties use party fund resources for a variety of purposes, with election expenses being just one of them. At any rate, parties in 2018 will count on plenty more money from the party fund than they did in 2014, and they have the possibility to invest (a part of) it in their campaigns. There were no changes in the criteria for distributing the party fund among parties.

Table 7: Tax Compensation for free electoral advertising time, 2014-2018

|  | 2014 | 2018 |
|---|---|---|
|  |  |  |
| **BRL** | 839,534,999.00 | 1,038,230,549.00 |
| **% increase in R$** | -- | 23.7 |
| **Cumulative inflation** | -- | 24.0 |

Source: Brasil, 2014, 2018

Secondly, the increased flow of public resources to electoral campaigns is also noticeable when attention is paid to the value of estimated tax exemptions as a result of free electoral advertising on radio and TV. The calculated value of tax exemptions for 2018 exceeds a billion reais, although the percentage increase in reais is very close to the cumulative inflation between October 2014 (at the time

---

[14] The values for 2018 were calculated by multiplying the total sum of transfers made in January to all political parties by twelve. Again, the values of fines and electoral penalties are not included.

[15] In 2018, inflation in Brazil is relatively low, so reasonably we may expect that the cumulative index will not vary greatly until 12/31/2018.

of the last national elections) and March 2018[16]. Here, it is important to add that Law no. 13,165/15 brought significant changes to free electoral advertising in national elections:

 i. the number of days for ads in the period prior to the first electoral round decreased from 45 to 35 (the number of advertising days in the period prior to the second round remained the same);
 ii. the duration of advertising blocks decreased from 50 to 25 minutes, from Monday to Saturday for the period prior to the first electoral round (the duration of advertising blocks remained the same for the period prior to the second round);
 iii. the time dedicated to insertion in advertising periods prior to the first and second rounds increased from 30 to 70 minutes per day[17].

The distribution of advertising time (in blocks and insertion) among parties in the period prior to the first election round became even more uneven: the share equally distributed among all parties dropped from one-ninth (i.e., 11.1%) to one-tenth (i.e., 10%). As a result, the share proportionally distributed according to the number of federal deputies in each party increased from eight-ninths (88.9%) to nine-tenths (90%). The distribution of advertising time among the candidates in the second round remained the same.

Therefore, with regard to free electoral advertising, Law no. 13,165/15 reduced the number of advertising days and the duration of block advertising in the period prior to the first round, but compensated those cuts by increasing the time spent on insertions in the periods prior to both rounds. Free electoral advertising on radio and TV has become leaner, albeit more dynamic and intense—and costlier for the public coffers.

---

[16] As stated in footnote 16, we may assume that inflation will not increase significantly until October 2018.
[17] In the period prior to the first round, time remains divided between majority and proportional candidacies, both in block advertising and in ad inserts. There may be a second round for president and governor. Should there be a second round for both, they receive thirty-five minutes each. If only one of such offices heads into a second round, it receives the entire amount of time.

The third and most important recent change that resulted in an increased flow of public resources to electoral financing was the creation of the "Special Fund for Campaign Financing" (FEFC in Portuguese), through Law no. 13,487/17. This fund will be available to parties in electoral years[18] and consists of federal budget resources at a minimum value corresponding:

i. to the sum of tax compensation granted to radio and TV broadcasters for the promotion of free party advertising in 2016 and 2017 (value updated at every election according to the IBGE's National Consumer Price Index—INPC);[19] and
ii. to 30% of the reserve fund for attending state benches' amendments of mandatory execution 20.

The estimated value of the FEFC for the 2018 elections could reach up to 1.7 billion reais[21].

The criteria for allocating the FEFC are as follows: 2% will be allocated equally among all parties, 35% among parties with at least one representative in the Chamber of Deputies in proportion to the percentage of votes obtained in the last general elections; 48% among parties in proportion to the number of representatives in the Chamber of Deputies, according to the parties of the elected parliamentarians; and 15% among parties in proportion to the number of repre-

---

[18] Elections in Brazil take place every two years. National elections will take place in 2018. In 2020 there will be municipal elections (for mayor and city councilor). Almost all mandates last four years. The only exception is the eight-year term for senators. The partial renewal of the senate happens every four years, sometimes for a third of the seats, sometimes for two thirds (as is the case for 2018).

[19] In addition to free electoral advertising, Brazil also had free party advertising in non-electoral semesters. Ruled by articles 45-49 of Law no. 9,096 (Law of Political Parties), free party advertising was ultimately extinguished by Law no. 13,487/17. The tax exemption resources saved with the end of free party advertising were passed on to the FEFC.

[20] The annual budget law predicts a reserve of resources for the mandatory execution of amendments by the benches (deputies and senators) of each state in Congress. In electoral years, 30% of these resources are transferred to the FEFC.

[21] http://www2.camara.leg.br/camaranoticias/noticias/POLITICA/545056-CAMARA-APROVA-CRIACAO-DE-FUNDO-PUBLICO-DE-FINANCIAMENTO-DE-CAMPANHAS.html

sentatives in the Federal Senate, according to the parties of the elected parliamentarians[22].

\* \* \*

The ban on corporate electoral donations was followed by a significant increase in the flow of public resources to political campaigns. Not only was there a reinforcement of previously existing public financing modalities (party fund and tax exemption for free electoral advertising), but also the creation of an entirely new modality—the FEFC—to the tune of billions. Electoral funding continues to be multifarious in Brazil, but the importance of public resources has now become much greater. That said, the distribution of resources continues to favor the larger parties.

## 4  Final remarks

In general, Brazil's electoral financing model has undergone an incomplete transition after the 2014 elections.

On the one hand, several attempts were made to reduce the importance of private resources as well as their concentration among a few major donors. The most successful initiative, headed by the OAB, resulted in a ban on corporate electoral donations since September 2015. Other initiatives—by the OAB via judicial routes and by Congress via legislation—sought to limit electoral contributions from wealthy individuals (voters and candidates). These initiatives, however, had little success. The ability of voters and candidates to fund the electoral race remains proportional to their financial means.

On the other hand, there has been a significant increase of public investment in elections. Unless we witness an unlikely upsurge of individual donations and self-donations in the upcoming 2018 elections, it seems that the predominance of

---

[22] For the 2018 elections, the amount of party representatives in the Chamber of Deputies and Senate will be determined on 08/28/18. For other elections, the amount will be determined on the last day of the legislative session immediately preceding the election year. Analysts believe that this redistributive criterion will promote party migration since the parliamentarian changing parties will bring a portion of the FEFC to his new party.

private resources (especially corporate resources, typical to the previous period) will give way to a preponderance of public resources.

It is hard to predict what the future holds and whether this transition will accelerate or reverse itself. The branches of the Brazilian government have behaved erratically on the issue of private electoral financing. The Supreme Court banned corporate contributions, but upheld rules allowing for the concentration of donations among wealthy voters and candidates. Within two years, the same legisla-legislature that approved a project reinstating corporate electoral financing against the restrictive decision of the Supreme Court, also endorsed a different project setting relatively low thresholds for individual donations and self-donations, pressing forward in a field that the Supreme Court had not dared to tackle. The presidency of the republic, under the Dilma Rousseff administration, vetoed the first decision of the parliament, while the Michel Temer administration vetoed the second decision. The branches of government are subjected to strong internal and external contradictory pressures when it comes to the role of private resources in electoral financing, and a restrictive or permissive position on the issue seems to depend on short-term issues, such as the preferences and strategic calculations of its current occupants. In such a scenario, while an intensification of the transition is a possibility, likewise the hypothesis of the reversion to the *status quo ante* cannot be excluded.

The stance of the Brazilian political class on public electoral financing is less controversial. There is little effective opposition to the increase of public resources earmarked for elections, even more so with the recent cuts in their main source of funding—corporate donations. However, this increase in public resources brings to surface relevant debates that may be resumed in the near future.

The first debate refers to the appropriate amount of public funding earmarked for electoral competition. Public investments in elections skyrocketed precisely in a period marked by an economic crisis and spending cuts across almost all areas of state action. The increase in public investments happened either indirectly (more tax benefits as a result of free election advertising) or directly (more budgetary resources for the party fund and the FEFC). The impact of this increase was partially diminished since a share of public resources came from collective parliamentary amendments as well as the end of free party advertising. Thus, the first question is whether public funding for the upcoming elections will be reduced, unchanged, or increased and, in case of an increase, if this would only replace or surpass inflationary losses.

The second debate concerns the distribution of public resources among political parties. The current distribution of the party fund, free electoral advertising, and the FEFC clearly favors the major parties. On the one hand, such asymmetric distribution reflects the choices of the electorate in the previous election. On the other hand, it hinders smaller parties from participating in political competition. In addition, access to public resources is one of the main incentives for creating new parties in the country[23]. New and smaller parties often use whatever public resources they can muster—such as free electoral advertising—to establish coalitions with larger parties and increase their odds of occupying elected and non-elected positions within the state. The second issue, therefore, is how to redistribute public resources through criteria that simultaneously respect the choices of the electorate, do not undermine political competition, nor artificially promote the fragmentation of the party system.

The third debate refers to the potential use of public resources to promote the candidacies of social groups historically underrepresented in Brazilian politics (such as women, black people, and the disabled). The existing rules simply fail to address this issue. This omission is all the more remarkable since recent studies (Mancuso et al., 2018) have shown that party leaders, when distributing resources, lean towards candidates with a predominant profile in Brazilian politics: highly educated white men seeking reelection. Thus, the third issue is how to use society's resources to make Brazilian politics more inclusive.

Evidently, all discussions regarding the desirable role and weight for private resources vis-à-vis public resources become meaningless if major private donors,

---

[23] Constitutional Amendment no. 97, approved on October 4, 2017, may provide an answer to this situation. The amendment established a barrier clause for accessing the party fund and free electoral advertising. From 2030, access to such public resources will be restricted to parties that obtained a minimum of 3% of valid votes in elections to the Chamber of Deputies, distributed across at least one third of the states, with a minimum of 2% of the valid votes in each. The amendment also established transition rules for the remaining three national elections until then (2018, 2022, and 2026).

although formally excluded from political financing, continue to fund elections in a fraudulent, unlawful, and unpunished manner. That is to say, the underlying premise of this article is that electoral financing in Brazil should become increasingly transparent and that deviations from existing legislation should be monitored, detected, and punished.

## References

Bourdoukan, A. (2009 [2009]) *O bolso e a urna: financiamento político em perspectiva comparada* (PhD thesis in Political Science, University of São Paulo) [Online].

Brasil (2002) *Demonstrativo dos benefícios tributários*, Brasília: Receita Federal.

Brasil (2006) *Demonstrativo dos gastos governamentais indiretos de natureza tributária (gastos tributários)*, Brasília: Receita Federal.

Brasil (2010) *Demonstrativo dos gastos tributários*, Brasília: Receita Federal.

Brasil (2014) *Demonstrativo dos gastos tributários*, Brasília: Receita Federal.

Brasil (2018) *Demonstrativo dos gastos tributários*, Brasília: Receita Federal.

Figueiredo Filho, D. (2009) *O elo corporativo? Grupos de interesse, financiamento de campanha e regulação eleitoral*, Master's dissertation in Political Science, Federal University of Pernambuco.

Heiler, J., Viana, J. P. and Santos, R. (2016) 'O Custo da Política Subnacional: a Forma como o Dinheiro é Gasto Importa? Relação entre Receita, Despesas e Sucesso Eleitoral', *Opinião Pública*, vol. 22, no. 1, pp. 56–92.

Katz, R. and Mair, P. (1995) 'Changing models of party organization and party democracy: the emergence of the cartel party', *Party politics*, vol. 1, no. 1, pp. 5–28.

Katz, R. and Mair, P. (1996) 'Cadre, Catch-All or Cartel? A Rejoinder', *Party politics*, vol. 2, no. 4, pp. 525–534.

Katz, R. and Mair, P. (2009) 'The Cartel Party Thesis: A Restatement', *Perspectives on politics*, vol. 7, no. 4, pp. 753–766.

Katz, R. and Mair, P. (2012) 'Parties, interest groups and cartels: a comment', *Papers in Regional Science*, vol. 18, no. 1, pp. 107–111.

LEMOS, L., MARCELINO, D., PEDERIVA and João Henrique (2010) 'Porque dinheiro importa: a dinâmica das contribuições eleitorais para o Congresso Nacional em 2002 e 2006', *Opinião Pública*, vol. 16, no. 2, pp. 366–393.

Mancuso, W. (2015a) 'A reforma política e o financiamento das campanhas eleitorais', in Ianoni, M. (ed) *Reforma política democrática: temas, atores e desafios*, São Paulo: Editora Fundação Perseu Abramo, Editora Fundação Perseu Abramo, pp. 83–104.

Mancuso, W. (2015b) 'Investimento Eleitoral no Brasil: Balanço da Literatura (2001-2012) e Agenda de Pesquisa', *Revista de Sociologia e Política*, vol. 23, no. 54, pp. 155–183.

Mancuso, W., Horochovski, R. and Camargo, N. (2018) *Financiamento eleitoral empresarial direto e indireto nas eleições nacionais de 2014*, Paper prepared for the XI Workshop "Empresa, Empresários e Sociedade", held in Maringá (Paraná, Brasil), 06/20-22/2018.

Mancuso, W. and Speck, B. (2014) 'Financiamento de campanhas e prestação de contas', *Cadernos Adenauer*, vol. 15, no. 1, pp. 135–150.

Mutch, R. (2016) *Campaign finance: what everyone needs to know*, New York, Oxford University Press.

Norris, P. and van Es, A. A., eds. (2016) *Checkbook elections?: Political Finance in Comparative Perspective*, New York, Oxford University Press.

Peixoto, V. d. M. (2010) *Eleições e financiamento de campanhas no Brasil* (PhD thesis in Political Science. University Research Institute of Rio de Janeiro) [Online].

Przeworski, A. (2011) *Money, politics, and democracy* (Paper presented at the Department of Political Science of the University of São Paulo) [Online].

Samuels, D. (2001) 'Money, Elections, and Democracy in Brazil', *American Politics and Society*, vol. 43, no. 2, pp. 27–48.

Samuels, D. (2002) 'Pork Barreling is not Credit Claiming or Advertising: Campaign Finance and the Source of the Personal Vote in Brazil', *The Journal of Politics*, vol. 64, no. 3, pp. 845–863.

Schumpeter, J. A. (1942) *Capitalism, socialism and democracy*, New York, Harper & Brothers.

Speck, B. and Mancuso, W. (2013) 'O Que Faz a Diferença? Gastos de Campanha, Capital Político, Sexo e Contexto Municipal nas Eleições para Prefeito em 2012', *Cadernos Adenauer*, vol. 14, no. 2, pp. 109–126.

Speck, B. and Mancuso, W. (2014) 'A Study on the Impact of Campaign Finance, Political Capital and Gender on Electoral Performance', *Brazilian Political Science Review*, vol. 8, no. 1, pp. 34–57.

Speck, B. W. (2016) 'Brazil', in Norris, P. and van Es, A. A. (eds) *Checkbook elections? Political Finance in Comparative Perspective*, New York, Oxford University Press., pp. 27–44.

Stratmann, T. (2005) 'Some talk: Money in Politics. A (partial) review of the literature', *Public Choice*, vol. 124, 1/2, pp. 135–156.

# 'Do not try to outsource dirty business into your value chain'. An interview with Matthias Kleinhempel

*Julian Klinkhammer*

**Julian Klinkhammer**: Mr Kleinhempel, you have provided your audience and discussants at the Herrenhausen Symposium with a knowledgeable perspective on the mechanisms of anti-corruption, based on your vast experience in South American Markets and in executive education. In hindsight, what was the most surprising insight with regard to anti-corruption that you have gained through your participation?

**Matthias Kleinhempel**: The "stick" approach by the sociologists.

**Julian Klinkhammer**: This is indeed a surprising insight as it does not square with the sociological self-perception. So, let's think about the 'carrots' for a moment. Of course, you are right; usually sociologists do not talk a lot about incentives. However, would you agree that careers are important to an understanding of the incentives for wrongdoing and for compliance in organizations?

**Matthias Kleinhempel**: I would say that incentives are an expression of the company culture. They show what the company really asks for. Executives' income package often has a big variable part. If the company's targets are short term financial goals, then those will most likely be perceived as an invitation to do what it takes to achieve them. Fortunately, some companies have started to change their incentive systems: a smaller percentage of the yearly income is variable; income depends more on the achievement of long-term goals, less on personal financial results; and more on company-wide goals.

**Julian Klinkhammer**: What's more, cultures might differ in the premiums that they put on goal attainment, or on the social status that you gain with economic success. Is this something that you have experienced in the context of South America?

**Matthias Kleinhempel**: There are differences between Anglo-Saxon and Latin American cultures. However, corporate culture is more relevant than national culture in the context of wrongdoing.

© Springer Fachmedien Wiesbaden GmbH, part of Springer Nature 2020
M. Pohlmann et al. (eds.), *Bribery, Fraud, Cheating*, Organization,
Management and Crime – Organisation, Management und Kriminalität,
https://doi.org/10.1007/978-3-658-29062-7_9

**Julian Klinkhammer**: The impact of multinational corporations (MNCs) on local institutional environments has been discussed controversially across the social sciences. Some see them as crucial allies in the international fight against corruption; some argue that their presence might even increase local corruption rates in vulnerable countries. What are the specific challenges for MNCs operating in South America?

**Matthias Kleinhempel**: I see challenges for MNCs in emerging markets in general, not only in Latin America: MNCs are the most risk exposed and therefore the most interested in improving the situation. They are additionally the most experienced, have already more or less sophisticated compliance systems and have the best resources available. They should support local companies (mostly SMEs and family businesses) in their anti-corruption efforts and eventually help them see the convenience of fighting corruption.

They can do so in various ways:

- More stringent due diligence processes in their local and regional value chains. Include sub-suppliers in the process. Put more emphasis on training of third party personnel;
- Organize collective actions among various levels of the value chain;
- Plus, "White Lists" of "clean" local companies as approved suppliers provide MNCs with a secure haven for doing clean business, which makes the MNCs less dependent on more difficult business relationships, and enables them economically to say "no".

For some MNCs, unfortunately, it starts with the basic: don't try to outsource dirty business into your value chain (distributors, vendors, agents etc).

**Julian Klinkhammer**: This is, indeed, a very important point, because we see in bribery cases as well as in recent revelations of investigative journalists (e.g., "Panama Papers", "Paradise Papers" etc.) that even decent corporations increasingly rely on offshore financial centers for all sorts of business. How would you describe the role of the private sector; what could top managers of non-financial companies do to prevent organizational deviance in (or via) such secretive jurisdictions?

**Matthias Kleinhempel**: By not using them. And, by the way, it's a reputational issue as well.

**Julian Klinkhammer**: So, you would argue that the increase in corporate profits offshore and the strong use of dot-tax-havens especially by firms from 'liberal market economies' is an issue for risk management that will eventually backfire?

**Matthias Kleinhempel**: Yes, I think so. On the one hand, we see this with Apple and other companies in Ireland for instance. They have reputational problems due to the delegitimization of mostly legal operations. Think of Bono [the lead singer of the rock band U2, eds.], and others, who have retreated their legal operations from offshore jurisdictions after public exposure in the Paradise Papers. On the other hand, for some companies, reputation doesn't matter. There are companies whose products are legal but ethically questionable, and some of them simply do not care much about their reputation. Companies with popular brands are way more vulnerable to public shaming and they are probably more affected than companies who sell to other businesses—instead of to end-consumers.

**Julian Klinkhammer**: At the Herrenhausen Symposium, you talked about organizations with strong corporate cultures, and you were optimistic that cultural change with regard to organizational deviance is possible. Could you please elaborate on this issue—e.g., by giving us an example from your experience?

**Matthias Kleinhempel**: I think that only a strong culture of integrity will be successful in the fight against corruption. Only when everybody in the organization has internalized that in this company certain behaviors are not only not well received but also not tolerated ('We simply don't do that …'), then the company can be reasonably sure that their executives won't commit corrupt acts. It's about culture (which is expressed and reinvigorated by a long list of topics like tone at the top, incentive systems, promotions and firings etc). The problem with culture in general is that companies aim at strong cultures. Once established, they are difficult to change because they are deep-rooted. So, if the way of doing business is perceived within the company as necessarily including corrupt practices (the famous 'everybody does it', 'it has always been that way'), it will not be easy to change that view.

**Julian Klinkhammer**: Do you think that corporate scandals are necessary drivers for change, or will good companies with a strong culture eventually purge themselves?

**Matthias Kleinhempel**: If I only knew. First, most companies do not have such a strong culture, and thus a scandal might help a great deal. Those companies that I know in Argentina that had to cope with scandals have benefited a lot. But the problem is that change might not last for a long time—e.g., the shareholders might not agree with a corporate management that aims strategically at long-term profitability through ethical business practices (beyond legal requirements). They could change the CEO or divest and then look for other more profitable companies without costly compliance measures.

**Julian Klinkhammer**: You have argued that companies do not have the freedom to violate the expectations of their shareholders anymore. Where do you see links between the short-termism that some institutional investors promote and the decisions of corporate management regarding anti-corruption?

**Matthias Kleinhempel**: In the end, no CEO will be able (and willing) to act against their shareholders. The CEO with the best intentions will not remain in office for long if shareholders focus exclusively on high short-term profits. That might be the case with most institutional investors and supporters of Milton Friedman, as their credo is that "the social responsibility of business is to increase its profits". Fortunately, we see some change in their views and expectations: look at BlackRock as an example.

**Julian Klinkhammer**: What is BlackRock doing better than other institutional investors?

**Matthias Kleinhempel**: I do not know if they really do business differently now, but recently BlackRock's CEO, Larry Fink, publicly announced that the company's investment decisions will no longer be taken based on financial results only, but instead on the triple bottom line. This company is the biggest institutional investor; it has a huge impact on companies worldwide.

**Julian Klinkhammer**: Could this be an example of American exceptionalism? I remember the CEO of a Swiss company who once told me that an institutional investor from the UK had been one of the main change agents, pushing him towards anti-corruption way back in the 1990s—which is why the company became a forerunner of anti-corruption.

**Matthias Kleinhempel**: If the institutional investor insisted on anti-corruption back then that's perfectly fine, but probably it was a consequence of risk management, not a matter of conviction.

**Julian Klinkhammer**: What could average middle managers do in an extreme situation—e.g., when their division is facing losses, their business partners are demanding favors, superiors turn their heads away, and business as usual has been paying bribes in the past? Should they just give up their job to keep their hands clean, or do you know any other ways for getting out of such a dilemma?

**Matthias Kleinhempel**: For their own good, and as a last resort, they should leave the company. But before they do, they should try speaking to upper management and the Compliance Officer to evaluate the situation and the chances for bringing change to the organization. But: It's easy to say this in an interview or a questionnaire …

**Julian Klinkhammer**: Are whistleblower hotlines of any use here?

**Matthias Kleinhempel**: They are necessary and useful. They are also a formal requirement if you want your compliance program to be considered effective by regulators (SEC, DoJ, and many others) and therefore able to mitigate fines etc. But it does not mean that you always take the high road. In my opinion, what is more appropriate to taking the high road is to establish a culture of speaking up, where your people feel free to speak about problems and wrongdoing that they observe to their superior, or compliance officer for that matter.

**Julian Klinkhammer**: In bribery cases on behalf of large bureaucratic organizations, scholars have claimed that social mechanisms on all levels are necessary to circumvent formal controls. Among the mechanisms that have been blamed so far you will find, i.a., the financial pressures of strong CFOs, the mindlessness of bribe paying middle managers, the close-knit social networks of conspirators, and strong corporate cultures. If you were in a top management position today, where you have to decide on the priorities of corporate compliance with regard to *organizational deviance*, how would you do it?

**Matthias Kleinhempel**: Here we are again: It's about culture. I'd start changing the culture. That means emphasis on moral integrity and a determined way of doing business. Education has to address the roots and consequences of scandals. And, most importantly, I'd start changing the incentive systems in the direction of rewarding long-term results and company results, not so much individual accomplishments. This would most likely relieve the individual from the pressure of having to use deviant means, in order to achieve his income goals. It will be perceived as a signal for the company to favour clean business with long-term success over short-term success risking dirty tricks.

**Julian Klinkhammer**: Mr Kleinhempel, this was a highly pointed summary. Thank you very much for your time and the valuable insights that you have conveyed to us.

# The FIFA's case and corruption in Brazil. An expert dialogue with Markus Asner and Fausto De Sanctis

*Elizangela Valarini and Wagner Pralon Mancuso*

**Wagner Wagner Pralon Mancuso**: Marcus Asner, could you please introduce us to the FIFA corruption case?

**Marcus Asner**: I think you are talking about the federal criminal case that is pending in the United States. There have been a number of other investigations, including investigations conducted by FIFA itself, for example, at an earlier point they hired Michael Garcia to conduct an investigation. However, with respect to the criminal case pending in the United States, as I understand it, the case really began in earnest with a cooperating witness who was arrested a number of years ago. He was part of the genesis of the case according to the press reports. His name was Chuck Blazer, and he was a high-ranking US soccer official, and a fairly high-ranking FIFA official. He cooperated with the government's investigation and I think ultimately that was key that led to the United States to bring down the case in May 2015. There is a big announcement, the Attorney General of the United States went to Brooklyn for the announcement, as did the Director of the FBI, James B. Comey. They announced a series of charges against a large number of people, including FIFA officials and marketing company officials. At the same time, they also announced that a number of people had been arrested previously and had already pleaded guilty, which, at least for people like me, suggests, that these people likely were cooperating with the government. Since then, a few months later, in December 2015, there was a second superseding indictment in which a number of other individuals were charged. So far, I think over forty people or entities have been charged. Over twenty have pleaded guilty. And the case is ongoing. In October [2017], we expect some sentences. There is also going to be a trial in November [2017] for some of the people who have elected to go to trial. The charges mainly have to do with bribery and corruption in connection with all sorts of things that FIFA is involved with. FIFA is involved in marketing rights, the granting of rights to hold certain tournaments, such as the World Cup, the selection of countries for the championships. As we all know, it's a pretty ground-breaking, very dramatic

© Springer Fachmedien Wiesbaden GmbH, part of Springer Nature 2020
M. Pohlmann et al. (eds.), *Bribery, Fraud, Cheating*, Organization,
Management and Crime – Organisation, Management und Kriminalität,
https://doi.org/10.1007/978-3-658-29062-7_10

case.

**Wagner Pralon Mancuso**: Fausto De Sanctis, how do you see FIFA's role in soccer regulation?

**Fausto De Sanctis**: In terms of soccer regulation, on the FIFA side, everything is relatively well. However, on the state side, it has not been enough, because despite the authorities' concerns about crime prevention, we still see many problems in football. This situation is worrying since many people, including the young ones, do not appreciate this sport anymore. They have learned about the problems of corruption and do not feel that it is a fair competition. My opinion is that we need better coordination between government agencies charged with investigating corruption, money laundering and FIFA itself. When we talk about a sector that is being regulated, historically, we have had issues with regard to crime prevention. This also occurs, for example, in the art sector. In the United States this sector is self-regulated and the results have not been satisfactory. Regulatory activity outside the industry would be important to fiscally monitor crime-related issues.

**Marcus Asner**: Just to comment on that, I think you see that issue not only in art, but also in real estate in London and in New York over the last years. I understand that one of the regulators, whether it was FINRA [Financial Industry Regulatory Authority] or one of the others, now requires you—if you buy a real estate in Manhattan, high-end real estate—to reveal the actual beneficial ownership because of concerns that people are using real estate to launder money.

**Fausto De Sanctis**: Yeah, but the real estate has the obligation now. At least there is a recommendation from the FATF [Financial Action Task Force] in that way. It has a concern to ask for real estate agents to report suspicious activities. For sports, although the FATF makes clear that the physical movement of players has been considered important since the circumstances surrounding the recruitment of them are not clear, there is no particular request as we see for real state. Rogue agents have established a network that leads to a number of irregularities. The recommendations of the FATF can play a special role in combating illegal gambling and money laundering. Particular attention was given to the designated non-financial businesses and professions (DNFBPs), such as casinos, real estate offices, etc., which must report suspicious operations (Recommendation no. 22, in combination with no. 18 through 21). Furthermore, the FATF has introduced rules (Recommendation 28) aimed at the effective supervision and prevention of money laundering specifically in casinos. Nothing, however, is said about the sport sector.

**Wagner Pralon Mancuso**: Marcus Asner, it is not that easy to understand why the US has jurisdiction over this specific case.

**Marcus Asner**: If we tweak the question a little bit and make it into: Why does the United States have jurisdiction and why is the United States asserting jurisdiction? Because those are two separate issues. The United States' jurisdiction in a criminal case in many circumstances is extremely broad, often surprisingly broad. The United States is able to assert jurisdiction in situations in which you will think there is a very thin connection with the United States. For example, in terrorism cases it doesn't take much of a link to the United States for the US to assert jurisdiction. In sanctions cases, for example, cases involving sanctions against Iran and North Korea, the United States will try to assert jurisdiction over transactions simply because they somehow are US-Dollar denominated. The transaction may go through a US bank or even a subsidiary US bank and may be dollar denominated, and the US may argue that the transaction therefore has a sufficient nexus to the US in order to assert jurisdiction. And the reason for this approach, of course, is that the United States, at least technically, should have a jurisdictional hook in order to support the United States' interests in enforcing sanctions and in fighting terrorism.

The more sort of run-of-the-mill jurisdictional hook that the United States has like every other country is territorial jurisdiction. In that sense, the FIFA case is very simple. They charged RICO [Racketeer Influenced and Corrupt Organizations Act] and they charged conspiracy and a number of other crimes. But if you look at the facts described in the indictments, a lot of the facts that are alleged to have been in furtherance of the scheme physically occurred in the United States. One of the checks was flown into JFK-Airport, CONCACAF was headquartered initially in New York and then in Miami, Chuck Blazer [Charles Gordon Blazer a former American soccer administrator] lived in New York City. So, there are a number of connections to the United States — the wires go through the banks in the United States and so forth. So, as a purely technical legal matter, the fact that the United States has jurisdiction to bring the FIFA criminal case is not actually difficult from a lawyer's perspective.

The more difficult point here is: Why is the United States doing this? Because if you think about it very broadly much of the financial world interacts with the United States in some way. In fact, you kind of have to do acrobatics to avoid the United States when you are conducting a major international financial transaction. The United States does not assert jurisdiction in every case and in fact it elects to assert jurisdiction in a small minority of cases. The interesting question to me is: Why did the United States assert jurisdiction, when we are not really a big soccer country, at least not compared to Switzerland, where FIFA is headquartered. Certainly you could imagine Brazil or other South American counties having a much stronger interest in this case than the United States has. That is one of the very interesting things about the FIFA case.

Ultimately, my own guess is that the United States decided to assert jurisdiction here it for a number of reasons. One is that it could bring the case as a practical matter, and because it is ultimately the most powerful law-enforcement country in the world. When it comes to white-collar prosecutions, the United States is way ahead of any other country. It has a lot of advantages that, of course we can go into, in the way it conducts white-collar prosecutions that gives it a head start, an advantage over other countries trying to bring these sorts of cases. Also, when you read the statements issued by the prosecutors and when you read the indictment you see they go out of their way to emphasize the US connections. They detail how the United States was involved and that some of these tournaments took place in the United States and that meetings took place in the United States. All of that is an advocacy tactic, to try to make it appear more and more of a United States case. However, there is almost a quality of they "protest too much". There is almost a sense when you read the indictment that the drafter were a bit embarrassed by the fact that this really should have been a case venued elsewhere. Nevertheless the United States did it because maybe they were the only ones who could and because the case was sitting there for them to take it.

**Fausto De Sanctis**: In Brazil, many investigations show the participation of offshore companies in tax havens and, in most of them, criminals usually have a bank account and a connection with American banks. So, when we try to get information directly about these accounts, it is very difficult to get them from tax havens. However, when we go through the United States, you get the information easily because of the obvious economic and political influence of this country. We are receiving a lot of support from the US. Sometimes people say: 'You are praising the US'. It is not that. In many cases, it is a fact that the US has helped a lot. When I talked to some American prosecutors in charge of the co-operation between Brazil and the US, they said that Brazil has requested a lot from the US and is receiving a strong support. However, the opposite is not true. When the US asks Brazil for support, there are a lot of legal obstacles. For example, we need to get the agreement of a superior court in most of the cases, etc. We have a lot of bureaucracy – in legal means – regarding the foreign requests.

**Marcus Asner**: In my past life I was co-chief of the Major Crimes unit in the Southern District of New York in Manhattan. It is now called Complex Frauds unit. We were in charge of the cases that involved money laundering and the banking system in New York City, in charge of the federal prosecutions in that area. We felt that it is very much in the interest of the United States to protect the financial center of the world. You want to make sure that the banks are clean, and that the world can rely on the banking system in the United States. That is a major interest of the United States. That there is enough of an argument to say that this is clearly something in the United States' interest. So the FIFA case is fairly in the United States interest. The question that I think is worth asking is whether the case isn't even more in Brazil's interest, or in Switzerland's or Germany's interest. It is plain why the United States brought the case. To me, the real question is: why didn't the other countries do it.

**Fausto De Sanctis**: Soccer is not a big concern for the United States, but for Europeans and Brazilians it is a sensitive issue. That is why I believe that investigations in European countries as well as in Brazil were not as effective. Until recently, it was due to the lack of public and institutional support.

**Marcus Asner**: Maybe it was easier.

**Fausto De Sanctis**: For us [Brazilians, Europeans] it's more complicated, because you have feelings for the sport and it is also difficult for soccer professionals. I could feel that when I was talking to the people.

**Marcus Asner**: It is breaking idols.

**Fausto De Sanctis**: Yes, exactly.

**Wagner Pralon Mancuso**: There is a kind of emotional dependence...

**Marcus Asner**: I think that might be part of it. I am not sure if the US is emotionally independent. The other countries are emotionally depended. And maybe that is why they didn't bring the case. Maybe you don't know who Pete Rose is. Pete Rose was a baseball hero when I was a little boy and he was prosecuted and he was kicked out of baseball for gambling. So we do prosecute our own heroes as well.

**Fausto De Sanctis**: FIFA dealt the issue, historically, in a romantic view of soccer to escape investigation. Usually it is said: 'Ah this is related to the organization of the sport'. So, in legal terms, we have to take care of it properly.

**Wagner Pralon Mancuso**: Fausto De Sanctis, the last world cup took place in Brazil. The results were not good for us, but how do you evaluate FIFA's role in Brazil's world cup 2014?

**Fausto De Sanctis**: Before the World Cup, there were concerns that it would bring organized crime [cartel formation] to Brazil to get all public contracts related to the World Cup. Now, we see that this was a reality in Brazil. Many plea agreements revealed that in order to build stadiums in Brazil, there was a kind of cartel that benefited politicians and businessmen. So, FIFA seems not to have that concern when it chooses the venues of the World Cup. They had no idea of the role they should play in dealing with this market. Historically, they wanted to protect what they call "FIFA friends" without worrying about the issue of crime prevention. On the other hand, the Brazilian government accepted FIFA's conditions very easily. This is surprising because such conditions violated sovereignty and cannot be bargained for. Everyone should respect the law. In terms of avoiding crime, FIFA has not played a good role or they couldn't do more in order to prevent crime.

**Elizangela Valarini**: Concerning the topic of the relationship between FIFA and governments, in your opinion: What is in the background of this relationship? What were the motivation and the interests of government for hosting the world cup? What are the benefits for governments and FIFA?

**Marcus Asner**: I'll give you my thoughts and I'm sure you have deeper thoughts, because, you know, I'm not from a soccer playing country. I think a lot of it has to do with nation building. Where football is, where people are very emotionally attached to sports generally, football takes everything to a whole different level. You know, there is a certain amount of hysteria that goes with sports, any sports. People are so emotionally attached to football. I remember being in Germany during the World Cup in 2010. And I have been in Germany off and on since the 70s and one of the things I always noticed about Germany is that Germans were decidedly non-patriotic and they go out of their way not to be patriotic. And I thought, that was kind of depressing because Americans are very patriotic. And I understand the history for why that is, but one of the things I noticed for the first time during the World Cup was that there were German flags out and people were proud of being German. And that was part of creating a nation, as a process after the war, being a nation you could be proud of. You see the same thing with Nelson Mandela. Saying: Okay, we have got to create a country. Let's create a country and use sport to help with that. So to bring the world cup to South Africa was obviously very important. So, I think, that's part of it, it's just the emotional connection and the governments recognizing that people love sports and that emotional connection to the team helps create a concept of nation, which is very important if you believe in a nation state.

**Fausto De Sanctis**: But real world is not behind the scene.

**Marcus Asner**: No, this is very open.

**Fausto De Sanctis**: However, I believe the sport is being used politically behind the scenes to get popular support. So, this seems to have become clear in dictatorial regimes, also in Brazil, and even democratic countries, with the evident demagogic appeal. The sport is used to win votes in the future, to stay in power, with the support of the nation, because of people's emotional involvement. So, I guess that's what goes on behind the scenes, not to mention the issue of organized crime. Criminals try to get contracts and dirty money. I say this based on my own judicial experience. Many only see money, not the sport, and do not care to protect the sport. They are so focused on doing business and enforce their interests. For me, behind the scenes, there is a lot of organized crime, allied to demagogy.

**Wagner Pralon Mancuso**: Emotional connections, organized crime, and political use, alright. Marcus Asner, how do you think FIFA got in this situation? Why did this happen?

**Marcus Asner**: Well, I think most financial crimes boil down to a little bit of supply and demand and then, rules and the ability to circumvent the rules to cheat. And, here the demand is just immense, because of what we were just talking about: the emotional connection that people have. Football is just wildly popular. Not only do you want to go to the games but you also want to watch the games on TV, you want to wear the t-shirts, you want the posters and all that makes you feel good. You root for your teams. Everybody has some merchandize from a sports team. I tend to have more baseball stuff but, if I were here I'm sure I would have a lot of football stuff. My children have football stuff. All that creates a huge amount of demand and once you have demand there is a lot of money floating around.

People then place a lot of importance on marketing rights, into hosting tournaments, and into having high positions within FIFA. Because if you have a high position within FIFA you are important. But it's also important because you then have opportunities to make yourself wealthy.

So, how do we get here? I think, if you believe the indictment (and since there are over twenty guilty pleas there is political reason to believe the indictment) FIFA has been full with corruption for a long time. There have been a lot of people within FIFA who have taken advantage of the fact that there were few controls and they saw an opportunity to make a lot of money. They took that opportunity—you know, it's the usual sort of criminal story. You have huge opportunities, its sitting there right in front of you.

Personally, I was a prosecutor for a long of time, and I put a lot of people in jail, but I think they were very few bad people. I think there are a lot of people who make bad decisions. We can make it easier for people to make bad decisions by putting a lot of money right in front of them and saying: we are not looking. And, you know, it's really hard to turn down money sitting right in front of you. And, I think that, over time people lose direction. You start out with a little bit of corruption and then, the next time, it becomes a little easier and so on.

**Fausto De Sanctis**: When you are emotionally involved, most people are not interested in whether there is organized crime behind the scenes. If my team is winning, e.g., my national team is a winner; I don't care if illegal things happen. But it's getting better now after the FIFA case in the US and people are more aware of the risk of leaving sports in the hands of organized criminals.

**Wagner Pralon Mancuso**: Fausto De Sanctis, in your position of a judge, how do you see the influence of organized crime in Brazilian soccer, especially related to betting?

**Fausto De Sanctis**: I think illegal gambling is international. It is a global problem that must be faced by many authorities, because you can bet on the internet and controlling it is very hard. Internet guarantees anonymity, confidentiality. That makes it harder to find these people, especially in the deep web. So, that's something we need to work on together. Every country tries to deal with this. 8.5% of bets are illegal. I have this number from a white paper of a European study. I also have acquaintances that have studied this and say that there is a great deal of room for illegal gambling practices, rather than legal ones. Now, the Brazilian football confederation has had this concern and made an agreement with a private company to investigate this issue because we have already seen previous illegal agreements for betting. There was a referee, not from the minor league, but from the major league, who was arrested. In Brazil, it was a major scandal, the first scandal involving football. It was also the first scandal involving sports betting there.

**Wagner Pralon Mancuso**: Marcus Asner, do you think the same happens in the US?

**Marcus Asner**: Organized crime often has been involved in American sports. There are famous stories of organized crime being involved in throwing the baseball World Series. In the US, organized crime generally has died down compared to what it was before. Another why of saying that is that it changed ethnicities. So probably a hundred years ago, you would say, there was Jewish, Irish organized crime and then came Italian and now, more recently, let's say it's Albanian, Russian organized crime, Chinese organized crime. So, there probably is organized crime. But does it impact, for example, American football, American baseball, the major sports? I wouldn't think so. Now, on the other hand, all this depends what you called organized crime. We just had a major take down involving the NCAA [National Collegiate Athletic Association] which is college sports, which is huge in the United States, involving college basketball. It's not a Cosa Nostra but on the other hand, you look at it and say was it organized? Yes. Is it crime? Yes. That's a major case going on right now in the United States in sports and certainly it was organized.

**Fausto De Sanctis**: So you said something important. When I say organized crime, I consider the definition of the convention of Palermo. If only three persons act together for criminal purposes, for me its organized crime then.

**Marcus Asner**: So much of this definitional. I mean, if you think organized crime people often think of Michael Corleone [of the Godfather] and the Dons and all of the Capos. You place on it a structure and call it organized crime. We also say this is narcotics trafficking, this is prostitution, etc. In fact it's just crime.

**Elizangela Valarini**: If you talk about FIFA or national soccer football, basketball teams, etc.—they all are a form of organization. In the case of FIFA and I think in other cases too, high ranked executives of these organizations were involved in the crime. If you compare FIFA to other forms of organizations, such as economic organizations, there are a lot of cases in which high ranked executives were involved. In the case of active corruption, in our empirical research, we could find that a major part of the executives who are involved don't directly benefit from the bribes, but the interest of their companies was the priority. Do you see some difference between organizational corruption cases in economic and sport organizations? What could you find out in the FIFA case? Were the benefits for the organization or a matter of individual gains?

**Marcus Asner**: I think the FIFA has a lot of different facets to it. Certainly, you could see awarding of certain matches to certain countries as working to the benefit of the local organization. Or is it to the benefit of FIFA? Certainly, you would say if there is a bribe that was paid it was to the benefit of the organization that wanted that result. The taker of the bribe obviously is doing it to the line of its own pockets. Take the NCAA case, the case that just came down. There allegedly were a series of recruiting violations and alleged bribery. If you believe the allegations, of course nobody has been proved guilty yet, if you believe the allegations, it looks like a lot of people really were just focused on getting the best players for their teams and it really hasn't anything to do with money. But they were facilitating crime if you believe the indictment or the complaints in order to further the interests of their teams. Of course, some people plainly made money out of it.

**Fausto De Sanctis**: I'd like to say something about it. I think that solidarity is more of a personal obligation, now it is a legal obligation. When you talk about FIFA, they think they have no obligation to contribute to the authorities to avoid crimes. The concern is the sport itself and also mainly business. There are other sectors that were also concerned only with business. However, they had an obligation to help the state avoid crime within their activities. So, that is why FIFA should, but not just FIFA, also clubs, federations, confederations, help states avoid crime within their scopes because you have a moral obligation to protect them from organized crime. Normally, sectors prefer to regulate themselves. Today it is different. All individuals have the burden of helping the state fight against crime in general. This is not just a state function. In the past, the obligation of solidarity was limited to the church, the school, the family, but today this obligation has passed through all fields, a universal value of solidarity for collective well-being.

**Wagner Pralon Mancuso**: We talked a lot about having a broader view of the problems and we could talk about solutions now. How is it possible for FIFA to overcome, to remedy this situation? Which solutions would you suggest for this problem?

**Marcus Asner**: What good organizations do when they are in the middle of a scandal, is completely self-investigate and then completely remedy it. That may mean that a lot of people get fired and you start over again. That could well mean that you bring in monitors who have maybe nothing to do with football, who monitor the situation. Essentially they need to put themselves on probation or more likely to put themselves (metaphorically) in jail for a while, so they are being supervised until they figure out how to right the ship. I think how they will go about doing that is going to be tricky. I think that there are obviously a lot of consultants out there, a lot of people who have studied organizational behavior who know a lot about that sort of approach. So I think they are going to have to make a concerted effort, e.g., a serious effort to do that. I think there are going to be a lot of resources for them to help them to do this. Part of the process likely will be that countries are going to insist that they clean up things. The fans are also going to have a role, as are the various corporations that advertise with FIFA. If I had a brand of being a good, wholesome, American company, I'm not going to advertise with FIFA unless they clean up their act. I think it would help a lot if the brands and consumers who put the pressure on the brands force the organizations to clean up their act. That will help a lot.

**Fausto De Sanctis**: It is important to establish compliance programs in sports organizations and, of course, in companies involved with sports. France gave us a good example because it set up an entity charged with supervising contracts between clubs and football players, as well as international transfers. Each individual contract must be submitted to this entity and they need the approval of this autonomous entity, composed of people from the sport, but also from government agencies. The creation of an agency similar to the National Directorate of Management Control (DNCG) of France would signal strong repudiation of the unlawful practice of money laundering. FIFA is improving, as you said, they are trying, they have changed the rules for transfer agents as intermediaries, but their definition is very limited, and should cover all situations involving intermediation between clubs and football players.

**Marcus Asner**: Also, the Department of Justice could do more to help out. Right now, we are in the situation that I deal with every day where nobody knows what the DOJ is doing and there is a lot of secrecy. If you are representing officials within FIFA, you would think twice, three times, ten times before you allow them to be interviewed by the people that FIFA hired to try to figure out what happened. Because you know that those interview notes will be provided to the United States government and so you are worried. And I think that the DOJ [Department of Justice] could help by making it clear, for example, that the following ten people are not targets of their investigation. That will help FIFA correct itself, because I think that things are going much slower than they could be of DOJ where more clear about where it going. But, on the other hand, I have been on the other side, and while I was in DOJ, it is in your interest to keep your cards very close to your chest, far as long as you can. There is a real world dynamic going on between how the investigations going and the reality of FIFA trying to go forward.

# Corruption in China

# Corporate compliance and industrial sophistication

*Xiuyin Shi*

## 1 Gradual increase in commercial bribery

In Chinese, *hegui* is translated from the English word "compliance". Compliance means "to abide by, to obey", which is usually understood as to proactively abide by rules that broadly include laws, moral teachings, contracts, etc. Opposite to compliance is non-compliance, which means to violate, to refuse to abide by or obey. Currently, one important part of corporate non-compliance is bribery, which means to seek illicit profits by breaking the rules and giving items of value to state employees or employees of other companies. Bribe taking and bribe giving are the two sides of the same coin. The former refers to the act of state or corporate employees who take advantage of their office to seek illicit interest for bribe givers, accepting or demanding items of value from bribe givers in return. This article focuses on acts of bribe giving by companies and their employees, whose targets for bribery in the Chinese context include not only state employees, but also employees of government-sponsored public institutions that have either administrative management functions or administrative law-enforcement authorities.

China is under one-party rule by the Communist Party of China (CPC). As early as 1950s, the CPC had been combating against bribe taking by state employees and bribe giving by corporate employees. In 1951, the third year of its rule in mainland China, CPC Central Committee decided to launch the so-called "anti-corruption, anti-waste, anti-bureaucracy" campaign (*San Fan Yun Dong*) and attached severe penalty to bribe-taking state employees. In that year alone, 9442 were sentenced to imprisonment of various lengths, 67 got life imprisonment, 9 got death penalty with a reprieve, and 42 were sentenced to death with no reprieve. In 1952, CPC Central Committee further launched the so-called "anti-bribery, anti-tax-evasion, anti-steeling-state-property, anti-shoddy-products, anti-steeling-state-economic-intelligence" campaign (*Wu Fan Yun Dong*). As many as 5% of all private enterprises were judged to have broken the law and were punished accordingly. After such a severe crackdown, followed by massive

© Springer Fachmedien Wiesbaden GmbH, part of Springer Nature 2020
M. Pohlmann et al. (eds.), *Bribery, Fraud, Cheating*, Organization,
Management and Crime – Organisation, Management und Kriminalität,
https://doi.org/10.1007/978-3-658-29062-7_11

nationalization of private enterprises, commercial bribery was rarely seen in China between late 1950s and 1970s. Due to lack of reliable statistical data on commercial bribe giving in that period, we could only catch a glimpse by looking at the statistical data on the receiving end. In 1980s, Chinese public prosecution authorities on all levels filed as few as 4,400 "corruption cases", in which 9,832 civil servants and employees of state-owned enterprises were convicted by the courts. These so-called "corruption cases", it must be noted, include not only bribe giving and taking, but also graft and embezzlement. Judging from these data, it's fair to say commercial bribery rarely occurred in China between late 1950s and 1970s.

With the market economic reform in the 1980s, commercial bribery re-emerged to be a widespread phenomenon. As for how widespread it was, a popular saying at that time went that when an entrepreneur self-proclaimed that he had never given a bribe, he was put on inquisition by his peers who insisted on knowing how he managed to keep his company afloat without bribing anyone. However, despite the fact that bribery was ubiquitous, there was no relevant statistics and one could only count on the best of guesses. According to the CPC Central Commission for Discipline Inspection (CCDI), in the period from late 2012 to 2016, there have been over one million corruption cases and over one million individuals have been punished. A case study shows that on average, one bribe-giver bribes eight bribe-takers. To extrapolate from these figures, over one million corruption cases (except for cases that involve no bribery) involve around a few million bribe-givers. The case study also finds that on average, each bribe-taker accepts bribes of various kinds on 23 occasions[1]. To extrapolate from these figures, over one million corruption cases (except for cases that involve no bribery) stand for tens of millions of individual instances of bribery. This does not include many more state employees who have so far managed to escape or hide from the crosshairs of anti-corruption investigations, nor does it include bribery among companies and among corporate employees, such as the widespread

---

[1] Li, Hui, "Self-Moralization in Bribery and Integrated Corruption: A Textural Study on the Dossier of Discipline Inspection and Supervision Authorities of H Municipality" (贿赂中的自我道德化与嵌入性腐败——基于H市纪检监察机关档案的一项文本研究), *The Society* (社会), Vol, 6, 2009.

bribery with hospital managers and doctors by sales-reps from pharmaceutical companies.

Not only Chinese companies, but also foreign companies, including renowned multinationals are involved in commercial bribery in China. Walmart has bribed a senior official in Yunnan Province[2]; IBM has bribed the Chairman of Board of Directors of China Construction Bank[3]; Siemens has bribed multiple officials and doctors[4]; GlaxoSmithKline has bribed government officials, medical industry associations, foundations and hospitals[5]. If we make a list of companies that have been investigated and punished, it would be a long one.

All in all, the trend is clear: commercial bribery is in the rise. Both Chinese and foreign companies pay bribes; bribes are paid in China and in many other countries, including advanced western economies. The research question of this article aims to answer is why commercial bribery is becoming widespread and why corporate compliance is increasingly becoming a tough issue even for companies from the developed world.

---

[2] Ding, Qiang, et al, "Yumu Peng, Ex-Director General of Yunnan Proivincial Dept. of Foreign Economic and Trade Repented in Court of Not Having learned of the Criminal Code" (云南省外经贸厅原厅长彭木裕当庭忏悔没学刑法), *Yunnan Daily* (云南日报), A4, 1 July, 2003.

[3] Tian, Yu, et al, "Enzhao Zhang, Ex-Chairman of the Board of Directors of China Construction Bank was Sentenced to 15 Years in Prison at the First Instance" (建行原黄事长张恩照一审被判15年), *Xinhua Daily Telegraph* (新华每日电讯), A2, 4 November 2006.

[4] Wang, Leiyan and Wang, You, "Legal Files Reveal Inside Stories of the Hidden Bribery by 3 Daughter Companies of Siemens AG in China" (司法文件曝西门子三家中国子公司隐蔽行贿内情), *First Finance Daily*(第一财经日报), A10, 17 December 2008.

[5] Li, Jianhua, Tian, Zan and Tian, Hui, "Root Causes of Commercial Bribery by Multinational Companies in China and Studies on Counter-measures: A Reflection on the Case of GlaxoSmithKlein"(在华跨国商业贿赂的根源与治理对策研究——葛兰素史克案反思), *Dongnan Academics*(东南学术), Vol. 12, 2014.

## 2   Corporate compliance theory

The current theory on corporate compliance and non-compliance can be broadly divided into four categories, or to be more precise, four perspectives.

### I.   Legitimacy belief theory

In Sophocles' tragedy *Antigone*, when Creon, the brother of Queen Jocasta, Oedipus's mother and wife, assumed the throne, he prohibited the burial of Polynices, who had just led an army to lay siege to Thebes, and he who violated the prohibition would be put to death. Antigone, the sister of Polynices, however, begged to disagree as she believed even a rebellious prince as Polynices deserved to rest in peace, for it was a law made by gods. Latter-day scholars added an extra layer judicial interpretation: Creon's prohibition stands for positive law, whereas Antigone's dissent stands for natural law. The latter prevails over the former, because the latter has more legitimacy and universal applicability as it espouses divine will, justice and affection.

Max Weber explains compliance with legitimacy from a divine source. Weber maintained that Calvinism believed one must glorify God in order to become God's chosen one, and to glorify God one must "do good works" and "fulfill His commandments". He who breaks His commandments will be abandoned by God. Religious belief and God in one's heart is a kind of legitimacy belief that motivates compliance.

Unlike the western Calvinist scholarship that emphasized on viewing legitimacy from a perspective of religious ethics, Chinese philosophy tends to approach legitimacy belief from a moral perspective. Confucius emphasized that ethics shall be inculcated by external force and then internalized: "If the people be led by laws, and uniformity sought to be given them by punishments, they will try to avoid the punishment, but have no sense of shame. If they be led by virtue, and uniformity sought to be given them by the rules of propriety, they will have the sense of shame, and moreover will become good."[6] Mencius, on the other hand, emphasized on moral ethics that flow from the inner mind of human beings: "he

---

[6] Confucius, *The Analects of Confucius: On the Exercises of Government* (论语·为政)

feeling of commiseration is the principle of benevolence; the feeling of shame and dislike is the principle of righteousness; the feeling of modesty and complaisance is the principle of propriety; the feeling of approving and disapproving is the principle of knowledge."[7] Wang Yangming also emphasized on the innate judgement on what is just and legitimate in one's mind, and maintained that "conscience is the principle of heaven".[8]

Psychological studies show that human beings possess a belief in a world that is just ever since childhood, believing that "one gets what he deserves and what he gets is what he deserves".[9] Such a belief prompts the mankind to abide by rules that are fair and just, whereas non-compliance of these rules is negatively correlated with this belief[10].

## II. Economic rationality theory

Economic rationality theory, also called rational choice theory, hypothesizes all men to be rational economic beings. Economic rationality is both the reason for compliance, as well as for non-compliance and bribery.

Economic rationality theory maintains that *homo economicus* always pursue maximum economic utility or profits. Such views date back all the way to Protagoras and Epicurus. Benthamism in the 19th century is another advocate, which insists on the https://en.wikipedia.org/wiki/Greatest_happiness_principle \o "Greatest happiness principle": "Nature has placed mankind under the governance of two sovereign masters, pain and pleasure. It is for them alone to point out

---

[7] Mencius, *Mencius: Gongsun Chou I* (孟子·公孙丑上), in *Mengzi* by Wan, Lihua (translator), and Lan, Xu (translator), Beijing: Zhonghua Book Company, 2006, p.69.

[8] Wang, Shouren, "Answer to Ouyang Chongyi" (答欧阳崇一), in *Collected Works of Wang Yangming* (Rev. Ed.), p81.

[9] Lipkus, I. The construction and preliminary validation of a global belief in a just world scale and the exploratory analysis of the multidimensional belief in a just world scale [j]. Personality and Individual Differences, 1991 (11)

[10] Cohn, E. S & Modecki, K. L. "Gender differences in predicting delinquent behavior: Do individual differences matter?"[j] . Social Behavior and Personality, 2007(3).

what we ought to do, as well as to determine what we shall do. ... They govern us in all we do, in all we say, in all we think."[11]

Gary S. Becker, who was awarded the Nobel Prize in Economics in 1992, came up with a crime deterrence hypothesis that builds upon economic rationality theory. It hypothesizes that men are rational agents that 1) pursue maximum profits; 2) could rationally weigh the costs and benefits of their actions; 3) choose to abide by the law when perceived costs exceeds benefits, and to violate the law when it is the other way round[12].

This hypothesis has been echoed by ancient thinkers in China. Sima Qian, one of ancient China's greatest historians, concluded in his masterpiece *Records of the Grand Historian* that "Jostling and joyous, the whole world comes after profit; racing and rioting, after profit the whole world goes."[13] Han Fei, a political philosopher living in the 3rd Century BC, expressed Hobbesian views 18 centuries earlier than Thomas Hobbes did, stating that "the very purpose of meting our heavy sentences is to make sure that criminals lose more than they gain; if nobody wishes to risk heavy penalties for small illegal gains, crime is necessarily deterred."[14] He opinionated that human beings possess the instincts of weighing costs against benefits, seeking advantages while avoiding disadvantages, and thereby deciding to abide by or violate the law. Contemporary scholars go from there to build more sophisticated arguments: the decision-making calculus of bribe-giving is a comprehensive one that carefully weighs direct cost, opportunity cost and penalty cost against anticipated benefits and profits[15]. Moreover,

---

[11] Bentham, Jeremy, *Principle on Moral and Legislation*, Translation in Chinese by Shi, Duanhong, Beijing: The Commercial Press, 2000, p.58.

[12] See Cart Becker, "Crime and Punishment: An Economic Approach", Journal of Political Economy, 76(1968), pp. 169—217; M. A. Polinsky and S. Shavell, "The Economic Theory of Public Enforcement of Law", Jour*nal of Economic Literature*, 38(2000), pp. 45-76; Harold G. Grasmick and Robert J. Bursik, Jr., Conscience, Significant Others, and Rational Choice: Extending the Deterrence Model, "Law & Society Review, 24(1990):pp. 837—840, 857.

[13] Sima, Qian, *Historical Records: Huo Zhi Biography*(史记·货殖列传).

[14] Han Fei Tzu, *The Complete Works of Han Fei Tzu : Six Contrarities* (韩非子·六反).

[15] Bao, Guoyou, "Cost Analaysis of Bribery Crime"(贿赂犯罪成本分析), *Jianghuai Forum*(江淮论坛), Vol. 5, 2008.

some researchers even regard bribery as a game between bribe givers (usually business people) and bribe takers (usually civil servants), with each party making its own calculation on costs and benefits, and finally settling on an optimal size of bribes[16].

Sociologists introduced the *homo economicus* hypothesis into studies on the society. Relevant sociological studies argue that in the Chinese context, civil servants pursue maximum monetary income while at the same time seeking maximum political promotion[17]. In the calculus of *homo economicus*, interest include not only money and material objects but also social objects such as identity, social status, power and authority. Some studies, for instance, argue that the willingness of complying with social norms partly hails from the calculation of eliciting social acceptance and recognition, as well as avoiding social non-acceptance and rejection by other members of the society[18].

*III. Institutional environment theory*

Institutional environment theory hypothesizes that social environmental, particularly the characteristics of the social institutions, determines whether people comply with rules or not. This theory can be roughly sub-divided into institutional loophole theory, institutional pressure theory, institutional iniquity theory or social atmosphere theory, depending on different perspectives taken to approach the issue.

Institutional loophole theory argues that the very existence of various loopholes in social institutions motivates *homo economicus* to capitalize upon them in

---

[16] Wang, Tianlong, "Optimal Bribery, Corruption and the Endogeneity of Mining Accident"(最优贿赂、腐败与矿难事故的内生性：解释与防治矿难的经济模型), *Journal of Liaoning University(Philosophy and Social Science Edition)* (辽宁大学学报[哲学社会科学版]), Vol, 2, 2010。

[17] Guo, Guangzhen, "Political Profits, Economic Bribery and Economic Performances: A Neo-Classic Political Economy Model" (政治收益、经济贿赂与经济绩效：一个新古典政治经济学模型), *South China Economy*(南方经济), Vol. 10, 2009.

[18] See Spitzer, M., Fischbacher, U., Herrnberger, B., Grön, G., and Fehr, E., "The Neural Signature of Social Norm Compliance", *Neuron*, 56 ( 2007) , pp.185-196.

order to gain the maximum return that is beyond the reach of rule-abiders[19]. Institutional loopholes include the lack of anti-commercial-bribery legislation, deficiency in economic and political institutions, weak law enforcement regime, etc[20]. Once these loopholes were filled and institutions strengthened, bribery would ebb away and the co-opting power bribery has upon bribe-takers would weaken[21].

Institutional pressure theory argues that commercial bribery happens because bribe-givers are under the pressure from bribe-takers to pay bribes. For instance, as the regulatory framework tightens, government regulations increasingly press companies to bribe the regulators[22]. Such pressure does not only come from the government, it also comes from the market, such as information asymmetry[23], companies' market status and the relationship between supply and demand[24].

制度不公平说认为制度对不同社会群体的不公平带来了遭遇不公平待遇者的行贿。例如中国私营企业因为与国有企业、外资企业相比处于不公平地位，所以不得不选择行贿。贫困地区的企业受制于创业资源约束和不利的制度环境，倾向于采取非合规行为来降低创业风险。

---

[19] Cheng, Baoku, et al., "Deficits in the Rule of Law on Transnational Commercial Bribery: Causes and Improvements" (跨国反商业贿赂法制缺陷的根源及完善), *Legal Studies*(法学), Vol, 7, 2010.

[20] Luo, Bin: Inspiration from Experiences of Countering Commercial Briberies in Colleges and Universities(高校商业贿赂专项治理经验的启示), *College Party Building and Ideological Education* (学校党建与思想教育), Vol. 10, 2009.

[21] Li, Houjian, "Bribery, Corruption and Allocation of Bank Credits: the Effects of Formal Institutions" (贿赂、腐败与银行信贷资源配置：审视正式制度的作用), *Nanjing Social Sciences*(南京社会科学), Vol, 2, 2014.

[22] Li, Huujian, "Turnover of Officials, Regulations by the Government and Bribery by Companies"(官员更替、政府管制与企业贿赂), *Public Administration Review*(公共行政评论), Vol, 3, 2016.

[23] Zou, Wei, et al., "An Economic Analysis on Commercial Bribery in the Pharmaceutical Industry: A Not-so-perfect Gaming Model" (药品市场中商业贿赂的经济学分析：一个不完美信息的博弈模型), *Journal of Wuhan University (Philosophy and Social Sciences Edition)* (武汉大学学报[哲学社会科学版]), Vol, 5, 2010.

[24] Wu, Jianping, "Rio Tinto Case: Weakness of China's Anti-Commercial-Bribery Regime and How to Improve It" (从"力拓案"看我国反商业贿赂的缺陷与改善), *Corporate Economics*(企业经济), Vol. 7, 2010.

Institutional iniquity theory argues that the fact that the same institution affords different sectors of the society unequal treatments encourages non-compliances. For instance, since privately-owned enterprises in China are given less favourable treatment than state-owned enterprises and foreign-owned enterprises, they have no other option but to bribe their way to success.[25] Companies that hail from economically less developed areas, who are in an inferior position vis-a-vis their competitors from more advanced regions in terms of operational resources and institutional environment, are thus more inclined to take non-compliant actions to lower operational risks.[26]

Social atmosphere theory maintains that social atmosphere is also an important factor in determining people's behaviour. The more one perceives the existence of corruption, the more likely one himself bribes, *ceteris paribus*. Moreover, personal experiences of corruption noticeably increase the likelihood of future bribe-giving behaviour.[27]

*IV. Indigenous culture theory*

In his 1961 article "A Theory of Corruption", M. McMullan investigated public service and government corruption in British colonies and ex-colonies in West Africa and concluded that the conflicts between old, traditional customs and perceptions on the one hand, and modern nation-building on the other form the indigenous cultural factors of corruption.[28]

---

[25] Zhang, Libo, Concept, Causes and Path Selection of Commercial Bribery As A Way of Maintaining Lawful Rights" (维权型商业贿赂"概念、成因及路径选择), *Economic Reform*(经济体制改革), Vol. 6, 2008.

[26] Long, Haijun, "Studies on Non-Compliant Startup Entrepreneurship in Undeveloped Regions: A Capital Perspective to Entrepreneurs' Political Connections" (贫困地区企业家非合规创业行为研究——企业家政治关系资本视角), *Technical Economics and Management Studies* (技术经济与管理研究), Vol. 11, 2016.

[27] Sun, Zongfeng, "A Study on the Public Willingness to Pay Bribes: Survey Data from Province G", (公众行贿意愿研究——来自G省的调查数据), *Journal of Northeast University*(东北大学学报[社会科学版]), Vol. 4, 2015.

[28] McMullan, M.1961."A Theory of Corruption." The Sociological Review,Vol. 9(2)(July). Moodie, Graeme C.1980."On Political Scandals and Corruption." Government and Opposition 15 (2):186.

The most prominent feature of indigenous culture in China is the so-called *guanxi*. For the lack of a proper social equivalent in western societies, scholars kept the Romanized spelling of the word's Mandarin pronunciation when translating this word from Chinese into English, as neither "connections" nor "relationships" sufficiently reflects the wide cultural implications that *guanxi* describes in the Chinese or Oriental context. To put it more graphically, western societies operate like dried haystack in the field, with each haystack containing many bundles and each bundle containing many bunches and each bunch containing many handfuls of hays, whereas *guanxi* in the Chinese society "is just like the ripples that spread out when one throws a stone in the water, ... one circle after another, the farther the thinner." [29] *Guanxi* is both individualistic and private, combining emotion and interest. The rule that governs *guanxi* is *renlun*, a Confucian term that means "moral and ethical obligations defined by inter-personal relationships", which commands full legitimacy that has received both official and social recognitions.

With the emergency of market economy, *guanxi* insinuates itself into the marketplace. In market transactions, trading goods for money and emotional exchange are two sides of the same coin, success in the latter could feed the former in a certain type of preferential treatment. Moreover, two need not happen at the same time, as emotional exchange could continue where trading activities stop.

With it comes to the relationship between giving and taking bribes, bribe-givers usually begin by subtly but steadfastly endearing himself to his target, trying to win his target's affinity by complying with *renlun* rules and presenting gifts that serve as the carrier of goodwill under such rules. Once the "friendship" is established, the bribe-giver will increase the value of gifts (bribes), suggesting that he be taken special care of. To respond in kind, the bribe-taker is expected to follow *renlun* rules too by granting his "friend" a certain type of preferential treatment. Thereafter, such a transactional relationship goes on and on. Legally speaking it is indisputably a relationship of giving and taking bribes; but viewed from a

---

[29] Fei, Xiaotong, *From the Soil: The Foundations of Chinese Society* (乡土中国), Shanghai: New Century Press, 2007, p26-27, 29-30.

*renlun* point of view, it is perfectly normal and justifiable. Almost all such relationships have integrated market relations; whereas both parties in the deal have realized the nature of market transaction, they have employed *renlun* rules to self-justify and justify the legitimacy of such transactions.

When modern, western legal institutions were introduced to crack down upon the aforementioned behaviour of bribes, they were not powerful enough to eradicate *renlun* rules. On the contrary, these rules were well-entrenched enough to survive. When these two sets of ideas are irreconcilably conflicting with each other, both bribe-givers and bribe-takers opt to disguise bribery as moral and ethical acts that fully comply with *renlun* rules. Thus the real intention of bribery has donned the cloak of courtesy and largesse that *renlun* rules encourage, while the various methods of bribery invariably appear to be endorsed by *renlun* rules, such as calling bribes "small souvenirs" for school-age children or patients among the bribe-takers' beloved ones[30]. These colourful costumes make it harder for law enforcers to distinguish between bribery on the one hand, and courtesy and largesse on the other, weakening the anti-bribery regime.

## 3   The limits of present theories

The four theories mentioned above are certainly powerful explanatory tools for commercial bribery and bribery by corporate employees, as these theories are induced from multiple cases in various historic periods, based on scientific research methods and supported by empirical data or survey data. Their interpretative power and evidential basis are not to be repeated here.

In the meantime, dissonances and discrepancies exist between these theories and the realities.

The inner core of legitimacy belief theory is natural law, which highlights human rationality. Rationality is mankind's capability to intelligently understand and deal with realities. Legitimacy belief evolves from rational understanding of the

---

[30] Li, Hui, "Self-Moralization in Bribery and Integrated Corruption: A Textural Study on the Dossier of Discipline Inspection and Supervision Authorities of H Municipality" (贿赂中的自我道德化与嵌入性腐败——基于H市纪检监察机关档案的一项文本研究), *The Society* (社会), Vol, 6, 2009.

universe, and is both scientific and normative. But when it comes to commercial bribery or bribery by corporate employees, legitimacy belief theory comes across something it struggles to explain: if compliance is a decision that derives from rationality, then widespread bribery illustrates the weakening of human rationality. However, rationality is not only essential to mankind but also evolves with human civilization; at least there is no evidence to support a weakening-rationality hypothesis. For millennia, the Chinese have a solid conviction in the maxim that "when there are adequate stores, they will know what are decorums; when the people have enough food and clothing, they will know what is honour."[31] In other words, they believe that economic developments and improved welfare serve to strengthen legitimacy belief. Max Weber did say that once capitalism achieved enormous success with the prowess of modern machinery and technology, it no longer needs spiritual pillars such as "calling".[32] However, "calling" is Weber's religiously tinged description of rationality, but Weber has never stated that the changes in Protestantism would result in weakened rationality. In short, legitimacy belief theory is unable to adequately explain widespread commercial bribery. One explanation may be that legitimacy rationality is a kind of value rationality, whereas bribery by companies belongs to instrumental rationality. The instrumental rationality of economics has nothing to do with value rationality of ethics. But this gives rise to a new question: why value rationality failed to regulate instrumental rationality, which has grown and strengthened, in the course of evolution of human rationality.

Economic rationality theory maintains that the decision of compliance or non-compliance is contingent upon one's rational judgement. However, whether the benefit of compliance outweighs that of non-compliance or vice versa, depends not on one's desire or wish, but on institutional setting. It is institutional design, above all, that determines the ways in which the maximum profit could be secured. According to economic rational theory, one tends to break the rules to achieve his goals where and when institutional designs are primitive and inferior.

---

[31] *Kuan Tzu,* Guanzi: Mu Min (管子·牧民)

[32] Weber, Max, *The Protestant Ethic and the Spirit of Capitalism* (Rev. Ed.), Translation in Chinese by Kang, Le, and Jian, Huimei, Guilin: Guangxi Normal University Press: 2007, p.187.

However, if nobody plays by the rules, transaction costs and behavioural risk are sky-high, which may end up in less profits for all instead of the expected maximum return. Under these circumstances, rational beings would undertake to build new institutions and improve old ones in order to ensure fair competition. That's how institutions and rules evolve. Yet when confronted with widespread bribery, economic rationality theory hypothesizes that this is because institutions have degraded and backtracked, which is difficult to understand when human rationality proceeds and grows. In reality, there is no evidence that long-term business success can build upon bribery; admittedly bribery may bring extra profits within a given period of time, but eventually it would backfire and drag the business into the abyss of catastrophe. In other words, in the long run bribery is not cost-effective. One recently published paper studied 103 companies publicly listed on Shanghai or Shenzhen Stock Exchange that were investigated for commercial bribery in 2001-2015 by analyzing the influence of bribery on each company's market capitalization. The findings are unmistakable: before the revelation, bribery was positively correlated with company's revenue growth; once the scheme was made known to the capital market, bribery was negatively correlated with the company's Tobin's q [33]. This study shows that institutions are in fact self-ameliorating.

There are at least two questions institutional environment theory struggles to answer. First, why some companies and some corporate employees bribe whereas others don't? After all, they all operate in the same institutional environment; second, in the Chinese context, institutional building is generally moving forward since the economic reform began in the late 1970s, and substantial strides have been made in governance and public policy-making. Why bribery has been increasing unabated while government policies have become more accountable and institutionalized? As if the case of China is not sufficient in making the point, the same malice is even haunting countries such as Germany and the US

---

[33] Zhou, Lili, "A Study on the Effect of Bribery by Listed Companies on Their Market Capitalization" (上市公司贿赂行为对企业价值的影响研究), Finance and Accounting Communication, (财会通讯), Vol. 36, 2016.

where institutions are far better-established but commercial bribery has persisted, even contracting a significant number of well-known companies.

Indigenous culture theory faces two challenges. First, *renlun* rules is unique to China's traditional rural society which builds on the small concentration and long-term stability of agricultural families. When the traditional rural society disintegrates in front of the onslaught of modernization, *renlun* rules fall apart. Second, in the process of urbanization, the amalgam of populations from various corners and the integration among them lead to the creation of new laws and social contracts, which in turn seep into rural areas, further undermining the soils for *renlun* rules. Under such a background, *renlun* rules play an increasingly dim role, if at all. Using *renlun* rules to explain widespread bribery, therefore, is obviously problematic. In addition, *renlun* rules are irrelevant when it comes to explaining widespread bribery in western countries.

## 4 Prospects for new explanations

### I. Extension of legitimacy belief theory

If legitimacy belief theory is the right interpretative tool and legitimacy belief evolves along with human rationality, the disturbingly paradoxical reality of widespread bribery can only be explained by "decoupling" that may have taken place between legitimacy belief and the act of bribery. There are three different situations of "decoupling".

In the first situation, legitimacy belief can no longer properly reflect reality as it has been lagged far behind reality. Ancient Greek philosophers were brimming with confidence in human rationality, but thanks to industrialization, urbanization and scientific progress, division of labour has become ever finer and average human beings are facing ever more complicated issues even on a day-to-day basis. Whereas it is relatively easy for those who lived in simpler social structures such as rural villages in ancient China or Greek polis in the Hellenic Age to rely on their rationality to make legitimacy norms that went through numerous tests in the real world to become beliefs, this is no longer feasible in a modern world that is characterized by explosive amount of information and ever-changing values. In other words, it has lost the dynamics to keep pace with the times.

In the second situation, legitimacy belief itself is pulled apart by complicated realities. Now legitimacy can be approached from more than one perspective, such as goals vs means, efficiency vs fairness, institution vs technique. Different social groups have different gauges for legitimacy, so do people in developing and developed countries. If a given company worships efficiency while ignoring fairness, it is likely to deviate from its former legitimacy belief and decides to bribe its way to success. In short, legitimacy belief has more than one variation since from day one and the number of variations grow as economic and technological divisions of labour, social stratification and intellectual progress deepen. Companies that are in different stages of development and of different natures may subscribe to different variations of legitimacy belief. Therefore, if a given company prefer efficiency legitimacy at the expense of equity legitimacy, it may be more susceptible to paying bribes due to its favoured variation of legitimacy belief.

In the third situation, corporate actors are engaged in unprecedentedly diverse activities. In agricultural societies, behavioural types were much simpler and behaviourable boundaries much clearer, it is therefore relatively easy to spot non-compliance. In industrialized, and particularly post-industrialized and digitized age, behavioural types become diverse and cover a broad spectrum. Distinguishing between compliance and non-compliance is easy at the two extremes of the spectrum but not in the middle. Companies are prone to committing non-compliant acts once a deviation in orientation occurs. In the meantime, the broad spectrum of behavioural types is reflected in the broad spectrum of legitimacy standards mentioned above. Due to the complex interactions between the two spectrums, companies are moaning under the heavy burden of "information bombshell" and struggling to figure out the right way to comply with rules and regulations, which usually lead to bewilderment or even cynicism of resigning to chances.

## II. Extension of economic rationality theory

Ancient Greek philosophers believed that human rationality knew no bounds. In human history, however, there were plenty of cases in which rational behaviour led to disastrous consequences, such as environmental pollution from industrial production, social risks of technological innovation. Based on these phenomena, Herbert A. Simon coined the notion of "bounded rationality".[34] Douglass C. North, who received Nobel Prize in Economics in 1993, added that "bounded rationality" is reflected in two ways: first, the real world is full of probabilities, the more people are involved, the more probabilities there are, highlighting the bounded nature of rationality; second, mankind's capability of understanding the environment is limited.

So why the notion of "bounded rationality" was not raised by ancient Greek philosophers? Indeed, why it was not raised until very recently? The answer is simple: modern companies and their activities had become so complicated recently that the limitation of rationality was increasingly felt. To put it in another way, the progress of human rationality lagged behind that in the sophistication of modern companies and the complication of their activities[35].

In fact, even Gary S. Becker's crime deterrence model no longer sticks in many cases when facing the sophistication of modern companies and the complication of their activities. Even though men pursue maximum profits, they don't exactly know how much is "maximum", and men are unable to exhaustively and rationally calculate the costs and benefits of each individual choice, particular in a working environment of sheer complexity, inexhaustible variants and unfixable perimeters. When making a decision on bribery, the bribe-giver is neither sure about the exact amount of profits, nor able to anticipate the fortunes or misfortunes that lie ahead. Bribery therefore picks up a shade of gambler's mania, which tends to encroach upon rational calculation.

---

[34] Deng, Hanhui, Zhang, Zigang, "An Overview on Herbert A. Simon's Bounded Rationality"(西蒙的有限理性研究综述)[J]. Journal of China University of Geosciences(中国地质大学学报), 2004(6):38.

[35] Lu, Xianxiang, *New Institutional Economics in the West (Rev. Ed.)* (西方新制度经济学), Beijing: China Development Press, 1996, p.10.

## III. Extension of institutional environment theory

The two questions facing institutional environment theory discussed in Part III could receive the following answer: first, some companies bribe while other don't because even though they live in the same institutional environment, they deal with different parts of it, which could vary radically thanks to the sophistication and diversification of the institutional environment itself, and therefore perceive the institutional environment in wildly different ways; second, while institutions generally improve over time, corporations and their activities adapt and evolve at a faster pace, and tend to go beyond the boundaries of existing institutions or dabble in new fields where institutions are non-existent. Moreover, institutions are becoming much more complicated than ever before, which exacts far higher compliance-costs on companies, who struggled to figure out the latest regulatory framework and how to cope with. Indeed, over-regulation has served to leave many companies in the limbo, who swayed between compliance and non-compliance, and may have pushed many to make the wrong decision.

## IV. Extension of indigenous culture theory

In ancient societies, there is a single set of rules of the game to follow, with no legitimate alternatives. Therefore the relationship between one's behaviour and its results is marked with certainty. With the dawn of marketization, industrialization, urbanization and globalization, market rules, urban rules and global rules come into the play, providing multiple choices. On the other hand, corporations and their activities cover a much broader range, each befitting a certain set of rules or adapting to one. Whereas Chinese companies may actively practice *renlun* rules, western companies, having established themselves in China, may also adapt to local realities by donning a Chekhovian gown that makes them look like converts to these rules.

All four extensions discussed above have one thing in common: sophistication and complication, both in corporate types, structures, behaviour, as well as in industrial structure and industrial and social environments. Sophistication and complication is both the result of innovations in technology and management, and the response to more complicated industrial structure and environment. It also goes a long way to explain why there is widespread commercial bribery. For researchers, the mission ahead is to propose paradigms that are able to reasonably explain compliance-related corporate behaviour under conditions of unprece- unprecedented complexity and what companies must do in order to achieve compliance.

# References

Baird, Douglas G., *Game Theory and the Law*, Translation in Chinese by Yan, Xuyang, Beijing: Law Press, 1999.

Becker, Gary S., *The Economic Approach to Human Behavior*, Translation in Chinese by Wang, Yeyu and Chen, Qi, Shanghai: Shanghai People's Press, 2002.

Bentham, Jeremy, *Principle on Moral and Legislation*, Translation in Chinese by Shi, Duanhong, Beijing: The Commercial Press, 2000.

Blau, Peter M., ed. *Approaches to the Study of Social Structure*. New York: Free Press, 1975.

Bodenheimer, Robert E., *Jurisprudence: The Philosophy and Method of the Law* (Rev. Ed.). Translation in Chinese by Deng, Zhenghai and Ji, Jingwu, Beijing: Huaxia Press, 1987.

Fei, Xiaotong, *From the Soil: The Foundations of Chinese Society*, Shanghai: New Century Press, 2007

Gao, Zhaoming, *Institutional Equity Theory: Studies on Moral Degradation in Times of Change*, Shanghai: Shanghai Literature and Arts Press, 2001.

Giddens, Anthony, *The Consequences of Modernity*, Translation in Chinese by Tian, He, Nanjing: Yilin Press, 2000

Giddens, Anthony, *Runaway World: How Globalization Is Reshaping Our Lives*, Translation in Chinese by Zhou, Hongyun, Nanchang: Jiangxi People's Press, 2001

Harvard-Yenching Institute and SDX Joint Publishing Company eds., *Rationalism and Its Restraints*, Beijing: SDX Joint Publishing Company, 2003.

Hayek, *The Constitution of Liberty*, Vol.1, Translation in Chinese by Deng, Zhenglai, Beijing: SDX Joint Publishing Company: 1997.

Liu, Junning, eds., *Market Logic and the Concept of States*, Beijing: SDX Joint Publishing Company, 1995.

Lu, Xianxiang, *New Institutional Economics in the West (Rev. Ed.)* (西方新制度经济学), Beijing: China Development Press, 1996.

March, James G., Schulz, Martin, *The Dynamics of Rules: Change in Written Organizational Codes*, Translation in Chinese by Tong, Genxing, Shanghai: Shanghai People's Press, 2005.

Weber, Max, *The Protestant Ethic and the Spirit of Capitalism*, Translation in Chinese by Yu, Xiao et al, Beijing: SDX Joint Publishing Company: 1987.

Wei, Sheng, *An Introduction to Economic Analysis of Social Order*, Shanghai: SDX Joint Publishing Company, 2001

Zheng, Liping, Economic Analysis of Corruption (Rev. Ed.), Beijing: Party School of the Central Committee of CPC Press, 2000.

# Corruption issues in China. An interview with Jianyuan Yang

*Anja Senz*

**Anja Senz:** Dear Ms. Yang, thank you for your willingness to speak with us and to answer the following questions. To start with, could you please give us some brief background information about Fangda Partners, a leading law firm in China, and your responsibilities there?

**Jianyuan Yang:** Fangda provides full-scale regulatory compliance services, and has the largest team dedicated to this practice in China. My responsibilities are related to the regulatory compliance services we provide. Our team assists clients with:

i. the implementation of compliance systems: We help leading multinational corporations (MNCs) and Chinese companies build state-of-art compliance systems according to international standards coupled with local expertise;
ii. corporate investigations: We lead investigations of complex fraud cases such as anticorruption violations, accounting fraud, and conflict of interest cases and assist clients in disciplining employees;
iii. compliance due diligence: We conduct anticorruption/compliance due diligence in connection with M&A transactions as well as due diligence on third parties;
iv. government enforcement: We act on behalf of clients in response to government investigations and inquiries from various government agencies in China and advise clients on law of the PRC law (People's Republic of China) in connection with oversea government enforcements;
v. criminal issues: We advise clients on a broad range of criminal issues, and
vi. dispute resolutions relating to compliance issues, for example, terminating joint ventures and distributor contracts due to compliance reasons.

---

© Springer Fachmedien Wiesbaden GmbH, part of Springer Nature 2020
M. Pohlmann et al. (eds.), *Bribery, Fraud, Cheating*, Organization, Management and Crime – Organisation, Management und Kriminalität, https://doi.org/10.1007/978-3-658-29062-7_12

We have a lot of experience advising clients on the FCPA (Foreign Corrupt Practices Act), PRC commercial bribery laws, the UK Bribery Act (UKBA) and Hong Kong anticorruption laws. Our clients are MNCs and Chinese companies from a broad range of sectors such as life science, TMT (technology, media, and telecom), financial service, consumer goods, automobiles and manufacturing industries.

**Anja Senz:** The phenomenon of corruption encompasses different punishable crimes like bribery, fraud, etc. Could you please tell us how corruption issues are defined according to the Chinese law and where do you see the biggest differences between Chinese and Western law? In addition, what are the main issues you are dealing with when giving legal advice to your clients with regard to corrupt and illicit practices?

**Jianyuan Yang:** In the Chinese legal framework, multiple legal sources are regulating commercial bribery activities. Both the PRC Criminal Law and the PRC Anti-unfair Competition Law (AUCL) penalize commercial bribery. Commercial bribery is also punished under several administrative regulations. However, there is not a unified and clear definition of "commercial bribery". Article 7 of the currently effective PRC Anti-unfair Competition Law defines commercial bribery as an unfair competitive activity and provides that "business operators should not conduct bribery by providing property or by other means in order to seek business opportunities or competitive advantages".

The Chinese commercial bribery laws are broad in four aspects:

i. not only bribes given to government employees, but also bribes given to non-government employees can be regarded as commercial bribery. The PRC Criminal Law covers bribery both public and private sectors. For example, bribing an employee of a private enterprise in order to exclude competitors and gain business opportunities could also trigger the crime of bribing non-government employees under the PRC Criminal Law;

ii. bribes to or given by a natural or legal person, such as companies, associations or other entities, can both constitute commercial bribery. Please note offering bribes to a private company does not constitute a crime though. Companies in China may face criminal or administrative punishments as a legal entity if they committed commercial bribery crimes;

iii. apart from what is commonly understood as "corruptive bribery" (bribery in exchange for improper benefits), "competitive bribery" (bribery in exchange for business opportunities and/or competitive advantages) can also fall into the category of commercial bribery. In some circumstances, even a business operation considered standard practice in a given industry could be defined as commercial bribery;
iv. lastly, according to the relevant commercial bribery laws and regulations in China, both bribe takers and bribe givers will be held liable. In addition, the current trend in enforcement is that bribe givers are facing harsher punishments than before.

In China, enforcement actions against competitive commercial bribery have become a more and more substantive legal risk that multinational companies need to pay more attention to when doing business in China. We are frequently instructed by clients to evaluate their business models from a commercial bribery perspective and represent the company if they have to deal with enforcement actions by the local Administration for Market Regulation (AMR, the agency that consolidates the market regulation functions previously exercised by Administration for Industry and Commerce (AIC) and functions of other two agencies since March 2018), the administrative enforcement agency for the punishment of commercial bribery. What companies encounter frequently are enforcement actions against commercial bribery under AUCL by the local AMR. As mentioned above, the AUCL is an administrative law that prohibits companies from "providing property or by other means" in exchange for business opportunities, improper competitive advantages, or other improper interests, so as to promote fair competition and protect the interests of consumers. Sometimes the line between competitive acts and commercial bribery is vague, thus local AMRs have broad discretion to interpret the commercial bribery clause.

With regard to criminal enforcement, many factors will be considered to distinguish between employees' individual liability and corporate liability. Pursuant to an applicable rule, a company is likely to be held liable if the bribe is provided in the name of the company and as a result the company benefits from the bribery. In practice, this issue is much more complicated as a company would unavoidably be a beneficiary party should their employee achieves a business opportunity. The bribes offered by the employee are often obtained from the company by illegal means, e.g., falsifying expense reports to claim reimbursement or colluding with third parties to fabricate transactions to obtain payments from the company, so the external bribery is likely to be interpreted as company sponsored misconduct. Nonetheless, in judicial practice, the employee who executes the bribery scheme is more likely to be held liable than the company due to evidence collection reasons.

**Anja Senz:** How did the anti-corruption laws develop in China in the last decades and what do you consider to be the most important changes?

**Jianyuan Yang:** The first PRC Criminal Law was passed in 1979 prohibiting both offering bribes to and accepting bribes by government employees. In 1997, the currently valid Criminal Law came into force. In the past few years, we have witnessed some significant changes made to the law regarding corruption and these changes will definitely have some positive effects on the anti-corruption campaign in China.

Traditionally, criminal punishment of accepting bribes is stricter than that of offering bribes under the PRC Criminal Law. However, the recent trend is towards stepping up government enforcement actions against bribe givers including MNCs. In 2015, the Criminal Law has been amended to strengthen monetary penalty of bribe givers and to reduce the credits given for cooperating with the authorities. Furthermore, the definition of bribe takers and bribe givers has been broadened in 2007 and 2015, respectively. The Criminal Law originally only penalized state functionaries who exercised their authority for the bribe giver's inappropriate interests. Since 2007, receiving bribes from state functionaries' close relatives, or other persons closely related to them, former state functionaries, or their close relatives or other persons closely related to them is punishable. Since 2015, giving bribes to the aforementioned individuals also constitutes a crime.

The Chinese Anti-unfair Competition Law (AUCL) has been amended recently for the first time since its enactment in 1993 in regard to commercial bribery and has come into force on January 1$^{st}$, 2018. After the amendment, commercial bribery is one of the seven unfair competition acts regulated by the AUCL. Revisions to the commercial bribery clause attracted the most attention.

Under the new AUCL, transaction counterparty is no longer a bribe recipient. The 1993 AUCL provides that the transaction counterparty is taking bribes where the benefit is made to transaction counterparty for obtaining business opportunity and/or competitive advantage, e.g., "entrance fee" paid by a commodity producer to the supermarket might be regarded a form of commercial bribery. The new AUCL prohibits a business operator from using cash, property or other means to bribe the following entity or individual:

i. employee of the transaction counterparty;
ii. entity or individual entrusted by the transaction counterparty to handle relevant affairs; or
iii. entity or individual that uses its power or influence to affect a transaction.

The new AUCL emphasizes the prohibition of utilizing power of entrustment or authority in exchange for monetary benefits, thus violating the duty of loyalty to the entrusting/third party or employer. The transaction counterparty is unable to take bribes in order to undermine its own interest. Since the scope of entity and individual under b) and c) is broad it is advised to keep an eye on the development of enforcement after the new law takes effect.

The new AUCL also protects companies when an employee undertakes commercial bribery acts. Under the 1993 AUCL, companies are held liable for its employees' wrongful acts. This presumption remains true under the new law unless the company has evidence to prove the employees' acts were "unrelated to obtaining business opportunities or competitive advantages for the company". Without a more detailed legislative interpretation, we can foresee difficulties to make use of this protective mechanism.

**Anja Senz:** How did the procedures at courts develop in the last years and what are the most relevant consequences for your work as a lawyer? Can you please give us an idea of the differences between courts of different levels and regions, too?

**Jianyuan Yang:** As a lawyer, one of the most relevant developments of procedures at courts is the "pre-trial meeting" system which was newly established by the amended Criminal Procedure Law in 2012. The "pre-trial meeting" is helpful to ensure efficiency of the hearing and provide more chances for lawyers to argue on procedural issues. The court can decide to call for a "pre-trial meeting" where the defendant applies for exclusion of illegally-obtained evidence, claims that the case involves complex issues, or argues that judgment of the case might have material social influence, etc. The "pre-trial meeting" is designed to resolve procedural issues, for example, jurisdictional objection, application of withdrawal of members of judicial personnel, application for obtaining evidence produced at investigation stage, application to submit new evidence, objecting to the choice of witness, appraiser and expert, exclusion of illegally obtained evidence, and application for hearing the case in a private session.

Since China adopts a uniform legislation system and the same legislation applies to cases adjudicated at courts of different hierarchical levels and regions (except Macau, Hong Kong, and Taiwan), there are no significant differences between courts in application of laws and procedures. From a hierarchical perspective, Chinese courts are divided into a four-level court system: supreme people's court (highest court), high people's courts (at the level of the provinces, autonomous regions, and special municipalities), intermediate people's courts (at the level of prefectures, autonomous prefectures, and municipalities) and basic people's courts (at the level of autonomous counties, towns, and municipal districts). The people's courts adopt the system whereby the second instance is the last instance. Against a sentence or ruling of a local people's court at any level as a court of first instance, the party shall have the right to appeal to the people's court at the next higher level. The people's court of second instance shall conduct a comprehensive review of the facts found and of the application of the law in the sentence of the first instance. Retrial is a process to review the legally effective judgment or ruling where the judgment or ruling does have an error. Only a court or a procuratorate has authority to initiate a retrial process. From a regional perspective, despite that the same procedures and laws are observed, unbalanced economic and social development as well as remnants of local protectionism have influenced law-enforcement capabilities of judicial personnel. In courts in less developed areas, problems like non-transparent exercise of judicial discretion and non-standardized judicial acts are common.

**Anja Senz:** In China, corruption is a hot topic, many Chinese citizens regard corruption as a big challenge and the Chinese government has started a harsh fight against corruption several years ago. According to your professional experience, which economic sectors are particularly susceptible to corruption and what are the major developments of the last 5 years?

**Jianyuan Yang:** Fangda has published a blue book on commercial bribery in China (The Blue Book) for four consecutive years since 2015. Based on empirical research, healthcare, manufacturing, automotive, real estate, and finance industries are those at the highest risk of anti-commercial bribery enforcement actions in China throughout the last four years. In 2017, the results show that of all reasons enterprises in the healthcare industry encountered enforcement actions, commercial bribery accounted for 70%, far more than for any other industry. The TMT industry held the second position at 38% and more than one third accounted for anti-commercial bribery enforcement actions in the automotive and real estate industries. The percentages for the manufacturing and financial/investment industries were 21% and 17%, respectively. Comparing to 2016, in 2017, the TMT industry has ascended to the list of industries most at risk of encountering anti-commercial bribery enforcement, while the Fast-moving Consumer Goods (FMCG) industry's enforcement risk has declined somewhat.

Anti-corruption is also the predominant reason Chinese enterprises encounter foreign enforcement actions. In recent years, more and more Chinese companies do business abroad and target markets overseas. Among the Chinese enterprises affected, the primary reason for penalties was corruption. 69% of those enterprises that were subjected to foreign enforcement actions encountered anti-corruption enforcement actions. Chinese enterprises from the healthcare, manufacturing, TMT, automotive, and energy/environmental protection industries account for more than 65% of the enterprises that are subject to the jurisdiction of foreign anti-corruption laws. Among these, the proportion of enterprises from the healthcare industry is as high as 93%. Of the enterprises that are subject to the jurisdiction of foreign anti-corruption laws, enterprises from the energy/environmental protection industry were most often involved in foreign investigations or enforcement actions (nearly 30%), followed by the healthcare industry, the financial and investment industry, followed by the manufacturing industry.

**Anja Senz:** Taking the healthcare and pharmaceutical sector as an example, what are typical problems related to corrupt practices and how does China—the agencies in charge—deal with these issues?

**Jianyuan Yang:** As discussed above, the pharmaceutical and healthcare sector encounters the most anti-corruption enforcement actions in China. Hospital management and doctors who have the right to prescribe drugs are key individuals in determining the purchase of drugs. They are therefore the major targets of corrupt schemes (in addition to officials at the supervising authority). Traditionally, bribes take the form of cash, gifts, meals or entertainment and are directly linked to the prescription volume. For example, in 2016, AstraZeneca (AZN) was accused by the U.S. Securities and Exchange Commission (SEC) of "making numerous improper payments in cash, gifts, and other items" to (Chinese) doctors at state-owned healthcare providers "as incentives to purchase or prescribe AZN pharmaceuticals". Many other bribes are provided in more secret ways. In November 2017, Bristol-Myers Squibb (BMS) was penalized by an AIC in Shanghai for sponsoring a doctor's trip to a conference in Europe because it was found to be related to the purchase of BMS products by the hospital. Moreover, there are some practices considered to be commercial bribery by AIC to which the industry holds a different opinion. For example, it is a prevalent practice for medical device companies to give for free, lease, sell at great discount, or offer the right to use the medical device to hospital on the condition that the hospital commits to purchasing relevant consumables at certain volume. AIC regards such practices as commercial bribery as it excludes fair competition.

The underlying reason for the corrupt practices is partially attributable to the healthcare reforms from 1992 to around 2003. As a result, hospitals are too dependent on revenues from drug sales and the use of medical devices. In addition, too many participants are involved in this circulation process of drugs and medical devices which causes a significant markup in the end prices for drugs/medical devices and also creates a profit margin for corruption.

In order to deal with such problems, China launched a new round of healthcare reform in September 2006. One of the primary purposes of this reform is to lower drug prices. Firstly, the state established a basic drug index and organized centralized procurement. Hospitals are not allowed to make very little or even no profit when selling drugs. Therefore, the price for medical services is raised to make up for the loss. Secondly, the Chinese government is exploring ways to reduce the number of participants in the circulation process. The "Two-Invoice System" is one of the most influential reforms recently. It is designed to limit the number of invoices between manufacturers and hospitals to a maximum of two, thereby reducing the number of participants in the circulation process and with it the price for the end consumers. The system has been implemented in public hospitals across the country by the end of 2018.

**Anja Senz:** Comparing Chinese State-Owned Enterprises (SOE) and foreign companies operating in China, what are major challenges those companies face according to your experience?

**Jianyuan Yang:** The number of employees of SOEs and the SOEs receiving domestic penalties for corruption were far greater than those of other types of enterprises. Based on the empirical research results published in the 2016-2017 Blue Book, 1/3 of all foreign companies that were subjected to investigations ultimately received penalties. In comparison, 2/3 of all SOEs that were investigated received penalties. The same goes for SOE employees compared to employees of foreign companies. There are two reasons for SOEs and their employees being at greater risk regarding domestic enforcement actions: (1) anti-corruption crackdowns mainly target bribery in the public sector; (2) SOEs and their employees are not only monitored by law enforcement agencies but also by the Commission of Discipline and Inspection, an internal-control institution of the Communist Party that is ordered to enforce disciplinary rules.

In recent years, Chinese SOEs also have to deal with challenges arising from foreign enforcement in the process of expanding business worldwide. It is worth noting that more than 50% of SOEs were subject to the jurisdiction of foreign anti-corruption laws. Among them, one out of every six SOEs has been subjected to investigation or enforcement actions in foreign countries. For example, in June 2012, a senior manager of Zhongxing Telecommunication Equipment Corporation (ZTE), a partially state-owned telecom enterprise, was found guilty of bribing an Algerian official and was sentenced to ten-year imprisonment. ZTE was banned from participating in bidding projects in Algeria for two years.

The primary reason for these enforcement actions is commercial bribery, especially enforcement of the AUCL by the AIC. For example, at the end of 2016, about 10 multinational tire companies were involved in commercial bribery enforcement actions by AIC in Shanghai, including Michelin, Goodyear, Dunlop etc. Of the foreign companies that had been subjected to domestic investigations, approximately 50% have encountered a dawn-raid, a rate far greater than that for SOEs (29%).

From a policy perspective, although many foreign companies already had a globalized compliance system, most of them lacked a compliance guide that specifically addressed Chinese commercial bribery laws. For example, less than 25% of foreign companies create policies that deal specifically with Chinese dawn-raids despite half of the investigations targeting foreign companies involve a dawn-raid. 15% of them referred to their pre-existing standardized global compliance policy. As said, Chinese commercial bribery laws have their own unique way of combatting anti-competition behaviors, thus a globalized anti-corruption compliance policy is not well-suited for addressing compliance issues relating to Chinese laws.

As foreign companies are subject to multiple jurisdictions, investigation or punishment in China may trigger anti-corruption enforcement actions in other countries. Following the sentence for offering bribes to non-government employees in China, GlaxoSmithKline (GSK) paid $20 million to settle civil charges with the SEC in the U.S. because the company had disguised bribes to foreign officials in China as legitimate travel, entertainment and marketing expenses in 2016. In May 2014, the UK Serious Fraud Office (SFO) launched an official criminal investigation after allegations were made that executives and employees of GSK engaged in widespread fraud and bribery in China.

**Anja Senz**: What are the biggest differences between these companies when trying to prevent corruption and when facing corruption?

**Jianyuan Yang**: SOEs and foreign companies attach equal importance to the prevention of corruption. Within foreign companies, the role of compliance is gradually becoming more independent. The Compliance Department is responsible for a full range of internal control matters mainly in order to comply with the PRC and other applicable laws in respect of anti-commercial bribery regulations.

Relatively few SOEs have established compliance departments; consequently, the Commissions for Discipline Inspection and legal departments have played an important role in dealing with both anti-commercial bribery matters and disciplinary violations.

In comparison, foreign companies started establishing policies to prevent corruption earlier. Over 70% of foreign companies have specialized mechanisms for reporting and handling compliance issues. About 50 to 60% of foreign companies have policies that deal with external bribery and internal fraudulent activity, respectively. Less than 50% of SOEs have general compliance policies, about 25% of SOEs have policies that deal with external bribery and about 35% of them have policies that deal with internal fraudulent activity. Although SOEs and foreign companies are both making progress in establishing policies to manage and control the risk of corruption, the implementation of measures to exercise this control remains somewhat weak in both of them. For example, only about 20% of foreign companies and 10% of SOEs conduct random compliance inspections of expense reimbursements, respectively.

When facing corruption, both SOEs and foreign companies will take proper measures to handle the matter and cooperate with the government regarding investigations. As foreign companies are also subject to laws of their home countries and third countries, some of them may need to take additional steps, e.g., conducting internal investigation and self-reporting corrupt practices as required by foreign laws.

**Anja Senz:** What role do compliance procedures and professional training play for those companies and which role do they play in legal terms?

**Jianyuan Yang:** Both the U.S. FCPA and the UKBA explicitly recognize the establishment of compliance procedures. An effective and adequate procedure is regarded a valid defence for companies to shield off bribery that aims to obtain or retain business advantages.

Although similar legislation has not yet been enacted in China, compliance procedures and professional trainings play an increasingly significant role in presenting a company's strength in compliance and in proving that they have procedures in place designed to prevent employees from undertaking bribery conduct. In May of 2017, a court in Northwestern China openly considered the milk powder manufacturer Nestle's compliance program in a criminal case. Several Nestle employees at its local office in Gansu Province in Northwestern China were found guilty of illegally obtaining personal information from hospital staff by offering benefits to doctors in local hospitals. The defendant's counsel argued that the offense should be viewed as a "unit crime", i.e., a crime committed by the Nestle company rather than the employees, but the court ultimately did not accept this argument and decided that Nestle was not liable for those employees' misconduct because a) Nestle had policies and guidelines that explicitly prohibited employees from providing cash or other items of value to a Healthcare Provider (HCP) in exchange for the promotion of Nestle's products by the HCP; and b) the employees had received training and tests regarding those policies and signed certificates of commitment.

We have been advising MNCs in localizing their compliance policies in regard to China and have been helping with the establishment of third party compliance programs. We have also been assisting Chinese companies in establishing compliance programs from scratch. Multi-national companies have had plenty of experience operating in the Chinese market. Many of them, especially those that are subject to the jurisdiction of the FCPA, have already established relatively elaborated compliance policies and implementation processes. The most prominent shortcoming of MNCs in this regard is that their compliance policies often emphasize on regulations that prohibit the bribery of government employees, but they often neglect the crime of "bribing non-government employees" in China as well as the act of "competitive bribery" that is prohibited by the AUCL. The SOEs are encouraged to establish compliance programs since the State-owned Asset Supervision and Administration Commission (SASAC) launched a pilot compliance system setting up program from 5 central enterprises in 2016. Many factors distinguish SOEs from other commercial companies. This is also the case with regard to the applicable compliance programs, e.g., SOEs are dually regulated by both laws and regulations and the communist party's disciplinary rules. Over the past few years, Chinese domestic firms doing business both in China and abroad have placed ever-greater importance on the establishment of compliance control systems. Domestic private companies are different from SOEs and

MNCs in that their compliance systems place special emphasis on internal anti-fraud in addition to anti-commercial bribery.

**Anja Senz:** According to your understanding, what is the role of international cooperation in the fight against corruption in China?

**Jianyuan Yang:** The Chinese government is willing to participate in international cooperation and is open to offering assistance in the fight against corruption. China had established bilateral and multilateral frameworks to jointly combat corruption worldwide. By February 2017, according to the latest rating of China's Foreign Ministry, China has signed a total of 135 criminal judicial assistance treaties with 70 countries, and extradition treaties with 48 countries. In addition, China has signed several important multilateral treaties, such as the UN Convention against Transnational Organized Crime in 2000, the UN Convention against Corruption in 2003 and the Beijing Declaration on Fighting Corruption in 2014. On 5 September 2016, the G20 leaders endorsed the High Level Principles on Cooperation on Persons Sought for Corruption and Asset Recovery and the 2017-2018 Anti-corruption Action Plan. Moreover, in the PRC Supervision Law (draft), international cooperation is covered in Chapter 7 with the supervision commission being authorized to coordinate global cooperation and communication.

Take the bilateral cooperation between China and the United States as an example. The two countries have communicated and cooperated through a Joint Liaison Group on law enforcement cooperation since 1998. The China-US Joint Liaison Group sets a good example for international collaborations on anti-corruption efforts. It is a major channel for China-US law enforcement cooperation and anti-corruption is one of the cooperation issues. It involves the two countries' foreign affairs authorities, security agencies and justice departments among others.

International cooperation plays an important role in the fight against corruption in China. According to the data of the Communist Party of China's Central Commission for Discipline Inspection (CCDI) in 2016, China has extradited 2,442 criminals from over 70 countries or regions, recovering illicit fund worth RMB 8.54 billion ($1.24 billion) between January 2014 and November 2016. The CCDI is the Communist Party's disciplinary arm and deals only with party members. It is in charge of supervising and investigating party member's corrupt activities.

**Anja Senz:** According to the law, different sorts of punishment are possible depending on the respective case. Can you please briefly tell us more about the possible types of punishment according to the law? In your understanding, what is the main function of punishment in China and how relevant is the idea of deterrence? Which type of punishment the companies fear most?

**Jianyuan Yang:** Serious consequences could arise from commercial bribery activities. If the AMR determines that the investigated case constitutes commercial bribery, they could impose several types of administrative punishments, including: Sanctions that could reach RMB 3,000,000 (~381,500 Euros) and confiscation of the unlawful income generated from commercial bribery. The AMR may revoke the business license of the offending company under serious circumstances. If the bribery misconducts reach the threshold of criminal offenses, criminal liabilities will be pursued against the offenders, i.e., imprisonment for natural person offenders (i.e., those who directly pay the bribes and those who organize, instruct, and decide on the commercial bribery), and criminal sanction to natural persons or entities, which may reach very high amount, such as billions of RMB.

Unlike many other violations or offenses which have specific victims and beneficiaries, corrupt practices undermine the fair market order and the positive social morality. Apart from penalizing the offender, administrative or criminal punishment of corruption is also important to encourage a fair business environment and foster healthy social conduct. For these reasons, offenders are not only subject to different sorts of legal punishment but also punishment arising from the social credit system which will have long-term and far-reaching impacts on the offender's reputation and business operation.

Companies doing business in China fear criminal punishment most as PRC Criminal Law imposes harsh punishment for corrupt behavior. The maximum statutory penalty for accepting bribes is the death penalty (e.g., Xiaoyu Zheng, former Director-General of the State Food and Drug Administration, was sentenced to death for accepting bribes in 2007) and for offering bribes it is life imprisonment. A company can also be regarded as the offender and be subject to monetary sanctions (e.g., GSK was found guilty of offering bribes to non-government employees and fined RMB 3 billion (~38,500,000 Euros) in 2014).

Punishment arising from the social credit system has the greatest impact on Chinese companies in regard to fighting corruption. The company may suffer severe reputational damage and lose credibility publicly as a result of corrupt practices. For example, an inquiry system for criminal bribery records was launched nationwide in 2012. Nowadays, criminal bribery records are easier to access as the court judgments are available online since 2014. The administrative agencies also create blacklist systems to restrict companies with a history of serious illegal and dishonest conduct, including commercial bribery. The trend is to integrate and share previously separated blacklist systems among various administrative agencies. Once a company is put on a blacklist due to bribery, the company may face serious restrictions regarding government procurement, tendering and bidding, finance and policy support from the central or local governments, etc. Last but not the least, compliance reviews have become one of the compulsory steps for more and more companies in the process of selecting and evaluating their business partners. In some major bidding projects, a corruption record alone is sufficient to disqualify a company from participating in further competition.

**Anja Senz:** Which further legal steps could China take to fight corrupt practices more effectively? Which ways of international cooperation could be helpful in this regard?

**Jianyuan Yang:** China has, from the Criminal Law to AUCL, set up a legal regime and has been constantly strengthening the law enforcement in the fight against corruption. However, since judicial resources are limited compared to the amount of corrupt practices, the Chinese government may consider mobilizing social resources to fight corruption. The FCPA legislation and enforcement is worth noting. The FCPA entails a well-established cooperation system. When a company voluntarily self-discloses, fully cooperates and remediates, this has an impact both on the charges and the penalty. In addition, there are detailed sentencing guidelines, which explicitly set out a cooperation credit a company may obtain. China does have a general rule of self-reporting under PRC Criminal

Law, but there is no such cooperation regime so it is uncommon for companies to self-report their misconducts to authorities.

Effective implementation of anti-corruption laws and regulations is also important. Although the Criminal Law had been amended to tighten penalties against bribe givers in 2015, enforcement did not move at the same pace. Additionally, both the central government and local governments are important in promoting a corruption-free economy. Recently, Shenzhen published the Anti-bribery Management System Shenzhen Standard in order to help organizations develop systems to prevent and expose bribery of their employees and partners. The management system will be a powerful tool for reducing bribery on the so-called "supply-side" just as President Xi's Anti-Corruption Campaign targets graft on the "demand-side."

**Anja Senz:** Ms. Yang, thank you very much for answering our questions!

## List of Abbreviations

| | |
|---|---|
| AIC | Administration for Industry and Commerce (工商行政管理局) |
| AUCL | Anti-unfair Competition Law (反不正当竞争法》) |
| AZN | AstraZeneca (阿斯利康) |
| BMS | Bristol-Myers Squibb (百时美施贵宝) |
| CCDI | Central Commission for Discipline Inspection (中央纪律检查委员会) |
| FCPA | U.S. Foreign Corruption Practices Act (美国《反海外腐败法》) |
| FMCG | Fast-moving Consumer Goods (快速消费品) |
| GSK | GlaxoSmithKline (葛兰素史克) |
| HCP | Healthcare Provider (医疗专业人士) |
| M&A | Mergers & Acquisitions (收购并购) |
| MNC | Multinational Corporation (跨国公司) |
| PRC | People's Republic of China (中华人民共和国) |
| SASAC | State-owned Asset Supervision and Administration Commission (国有资产监督管理委员会) |
| SEC | U.S. Securities and Exchange Commission (美国证券交易委员会) |
| SOE | State-owned Enterprise (国有企业) |
| TMT | Telecom, Media, and Technology (电信、媒体和技术) |
| UK SFO | UK Serious Fraud Office (英国严重欺诈办公室) |
| UKBA | U.K. Bribery Act (英国《反贿赂法》) |
| UN | United Nations (联合国) |
| ZTE | Zhongxing Telecommunication Equipment Corporation (中兴通讯股份有限公司) |

# Fraud in medicine

# Manipulation of medical patient data in organ transplantation as attempted homicide?

*Torsten Verrel*

## 1 Introduction[1]

In June of the past year, the criminal investigation of a case of data manipulation that has shocked German transplantation medicine came to an end. The Federal Court of Justice confirmed the acquittal of a liver surgeon from the accusation of attempted homicide through the false indication of allocation-relevant patient data.[2] This case, which is referred to as the "Göttingen Transplant Scandal" represents a caesura for German transplantation medicine, for it led not only to a sharp drop in the already decreasing number of postmortal organ donations, but also to a regular monitoring of all transplant centers in Germany since 2012. Before getting closer to the decision of the Federal Court of Justice and the problems of the criminal law assessment of the waiting lists manipulations, the German organ transplantation system and the Göttingen case have to be described.

## 2 Organ transplantation in Germany

In Germany, the organization of the transplantation of postmortally donated organs, heart, kidney, liver, lung, pancreas and intestine is not in the hands of the state, but is a joint task of health insurance companies, hospitals and the German Medical Association. The legal basis for the removal and allocation of organs is the Transplant Act. This statute confers on the German Medical Association the task of drawing up the guidelines, which are relevant for organ removal and distribution,[3] and to supervise their compliance.[4]

---

[1] The author would like to thank his researcher Tatjana Windgassen for her assistance during the preparation of this article.
[2] Federal Court of Justice, judgement of 28 June 2017 – 5 StR 20/16, NStZ 2017, p. 701 et seq.
[3] Sec. 16 (1) Sentences 2 no. 2 and 5 of the Transplant Act.

To this end, it has set up interdisciplinary commissions that are composed of representatives of the Federal as well as the state ministries of health.[5] The guidelines are drafted by the Standing Committee for Organ Transplant, while the Assessment and Monitoring Commission is in charge of monitoring organ removal and allocation. Germany has teamed up with seven other European countries for an organ exchange program—Eurotransplant.[6] The allocation of the organs donated in areas covered by Eurotransplant is carried out by the allocation office based in Leiden. The transplant centers report the health data of their patients on the waiting list to Eurotransplant. If a donor organ is reported to Eurotransplant, a computer-based allocation program identifies a list of appropriate recipients. The relevant distribution criteria according to the Transplant Act are the urgency and chance of success of an organ transplantation, section 12 subsection (3) sentences 1 of the Transplant Act. The allocation of livers, which was the subject of the "Göttingen Transplant Scandal", is primarily based on the criterion of urgency and follows the Model for End-Stage Liver Disease (MELD) system borrowed from America. Using this system, a MELD score is calculated to predict the mortality within 3 months.[7] The MELD score is based on three laboratory values or assigned on the grounds of specific symptoms. Organs are allocated to patients with the highest MELD score. For patients who suffer from alcohol-induced liver cirrhosis, the guidelines provide that they may only be admitted onto the waiting list if they have maintained alcohol abstinence for at least six months.[8]

---

[4] Sec. 11 (3) Sentences 3 and Sec. 12 (5) Sentences 3 of the Transplant Act.

[5] Sec. 11 (3) Sentences 4 and Sec. 12 (5) Sentences 4 of the Transplant Act.

[6] Currently Austria, Belgium, Croatia, Hungary, the Netherlands, Luxembourg and Slovenia are cooperating within the Eurotransplant region in addition to Germany.

[7] German Medical Association, Guidelines for Liver Transplantation acc. to Sec. 16 of the Transplant Act, III.5.2.2., in the version of 26 March 2011.

[8] German Medical Association, Guidelines for Liver Transplantation acc. to Sec. 16 of the Transplant Act, III.2.1., in the version of 26 March 2011.

## 3 The Göttingen case

The "Göttingen Transplant Scandal" arose due to the fact that the head of the liver transplantation program of the Göttingen University Hospital increased the MELD score of his patients through incorrect information about their medical condition in the years of 2010 and 2012. Thereby he helped them to secure a better position on the waiting list.[9] This was done, among other things, through the untruthful indication of a dialysis treatment. In addition, even patients who had not yet completed the six-month alcohol abstinence were admitted onto the waiting list in Göttingen. As a result, in terms of organ allocation these patients were given preference over patients from other hospitals. Regular examinations of nearly 50 German transplant centers and their 120 transplantation programs have been carried out since 2012. They have shown that the vast majority of transplant surgeons work correctly, but false reports and data manipulations have also come to pass at other transplantation centers.[10] This applied not only liver but also to heart and lung transplants. However, these further conspicuous cases can be left out for the moment, since up until now the only charges that were filed are in relation to the Göttingen case. A surgeon was indicted for multiple attempted homicides. This criminal proceeding acted as a test case for all others.

## 4 Criminal law assessment of waiting lists manipulations

The discussion about the criminal law assessment specifically focused on the question whether waiting list manipulations can be judged as an attempted homicide because of the induced detriment of the other patients on the waiting lists. The fact that only culpability concerning attempting comes into consideration has to do with the problems of establishing the causality between a waiting list manipulation and the death of a patient further ahead on the waiting list. It would have to be proven that the death of a privileged patient had occurred because of the manipulation and would have been prevented if he had received the organ

---

[9] Cf. to the facts of the case Federal Court of Justice, NStZ 2017, p. 701 et seq.
[10] Cf. the Annual Reports of the Assessment and Monitoring Commission 2012/2013, 2013/2014 and 2014/2015, available at http://www.bundesaerztekammer.de/aerzte/medizin-ethik/transplantationsmedizin/(last accessed on 5 April 2018).

designated to him.[11] This is nearly impossible not only because of the transplantation mortality rate of up to 10% but also because of the fact that it is by no means certain that the disadvantaged patient or their doctors would have accepted the organ that would have been offered to him without the manipulation.

Even when limiting the scope to the culpability for attempting, there are also a whole series of problems that have been controversially discussed in the literature before the decision of the Federal Court of Justice. The present article shall be confined to the reasons the Federal Court of Justice has given for the acquittal in the Göttingen case. Admittedly, the Federal Court of Justice can be agreed in the conclusion, since the transgression of the rules of organ distribution does not constitute the injustice of homicide.[12] However, the justification given by the Federal Court of Justice for the acquittal is questionable.

The Federal Court of Justice distinguishes between the non-compliance of the six-month alcohol abstinence and the manipulation of the MELD score.

*a) Alcohol abstinence cases*

The Federal Court of Justice cites several reasons why violations of the alcohol abstinence rule cannot be sanctioned as attempted homicide. The criticism which was already expressed in the literature so far is certainly correct: This rule in its applicable version at the time of the offense failed to provide any exceptions.[13] According to the rule's wording, alcoholics who have not yet been abstinent for six months are excluded from organ allocation even if they are in acute danger of life, that is, they would not survive the six-month abstinence period.[14] Such a

---

[11] On this and the arguments that follow, see for example Schroth, NStZ 3013, 437, 442; Verrel, MedR 2014, 464, 465 et seq.; Rosenau, MedR 2016, 706, 708 et seq.; Bornhauser, Die Strafbarkeit von Listenplatzmanipulationen, S. 135.

[12] Cf. details in Verrel, MedR 2014, 464, 467 et seq.; also Bülte, StV 2013, 749, 755; different view for example Rissing-van Saan, NStZ 2014, 233, 240 et seq.; Haas, HRRS 2016, 384, 390 et seq.; Koppe, Zur strafrechtlichen Verantwortlichkeit der Wartelistenmanipulation, S. 156 et seq.; Bornhauser, Die Strafbarkeit von Listenplatzmanipulationen, S. 197.

[13] Cf. already Rissing-van Saan/Verrel, NStZ 2018, 57, 59 et seq.

[14] German Medical Association, Guidelines for Liver Transplantation acc. to Sec. 16 of the Transplant Act, III.2.1., in the version of 26 March 2011.

scenario, which is rare in practice, has now been taken into account. The new version of the rule, which has been in effect since 2015, provides that a patient with acute decompensated alcoholic hepatic disease may be exempt from the six-month rule.[15]

However, the Federal Court of Justice also expresses fundamental doubts that violations of guidelines issued by the German Medical Association may lead to criminal liability, while the Transplant Act, which authorizes these guidelines, does not specify the content of these guidelines.[16] The criticism overlooks the fact that laws always have a certain degree of abstraction, and that the criteria of urgency and chance of success provide a sufficient basis for the concretization to be constituted by the guidelines. Looking at the scope and medical details of the current organ distribution guidelines, as well as the dynamics of medical developments and the resulting changes in guidelines, the demand for a more precise legal regulation is barely practical.[17]

The court furthermore questions the medical justifiability of alcohol abstinence as a prerequisite for the admission onto the waiting list.[18] This point is of particular importance because, according to the Transplant Act, it is exactly in the German Medical Association's responsibility to establish the "state of knowledge of medical science" in its guidelines, section 16 subsection (1) of the Transplant Act. The medical justification for demanding alcohol abstinence is based, on the one hand, on the fact that a continued alcohol abuse reduces survival rate after transplantation, thereby narrowing the chance of success.[19] On the other hand, when it comes to alcoholic liver cirrhosis, in contrast to other

---

[15] German Medical Association, Guidelines for Liver Transplantation acc. to Sec. 16 of the Transplant Act, A.III.2.1., in the version of 20 June 2017, available at http://www.bundesaerztekammer.de/fileadmin/user_upload/downloads/pdf-Ordner/RL/RiliOrgaWlOvLeberTx20170616.pdf (last accessed on 5 April 2018). (last accessed on 5 April 2018).

[16] Federal Court of Justice, NStZ 2017, 701, 703.

[17] Nickel/Schmidt-Preisigke/Sengler, Transplant Act Commentary, Sec. 16 Point 1; Augsberg, Die Bundesärztekammer im System der Transplantationsmedizin, in: Höfling, Die Regulierung der Transplantationsmedizin in Deutschland, p. 46 with further references.

[18] Federal Court of Justice, NStZ 2017, 701, 704.

[19] Strassburg, Der Chirurg 2013, 363, 367; Rissing-van Saan/Verrel, NStZ 2018, 57, 60.

liver damage, the special feature is that an improvement of the liver function can be achieved by terminating the injurious action, i.e., by abstinence, so that a transplant is rendered unnecessary, whereby the limited resources of donor organs can eventually be spared.[20]

The Federal Court of Justice, however, invokes the experts consulted during the first instance trial and argues that a liver transplant is also promising in the case of continued alcohol consumption, and that it rarely results in loss of transplant losses.[21] Against the point of view of recompensation, the court alleges that admittedly, alcohol abstinence can lead to an improvement in the liver function, but liver cirrhosis itself is irreversible and therefore the patient constantly remains at risk of an acute liver decompensation.[22]

This argument, however, appears doubtful in light of the fact that most transplantation programs in Europe and the United States require alcoholic abstinence as a prerequisite for admission onto the waiting list, based on studies showing increased survival rate through abstinence.[23] In any case, the reference to persistent liver cirrhosis with the risk of an acute decompensation falls short of the mark. This risk is significantly lower in a liver cirrhotic in case the patients remains abstinent than in a patient who continues to drink. Thus, the Federal Court of Justice equates the mere abstract risk of a life-threatening decompensation with the acute threat, thereby undermining the central criterion of organ distribution, namely urgency.[24] In addition, the Federal Court of Justice overlooks the fact that the risk of dying during transplantation must be weighed against the risk of suffering from an acute decompensation despite abstinence.

---

[20] Strassburg, Der Chirurg 2013, 363, 367; Webb/Neuberger, BMJ 2004, 63, 63; Rissing-van Saan/Verrel, NStZ 2018, 57, 60.
[21] Federal Court of Justice, NStZ 2017, 701, 703.
[22] Federal Court of Justice, NStZ 2017, 701, 703 et seq.
[23] Strassburg, Der Chirurg 2013, 363, 367; Rissing-van Saan/Verrel, NStZ 2018, 57, 60.
[24] Cf. already Rissing-van Saan/Verrel, NStZ 2018, 57, 60.

## b) Manipulation of the MELD score

Even more problematic are the observations, based on which the Federal Court of Justice justifies why the manipulation of the MELD scores through fictitious dialysis treatments cannot be punished as an attempted homicide.

In this respect, the Federal Court of Justice again expresses doubts not only about the sufficient preciseness of the Transplant Act, but also on whether the MELD score is a suitable method for establishing the urgency of a transplantation.[25] The court argues that the MELD score determined by blood count cannot indicate the urgency in each individual case in a reliable way, and that significant fluctuations of the MELD scores can occur as a result of high "inter-laboratory variability".[26]

These arguments also fall short of the mark for various reasons. First of all, the absence of a fully valid organ distribution system, which is probably not attainable, cannot be inferred from the fact that manipulations of this system have no criminal relevance.[27] Measurement tolerances, which are by no means unusual in medicine, affect each patient equally, whereas manipulations modify this general risk unilaterally. Secondly, it has to be examined in detail, whether the increases in the MELD scores caused by the manipulation of the Göttingen surgeon lie within the scope of fluctuations inherent in the system or beyond. Furthermore, it must also be precisely pointed out that the patients involved in the manipulation cases were actually those whose urgency was not adequately described by the MELD score.[28]

However, the Federal Court of Justice does not base the acquittal on the alleged shortcomings of the MELD system, but denies the Göttingen surgeon the intent to kill.[29] Because of the general risk of death in transplantation, frequent organ rejection, and the possibility of alternative organ offerings, the surgeon had not

---

[25] Federal Court of Justice, NStZ 2017, 701, 704.
[26] Federal Court of Justice, NStZ 2017, 701, 704.
[27] Rissing-van Saan/Verrel, NStZ 2018, 57, 61; see also Bornhauser, Die Strafbarkeit von Listenplatzmanipulationen, p. 187 et seq.
[28] Cf. already Rissing-van Saan/Verrel, NStZ 2018, 57, 61.
[29] Federal Court of Justice, NStZ 2017, 701, 705.

assumed that a patient standing further ahead on the waiting list would die simply because a particular organ was withheld—and for that reason alone.[30] Especially the surgeon must have been aware that the rescue would probably be successful without the manipulation.[31] The limited length of this article does not allow going further into this argumentation, which overstretches the requirements for the conditional intent in the court ruling indicates that it wasn't an attempted crime. It may suffice to point out that this passage of the court's ruling also has very significant consequences for assessment of intent outside transplantation medicine and certainly will receive considerable criticism in literature as well as jurisprudence. It would be an abolition of the conditional intent not only in the case of an attempted crime.[32]

## 5 Outlook

What are the consequences for transplantation medicine from the acquittal in the Göttingen case?

(1) An already foreseeable consequence is the uncertainty about the binding effect of the organ allocation guidelines. Admittedly, the Federal Court of Justice has only ruled these guidelines not safeguarded by offenses of homicide. However, the court's remarks about the allegedly lacking medical justification for the guidelines are very problematic. In this respect, it should be noted that these guidelines do not in any way characterize a special "German way" but are in accordance with international organ distribution rules. It would be fatal if the ruling of the Federal Court of Justice left transplant surgeons with the impression that the guidelines are now non-binding.

(2) The acquittal in the Göttingen case also has the consequence that the investigation proceedings in all other cases, in which manipulations were established, will now be closed by the public prosecutors, and likewise will have no criminal

---

[30] Federal Court of Justice, NStZ 2017, 701, 706.
[31] Federal Court of Justice, NStZ 2017, 701, 706.
[32] Critical already Hoven, NStZ 2017, 701, 707 et seq.; Kudlich, NJW 2017, 3249, 3256; Rissing-van Saan/Verrel, NStZ 2018, 57, 65.

consequences either. This does not apply, however, to manipulations that were committed after August 1st, 2013. As a consequence of the Göttingen case, the legislature introduced a rule into the Transplant Act in 2013, which makes deliberate false indications of the medical condition of patients on the waiting lists punishable by a fine or imprisonment for up to 2 years, section 19 subsection (2a) i.c.w. section 10 subsection (3) sentences 2 of the Transplant Act. The Assessment and Monitoring Commission has also identified incidents of false indication after 2013,[33] so that a punishment of the responsible surgeons is possible under the new penal provisions. It remains to be seen what will happen in these cases.

"Fraud in Medicine" in the Göttingen Transplant Scandal had no criminal consequences. This result, however, must not be misunderstood as a free pass for manipulations in transplantation medicine. Apart from the fact that there is a specific criminal offense for subsequent cases, all transplant surgeons must be aware of the dramatic impacts manipulations in organ allocation have for organ donations. This awareness is present among the vast majority of transplant surgeons. In conclusion, it can be noted that the violations established by the Assessment and Monitoring Commission have always involved only few transplant centers and have become increasingly rare in the course of the five-year examinations. So it seems to have achieved a change in behavior without the pressure of criminal law.

---

[33] Annual Report of the Assessment and Monitoring Commission 2015/2016 and 2016/2017, available at http://www.bundesaerztekammer.de/aerzte/medizin-ethik/transplantationsmedizin/ (last accessed on 5 April 2018).

# How to explain and to prevent corporate crime?

# Esprit de corps as a source of deviant behavior in organizations. Applying an old concept with a new livery

*Peter Graeff and Julia Kleinewiese*

## 1 Introduction

Deviance and misconduct refer to the "dark side" of organizational actors, which has been studied since the early days of Organizational Sociology (cf. Vaughan, 1999). Scrutinizing this topic, several sociological studies consider deviance on an aggregated level, such as the company as a whole. An example of this is the refinement of the term "useful illegality", by Pohlmann et al. (2016), which was originally developed by Luhmann (1964). Some of the behavioral strategies that organizations' members apply in legal (and corporate) border zones might be considered as "useful" and also as legitimate if—for example—they contribute to an overall organizational gain. Considering specific forms of deviance in companies under this theoretical notion delivers a consistent sociological analysis suitable for inspecting criminal incidents like the Siemens corruption scandal in Argentina (Pohlmann et al., 2016). Pinto et al. (2008) suggest a theoretical framework that also adds to such an analysis. Focusing on corruption in organizations, the authors take two aspects into consideration: The beneficiary of deviant actions and the number of actors involved. In their conceptualization, deviant actions at the level of the organization can emerge either because most of the corporation's members behave in a deviant manner or because a corporate collective deviates for the benefit of the company (Pinto et al., 2008, p. 688). In either case, deviance (e.g., corruption) is considered to be an organizational challenge—with a focus on the organization itself.

As single actors or groups of actors commit deviant deeds, in this paper, we will try to explore the validity of a theoretical perspective that focuses on the *dynamics* of actors that could deviate. We are not primarily interested in classifying potential deviant actors as not following legal standards or being law-abiding organizational members. We are more interested in the social processes that increase the likelihood of deviant behavior, regularly and regardless of the particular characteristics of the specific "offenders".

As a point of departure, we pick up results from Social Capital research (e.g., Fuchs, forthcoming; Graeff, 2009; Putnam, 2000) with regard to the positive and negative effects of social capital. Findings from these studies suggest that positive social bonds and obligations may turn into relationships with negative social outcomes. Regarding this assumption, *esprit de corps* is a prime example. In consequence, we argue that high degrees of social cohesion between group members might increase the likelihood that social norms (for the purpose of group protection) emerge; these are known to enhance group performance, however, they may also normalize or trivialize deviant behavior of group members.

Using such a concept for *explaining* deviant phenomena in organizations requires the clear definition of research terms (Manzo, 2014, p. 7), in order to warrant its transmissibility to empirical research. The theoretical concept and its specific terms are not considered in an abstract or normative manner. They provide the foundation for operationalization and testing. Furthermore, the empirical tests should be unbiased in regard to the results. Therefore, the testing process must allow for rejecting a theoretical explanation.

Applying a theoretical explanation to a certain social outcome also necessitates that causes bring about a postulated consequence regularly. The theoretical conception should identify the components that are necessary for explaining the outcome. Correspondingly, in order to connect these necessary constituents, we will introduce the concept of esprit de corps in the subsequent section. While this concept denotes positive within-group relations, the out-group effect of these relations may not be positive at all. In the third section, we discuss studies related to esprit de corps and eventually identify it as a potential source of deviant behavior. In the final section, we embed our conclusions into a broader theoretical context and provide suggestions for future empirical research.

## 2 Esprit de corps as a form of social cohesion and as a source of deviance?

Putnam (2000) suggests that bonding social capital is a form of social support within a rather closed group. The supportive function is primarily directed towards group members (in contrast to bridging social capital, in which case supportive actions are also directed towards out-group individuals). Relations relying on bonding social capital, benefit from strong reciprocal exchange between group members. Specifically, this applies to (team) partners in crime (Graeff, 2016a). Consequently, such actions are associated with the loyalty of each group member.

Framing it in a broader notion, bonding social capital can be considered a specific form of *social cohesion* (Blufarb, 1989). Such a concept becomes of immediate relevance in workgroups if their profession implies the occurrence of life-endangering actions. In consequence, social cohesion was important for all types of military organizations. The military perspective often differentiates between forms of social cohesion. This includes a categorization into horizontal cohesion (e.g., teamwork) and vertical cohesion (e.g., the superiors' concern for the soldiers) (Stewart, 1988). Another delineation is drawn between types of horizontal cohesion, such as those present amongst leaders in contrast to those amongst squad members (Mael, 1989). Social cohesion can be defined as based on attraction to and identification with the group (Boyt et al., 2005) and presumably produces positive effects for the individual and the organization (Boxx et al., 1991; Johnson and Johnson, 1991). While Boyt, Lusch and Schuler (1997) maintain that esprit de corps is equivalent to solidarity rather than to team spirit—presenting a definition that focuses on common feelings, beliefs, values and (work) goal achievement—literature has generally struggled to draw a clear line between these two concepts of group cohesiveness (esprit de corps/team spirit). They are predominantly used interchangeably in organizational theory and studies, either placed in direct equivalence (e.g., Agarwal and Adjirackor, 2016; Pahi et al., 2016; Silva et al., 2013) or indirectly paired through inconsistent application, in reference to the same manifestation of cohesiveness (e.g., Abdullah, 2017; Shoham et al., 2005). As indicated above, currently, within the academic literature, there is no prevailing consensus on what aspects demarcate esprit de corps from team spirit.

For a first step of the analysis, e*sprit de corps* can be conceived as a specific form of social cohesion. Frequently, the origins as well as current relevance of esprit de corps are associated with military and organizational research. While the military background of the concept of esprit de corps is not incorrect per se, this background goes back farther in time and thus has more facets than is commonly assumed (e.g., by Boyt et al., 2005; their overview of the concept begins with "horizontal/vertical/organizational cohesion" by Stewart [1988] and first mentions "esprit de corps" in relation to Blufarb [1989]).

Historically, esprit de corps is ascribed to the contemporary elites (nobles), especially in regard to those engaged in military work. In the eighteenth century, military officers had a common esprit de corps, which they considered to be a manifestation of being members of an exclusive social class (Rogg, 2004). In the German military for instance, beginning at the end of the nineteenth century (when officers were still predominantly of noble birth) esprit de corps functioned as a marker of "nobility of the spirit"—which reflected a fundamental attitude and constituted a guideline for officers regarding behavioral dispositions (Elbe, 2004). An early German definition of a likely related concept of French origin *"esprit du corps"* describes it as "the common spirit that stimulates the members/constituents of a specific stand, of a specific community/society" (Brockhaus, 1809). In 1911, *"esprit de corps"* is defined as "corps spirit, in corporations, especially the military, the most active participation of each individual towards the common good of all, (…) under the setting aside/disregard of all egoistic-personal considerations" (Brockhaus, 1911). Socio-linguistically, the relative semantic stability of this concept (viewing them as one concept) is noteworthy, from 1809, to 1911 and the present early twenty-first century. In his article *Esprit de Corps* (1899), Georges Palante distinguishes between two forms of the concept. Esprit de corps in a narrow sense in which it is "a spirit of solidarity animating all members of a same professional group" (1899, p. 1) and esprit de corps in a broad sense, which is "the spirit of solidarity in general, not only in the professional group, but in all those social circles, (…) in which the individual feels himself to be more or less subordinated to the interests of the collectivity" (1899, p. 1). This dual definition of esprit de corps, in connection with Palante's ample criticism of the concept from a Marxist perspective in the late nineteenth/early twentieth century, indicates the shift from the first to the second Brockhaus definition.

Furthermore, the latter is in close proximity to more recent (later $20^{th}$ – early $21^{st}$ century) sociological usage in organizational and military research. In this more recent literature, esprit de corps is often conceived of as a foundation for group cohesiveness at the individual level; for example by Blufarb (1989), describing it from the perspective of a military concept, defines it as individuals' "esprit" towards a cause/goal. Additionally, along this perspective it is assumed to have the potential of intensifying group unification (Boyt et al., 2005). However, other (organizational) research is centered on the assumption that esprit de corps operates at several levels within the organization (Jones and James, 1979), or views esprit de corps as merely one dimension of social cohesion and as a strong form of team spirit (Koys and DeCotiis, 1991). Generally agreed upon aspects of esprit de corps include: Individuals' shared perceptions of and in a group, that it is a multi-dimensional concept (although the dimensions are not commonly agreed upon) and that it involves taking pride in the group's work as well as its achievements. Prevalently, it is postulated that esprit de corps presumably grows when individuals in the group face a threatening or antagonistic atmosphere (Boyt et al., 2005).

Building towards a perspective of esprit de corps as a potential source of deviant behavior in organizations, (early) organizational and military research delivers some theoretical input. This includes general approaches for analyzing work processes, concepts of group cohesiveness as well as a focus on the (social) effects of team cohesion. The issue arises whether or not the emphasis of previous literature on the positive effects of cohesion should be amended by a more neutral perspective that also allows for the examination of possible negative effects.

Henri Fayol's theory of management can be counted as one of the early approaches towards the examination of organizations and groups. Fayol identified 14 principles and 5 processes (Fells, 2000), naming esprit de corps as one of the former. In this framing, esprit de corps refers to accord and coherence between employees (Fayol, 1949). In the context of organizational research, typical means for reaching a higher degree of social integration are, for instance, measures of corporate identity and team building. These instruments are implemented in an attempt to raise the group cohesion (manifested, for instance, as an esprit de corps) in workgroups and organizations. This is already a central issue in early Organizational Sociology, for instance in the Hawthorne studies—for detailed descriptions see Roethlisberger and Dickson (1939) and Mayo (1933). The *Hawthorne Studies*, conducted in the 1920s and 1930s, of Western Electric Company presumably constitute the foundation for examining people's social behavior in the work place. They postulate that in addition to work as means to personal economic ends, employees form informal social groups (Roethlisberger and Dickson, 1939; Turner, 1933). The studies discovered that the informal associations and behavioral norms within organizations greatly affect work (group) efficiency. The "bank wiring room experiment" (conducted by Mayo and Warner), which commenced in 1931 and was concluded in 1932, was especially relevant for the development of research on group and team behaviors and mechanisms; it revealed the existence of informal groups parallel to formal groups, with informal behavioral norms and mechanisms to enforce them. More specifically, the informal groups controlled their members and attempted to manage supervisors. For example, when the supervisors asked questions, group members gave the same responses—even if these were untrue (Mayo, 1933; Roethlisberger and Dickson, 1939). Merton (1940) maintains that within groups there is a higher rating of particularistic group interests above the interests of the general public. O'Reilly and Wyatt (1994) further argue that contemporarily, this may be primarily derived from teamwork because in teams there is a social interdependency between members and a collective dependence on each other to reach work goals. Furthermore, group cohesion has been described as a phenomenon in which the team members are not required to have a face-to-face relationship (e.g., Faris, 1932). This can be interpreted as an indication of a normative regulation, existing independently of specific people. In consequence, cohesion would exist independent of individuals but have stimulating effects on the individual level (including processes of reciprocity and trust) and decrease the transaction costs of work procedures.

As a prerequisite for differentiating between the closely related (sometimes overlapping) concepts that are applied for different manifestations of the *cohesiveness of groups* as well as organizations, these concepts require clear definition in accordance with their previous usage in scientific literature and contemporary social as well as historical backgrounds. Moreover, if the concept of esprit de corps is to be used in an explanatory way, its applicability in regard to organizational research must be warranted.

Against this backdrop, we consider *esprit de corps* to be the crucial component of a mechanism that creates an internal social order and strengthens inner solidarity; moreover, it has a number of functions within an organization (Behr, 2010; Boyt et al., 2005). One function that is already mentioned in earliest research is social categorization; it implies a differentiation between individuals within and exterior to the group (Faris, 1932; Merton, 1940). In addition to this, primarily protecting functions as well as a particularistic character are stated in regard to esprit de corps (Blau et al., 1991; Parsons, 1951) because, in demarcation to other people, it refers exclusively to group members. The esprit de corps mechanism presupposes high internal social cohesion and is independent of individuals but exerts pressure on individual group members (Dungan et al., 2014). In consequence, it may exist independently of a specific group and in newly founded groups. For reasons of linguistic simplicity, we use the general term *group* for the target unit to which the esprit de corps relates. In this sense, the term is defined very broadly, to refer to specific workgroups, departments as well as entire organizations. Specifically, esprit de corps supports unwritten norms and rules within a group thus contributing towards particularistic organizational practices. Our suggestion is that these particularistic practices increase the probability of crimes.

However, most literature has focused on *positive* (social) effects of group or team cohesion and related concepts—such as team spirit or esprit de corps. As a consequence, these positive effects of cohesion (especially on work efficiency) have predominantly been examined; these are presumed for both the organization/group and its individual members (e.g., Boxx et al., 1991; Grant, 2007; Johnson and Johnson, 1991). A limited amount of theoretical work has also been conducted on possible negative effects. To illustrate the latter: It has been argued that particularistic norms of (informal) groups at the workplace may also inhibit instead of increase work efficiency (e.g., Wren, 1994). It would appear that a more balanced approach, considering both sides of the same coin (positive as well as negative effects), has rarely been illuminated theoretically, with few exceptions (e.g., Boyt et al., 2005).

Turner (1933) indicated that social factors, including esprit de corps, could increase the productivity and utility of workers. If one assumes that, for reasons of career advancement, members of an organization are in competition with one another, then group-oriented loyalty can serve to suppress competitive and possibly unethical behavior of employees (Graeff, 2016b). One could set incentives for group achievements and reduce the importance of individual achievements, in consequence, strengthening cooperation and group cohesion, thus, meeting the need to contribute towards the benefit of others in a community (Grant, 2007). A well-functioning community, in turn, has demonstrable effects on the general job satisfaction (Chiaburu and Harrison, 2008). It also increases the feeling of belonging to the group (Bishop and Scott, 2000).

Therefore, social cohesion is oftentimes connoted as positive and desirable from a company or organizational point of view. This is because in teams the primary focus is not on the individual's outstanding performance but rather on the achievement of the entire group. In various types of work organizations, integration and cohesion in workgroups are systematically promoted through measures of corporate identity or personnel development, for instance team trainings (Guzzo and Dickson, 1996; Wenger and Snyder, 2000). Core processes of team building measures administered by organizations aim at increasing the amount of communication and cooperation, fostering the degree of coordination or reducing conflict levels in a team (Salas et al., 2015). These social processes are considered crucial for the reduction of transaction costs, thus presumably leading to higher work performance. Such positive effects support and form a basis for contemporarily popular "team-building" projects within (work) organizations—aimed primarily at increasing group cohesion and, in consequence, work efficiency and employees' work satisfaction. Similarly to social cohesion in general, the specific manifestation as esprit de corps can be used to connect team behavior in groups to work performance (Boyt et al., 2005).

Some literature, however, suggests that an increase of group cohesion may have negative "side-effects". Such effects can potentially emerge, according to the "in-group and out-group" construct located at the group level (Boyt et al., 2005);

the construct is based on the assumption that in-group members rate each other very highly and share characteristics, interests as well as a mutual concern (Earley, 1993; Triandis et al., 1988). This differentiation between in-group and outgroup members has special relevance in situations of competition between (work)groups. In such instances, individual group members' demand of reciprocal loyalty increases and work assignments are rated more highly than social exchange. On the attitudinal level, this manifests itself in the higher rating of one's own group's achievements in comparison to those of other groups, which leads to identity-building and demarcation between the groups. As this illustration of the "in-group and out-group" construct implies, a strong orientation towards the group can work to the disadvantage of others outside of the group because higher group cohesion is often accompanied by heightened distancing from non-group members (Waytz and Epley, 2012). In consequence, conflicts between team members are reduced but intergroup conflicts become more likely (Meier and Hinsz, 2004).

Furthermore, esprit de corps can lead to situations in which different norms come into conflict with each other, rendering a situation of decision-making rather difficult for individuals. Clashing norms can cause situations of normative *ambivalence* (Graeff, 2012). In accordance with Eugen Bleuler (1914), we understand ambivalence to denote opposing tendencies in situations of making action-related choices; ambivalence should not be confused with the possibility of interpreting every situation in a dialectic manner (*ambiguity* would be the more fitting term for describing the possibility of a dialectic interpretation). A first instance is given if group norms stand in conflict with one another. This can arise in situations when an individual is a member of two (or more) separate groups whose norms or rules come into conflict with each other; under the assumption that esprit de corps in groups strongly impacts normative judgments, it is likely that individuals would, in consequence, choose to orient their decisions along the norms of the group in which they are most highly immersed in an esprit de corps (cf., Boyt et al., 2005). A second instance arises when individuals influenced by cohesive group processes are required to make normative decisions in situations in which the group's norms come into conflict with general norms or laws (Pfarrer et al., 2008), due to the circumstance that esprit de corps activates norms which are directed at the protection of the group. At the level of action, such normative ambivalence is present when one would prefer to observe and maintain the group norm as well as the general norms and laws (Lüscher, 2013; Merton and Barber, 1963). Likewise, strong internalization of a group's esprit de corps might provoke a "trade-off" between the group norms and the generally applicable norms.

It is usually assumed that high esprit de corps in a (work)group leads to higher work performance and while the extent to which this is accompanied by negative effects has been tentatively indicated, it has not been discussed to a sufficient extent. To exemplify, because high esprit de corps leading to higher work performance is effected through higher social cohesion within the group, conflicts with general rules or laws may arise (cf., Pfarrer et al., 2008; Portes and Vickstrom, 2011; Waytz et al., 2013). As the normative ambivalence between group and generally applicable rules and norms, in which team or group members can be situated indicates, cohesion in groups (such as in the specific form of team spirit or esprit de corps) can potentially also have negative effects. Thus, for example, expectations of loyalty are placed on the group members, should the group undertake deviant actions or come into conflict with legal regulations during the enforcement of their work goals. A very strong form of esprit de corps may, in consequence, only meet most compliance requirements to a limited extent. This can be seen, for instance, in the absence of "whistleblowing" (the reporting of crimes) in cases of colleagues' deviance (Gottschalk and Holgersson, 2011; Savage, 2016). "Whistleblowing" has the tendency to be contrary to group norms but is in accordance with formal compliance norms (Dungan et al., 2014).

A further likely negative effect of group cohesion in the form of an esprit de corps is that, within the group context, in instances of deviant actions, such as corruption, by keeping silent, members conform to the expectation of not bringing their organization into disrepute or betraying a colleague (Waytz et al., 2013). This may be caused by deeply embedded, highly developed cohesive group mechanisms (e.g., Behr, 2010; Blufarb, 1989) in organizations, departments, groups or teams, which modify employees' judgments of deviance in favor of the group and establish taboos against reporting infringements of rules (Niemi and Young, 2013). Independently of individuals, these mechanisms can be normatively fixed and, nevertheless, exert high pressure on every single group member (Dungan et al., 2014).

In the light of the previous illustrations of possible negative effects of esprit de corps and related mechanisms, a further conceptualization that is closely connected is the "code of silence". It refers to informal regulations, which lead to colleagues reciprocally covering for each other in instances of misconduct or maintaining silence on collectively performed acts of corruption (cf., Cottler et al., 2014; Hagedorn et al., 2013). The code of silence is a prominent research topic in studies on the police (Ivkovich and Sauerman, 2013) and organized crime (such as committed by the Mafia; Gambetta, 1988). This code may prevent the detection of deviant actions and the ensuing negative consequences (e.g., damage to the group's reputation), potentially constituting an act of deviance in the form of covering for a team member's misconduct. While conflicting with general rules and norms, the "code of silence", nevertheless, conforms to the group's particularistic norms. In that sense, the esprit de corps may cause or increase a "code of silence" and thus effect deviant behavior in groups/organizations.

## 3  Studies related to esprit de corps

A number of empirical studies have been conducted on issues related to cohesiveness in groups, such as esprit de corps. This previous research mainly refers to the conditions of labor situations. More recently, neighboring disciplines have contributed towards this topic, including criminological and urban-sociological studies. In consequence, findings that are connected or border with the current topic of esprit de corps as a source of deviance are from diverse subfields.

The previously addressed mechanism esprit de corps is based on norms, which have a socially cohesive character, connected to the protection of the group. Initial research on group cohesion discusses the protective function for workgroups in politics and in bureaucracies (e.g., Merton, 1940). Later studies primarily relate to workgroups that are exposed to dangers and collective threats in their work environment. This includes specific physical dangers, as in the case of the police and military (Behr, 2013; Westley, 1970). In empirical studies concerning such occupational groups (that are also exposed to physical dangers) the function of group protection in a threatening environment is foregrounded. Contrary to this work setting, the threat of physical dangers for groups working in the economy is exceedingly rare or minimal in form, but economic threats can become meaningful. Such threatening situations may arise, for instance, in times of crises or increasing competition; this includes threats to job security due to such economically challenging situations (Andersen, 2010).

Some studies have been conducted explicitly on aspects related to group cohesiveness in organizations. Research from the overall categories of organizational behavior and group effects, emphasizes numerous facets and utilizes (as well as examines) differing constructs related to social cohesion. The studies focus on several conceptions of group cohesiveness, such as cohesion, commitment, group consciousness and in-group versus out-group categorization (e.g., Back, 1951; Becker, 1992; Blake and Mouton, 1961; Boxx et al., 1991; Elliott, 1986). The most explicit connections to organizational research are given where authors directly address a clearly defined esprit de corps (e.g., Halpin, 1966; Halpin and Croft, 1962; Jones and James, 1979; Koys and DeCotiis, 1991) as well as its manifestations. In research on workgroup, professional and organizational esprit de corps, Jones and James (1979) treat team integration as a function of the work climate, wherein in attitudinal measurements it is correlated with typical features of commitment (such as longer membership in the organization). Subsequent studies mapped out clear connections of the esprit de corps to social cohesion; for example by Koys and DeCotiis (1991), who consider the former to be one dimension of the latter.

In economic organizational studies, team integration primarily increases financial profit and concomitantly heightens work efficiency. Furthermore, studies from an economic or socioeconomic perspective show that teamwork is significantly positively related to employees' performance; furthermore, they support the assumption that esprit de corps has a similar impact on work performance (e.g., Manzoor et al., 2011). Likewise, it is shown that teamwork—including a number of factors such as esprit de corps—has a positive effect on the overall organizational productivity (Agarwal and Adjirackor, 2016). Additionally, sociological and psychological studies that identify the advantages of coherent workgroups are of relevance—for example esprit de corps as a factor that increases production (Turner, 1933). In a socio-psychological approach examining the relationship of organizational climate and job satisfaction, a positive connection between team spirit and job satisfaction is established (Hashemi and Sadeqi, 2016).

Further emphases of examinations of social mechanisms in organizations include possible synergy effects of cooperative task sharing and regarding the improvement of work conditions (e.g., Johnson and Johnson, 1991; Livi et al., 2015). Within this framework, socio-psychological aspects, such as identification with the group (e.g., within social identity theory; Tajfel and Turner, 1986), or the level of attractiveness that a group has for the specific members (e.g., Back, 1951), play key roles. These aspects may become all the more meaningful, the more important a work context causes identification with the occupational field to be (cf., Hatch and Schultz, 2004), or the more explicitly the formation of an organizational identity (Whetten, 2006) takes place. That identification with the tasks and goals of the group has been shown to be central for dedication, results in connections with commitment research (Becker, 1992; Meyer and Allen, 1997); "team commitment" is related to research themes such as esprit de corps (Bishop and Scott, 2000; Kukenberger et al., 2015).

Beyond organizational research, factors related to social as well as group cohesiveness and its positive effects have also been a focus of urban-sociological research, which substantiates that perceptions connect higher social cohesion in neighborhoods to higher (reciprocal) levels of informal social control amongst neighbors. Additionally, that an increase in neighborhood racial homogeneity amplifies the relationship between social cohesion and social control (Collins et al., 2016).

While the preceding studies prevalently take recourse to individual assessments concerning esprit de corps and related constructs, through questionnaire and interview methods (in which the connected attitudes and sentiments are inquired), most presume that this mechanism represents a superordinate group phenomenon, which exists independent of the specific constellation of individual group members. As a result of this, effects of an internalized esprit de corps may also exist independent of specific groups or in newly founded groups. Furthermore, the previously elaborated research underlines that certain forms of esprit de corps continue relatively unabridged and untransformed when the specific individuals within a group change. This indicates that the normative effects of esprit de corps might continue to exert influence on individuals who have departed from the group. It is shown that—spanning a majority of the above studies—team integration is observed together with high self-commitment towards a specific form of work execution. This observation is always accompanied by a positive evaluation, oftentimes to the extent of pride. At the group level, commonly shared values and goals exist, which have cohesive effects and form a foundation for identification. Essentially, esprit de corps is conceived of as a positive social force. Consequently, these described studies are generally in deficit regarding the examination of possible negative consequences of esprit de corps.

A limited number of studies have been conducted that underline the disadvantages of workgroup cohesiveness—for instance production-diminishing work norms in informal groups (Roethlisberger and Dickson, 1939). In an urban framework, social cohesion appears to have a negative consequence in the form of increasing binge drinking in a neighborhood or community. Specifically, this effect is shown to be prevalent amongst students (Martins et al., 2017). From the organizational perspective, initially, it may appear that the effects of interactions between group cohesion and other organizational concepts might coalesce with the previously addressed implication of a positive relationship—indicated by Hashemi and Sadeqi (2016)—between team spirit and job satisfaction. While the direct positive relationship between the level of group cohesion and job satisfaction is confirmed, a negative relationship of role ambiguity and job satisfaction is found. Somewhat contrasting its direct effect on job satisfaction, group cohesion strengthens the negative effect of role ambiguity on job satisfaction (Urien et al., 2017).

For the social categorization in organizational research there is an evident parallel to the scientific work by Blake and Mouton (1961), who establish that—in business rivalry situations—"in-group" affiliation increases in the form of group cohesion and reciprocal solidarity. Empirically, it is shown that in-group members possess common interests and personality traits, furthermore, that they are interested in the wellbeing of the group (Earley, 1993). The categorization into in-group and out-group is not necessarily congruent with a more confrontational "us against them" attitude, since high in-group cohesion can be achieved without animosity towards (the) other groups. Nevertheless, conflicts that arise between groups can turn an in-group and out-group categorization into "us against them" positions (Rabbie, 1982).

Since esprit de corps is always linked to loyalty towards a group or an individual within it, the studies by Waytz et al. (2013) offer a more explicit connection between loyalty (and, accordingly, the normative foundations of esprit de corps) and deviance through the application of several research designs. These studies are able to demonstrate that test subjects who position general fairness norms above particularistic loyalty norms are more inclined to exhibit "whistleblowing" behavior, than test subjects who prefer loyalty norms. This empiric result suggests that, in situations involving deviant actions, individuals differentiate between particularistic group norms (and, in connection with them, group loyalty) and generally applicable norms (such as fairness). In addition, the results of the study explicated above are relevant because they show that these tendencies are neither inborn nor determined long-term (see Waytz et al., 2013).

Closely related to the dilemma of "whistleblowing" resides the manifestation of group norms in the form of a "code of silence". In a police work context, it is shown that adherence to a code of silence is a complex, multifaceted construct. Factors that play significant roles are impulsivity or temper, job satisfaction, cynicism and agency or group of employment as well as race, age and whether individuals have family members working in law enforcement (Donner et al., 2018). Examining attitudes about reporting fellow students carrying weapons in school has shown that the amount of perceived support for telling authorities among peers influences their personal support for reporting such infringements. It is thus deduced that misconceptions of the peer norm—estimating the peers' support to be lower than it is—may be a cause increasing an existing code of silence (Perkins et al., 2017).

Even though studies on the positive effects of group cohesion and esprit de corps have dominated earlier research and are still in the majority, a number of (more recent) studies have focused on possible negative effects and the related mechanisms, such as a code of silence. Notably, the newer empirical endeavors—especially in regard to aspects of deviance—have come from a more diverse background of disciplines. However, as of yet the direct connection of esprit de corps and deviance, in the form of corruption or the "silencing" of corrupt actions by not externally reporting them, has not been specifically examined.

## 4  Conclusion

The aim of our paper is to deliver a theoretical proposition for explaining deviant behavior with reference to social processes that are caused by esprit de corps. The aim is not to build a classification of groups, units or entire organizations as deviant or not. Nor is the aim to explain *every* type and incident of deviant behavior. On the contrary: Many deviant practices may happen without any social underpinnings—even if they have social consequences. Nevertheless, if there is an esprit de corps that clashes with universalistic norms (or a company's specific code of conduct), there might also be an increase in the likelihood of deviant behavior.

Esprit de corps can be considered a normative nexus that affects all of an organization's members (such as in the military), but it may also apply to groups within an organization (such as highly functional task forces). However, it differs from concepts such as "useful illegality" or the classification of groups and organizations into deviant as opposed to non-deviant. The theoretical connectedness to Social Capital theories (in which esprit de corps is merely considered to be a rather particular form of social support with strong normative obligations) is not yet clear and requires further exploration. As a major difference to these approaches, our theoretical modeling suggests that esprit de corps affects the *decision-making* of group members in work organizations. Esprit de corps offers the amenities of group protection and the feeling of belonging, in return for loyalty towards the group and its members. We consider the normative impact to be highly important, to the extent that—in situations of conflicting norms—individual group members are torn between universalistic norms and particularistic (group) norms. If situational conditions, such as collective threats (e.g., economic crises), activate feelings of loyalty due to an esprit de corps, then higher group performance *and* an affinity towards deviant behavior become more likely. As we expect this to happen regularly, esprit de corps becomes an explanation for deviance.

That being said, we consider esprit de corps to be the central component of a *social mechanism* causing the emergence of deviant behavior, suggesting that—if activated—esprit de corps can be of *causal influence* on the occurrence of deviance in organizations. In this step, we pick up the ideas of Hedström (2008) and other adherents of Analytical Sociology. Contrary to sociological approaches which primarily consider the influence of aggregated levels on social phenomena, this approach explains a social phenomenon (like deviance) in a hierarchical process. Mechanisms that apply at the micro level of individuals are taken—in conjunction with properties at the macro level—as starting points for the mechanisms' effects on other aggregated levels (Hedström and Bearman, 2009) . Our line of argumentation begins with normative influences (of social cohesion), which affect individuals as well as groups, produce certain group outcomes and also produce (sometimes non-intended) effects on aggregated levels, such the organization itself. The mechanisms approach assumes individuals as actors, who make decisions under the influence of esprit de corps. From our theoretical perspective, the decision-making behavior of a group member or the group as a whole is the crucial factor. The decision-making process is regulated by organizational conditions (such as administrative directives) on aggregated levels and social conditions (such as the degree of social cohesion) on the level of individuals. These influences concur at the level of individuals and produce the mechanisms' outcomes: The performance improvements of groups (approved by organizations and expected in accordance with previous literature) and the social phenomenon of deviance in groups (not approved by organizations and rather ignored by scholars). The mechanisms bring about these effects frequently and systematically, in other words: regularly.

To illustrate this, consider the *hypothetical* case of an automobile manufacturer, operating under strict laws limiting the exhaust emissions (e.g., carbon dioxide and nitrogen oxide) of cars. The technological adaptations required for meeting these emission threshold values would render the cars economically unviable. Therefore, management is increasing the pressure on engineers and technicians to meet both emission requirements and economic viability, demanding that the workgroup must solve the condition. If they are not successful, management will fire the entire development team (*threatening situation*). The workgroup calls in an emergency meeting to discuss solutions (*esprit de corps*) and comes up with ideas that would, however, in all likelihood exceed the time limit for conquering the challenge. As a result of collaboration and teamwork, they manage to increase their work progress (*positive effect*) but time is slipping away and the threat remains. One (software) engineer decides—in order to protect the group from the consequences of failure—to manipulate the software (*negative effect*). The changes he makes will automatically, for example through the antilock braking system, cause cars to slow down their engines and activate an additional filter in test facilities, thereby decreasing emissions. Another group member notices this function of the manipulated software. In this situation, the witnessing group member can be caught between two conflicting norms (*ambivalence*)—the generally applicable norm of reporting the colleague's fraud and the particularistic norm demanding the protection of the group, including fellow team members. As long as the fraud is not discovered, the manipulated software can be considered to be in the interest of the workgroup and the entire company. The action that is pursued can lead to two outcomes: (1) "Whistleblowing" if the individual reports the colleague and goes against the group or (2) adherence to the "code of silence" if the individual maintains silence on the misdeed for the sake of the group. It follows that the individual's action may directly impact whether or not the fraud is detected and, arguably, the non-reporting itself would constitute a (second layer) form of deviant action, related to group norms and group protection.

This case exemplifies a key component of the mechanism: Suggesting the ramifications for consequences at aggregated levels in an organization. Likewise, ambivalence (as a symptom of normative clashes) is a phenomenon applying at the individual, not at the organizational, level. Taking recourse to the frequent issue of who is perpetrator—the "wrongdoer"—in cases of deviant or corrupt actions in companies and other organizations, previous literature has positioned itself in differing perspectives; one assuming that the individual is the cause and the other emphasizing the role of the organization (Pinto et al., 2008). At first sight and in fact, our approach is more affiliated with the camp that focuses on individuals. As a consequence, an explanation based on mechanisms is in line with several economic, psychological and sociological approaches that adopt a micro perspective, starting from the individual level and deriving aggregated (sometimes non-intended) effects of deviance at the organizational level, from the individual and collective actions of organizational members (Hedström and Bearman, 2009). As the example illustrates, ideas from the organizational approaches are suitable for being transferred into our mechanisms approach and complete, rather than contradict it. This appears evident when assuming that because esprit de corps norms differ from their actual real life manifestations in individuals and in groups or organizations (e.g., companies), moral choices made on normative esprit de corps issues at the organizational level are not necessarily congruent with the choices that arise out of the sum of individuals' moral attitudes (individual level). This is tantamount to the conceptual differentiation in Wikström's situational action theory (2006) between moral context and morality. It follows that we do not see the organizational approach as a competitor but rather as a source of inspiration. However, the results of studies based on the mechanisms approach should be empirically reproducible.

Our approach offers deeper insights into the causes of deviant actions, such as socially-based forms of deviance (like corruption in networks), through an explanation presuming that these crimes frequently happen in favor of the (work)group and sometimes in favor of the entire organization (Graeff, 2016b). Assuming that this is given in actual real-life instances of organizational deviance, the mechanisms perspective could amend and potentially substitute other concepts such as "useful illegality"—in certain cases. Whether it is really suitable for replacing the previous conceptualizations, is a preliminary proposition that requires empirical testing. Furthermore, it remains to be examined under what conditions such mechanisms apply and to what specific extent. It is possible that the mechanisms are triggered in situations of economic or physical threats as well as situations of success (e.g., in the banking sector). It should be explored, if these or alternative/additional circumstances are necessary for the formation and heightening of such mechanisms and to what extent these can be generalized, in their applicability, to further organizational settings and situations. In companies, the situational parameters causing mechanisms such as esprit de corps and a code of silence have direct implications for compliance measures that are aimed at preventing or reducing the prevalence of deviance.

It follows that we propose empirical testing of the *causal* inference of the (social) mechanisms through experiments, for example a factorial survey (Dickel and Graeff, 2016) or simulation (Manzo, 2014). While this should initially be conducted with a focus on the specific experimental setting (e.g., in companies), as it is assumed that the mechanisms measured in the particular framework of the situation are, nevertheless, general in their causalities in the sense of middle range theories (Hedström, 2008), studies should eventually be conducted in parallel manner across different business settings and sectors. This would allow for the comparison of the causal mechanisms' effects across business areas, similar companies in different countries as well as diverse cultural settings. Through such applications, the mechanisms approach could be useful, for example, in drawing comparisons between the prevalence of deviant actions in companies, which are affected by the consequences of deviant decisions in specialized workgroups. Beyond offering valuable insights indicating the mechanisms at work in particular real-world situations, coalescing results would also approve the mechanisms' validity. This has implications for the causes and the assignment of "blame" for deviant behavior, showing that group dynamics—such as the mechanism esprit de corps—beyond their positive effects may function to increase deviance.

## References

Abdullah, R. (2017) 'Impact of teamwork, esprit de corp, team trust on employee performance in Royalindo Expoduta Jakarta Indonesia', *International Journal of Advancement in Engineering Technology, Management and Applied*, vol. 4, no. 3, pp. 106–113.

Agarwal, S. and Adjirackor, T. (2016) 'Impact of teamwork on organizational productivity in some selected basic schools in the ACCRA metropolitan assembly', *European Journal of Business, Economics and Accountancy*, vol. 4, no. 6, pp. 40–52.

Andersen, M. A. (2010) 'Creating esprit de corps in times of crisis: Employee identification with values in a Danish windmill company', *Corporate Communications*, vol. 15, no. 1, pp. 102–123.

Back, K. W. (1951) 'Influence through social communication', *The Journal of Abnormal and Social Psychology*, vol. 46, no. 1, pp. 9–23.

Becker, T. E. (1992) 'Foci and bases of commitment: Are they distinctions worth making?', *Academy of Management Journal*, vol. 35, no. 1, pp. 232–244.

Behr, R. (2010) 'Korpsgeist oder Binnenkohäsion? Ein Essay zur Organisationskultur in der deutschen Polizei', *Die Polizei*, vol. 11, pp. 317–322.

Behr, R. (2013) 'Polizei.Kultur.Gewalt. Die Bedeutung von Organisationskultur für den Gewaltdiskurs und die Menschenrechtsfrage in der Polizei', *SIAK-Journal - Zeitschrift für für Polizeiwissenschaft und polizeiliche Praxis*, vol. 1, pp. 81–93.

Bishop, J. W. and Scott, K. D. (2000) 'An Examination of organizational and team commitment in a self-directed team environment', *Journal of Applied Psychology*, vol. 85, no. 3, pp. 439–450.

Blake, R. R. and Mouton, J. S. (1961) 'Reactions to intergroup competition under win-lose conditions', *Management Science*, vol. 7, no. 4, pp. 420–435.

Blau, P. M., Ruan, D. and Ardelt, M. (1991) 'Interpersonal choice and networks in China', *Social Forces*, vol. 69, no. 4, pp. 1037–1062.

Bleuler, E. (1914) 'Die Ambivalenz', in *Festgabe zur Einweihung der Neubauten 18. IV. 1914*, Zürich: Schultheiss & Co, pp. 95–106.

Blufarb, P. N. (1989) *Air force officer cohesion (Air War College research report)*, Maxwell Air Force Base, AL.

Boxx, W. R., Odom, R. Y. and Dunn, M. G. (1991) 'Organizational values and value congruency and their impact on satisfaction, commitment, and cohesion: An empirical examination within the public sector', *Public Personnel Management*, vol. 20, no. 1, pp. 195–205.

Boyt, T. E., Lusch, R. F. and Mejza, M. (2005) 'Theoretical models of the antecedents and consequences of organizational, workgroup, and professional esprit de corps', *European Management Journal*, vol. 23, no. 6, pp. 682–701.

Boyt, T. E., Lusch, R. F. and Schuler, D. K. (1997) 'Fostering esprit de corps in marketing', *Marketing Management*, vol. 6, no. 1, pp. 20–28.

Brockhaus Konversations-Lexikon Bd. 1. (1809) 'Esprit du Corps', Amsterdam, p. 394.

Brockhaus' Kleines Konversations-Lexikon Bd. 1. [5th Ed.] (1911) 'Esprit de Corps', Leipzig, p. 535.

Chiaburu, D. S. and Harrison, D. A. (2008) 'Do peers make the place? Conceptual synthesis and meta-analysis of coworker effects on perceptions, attitudes, OCB´s, and performance', *Journal of Applied Psychology*, vol. 93, no. 5, pp. 1082–1103.

Collins, C. R., Neal, Z. P. and Neal, J. W. (2016) 'Transforming social cohesion into informal social control: Deconstructing collective efficacy and the moderating role of neighborhood racial homogeneity', *Journal of Urban Affairs*, vol. 39, no. 3, pp. 307–322.

Cottler, L. B., O'Leary, C. C., Nickel, K. B., Reingle, J. M. and Isom, D. (2014) 'Breaking the blue wall of silence: Risk factors for experiencing police sexual misconduct among female offenders', *American Journal of Public Health*, vol. 104, no. 2, pp. 338–344.

Dickel, P. and Graeff, P. (2016) 'Applying factorial surveys for analyzing complex, morally challenging and sensitive topics in entrepreneurship research - the case of entrepreneurial ethics', in Berger, E. S. C. and Kuckertz, A. (eds) *Complexity in entrepreneurship, innovation and technology research: Applications of emergent and neglected methods*, Cham, Springer, pp. 1–20.

Donner, C. M., Maskaly, J. and Thompson, K. N. (2018) 'Self-control and the police code of silence: Examining the unwillingness to report fellow officers' misbehavior among a multi-agency sample of police recruits', *Journal of Criminal Justice*, vol. 56, pp. 11–19.

Dungan, J., Waytz, A. and Young, L. (2014) 'Corruption in the Context of Moral Trade-offs', *Journal of Interdisciplinary Economics*, vol. 26, 1-2, pp. 97–118.

Earley, P. C. (1993) 'East meets west meets mideast: Further explorations of collectivistic and individualistic work groups', *Academy of Management Journal*, vol. 36, no. 2, pp. 319–348.

Elbe, M. (2004) 'Der Offizier – Ethos, Habitus, Berufsverständnis', in Gareis, S. B. and Klein, P. (eds) *Handbuch Militär und Sozialwissenschaft*, Wiesbaden, VS Verlag für Sozialwissenschaften / Springer Fachmedien Wiesbaden GmbH Wiesbaden.

Elliott, W. A. (1986) *Us and Them: A study of group consciousness*, Aberdeen, Aberdeen University Press.

Faris, E. (1932) 'The Primary Group: Essence and Accident', *American Journal of Sociology*, vol. 38, no. 1, pp. 41–50.

Fayol, H. (1949) *General and industrial management*, London, Sir Isaac Pitman & Sons Ltd.

Fells, M. J. (2000) 'Fayol stands the test of time', *Journal of Management History*, vol. 6, no. 8, pp. 345–360.

Fuchs, S. (forthcoming) *Sozialkapitalindikatoren in Deutschland*, Berlin, Springer.

Gambetta, D. (1988) 'Fragments of an economic theory of the mafia', *European Journal of Sociology*, vol. 29, no. 01, p. 127.

Gottschalk, P. and Holgersson, S. (2011) 'Whistle-blowing in the police', *Police Practice and Research*, vol. 12, no. 5, pp. 397–409.

Graeff, P. (2016b) 'Ethics and corruption: An introduction to the special issue', *German law journal*.

Graeff, P. (2016a) 'Social Mechanisms of Corruption: Analytical Sociology and its Applicability to Corruption Research', *Analyse & Kritik*, vol. 38, no. 1.

Graeff, P. (2012) 'Ambiguitätstoleranz und Anfälligkeit für Korruption in der Organisationsberatung', in R. Haubl, H. Möller, & C. Schiersmann (eds.) *Positionen. Beiträge zur Beratung in der Arbeitswelt*, Calden, Kassel University Press, Ausgabe 3 (pp. 1-8).

Graeff, P. (2009) 'Social capital: The dark side', in Svendsen, G. T. and Svendsen, Gunnar Lind Haase (eds) *Handbook of Social Capital: The Troika of Sociology, Political Science and Economics,* Cheltenham, Edward Elgar, pp. 143–161.

Grant, A. M. (2007) 'Relational job design and the motivation to make a prosocial difference', *Academy of Management Review*, vol. 32, no. 2, pp. 393–417.

Guzzo, R. A. and Dickson, M. W. (1996) 'Teams in organizations: Recent research on performance and effectiveness', *Annual review of psychology*, vol. 47, pp. 307–338.

Hagedorn, J., Kmiecik, B., Simpson, D., Gradel, T. J., Zmuda, M. M. and Sterrett, D. (2013) *Crime, corruption and cover-ups in the Chicago Police Department,* University of Illinois, Anti-Corruption Report Number 7.

Halpin, A. W. (1966) *Theory and Research in Administration*, New York, Macmillan.

Halpin, A. W. and Croft, D. B. (1962) *The organizational climate of schools*, Chicago, IL, Chicago University Press.

Hashemi, J. and Sadeqi, D. (2016) 'The relationship between job satisfaction and organizational climate: a case study of government departments in Divandarreh', *World Scientific News*, vol. 45, no. 2, pp. 373–383.

Hatch, M. J. and Schultz, M., eds. (2004) *Organizational identity: A reader*, Oxford, Oxford University Press.

Hedström, P. (2008) 'Studying mechanisms to strengthen causal inference in quantitative research', in Box-Steffensmeier, J. M., Brady, H. E. and Collier, D. (eds) *The Oxford handbook of political methodology,* Oxford, New York, Oxford University Press, pp. 319–335.

Hedström, P. and Bearman, P. (2009) 'What is analytical sociology all about? An introductory essay', in Hedström, P. and Bearman, P. S. (eds) *The Oxford Handbook of Analytical Sociology,* Oxford, Oxford Univ. Press, pp. 3–24.

Ivkovich, K. and Sauerman, A. (2013) 'Curtailing the code of silence among the South African police', *Policing: An International Journal of Police Strategies & Management*, vol. 36, no. 1, pp. 175–198.

Johnson, D. W. and Johnson, F. P. (1991) *Joining together: Group theory and group skills*, 4th edn, Englewood Cliffs, NJ, Prentice-Hall.

Jones, A. P. and James, L. R. (1979) 'Psychological climate: Dimensions and relationships of individual and aggregated work environment perceptions', *Organizational Behavior and Human Performance*, vol. 23, no. 2, pp. 201–250.

Koys, D. J. and DeCotiis, T. A. (1991) 'Inductive measures of psychological climate', *Human Relations*, vol. 44, no. 3, pp. 265–285.

Kukenberger, M. R., Mathieu, J. E. and Ruddy, T. (2015) 'A cross-level test of empowerment and process influences on members' informal learning and team commitment', *Journal of Management*, vol. 41, no. 3, pp. 987–1016.

Livi, S., Alessandri, G., Caprara, G. V. and Pierro, A. (2015) 'Positivity within teamwork: Cross-level effects of positivity on performance', *Personality and Individual Differences*, vol. 85, pp. 230–235.

Luhmann, N. (1964) *Funktionen und Folgen formaler Organisation*, Berlin, Duncker & Humblot.

Lüscher, K. (2013) 'Das Ambivalente erkunden', *Familiendynamik*, vol. 38, no. 3, pp. 238–247.

Mael, F. A. (1989) *Measuring leadership, motivation, and cohesion among U.S. army soldiers*, U.S. Army Research Institute for the Behavioral and Social Sciences, Technical Report 867.

Manzo, G. (2014) 'Data, generative models, and mechanisms: More on the principles of analytical sociology', in Manzo, G. (ed) *Analytical Sociology: Actions and Networks*, New Jersey, John Wiley & Sons, pp. 4–52.

Manzoor, S. R., Ullah, H., Hussain, M. and Ahmad, Z. M. (2011) 'Effect of teamwork on employee performance', *International Journal of Learning and Development*, vol. 1, no. 1, pp. 110–126.

Martins, J. G., Paiva, H. N. de, Paiva, P. C. P., Ferreira, R. C., Pordeus, I. A., Zarzar, P. M. and Kawachi, I. (2017) 'New evidence about the "dark side" of social cohesion in promoting binge drinking among adolescents', *PloS one*, vol. 12, no. 6, 1-12.

Mayo, E. (1933) *The Human Problems of an Industrial Civilization*, New York, Macmillan Company.

Meier, B. P. and Hinsz, V. B. (2004) 'A comparison of human aggression committed by groups and individuals: An interindividual–intergroup discontinuity', *Journal of Experimental Social Psychology*, vol. 40, no. 4, pp. 551–559.

Merton, R. K. (1940) 'Bureaucratic structure and personality', *Social Forces*, vol. 18, no. 4, pp. 560–568.

Merton, R. K. and Barber, E. (1963) 'Sociological ambivalence', in Tiryakian, E. A. (ed) *Sociological theory, values, and sociocultural change*, New York, Free Press, pp. 91–120.

Meyer, J. P. and Allen, N. J. (1997) *Commitment in the workplace: Theory, research, and application*, Thousand Oaks, CA, Sage Publications.

Niemi, L. and Young, L. (2013) 'Caring across boundaries versus keeping boundaries intact: Links between moral values and interpersonal orientations', *PloS one*, vol. 8, no. 12, 1-12.

O'Reilly, B. and Wyatt, J. (1994) 'The new deal: What companies and employees owe one another', *Fortune*, vol. 129, no. 12, pp. 44–52.

Pahi, M. H., Shah, S. M. M., Ahmed, U. and Umrani, W. A. (2016) 'Investigating the issue of nurse job satisfaction: Role of esprit de corps, task significance, self-efficacy and resilience: A case study', *International Journal of Academic Research in Business and Social Sciences*, vol. 6, no. 4, pp. 339–355.

Palante, G. (1899) 'Esprit de Corps', *La Revue Philosophique de la France Et de l'Etranger*, vol. 48, no. 135.

Parsons, T. (1951) *The social system*, England, Routledge & Kegan Paul Ltd.

Perkins, J. M., Perkins, H. W. and Craig, D. W. (2017) 'Misperceiving a code of silence: Peer support for telling authorities about weapons at school among middle school and high school students in the United States', *Youth & Society*, vol. 1.

Pfarrer, M. D., Decelles, K. A., Smith, K. G. and Taylor, M. S. (2008) 'After the fall: Reintegrating the corrupt organization', *Academy of Management Review*, vol. 33, no. 3, pp. 730–749.

Pinto, J., Leana, C. R. and Pil, F. K. (2008) 'Corrupt organizations or organizations of corrupt individuals? Two types of organization-level corruption', *Academy of Management Review*, vol. 33, no. 3, pp. 685–709.

Pohlmann, M., Höly, K. and Klinkhammer, J. (2016) 'Personal gain or organizational benefits? How to explain active corruption', *German law journal*, vol. 17, no. 1, pp. 73–100.

Portes, A. and Vickstrom, E. (2011) 'Diversity, social capital, and cohesion', *Annual Review of Sociology*, vol. 37, no. 1, pp. 461–479.

Putnam, R. D. (2000) 'Bowling alone: America's declining social capital', in Crothers, L. and Lockhart, C. (eds) *Culture and politics: A reader*, New York, St. Martin's Press, pp. 223–234.

Rabbie, J. M. (1982) 'The effects of intergroup competition and cooperation on intragroup and intergroup relationships', in Derlega, V. J. (ed) *Cooperation and helping behavior: Theories and research*, New York, NY, Academic Press, pp. 123–149.

Roethlisberger, F. J. and Dickson, W. J. (1939) *Management and the worker*, Cambridge, MA, Harvard University Press.

Rogg, M. (2004) 'Der Soldatenberuf in historischer Perspektive', in Gareis, S. B. and Klein, P. (eds) *Handbuch Militär und Sozialwissenschaft*, Wiesbaden, VS Verlag für Sozialwissenschaften / Springer Fachmedien Wiesbaden GmbH Wiesbaden, pp. 396–408.

Salas, E., Shuffler, M. L., Thayer, A. L., Bedwell, W. L. and Lazzara, E. H. (2015) 'Understanding and improving teamwork in organizations: A scientifically based practical guide', *Human Resource Management*, vol. 54, no. 4, pp. 599–622.

Savage, A. (2016) 'Whistleblowing in the police service: Developments and challenges', *European Journal of Current Legal Issues*, vol. 22, no. 1.

Shoham, A., Rose, G. M. and Kropp, F. (2005) 'Market orientation and performance: A meta-analysis', *Marketing Intelligence & Planning*, vol. 23, no. 5, pp. 435–454.

Silva, T., Cunha, M. P. e., Clegg, S. R., Neves, P., Rego, A. and Rodrigues, R. A. (2013) 'Smells like team spirit: Opening a paradoxical black box', *Human Relations*, vol. 67, no. 3, pp. 287–310.

Stewart, N. K. (1988) *South atlantic conflict of 1982: A case study in military cohesion*, U.S. Army Research Institute for the Behavioral and Social Sciences, Research Report 1469.

Tajfel, H. and Turner, J. C. (1986) 'The social identity theory of intergroup behavior', in Worchel, S. and Austin, W. G. (eds) *Psychology of intergroup relations*, 2nd edn, Chicago, Ill., Nelson-Hall, pp. 7–24.

Triandis, H. C., Bontempo, R., Villareal, M. J., Asai, M. and Lucca, N. (1988) 'Individualism and collectivism: Cross-cultural perspectives on self-ingroup relationships', *Journal of Personality and Social Psychology*, vol. 54, no. 2, pp. 323–338.

Turner, C. E. (1933) 'Test room studies in employee effectiveness', *American Journal of Public Health and the Nations Health*, vol. 23, no. 6, pp. 577–584.

Urien, B., Osca, A. and García-Salmones, L. (2017) 'Role ambiguity, group cohesion and job satisfaction: A Demands-Resources Model (JD-R) Study from Mexico and Spain', *Revista Latinoamericana de Psicología*, vol. 49, no. 2, pp. 137–145.

Vaughan, D. (1999) 'The dark side of organizations: Mistake, misconduct, and disaster', *Annual review of psychology*, vol. 25, no. 1, pp. 271–305.

Waytz, A., Dungan, J. and Young, L. (2013) 'The whistleblower's dilemma and the fairness–loyalty tradeoff', *Journal of Experimental Social Psychology*, vol. 49, no. 6, pp. 1027–1033.

Waytz, A. and Epley, N. (2012) 'Social connection enables dehumanization', *Journal of Experimental Social Psychology*, vol. 48, no. 1, pp. 70–76.

Wenger, E. C. and Snyder, W. M. (2000) 'Communities of practice: The organizational frontier', *Harvard Business Review*, vol. 78, pp. 139–145.

Westley, W. A. (1970) *Violence and the police: A sociological study of law, custom, and morality*, Cambridge, MA, The MIT Press.

Whetten, D. A. (2006) 'Albert and Whetten Revisited: Strengthening the concept of organizational identity', *Journal of Management Inquiry*, vol. 15, no. 3, pp. 219–234.

Wikström, P.-O. H. (2006) 'Individuals, settings, and acts of crime: Situational mechanisms and the explanation of crime', in Wikström, P.-O. H. and Sampson, R. J. (eds) *The explanation of crime: Context, mechanisms and development*, Cambridge, Cambridge University Press, pp. 61–107.

Wren, D. A. (1994) *The evolution of management thought*, 4th edn, New York, John Wiley & Sons.

# Corporate non-compliance and corporate identity building – A management dilemma. Early indicators of organizationally driven deviance traps[1]

*Christiane Gebhardt*

## 1 Introduction: Non-compliance and identity building A management problem

The current scientific debate demonstrates that present research models fail to assess the effectiveness of corporate compliance systems for the prevention of non-compliant behaviour. While research is intensified in this field, the *Foreign Bribery Report* (OECD, 2014) confirms an increase of non-compliance incidents and the involvement of corporate management and central executive officers in non-compliant behaviour. Most recent scandals in the German automotive industry show that origins of non-compliant behaviour with regard to formal rules are not only motivated by individual and financial gain, but explanations must be considered as being organisationally and culturally embedded. Regrettably, to date, there is no integrated theoretical approach towards compliance to explain the complex mechanism between economically and structurally determined behaviour and informal behaviour from a managerial perspective. Corporate performance and corporate culture appear to develop on different tracks and effective prevention of non-compliant behaviour seems to be a lucky shot despite elaborate corporate compliance systems to prevent it (overview in: Behringer, 2015; Roth, 2014; OECD related systems: Reindl, 2014; formal vs. informal: Tacke, 2015).

---

[1] I would like to express my appreciation to all those who provided me the possibility to complete this study. A special gratitude I give to Dr. Sebastian C. Fink, Postdoctoral Researcher, Faculty of Theology at Helsinki University (Co-Occurrence Analysis) and Roxane C. Diesing, Bachelor Student at University of Constance (Literature study on the Relation between Perceived Organizational Support (POS) und Affective Commitment (AC)). A special thanks goes to the interdisciplinary research team Organizational Deviance Studies at Heidelberg University, who encouraged me to discuss my empirical knowledge in the light of their theoretical framing.

© Springer Fachmedien Wiesbaden GmbH, part of Springer Nature 2020
M. Pohlmann et al. (eds.), *Bribery, Fraud, Cheating*, Organization, Management and Crime – Organisation, Management und Kriminalität,
https://doi.org/10.1007/978-3-658-29062-7_15

When in December 2017 Larry Thompson, US Justice Department-appointed compliance monitor for Volkswagen, stated how the firm intended to change, in his words, corruptive culture his answer was simple: "For instance, one of the initial changes involved splitting engine development and vehicle approval into two separate divisions [*to eradicate conflict of interests, author*]. Aside from that there are new company rules, the Code of Conduct, an integrity program—and all of these are continuously accompanied by staff training sessions. Compliance and integrity must be afforded the same significance within the company as vehicle development, manufacturing, or sales and marketing." (Menzel, Murphy 2017). The managerial challenge of selling cars in the US market has always represented a perfect opportunity structure for non-compliance despite the existence of an elaborate compliance and risk management scheme at Volkswagen: "After VW US sales dropped 7 percent in 2013—and market share to just over 2 percent CEO Martin Winterkorn replaced then CEO of VW Group of America who pushed for shorter product life cycles more in keeping with US consumer expectations of new, or at least new-looking models at a maximum of every five years. […] In 2014, VW sold 6.1 million cars, but only a fraction of that in the US—around 370,000." (Dumalaon, 2015). With a non-defendable market share, below 15% of the addressed market, a product design and business model not adequate for the US market and dominated by German Headquarter Wolfsburg, the pressure was on and the US market was a Kamikaze mission. The prelude for the scandal was a power struggle between the powerful member of the board Ferdinand Piëch, then chairman of the board, and CEO Martin Winterkorn. US sales figures fuelled the personal conflict behind the strategic dissonances. In a last fight, CEO Winterkorn was backed by labour leaders and representatives of the state of Lower Saxony, which owns a 20 percent voting stake of VW. He won the battle against Ferdinand Piëch, a patriarch who was notorious for pushing his managers to the limits—but he lost the war and had to resign because of Dieselgate after a period of denials. Martin Winterkorn, who was a representative of a similar leadership style to that of Ferdinand Piëch, remained a soldier of the organisation until the very end and handed in his resignation in September

2015 with the following words: "With my resignation, I am making the way clear ... VW was and remains my life ... I am convinced that VW and its team will overcome this difficult crisis." (Financial Times September 23, 2015)[2]. During Dieselgate, organisational conditions, corporate culture, power struggle, and routines culminated in a scandal of unknown dimension—but there was no direct personal financial gain. Paradoxically, despite ongoing scandals, US business is rather stable. Volkswagen of America, Inc. (VWoA) reported on the 2$^{nd}$ October 2018 that "today reported sales of 30,555 units delivered in September 2018, [constitute] a decrease of 4.8 percent over September 2017. With 266,228 units year-to-date in 2018, sales have now risen 5.5 percent this year to date." (Volkswagen US Media Site, 2018).[3] What scientific research tends to neglect is that customers buy products, not culture and even bad news are good marketing. The Volkswagen case illustrates that corporate identity is not just an ephemeral marketing strategy but also a strong governance device or *control* to economically survive turbulence in the markets, high fluctuation and all sorts of crises.

While the strategic situation of the US market is back to square one and will be answered with new car models the questions remain the same: How can the *mis*behaviour be explained? Who could have foreseen the problems? What cultivates the resilience? What were indicators at an early stage that showed that things went wrong? Is a strong corporate identity a problem or rather a benefit?

In this paper we discuss to what extent a comprehensive, interdisciplinary approach can be employed to build prevention of non-compliant behaviour. We discuss non-compliance as an organisational and cultural problem and subsequently reintegrate the management perspective into the current debate. We argue that organisational conditions provide answers to explain informal culture. Furthermore, we claim that environmental challenges and the need for organisational transformation affects organisational culture in a way that organisational fragmentation increases the gap between formal organisational structure (rules and standard organisational procedures) and informality. We assume that man-

---

[2] https://www.ft.com/content/da8d1240-6206-11e5-9846-de406ccb37f2%20accessed%2007.11.2018
[3] https://www.volkswagenag.com/en/news/2018/10/VW_US_deliveries_Sep_18.html# accessed 07.11.2018

agers fill this gap with an approach of identity-based leadership. That explains the persistence of informality which survives all corporate clean ups and formal compliance schemes. We employ constructs rooted in organisational behaviour to understand managerial practice in managing conflicts of interest between outside and inside as well as between formality and informality of the organisation (Simon, 1947; Gilley et al., 2015). *Managerial practice* is expressed as *opportunity structure* for non-compliant behaviour and the *deviance traps* are a model for further research on prevention and early intervention.

In the following theoretical chapter we describe the current theoretical framing of compliance and discuss the contributions and limits of different disciplines to build a valid research approach towards prevention of non-compliance. We introduce the management perspective to explain the complex relationship between the dynamics of *corporate environment* (organisational level), *corporate identity building* (managerial level) and *deviant behaviour* as an additional explanatory element for the occurrence of non-compliance.

In the subsequent section we introduce and discuss the Siemens business compliance systems—as best practice of a large corporation that intends to prevent non-compliant behaviour after the bribery scandal in the '90s. We discuss the management context in which formal corporate compliance schemes are employed. Learnings from the case are considered in the research design: For instance, that the most affected and influential group in this context within corporate organisations is the leadership level or top managers.

In the research design section we outline our qualitative research design which tests the constructs of *identity management / informality* and *behavioural deviance / non-compliance* and their interrelation. The interviews contribute to the explanation of non-compliant behaviour and provide insights with regard to *organisational grounds for managerial practices*. The categorization of managerial practice in form of *deviance traps* constitute a results that must be further validated in research and for prevention as well as early intervention.

We conclude in the discussion section that the correlation of corporate challenges and organisational dilemmas prepares the ground for *a specific opportunity structure* that we call *deviance traps*. These traps set an adequate and novel path for the development of effective prevention approaches. The heuristic of managerial practice is a first step to close a blind spot in non-compliance research, which only shows from a management and organisational angle.

## 2 Theoretical framing

Non-compliance to formal rules is linked to corporate criminal responsibility—the vicinity of illegality and corruption is evident. The existing data on corruption and non-compliance is based on various empirical grounds. The data rely on *outsider perception* (Transparency International, 2017b), *directors' and officers' liability insurance statistics* (e.g., Allianz Global Corporate & Speciality), *press coverage of spectacular cases* and the *number of compliance systems and checklists* employed, as well as on *narrative interviews of corporate manager*s in the context of organisational deviance studies and corruption in a transnational and institutional perspective (Pohlmann, 2007, 2008).

Predominantly, in a corporate context, non-compliant behaviour is discussed as a legal problem with the possibility of great reputational and financial loss for the organisation and the responsible managers who fail to implement effective control and surveillance duties. On 7$^{th}$ May 2017, the German Federal Court of Justice (1 Criminal Law 265/16) held that a compliance management system can lead to a reduction of a fine against the company (Behr, 2017). This legal and truncated perspective leads further away from the issue of prevention and the complex managerial problems that arise in the leadership context and make the reception of legal studies in empirical social sciences research difficult (Leeuw and Schmeets, 2016; Petersen, 2010). The question remains open as to why formal and legal rules are ignored.

Legal researchers admit that "What is also at stake is the problem of adding *normative value to facts*: no legal obligation follows from empirical facts." (Lepsius, 2005, emphasis added). In this line of reasoning, qualitative studies in the reference model of *organisational deviance* argue that actions of managers are in many cases related to the *corporate value system* and what seems to be "best" for the company, disregarding compliance with legal rules (Pohlmann et al., 2016; Gonin et al. 2012; Ilie, 2012; Umphress et al., 2010). This suggests that compliance systems are not effective because they are not supported by *social norms and belief systems* of the *relevant social group or individuals* which informally define appropriate and inappropriate conduct. As a necessary outcome, strong organisational identity and leadership behaviour, which are not in line with compliance rules, will increase the likelihood of deviant behaviour (Pohlmann et al., 2016; Klinkhammer, 2013, 2015). Accordingly, the sociological perspective of organisational behaviour is represented by Ashforth & Anand (2003); Ashford et al. (2008); Pinto et al. (2008); Palmer (2012). It opens the debate for cultural and organisational factors that can be linked to (compliant or non-compliant) *collective* behaviour. In this line of reasoning, non-compliance is no longer classified as opportunity-driven criminal behaviour of individuals nor as management failure to establish a control and surveillance system but rather is a "normal" individual adaptation to organisational routines, or so called "business as usual" procedures (Anand et al., 2004; Anand and Ashforth, 2005). The legal and organisational discourse is enriched by an explanatory effort from psychological research which adds valuable explanatory factors by research on *stress induced recognition and memories* and leadership behaviour (Payne et al., 2002; Payne et al., 2006; Payne et al., 2007; Nadel et al., 2002). Another explanatory arena is psychological research of mental disorders in relation to top management careers. Studies show that certain mental disorders like narcissistic, or extraverted behaviour facilitate managerial careers (Mischkowski and Klauk, 2011). This research can be relevant to explain *cognitive dissonance*, e.g., the *acceptance of co-existence* of deviant behaviour and compliance rules in companies. Sectorial in-depth studies show how common double standards are, or how hubris disturbs self-perception (Honegger et al., 2010).

New research in neurobiological and cognitive mechanisms of social behaviour and social interaction also adds to the explanatory set of non-compliance and collective silence, tolerance or forgetting. Neurobiological mechanisms may facilitate social influence, linking these mechanisms to broad-scale and emergent properties of social groups (Jordan, Couzin & Farin, 2018).

Practical impact of these approaches on management studies can be found by the rising importance of *integrity management* in relation to compliance and of *internalization of norms and values* for the selection of young talents and as a criterion to assess managerial careers. These ideas stand in marked contrast to compliance systems that work with controls and sanctions. Alas, integrity management has not only failed to prevent non-compliant behaviour but is also criticized as an intrusion in the employees' personal sphere (Pohlmann, 2017).

Studies demonstrate that the assessment of integrity is mainly embedded in *organisational identity* as an organisational reference model—and the bias built into it will apply. If non-compliance is part of the organisational identity, the assessment of integrity will be congruent. Several time studies in organisational development show that *Organisational Commitment* and *Organisational Citizenship Behaviour* correlate positively (Cetin, Gürbüz, & Sert, 2015) and significantly contribute to a decrease in employees' *Turnover Intention* (Meyer et al., 2002; Meyer & Maltin, 2010). A positive relationship exists between *Affective Commitment* (Caesens, et al., 2014) and *Conceived Wellbeing* of employees (Meyer et al., 2002; Typology of commitment in: Meyer & Allen, 1991). In the Meyer Study is it the variable *Perceived Organisational Support* (Lam et al., 2015) that closely correlates to *Affective Commitment* (Meyer et al., 2002)[4]. This result is confirmed by *Social Exchange Theory* which assumes that *Perceived Organisational Support* increases *Affective Commitment* by causing a *sentiment of obligation towards the organisation* (Eisenberger et al., 1986). We consider the proven relationship between *Affective Commitment* und *Perceived Organisational Support* as a strong explanation *for corporate identity building in organisations* which in turn allows for obligations that can lead to deviant behaviour, and to organisational routines that may stand in conflict with corporate compliance rules despite personal integrity of individuals. "Forgive and remember" can be the determining relationship for corporate identity building and explains *decision making* in supposed favour of the organisation or on the dominant group (e.g., on managing medical failure in hospitals: Bosk, 2003). We note that identity building also relates to forms of forgiving and remembering in an organisational context and on tolerance and ignorance of deviant behaviour as a strain of collective behaviour.

---

[4] '[...] commitment, as a psychological state, has at least three separable components reflecting (a) a desire (affective commitment), (b) a need (continuance commitment), and (c) an obligation (normative commitment) to maintain employment in an organisation.' (Meyer & Allen, 1991, p. 61)

In management literature a strong corporate identity has positive characteristics: *High robustness of the leadership context that compensates for organisational insecurity; a strong commitment to the organisation and its mission and organisational resilience which is needed to survive in turbulent times.* All characteristics have proven favourable for managing challenging situations and corporate change (Malik, 2002).

Moreover, corporate identity is an *emergent cultural phenomenon* resulting from an intricate mix of conceived purpose of the organisation and organisational practice. Formal changes do not affect culture directly and do not change behaviour immediately (Schein & Schein, 2016). Management studies related to transformation and organisational change emphasize corporate identity building as a managerial device or a favourable skill. Authors in organisational development go even further and do not differentiate between formal and informal rules but concentrate on organisational behaviour, perception and modes of functioning (Weick, 1999; Moss Kanter et al., 1992).

We conclude that managers face the challenge on how to balance organisational paradoxes such as "building" a robust organisational identity in order to retain human resources that are capable and committed to organisational goals and meeting economic and structural objectives of transformational challenges which have their origin in changing markets and strategic decisions towards them. Herein managers face a dilemma: From the legal perspective managers must avoid and prevent non-compliance with formal rules or a decoupling of informal and formal behaviour. But they adapt the organisation to new situations at the same time. With faster product cycles and the need for global (re)integration organisational change becomes a permanent task and the half-life of formal rules develops at an equal pace.

## 3 The management context defines managerial practice: Best practice compliance systems made by Siemens

Corporate management cases show the rationalities that motivate business practices and shed light on the belief systems behind them: For instance, Siemens links managerial integrity and compliance to communication rules. The company conceives non-compliance (e.g., resulting in bribery in the worst case) as a *cor-*

*porate risk*. Corporate risks can be linked to liabilities arising from organising the business in a way that (financial) damage can occur. The *top management* is accountable for damages deriving from organisational risks. In the company, risk management systems and compliance rules focus on *critical fields* where empirical evidence of "misconduct" are frequent.

"The Foreign Bribery Report published by the OECD in December 2014 offers a detailed description and analysis of transnational corruption based on data from the (then) 427 foreign bribery cases concluded since the OECD Anti-Bribery Convention entered into force. The results of the study paint a clear picture and are also an important indicator of potential risks. For Siemens, Transparency International's Corruption Perceptions Index (CPI) and the Foreign Bribery Report are important sources for their compliance risk management (Siemens, 2016). The company's anti-compliance system is based on the following facts:

- Fifty-three percent of all cases examined involve corporate management or CEOs.
- Fifty-seven percent involved bribes to obtain public procurement contracts.
- Seventy-five percent of the cases involved payments through intermediaries, i.e. business partners acting on behalf of or for companies.
- In two percent of the cases, investigations and sanctions were instigated by whistle-blowers." (Siemens, 2016, emphasis added)

The Siemens Compliance System (Siemens, n.d.) distinguishes between *prevention, detection and response* and offers an elaborate catalogue of actions in the respective categories. In terms of good governance, setting up a compliance system remains a management responsibility and a leadership task.

Following this rationale, managing dilemmas and conflicts of interest arising in the complexity of legal compliance and organisational identity are *top management problems* that must be answered by a more enlarged interdisciplinary approach to analyse the nature of this dilemma correctly. The main challenge is to change culture on the operational level and to break *routines (managerial or organisational practices.* Joshi et al., 2007*)* that are non-compliant, systematic and systemic in nature, as well as those seen as a corporate risk by auditors.

|  | Prevention | Detection | Response |
|---|---|---|---|
| **Management Responsibility** (To employ and to communicate the Corporate Risk Management System) ||||
| **Tools and Methods** ||||
| | • Compliance risk management<br>• Policies and procedures<br>• Training and communication<br>• Advice and support<br>• Integration in personnel processes<br>• Collective action | • Whistle blowing channels (Tell us and Ombudsman)<br>• Compliance controls<br>• Monitoring and compliance reviews<br>• Compliance audits<br>• Compliance investigations | • Consequences for misconduct<br>• Remediation<br>• Global case tracking |
| **Approach** ||||
| | • Create *transparency* and manage the corporate discourse' narratives<br>• Break wrong *routines* (*behaviour*)<br>• Selection of personnel (change culture via adequate *role models*)<br>• *Self organized* (collective, group pressure) | • Break the *Code of Silence*<br>• Open the *Black Box* (of closed systems)<br>• Standard procedures run by *specialized experts* (element of surprise, involvement of revision and/or outsiders) | • Crime and Punishment<br>• Find and eliminate *corruptive systems* within the corporation<br>• Correction (self-organized within the corporate context, and beyond) |

**Figure 1: Report on Responsible Business Behaviour Compliance at Siemens, Dec 2016 p. 19 (accessed 22.02.2018, adapted by the author (approach section))**

Although this framework appears to be a comprehensive set of rules and adequate to build an effective compliance system, it must also be reviewed in the leadership context and checked for potential conflicts that arise from current organisational and managerial challenges. Tools and methods lie in the domain of HR and specialized departments while the management responsibility is to employ and communicate the system (Figure 1). Does this setting spur self-reflection on deviant behaviour? Given the effort to clean itself up following the bribery scandal, Siemens' compliance effort may be in vain because it blends out managerial challenges.

*The leadership context: Managerial practice in turbulent times*

The Siemens example of a corporate compliance system illustrates the limitations of an approach which has a focus on an opportunity structure driven "misconduct" and on "accountability" for managing people in turbulent times (Becker, 1968; and adaptions: Gottfredson & Hirschi, 1990; Shover & Hochstetler, 2002; Shover & Hochstetler, 2012; Matsueda, 2013; Perrson et al, 2013; Simpson, 2013). It addresses common issues with regard to prevention and detection of corporate risk relevant non-compliance in closed social systems such as creating transparency, breaking the code of silence or introducing new routines (see approach section, Fig. 1). However, the question remains as to whether there are valid indicators for prevention that *constitute a difference in top management decision making and behaviour*, especially in the case of conflicts of interest with regard to respecting formal and informal rules. Can managers meet strategic and organisational objectives and be in line with the organisational culture? The Siemens corporate risk management system remains a misconduct (crime) and punishment catalogue unlinked to the specific leadership situation.

In fact, the question of compliant behaviour with regard to formal rules is a subsequent problem in management: "Management deals with the integration of people into a common venture, it is deeply embedded in culture". (Drucker, 2001). The mantra and paradigm of a whole management generation that currently constitutes the boards of big companies is: *Managers manage for results* (Drucker, 2001). And the success and smooth functioning of the corporate organisation, implies that the ends, which are of financial nature and aim at securing shareholder value, will somehow justify the means. Interviews with top management demonstrate the high pressure for financial results and the lack of time for thorough analysis before decision making (see Interviews in: Nolte & Heidtmann, 2009). In an interview carried out by Nolte and Heidtmann, former Siemens Board President (1992–2005) and later supervisory Board Chairman (2005–April 2007) Heinrich von Pierer reflects on his behaviour in the Siemens bribery case. He states that he relied on the vast compliance rules and voluntary commitment of Siemens employees which gave no hints for the bribery scandal Siemens was involved in. In the interview he states "[…] I should have spoken to the people who were responsible for the daily business and maybe they knew something. However, as a member of the board you cannot ignore hierarchies. Doing so you will undermine the authority of colleagues and board members." (Nolte & Heitmann, 2009, p. 78)

The Siemens bribery case coincides with drastic changes in the Western managerial context, such as the *financial crisis*, the *end of traditional business models in mature industries*, *saturation of existing and domestic markets*, as well as the *emergence of new competitors in (culturally) new markets such as China and India, demographic and technological changes*. On the one hand, the corporate context is characterized by the disintegration of the leadership context: Traditional roles, hierarchical structure, formal rules are lost. There are rapid technonogical changes. Lack of continuity and clear responsibilities cause strain. On the other hand, trust, identity and organisational coherence are well known, quasi archetypical phenomena which provide stability in this ever-changing picture. They must be considered important factors in a management context that is characterized by strategic and structural challenges and confusion with regard to socio-technical solutions.

In management studies, *leadership* is a key field for research. It addresses the impact of individuality and social hierarchy on corporate culture and emergent group behaviour (Schein & Schein, 2016). In hierarchical social systems, such as those found in organisations, individual managers may differ in their influence on emergent group properties. This may be due to specific behavioural interactions within networks that either facilitate or inhibit social influence (Pohlmann, 2007 and 2008 for a sociological perspective on elite profiles and Top Management belief systems). Social stimuli proliferate in social (organisational) networks as a function of the social relationships among individuals. Management techniques addressing organisational change and development are based on these social mechanisms. However, they must be classified as experimental knowledge as they lack empirical support in the corporate context.

## 4 Research design

In line with the literature discussed above which guided the aims of this study we operate with two central constructs: *Identity building / informal behaviour* and *deviant behavior / non-compliance* which both need to be validated and discussed in terms of their interrelation. In a second step, we focus our research on the impact of that interrelation on the effectiveness of compliance systems to add to the explanation of non-compliance in large organisations and to design an adequate prevention system.

In our search for valid explanatory indicators of non-compliant behaviour we focus on leadership behaviour in challenging management situations as a strong determinant for social norms (informal rules) and collective behaviour within organisations.

Very rarely top managers will tell you about deviant routines within their organisation or reflect on their own behaviour in the non-compliance context with outsiders. In our research design we took this difficulty into consideration.

In a secondery analysis of an unpublished management study, we used the data of 37 top management interviews in large German MNE to analyse the perceived organisational and leadership context and took these findings as a starting point to define deviance traps that may trigger typical behaviour (managerial practice). They create an opportunity structure for non-compliance, consequently we asked middle managers of German MNE to assess their personal leadership context and the corporate organisational and cultural blockages for strategy implementation in order to obtain information on conflicts and learn about practices.

## 4.1 Construct 1: Identity building / informal behaviour

*Hypothesis*

Leadership in turbulent times is expressed by identity management to improve organisational coherence and retain personnel despite formal changes. Organisational transformation is encouraged by changes in the environment of the organisation. Do managers conceive their organisational context as transformative and complex and what do they consider adequate leadership in this context?

*Operationalization*

The focus on top management can be explained by hierarchical pressure in the corporate context: As a general rule, organisational players high up in a hierarchy define informal expectations or tolerate deviant practices (Ashforth & Anand, 2003; Anand et al., 2004; Palmer, 2012; Campbell & Göritz, 2014). 37 unstructured and open interviews were conducted with top management executives, company owners, chief executive officers (CEO) and CEOs with HR responsibility in German companies with 5,000 to 500,000 employees. The interviews were carried out in peer to peer mode and on eye level, by a senior researcher who is an owner of a company and board member in a corporate context. Interviews were transcribed and recorded data destroyed subsequently. All personal data was rendered strictly anonymous. The analysis was conducted with the aim to understand how leading managers think and talk about the challenges of the present and the future. Therefore we closely investigated the language of the interviews. The most common terms were analysed guided by Ludwig Wittgensteins statement: "In most cases, the meaning of a word is its use." (Wittgenstein 1953, 41) The easiest way to understand how people think is to analyse the language they use.

Data was analysed using semantical co-occurrence analysis. The text of 37 interviews was first separated into 1.193 meaningful sub-units. Then all terms that convey a meaning of their own of all those sub-units were coded, which resulted in 6.473 entries. Then the list of these terms was solidified, meaning that synonyms and different formulations of the same concept (many participants used "change", "Wandel", "transformation" in the same way) were analysed as if one term. Then a list of the most mentioned terms was created and the co-occurrences of the most common terms were analysed. As many terms are closely connected, the analysis of terms was stopped when the results became redundant and offered no new insights. In that way we identified thematic clusters or so-called neighbourhoods of importance. In the interviews we asked for the *biggest perceived challenge*, the *opportunity and risks alongside them* and the *way the managers address or will address these challenges*. Typical questions to spur narratives were: *What keeps you awake at night? What happens outside and inside your organisation? What changes do you face from customer side and competitors? What methods do you employ to master change?* These questions prompted answers in form of belief systems with regard to the managerial challenges and the leadership context as perceived by the managers.

### 4.2 Construct 2: Deviant behaviour / non-compliance

*Hypothesis*

Deviance is not perceived as a criminal act by managers, it may occur unintendedly and relates to complexity management and pragmatic solutions for occurring conflicts of interest. Sometimes, compliance to formal rules is in conflict with identity building and, when it is, there is opportunity for non-compliance. There are typical opportunity structures / situations in which this conflict becomes prominent and pathological. Social pressure and traditions, rather than compliance rules determine behaviour. Moreover, behaviour takes time to change because top management careers rely on social networks and long-term projects. Socialization may occur according to unwritten rules (Ashforth & Anand, 2003) that accompany trust building in organisations (Luhmann, 1964: 311, in: Pohlmann et al., 2016). Studies show that *Organisational Commitment* and *Organisational Citizenship Behaviour* correlate positively (Cetin, Gürbüz & Sert, 2015) and significantly contribute to a *decrease in Employees' Turnover Intention* (Meyer, Stanley, Herscovitch, & Topolnytsky, 2002 and Meyer & Maltin, 2010). Long lasting personal relationships of top management members and their behaviour gradually form an *organisational identity* and build up *organisational obligation*. The timeline of career building correlates with the typical career paths of a highly connected elite (Pohlmann, 2007) which reinforces informal ties through experiences related to this correlation. All this favours a rule of men rather than a rule of law. Those managerial practices evolve in a slow and informal manner and are more evident on the level of middle management where strategies must be implemented and daily routines are in conflict with compliance rules.

*Operationalization*

The operationalization must verify managerial practice. For that, additional interviews were obtained in the context of strategy and organisational development projects, conducted by the author (marked as own interviews). About 30 Interviews were carried out in action research with individuals at managerial levels (middle management with reporting lines to the CEO level, in a leadership context with superiors, employees, colleagues, and with responsibility for personnel and results) in German MNE (partly the same as the top management interviews) in the period of June 2017 to June 2018. All personal data was rendered strictly anonymous.

In our interviews we were asking for conflicts, contractions with regard to rule and practice, and difficult situations. In our research we were guided by two common managerial tools in systemic management (Drucker and Malik) in order to spur narratives:

1. Self-evaluation of the professional situation in terms of five interconnected management dimensions: Managing oneself, your superior, your employees, colleagues and external partners/clients (Drucker, 1997; Drucker, 1973; Drucker, 1977).
2. General management model: Assessment of the fit between corporate strategy, organisational structure and corporate culture. Are there blockages to implement strategies? Self-assessment of the personal assignment to implement strategies (Malik, 2013).

Linking perception of challenges and leadership behaviour to conflicts of interest, we identified six typical situations that can trigger organisational deviance or lead to bypassing of formal rules. We call them *deviance traps*. They constitute categories for specific opportunity structures and open up a novel path towards the prevention of non-compliant behaviour in form of indicators as a tentative model for further validation in theory and practice.

## 5 Findings: Managerial challenges

The findings of the co-occurrence analysis were clustered in order to frame the main challenges top managers conceive in the managerial context. A key statement of an interviewed manager summarizes the dominant perception: *"We are facing an era of grand transformations, we see the end of business models and a paradigm change of how to manage. We cannot master the current challenges with the existing methods, tools and solutions."* (top management interviews)

The interviews were subdivided into 1.193 text units of which 206 ranked around the term employees. Similarly, there was a high frequency of *Change* (190). The highest number of co-occurrences in the interviews were found between both *Management and Leadership* (102) and *Change (190)*, and *Speed* (70) and *Change (190)*. Finding personnel, and integrating employees in the changing organisational context is expressed in the categories *Employees (206) / Human Resources (76)* (which includes expressions such as HR development and retention, training organisation of teams, recruiting, training, competences). Top Managers conceive *Communication* (64) as an important tool to master the speed of transformation within the *Organisation* (55).

There is a common feeling that there is an exhaustion of existing business models, which is expressed in an *Increasing Competition* (42) and *China* as a driving force for business (31), also included in terms like *Globalisation / Internationalisation* (24) and *Digitalization* (48).

The following statements from the top management interviews illustrate that the current business is not perceived as business as usual: *"We must be better and faster, but can we master the necessary speed?"* (top management interviews). *"The work load remains high but, the implications of decisions, the speed and the accelerated speed of ever new challenges is frightening".* (top management interviews) In turbulent times, cooperation and the sense of inter-connectedness are hampered and both corporate culture and communication are in danger of disintegration: *"I call us [company name] Babylon. [...] it is interesting that firms code their specific language. If they do this you can understand the meaning. Each company invents its own language".* (top management interviews)

The interviews indicate that top management perceives change as a constant and natural challenge. However, what is happening at the moment seems to be bigger and more complex to manage. The frequency of the terms "transformation process" or "paradigm change", "multidimensional transformation process" (summarized as *change* in the co-occurrence analysis), are linked to the clusters of global integration, customers, and digitalization and success and appear to be the biggest transformational challenge top managers ever faced during their career. The clusters illustrate managerial challenges in which a high level of insecurity, complexity, pressure, change, competition and time constraints may cause a regression into *informal behaviour* (Ashforth & Anand, 2003; Pinto et al., 2008; Campbell & Göritz, 2014 in: Pohlmann et al., 2016).

*Main challenges and their implications*

*Performance pressure:* It is caused by competition and shareholder value or ambitious goals set by the top management. Ambitious, financial targets are set in a top-down style: the way to achieve these targets is not defined and performance evaluation is not transparent. Digitalization as a driver of speed and transparency enhanced the dynamics of competition, growth requirements and/ or need for new business models to face competition. The growth and competitive economic power of China are perceived as a game changer.

*Complexity and insecurity:* The search for new business models, frequent strategy and structural changes imply that the shared framework for interpretation of data and figures disintegrates or is in question. Nota bene: A shared (informal) framework for interpretation of insights, or a belief system that adds rationality and legitimatization to actions, is not readily available anymore (see the expression *Babylon* above). A common identity framework as a solid base for new socially accepted routines seems to have disintegrated and not been replaced by a new one. There is no time for learning new routines, as managers perceive their agenda dominated by the following issues:

a. Managing conflicts of interests under time constraints, financial pressure, and high uncertainty
b. Retention and Integration of (new) employees
c. Rising complexity and speed of business activities
d. Increase of decision making in non-standard situations
e. Unclear responsibilities in a networking context add to the managerial stress level and the general state of insecurity.

## 6  Findings: Managerial practice and deviance traps

The findings show that in transformational periods there is no time to develop new formal rules and even new routines. Trial and error and the search for new solution designs direct corporate behaviour. What is happening in daily managerial practice? Is compliance hampered?

The self-assessments of the leadership context in the interviews show that life is extremely difficult for *middle management* that must steer the operational implementation of strategies together with employees, partners and clients. The organisational readiness for the implementation is assessed low by this group and they perceive the buy in of employees into organisational goals to become more difficult to obtain with increasing frequency of strategy programs and organisational changes. Importantly, not all problems can be escalated to the top level as there is not enough time for explanations in the leadership contexts with superiors. Also, middle managers are afraid that reporting problems will be considered a competence issue and career stopper. The own managerial situation within the environmental turbulence and constant change is perceived as being in a hamster wheel.

The incompatibilities between managerial challenges, identity building for turbulent times, and (legal) compliance systems integrate into opportunity structures or deviance traps. Those dilemmas constitute a problem that can be addressed very differently on an individual basis: ignorance, bypassing, breaking of the rule, dismissal, putting down the assignment, open reflection with the team, escalation, change of the rule, parallel actions and so on. We summarized the findings of the middle management interviews and clustered them below in six deviance traps.

## 6.1 Deviance trap 1: The leadership context – The disintegration of strategy, structure and culture

If targets are not realistic and achievable, a so-called killer job is created. If strategic targets are too ambitious and not feasible or objectives cannot be achieved because of structural blockages, informal bypassing of formal rules and regulations and reinterpretation of data (facts and figures) is likely to occur[5]. The reliance on organisational development for strategy implementation is still a blind spot in financial management. Feasibility studies related to strategies respect figures but frequently overlook organisational resistance and the time-consuming struggles of implementation management. Organisational silos, bureaucracies and resort egoism are organisational show stoppers and a time factor often overlooked by shareholders, top managers and strategy boards.[6]

Ideally, and in an integrated management perspective, structure follows strategy and a new reward system must replace the old one. This would include new behavioural rules and work flows, to allow for a buy-in into new chains of command, new key performance indicators (KPI), targets or jobs. The crucial managerial task, to define individual goals from high level strategy, is a common procedure but the clarification needs time and comes with the double risk of inflexibility and liability. Also, reporting lines are limited to a leadership control span and follow a cascade logic of the organisational hierarchy—in a worst-case scenario, reflection and communication of organisational behaviour is limited to small groups which are related by solid or dotted lines, and group meetings.[7]

If strategy and organisational structure frequently change and systems are not aligned, the constant disintegration and alignment of strategy and structure can lead to indifference[8], insecurity, or outright resistance to adopt new assignments

---

[5] "Only what gets measured gets attention". (own interviews)

[6] "Our organisational culture is very complex and not transparent and dominated by informal networks—there is turf protection in many areas". (own interviews)

[7] "We have an inefficient organisational structure with regard to leadership and decision-making". (own interviews)

[8] "It can also lead to a situation where the mission and purpose of the company is the true north for everything and we have no guidance for the nitty gritty operational issues"; "The legacy of German engineering overpowers everything". (same interview; own interviews)

and goals[9,10]. In flat hierarchies, peer behaviour matters and colleagues become important role models. As a consequence, lateral communication becomes more important and sometimes decouples from the strategy discourse of the top management boards.

*Key indicators*

- Strategy not feasible
- Creation of so-called killer jobs and over-ambitious individual assignments
- No open consideration of strategy operationalisation (no participation, goal setting, institutionalized feedback on strategy implementation / blockages)
- No strategic fit (incongruences between strategy, organisational structure and corporate culture)
- Figures cannot be made within the existent organisational setting
- Constant organisational change
- Exponential amount of culture programs on employee level which are not linked to strategy implementation and hard facts (co-occurrence of agility programs and unrealistic shareholder value driven financial targets)
- Appraisal system (informal or HR-driven only) and performance indicators (formal) not aligned
- Unclear or no assignments, financial goals only (why and how are not discussed)

---

[9] "The interconnections between systems is usually the hardest thing [] What we are missing is the interconnections". (own interviews)

[10] "[...] structure must be optimized with regard to the value chain and not be a purpose in itself". (own interviews)

## 6.2 Deviance trap 2: Middle management – Put them on dying ground and they will fight (Sun Tzu)

The sandwich position of *middle managers* who must quickly meet new targets and manage structural change can be difficult due to increased communication requirements and conflict mitigation[11].

Peter Drucker stated that "Culture eats strategy for breakfast". For instance, behaviour of superiors and role models in the hierarchy are important for compliance. If the superior accepts a killer job or does not comply with formal rules why should the middle management? If achievement of strategy implementation and meeting targets seem impossible, informal groups become important opinion makers and will define bypassing working procedures. Often, they are bound by a code of silence with regard to illegitimate ways to meet the ambitious targets.

In this group, loyalty and commitment to organisational targets and values can decline rapidly if the position is conceived an isolated stance and (social) reward and praise becomes unlikely. Equally, lack of transformational leadership properties (such as good judgment, communication skills, competence or knowledge, interpersonal skills, confidence etc.) can bring out a troubling darker side in character. Preselection of managers with high integrity and value orientation might explain the high number of burn-outs in this sandwich position.

*Key indicators*

- Isolated, unskilled, unexperienced and unprepared middle management
- High values (integrity), organizational turbulence and management by objectives (Fixed targets and no routines)
- Revising, controlling body is not independent, is not guided by a professional but organisational culture, is part of the organisation, and reporting to the same board as operations/ execution, has relationships outside the institutional context

---

[11] "It is like a patchwork. We manage sometimes with key indicators and sometimes not—but there are no results". (own interviews)

- Milestones are set by shareholder value or rent seekers in family owned enterprises
- High turnover of middle managers
- Detached boards (communication, spatial, backgrounds, culture)
- Corporate health indicators (burn outs, etc.)

### 6.3 Deviance trap 3: Crisis mode as business-as-usual – All is fair in love and war (John Lyly)

Marathon meetings, jam packed schedules, a sense of urgency, immense travel requirements, and unreliable working hours with a loss of private social life negatively influence risk awareness and judgement, as well as reflexive capacity[12]. If supported by a respective work ethic, management is likely to be affected and efficiency and speed of decision making supersede due diligence. The longer the state of exception and emergency rules dominate organisational culture, the more good governance suffers and managerial practice is not in line with written rules[13]. Some professions (medicine, consultants, and military) may be more inclined to accept this mode as a common rule and build this into their professional ethics rather than to follow the rules of the organisation[14]. Time aggressiveness in managerial behaviour can lead to non-compliant behaviour, and a hit and run mentality of an *après moi le déluge* behaviour.

*Key indicators*

- Work ethics and communication style (celebrating martial law vs. peace time code of conduct)
- Organisational mode (stress is standard)
- Number of meetings
- Duration of the state of emergency

---

[12] "We lack honest self-assessment, there is no culture of discipline". (own interviews)
[13] "We need a binding code of conduct and a disciplined culture—we must come from paper (and meetings) to reality". (own interviews)
[14] "You can learn that structures and systems are ignored in a stubborn manner". (own interviews)

## 6.4 Deviance trap 4: Top manager as a role model – All the Shakespearos (Stranglers)

If you are no longer criticized on a daily basis it is hard to check your ego. When placed in a position of power, your ego may get the best of you. Considering the homogeneity of leadership boards with regard to gender, age and cultural background, we live in an era of the silver generation: the boards are dominantly male, white, bourgeois and over 60. In these closed societies, tactics can be more relevant than strategy. Experience and gut feeling channel information and dominate the decision-making process[15]. *Forgive* (failure) and *remember* (take no action in the face of misconduct and trade favours) behaviour can lead to a bargaining culture and a code of silence of the elite. Both features uncouple the top management from the operational management and will soften the path to non-compliant rules[16][17].

*Key indicators*

- Homogeneity/ diversity of board members in terms of age, gender, cultural background
- Lengths of service (individuals in the same position / function)
- Stability of peer and leadership and supervisory context
- Narratives (What is success? Are there heroes in the company history? What are leadership attributes?)

## 6.5 Deviance traps 5: Complexity – Now only an expert can deal with the problem (Laurie Anderson)

It needs time and training to understand complex problems and discuss the pros and cons of intervention in complex systems. The transformational power of current business challenges asks for relentless questioning, close monitoring of effects, reflection and open discourse.

---

[15] "We have a weak corporate governance—no clear policies—we are too slow to come to an important decision". (own interviews)

[16] "[...] many top executives will not take on responsibility". (own interviews)

[17] "What if the rules are not followed? Until now there are no consequences". (own interviews)

If there is no time and no openness, the likelihood of risk (easy solutions for complex problems increase the likelihood of collaterals) is augmented. Therefore, decision making boards under time and performance pressure frequently rely on experts and consultants[18]. This is a widely accepted procedure, as risk of failure can be transferred to group outsiders. There is a positive correlation between risk avoidance and high control density compliance rules as well as be-between risk avoidance and the track record of claims of organisational liability in the company. If the company is still successful and functioning in a saturated and market despite these indicators, non-compliant behaviour is likely to be found. Compliance experts are very specialized and concentrate on accountability, processes and conflict of interest built into business processes. Leadership responsibility is reduced to accountability.

*Key indicators*

- Number of consultants, experts
- External compliance/ risk management experts
- Risk management department
- Ways/ processes of analysis and decision-making time
- Cases of organisational liability
- Number of Directors-and-Officers liabilities insurance contracts
- Risk at stake
- No reflection of leadership role

### 6.6 Deviance trap 6: Networks or hierarchies – I'm on a tightrope trying to keep my balance (Laurie Anderson)

The rise of the network society gave way to the rise of lateral leadership but also to disorientation with regard to chain of command, responsibility and organisational boundaries. Who is the boss can change on a case to case basis. When orientation systems like organisational charts fail and shared IT platforms supersede internal leadership, the informal framework of reference is shifting. In many

---

[18] "Operation management leaves no room for innovation". (own interviews)

organisations, the formal compliance rules originate from a structure that is counteracted by daily practice[19].

Professional networking is attributed many positive outcomes such as the promotion of career and faster innovation and rapid prototyping. In these situations, informality, swarm behaviour and collective behaviour might be predominant dynamics within the organisation. The assignment of liability and accountability remains difficult in networking relationships and public private partnerships. There might be technical real-time knowledge and IT based organisation of a multitude of interdependencies and scenarios but the managerial capability to manage social networks and technical systems at the same time is in question. Studies in neurobiological and cognitive mechanisms of social behaviour might inform us about the human opportunities and limits to manage complexity. This research provides a strong explanatory momentum and explains why managers tend to ignore work floor complexity[20].

*Key indicators*

- Platforms, systems, network organisations
- Artificial intelligence/ IT programs to automate decision making
- Lateral leadership or intricate matrix organisation
- Joint decision, public private partnerships or other forms of shared accountability
- No reflection of the new leadership context in terms of responsibilities

## 7    Discussion

In the context of our research we identified six deviance traps that rely on organisational and cultural characteristics in relation to the management of an organisation. The indicators listed above allow for prevention at an early stage—

---

[19] "They never report back to us... Do we need to be the Black Sheriff and punish misbehaviour or will we rather be Santa Claus who rewards compliance to rules and for fast implementation? IT department and decentralized operations—same leadership level". (own interviews)

[20] "We lack discipline—sometimes we say what we are going to do, but then we still don't do it. We don't have time for thinking it through". (own interviews)

before breaking the rules takes place. Deviance traps are an opportunity structure that can lead to non-compliant behavior.

*Overview: Six deviance traps*

1. Turbulence: strategy, structure and culture
2. Assignment of middle managers
3. Crisis mode as a management model
4. Top managers are role models
5. Degree of complexity
6. Responsibility in networks

We discussed non-compliant behaviour not from the legal perspective, e.g., as a criminal act, but as a management problem. The results of our empirical study display that the managerial context is characterized by a new dimension of transformational challenges and complexity, perceived as threatening and unmanageable. This seems to be the case for at least the mature and globally integrated corporations. We showed that managers who are coping with complexity and disruption will set new priorities in management which are based on corporate identity building—thereby addressing informality and the cultural side of the organisation to increase loyalty to themselves and/ or to the organisation for robust leadership and organisational resilience. At the same time, performance management—the management of facts & figures—is followed on a parallel track.

In our approach we exemplified the importance of corporate identity building for transformative management in times of turbulence and disruption and discuss the opposing effects on formal compliance rules. The study shows the apparent irrelevance and ineffectiveness of formal compliance rules in turbulent times for corporate governance (in the conducted interviews, not being asked about compliance systems, managers did not even mention legal rules). The current management problems are dominated by disruptive innovation, organisational disintegration, transformation and retention and integration of personnel along that tricky path. The study illustrates the opposing effects of identity building on formal compliance rules. Accordingly, over ambitious targets, organisational incongruences, outmoded role models and narratives, as well as a corporate management that lacks adequate tools and methods for managing the socio-economic transformation and operates on a reduced and insufficient governance model, provide an additional and strong explanatory element for the relationship between non-compliant behaviour, the corrosion of formal organisational structure and the shortcomings of traditional concepts.

The integration of management studies in the interdisciplinary approach sheds new light on non-compliance: Legal compliance rules to prevent, detect and respond to misconduct and lack of integrity that are developed in isolation, often prove to be irrelevant and ineffective to control collective behaviour in firms. Corporate identity is an intricate pattern, emerging from action, non-action, tolerance and forgetting that supersedes formalities. It remains to be seen whether the opposing effects of corporate identity and formal rules become even more prominent in the turbulent and transformative times ahead of us. In light of these findings it can be expected that non-compliant behaviour will proliferate alongside the dynamics of corporate transformation triggered by the socio-technological factors of the sixth Kondratieff as perceived by the managers of our empirical study. Eventually, it may lead to further disintegration of large corporations, the break down into smaller units and even to the replacement of a corporate governance elite that has grown dysfunctional.

On the managerial level it is important to know that corporate identity cannot be designed; instead, it evolves as an emergent cultural phenomenon evolving over a long period of time. By managing conflicts of interest and reacting to contradictions, the top management contributes to corporate identity building and 'forms' a specific culture that is hibernating in the organisations. Identity provides robustness and resilience. However, as the perils of managing with formal non-compliance and anti-corruption systems show, identity turns out to be an element that cannot be tackled directly and immediately. To run on these terms, flexibility to react in a swift mode is hampered and it is difficult to embark on a new organisational practice. Hence, the disintegration of organisational structures and the retreat into informal rules unleash organisational features such as resistance to change and strength for survival as two sides of the same coin.

They also unlock the various factors that cumulate to opportunity traps for non-compliant behaviour and shed lights on the shortcomings of criminal law in terms of prevention and early indicators in a *grey zone* of non-compliance. Incongruities in the management system or governance model are weak signals with strong explanatory importance to identify opportunities for non-compliance.

When our top management and middle management belief systems are brought together in the organisational context and manifest themselves in decision making and managerial practice we must paint a dark picture for compliance systems. Top Management sees environmental drivers as a major force that will shatter traditional management paradigms. They admit that they are lacking methods and tools to cope with the situation. Transformational and performance management is left to middle management who is tying together the loose ends with identity 'management' to retain personnel and maintain organisational coherence for further action. They also lack a clear perspective with regard to new business models, strategies and the future of work.

In a negative interpretation, identity building and informal behaviour can be seen as a creditor of last resort to keep the boat going and activate self-organisation to master the complexity that large and globally integrated organisations are facing. Up to now, Human Resource Management as well as the legally coined Compliance Management work within their silos that disregard the fact that strategy, identity building, deviant behaviour and non-compliance are interrelated. Simply put, managerial routines are very often not in line with compliance rules, because these rules are inadequate to manage the current transformation and to implement strategies in a successful way—especially when managers are considering a career in top management.

## 8   Conclusion and outlook

Management is a multifaceted concept. It deals with the management of people, the interpretation of data, and difficult decision-making in complex situations. We tried to narrow the gap that addresses this particular problem with the help of the unbiased concept of organisational deviance and with empirical research. We have shown that corporate governance comprises formal rules but also informal ways which manifest itself in corporate identity, corporate narratives and managerial belief systems. All of them are elements of a sometimes fuzzy, qualitative and difficult-to-nail-down concept of governance. We state that *managerial behaviour* seems to be a valid element of *governance* among many others. Therefore, methods to collect and assess critical incidents with regard to on-the-job behaviour of top and middle management might have their justification. Additionally, an open self-reflection of the leadership role in turbulent times will give insights into whether a silent non-compliance is perceived a trivial offence, a crime, a lack of integrity, or an unaddressed organisational problem. For further research, it is important to note that organisational *accountability* and leadership *responsibility* are two very diverse concepts in a leadership perspective. This crucial detail may be forgotten in times of high need for large numbers of managers. The debate on managing self-organising, fully automated risk management systems in order to avoid organisational and financial damage blends out the human side of the enterprise and the responsibility that comes along with the managerial profession. Although the new leadership context outlined in the paper has blurred the simplicity and clarity of the old and trusted *chain of command* principle, it has also shed new light on the *integrity of character* of those who manage themselves and others in a professional way and in an organisational context. Accordingly, responsibility might take new manifestations such as the bravery to say no to killer jobs and to silently accepted incongruences. It takes courage to decide against (very often) self-inflicted social pressure and to reject long gone career pathways of a manager generation that has experienced a very different management context.

A new generation of managers will need to identify weak signals in order to manage shorter life cycles and orchestrate people in smaller and changing organisations and teams rather than rely on solid and dotted lines. This will go along with the questioning of management methods that had their value in the organisational context of the last century, were less experimental, dominated by formalities and based on a top down approach. In this line of thinking, non-compliance is a symptom rather than a disease and it might also be a good start for a renewed reflection of the management role in transformative times and the role of responsible leadership in an organisational context.

## References

Anand V., Ashforth B.E. and Joshi M. (2004) 'Business as usual: The acceptance and perpetuation of corruption in organizations' *Academy of Management Executive* 18(3):9–23.

Anand, V., and Ashforth, B.E. (2005) 'Business as Usual: The Acceptance and Perpetuation of Corruption in Organizations' *The Academy of Management Executive* (1993-2005) 19:9–23.

Ashforth B.E. and Anand, V. (2003) 'The normalization of corruption in organizations' *Research in Organizational Behavior* 25(1):1–52.

Ashforth, B.E., Gioia, D.A., Robinson, S.L, and Trevino, L.K. (2008) 'Re-Viewing Organizational Corruption' *The Academy of Management Review*, 33:670.

Ashforth, B.E. and Anand, V. (2003) 'The Normalization of Corruption in Organizations' *Research in Organizational Behavior* 25:1–52.

Behr, N. (2017) 'German Federal Court of Justice: Compliance Management System can lead to reduction of fine' *Global Compliance News* [Online]. Available at https://globalcompliancenews.com/german-court-cms-can-reduce-fine-20170829/ (Accessed 17 October 2018).

Behringer, S. (2015) 'Compliance-management', in Passarge, M. and Behringer, S. (eds) *Handbuch Compliance International*. Erich Schmidt Verlag, Berlin, 5–25.

Bosk, C. L. (2003) *Forgive and Remember: Managing Medical Failure*. University of Chicago Press, 2d ed.

Caesens, G., Marique, G., & Stinglhamber, F. (2014). 'The Relationship between Perceived Organizational Support and Affective Commitment' *Journal of Personnel Psychology*, 13(4), 167–173.

Campbell J.L. and Göritz, A.S. (2014) 'Culture corrupts! A qualitative study of organizational culture in corrupt organizations' *Journal of Business Ethics*, 120(3):291–311.

Cetin, S., Gürbüz, S., and Sert, M. (2015) 'A Meta-analysis of the Relationship. Between Organizational Commitment and Organizational Citizenship Behavior: Test of Potential Moderator Variables' *Employee Responsibilities and Rights Journal*, 27(4), 281–303.

Drucker, P. (2001) *The Essential Drucker*. Harper Collins.

Drucker, P. (1997) *The Effective Executive*. Harper & Row, New York.

Drucker, P. (1973) *Management: Tasks, Responsibilities, Practices*. Harper & Row, New York.

Drucker, P. (1977) 'Managing oneself' *Harvard Business Review*, 1999 Mar-Apr. 77 (2):64-74, 185.

Dumalaon, J. (2015) 'The US Market: Volkwagen's Waterloo' *Deutsche Welle* [Online]. Available at https://p.dw.com/p/1GZte (Accessed 10 October 2018).

Eisenberger, R., Huntington, R., Hutchison, S., & Sowa, D. (1986) 'Perceived Organisational Support' *Journal of Applied Psychology*, 71(3), 500–507.

Gilley, J. W., Gilley, A. M., Jackson, S. A. and Lawrence, H. (2015) 'Managerial Practices and Organisational Conditions That Encourage Employee Growth and Development' *Performance Improvement Quarterly*, 28: 71-93.

Gonin M., Palazzo, G. and Hoffrage, U. (2012) 'Neither bad apple nor bad barrel: How the societal context impacts unethical behavior in organisations' *Business Ethics: A European Review*, 21(1):31–46.

Ilie, A. (2012) *Unethical Pro-Organisational Behaviors: Antecedents and Boundary Conditions, Graduate Theses and Dissertations.* https://scholarcommons.usf.edu/etd/4085

Joshi, M., Vikas A., und Henderson, K. (2007). ,The role of organisational practices and routines in facilitating normalized corruption', in Langan-Fox, J., Cooper, C., and Klimoski, R.J. (eds) *Research companion to the dysfunctional workplace: Management challenges and symptoms*, Cheltenham, Northampton: Edward Elgar Publishing, 235-251.

Klinkhammer, J. (2013) 'On the dark side of the code: Organisational challenges to an effective anti-corruption strategy' *Crime, Law and Social Change* 60(2):191–208.

Klinkhammer, J. (2015) 'Varieties of corruption in the shadow of Siemens. A modus-operandi study of corporate crime on the supply side of corrupt transactions', in Erp, J., Huisman, W., Vande Walle, G., Beckers, J., *Routledge Handbook of White-Collar and Corporate Crime in Europe*: 318–335.

Lam, L.W., Liu, Y. and Loi, R. (2015) 'Looking intra-organisationally for identity cues: Whether perceived organisational support shapes employees' organisational identification'. *Human Relations*, 69(2), 345–367.

Lepsius, O. (2005) 'Sozialwissenschaften im Verfassungsrecht — Amerika als Vorbild?' *JuristenZeitung*, 60(1), 1-13.

Leeuw, F.L., & Schmeets, H. (2016) *Empirical legal research: A guidance book for lawyers, legislators and regulators*, Edward Elgar Publishing.

Malik, F (2002) 'Die neue Corporate Governance. Richtiges Top-Management - Wirksame Unternehmensaufsicht' Verlag *Frankfurter Allgemeine Buch* (3 Auflage).

Malik, F. (2013) *Corporate Policy and Corporate Governance*. Campus, Frankfurt/ New York

Marique, G., Stinglhamber, F., Desmette, D., Caesens, G., & Zanet, F. (2013) 'The Relationship Between Perceived Organisational Support and Affective Commitment' *Group & Organization Management*, 38(1), 68–100.

Menzel, M. and Murphy, M. (2017) 'US monitor: VW had corrupt culture, flawed leadership' *Handelsblatt Global* [Online]. Available at https://global.handelsblatt.com/mobility/us-monitor-vw-had-corrupt-culture-flawed-leadership-867040 (Accessed 10 October 2018).

Meyer, J.P., & Allen, N.J. (1991) 'A three-component conceptualization of organisational commitment' *Human Resource Management Review*, 1(1), 61–89.

Meyer, J.P., & Maltin, E.R. (2010) 'Employee commitment and well-being: A critical review, theoretical framework and research agenda' *Journal of Vocational Behavior*, 77(2), 323–337.

Meyer, J.P., Allen, N.J., & Smith, C.A. (1993) 'Commitment to organisations and occupations: Extension and test of a three component conceptualization' *Journal of Applied Psychology*, 78(4), 538–551.

Meyer, J.P., Stanley, D.J., Herscovitch, L., and Topolnytsky, L. (2002) 'Affective, Continuance, and Normative Commitment to the Organisation: A Meta-analysis of Antecedents, Correlates, and Consequences' *Journal of Vocational Behavior*, 61(1), 20–52.

Mischkowski, A.D., and Klauk, B. (2011) 'Narcissists as Risk Factors for Companies. Psychology and Empiricism of the Narcissistic Disorder' *Personalführung*, 2, 16-24.

Nadel, L., Payne, J.D. & Jacobs, W.J. (2002) 'The relationship between episodic memory and context: Clues from memory errors made while under stress' *Physiological Research*, 51 Suppl 1, S. 3-11. Netzwerke – Cluster – Allianzen. Stuttgart. Kohlhammer.

Nolte, B., Heidtmann, J. (2009) *Die da oben: Innenansichten aus deutschen Chefetagen*. Suhrkamp Frankfurt am Main.

OECD (2014) 'Good practice guidance on internal controls, ethics and compliance' *OECD, Paris*. Available at: http://www.oecd.org/investment/anti-bribery/anti-briberyconvention/44884389.pdf (Accessed 15 September 2015).

Onur, O.A., Walter, H., Schlaepfer, T.E., Rehme, A.K., Schmidt, C., Keysers, C., Maier, W., and Hurlemann, R. (2009) 'Noradrenergic enhancement of amygdala responses to fear' *Social Cognitive and Affective Neuroscience*, 4, 119-126.

Palmer D. (2012) *Normal organizational wrongdoing: A critical analysis of theories of misconduct in and by organizations*, Oxford University Press, Oxford.

Payne, J.D., Jackson, E.D., Hoscheidt, S., Ryan, L., Jacobs, W.J., and Nadel, L. (2007) 'Stress administered prior to encoding impairs neutral but enhances emotional long-term episodic memories' *Learning and Memory*, 14, 861-868.

Payne, J.D., Jackson, E.D., Ryan, L., Hoscheidt, S., Jacobs, J.W., and Nadel, L. (2006) 'The impact of stress on neutral and emotional aspects of episodic memory' *Memory*, 14, 1-16.

Payne, J.D., Nadel, L., Allen, J.J., Thomas, K.G., and Jacobs, W.W. (2002) 'The effects of experimentally induced stress on false recognition' *Memory*, 10, 1-6.

Petersen, N. (2010) *Does Legal Scholarship Need an Empirical Turn?* MPI Collective Goods Preprint, no. 2010/10.

Pinto J., Leana C.R. and Pil F.K. (2008) 'Corrupt organizations or organizations of corrupt individuals? Two types of organization-level corruption' *Academy of Management Review*, 33(3):685–709.

Pohlmann, M. 2008. 'Management und Moral', in Blank, T., Münch, T., Schanne, S., & Staffhorst, C. (Hrsg.). (2008). Integrierte Soziologie: Perspektiven zwischen Ökonomie und Soziologie, Praxis und Wissenschaft ; Festschrift zum 70. Geburtstag von Hansjörg Weitbrecht. München: Hampp. 161-175.

Pohlmann, M., Bitsch, K., Klinkhammer, J. (2016) 'Personal Gain or Organizational Benefits – How to Explain Active Corruption?' in: Graeff, P., Wolf, S.(eds) *Ethical Challenges of Corrupt Practices: Formal and Informal Conflicts of Norms and Their Moral Ramifications*, in: *German Law Journal* 17(1): S. 73-100.

Pohlmann, M. (2007) 'Management und Führung: eine managementsoziologische Perspektive', in: *Sozialwissenschaften und Berufspraxis*, 30 (2007), 1, 5-20.

Reindl, A. (2014) 'Der Beitrag der OECD zur Entwicklung von Corporate Compliance Standards', in: Bungenberg, M., Dutzi, A,. Krebs, P., and Zimmermann, N. (eds) *Corporate compliance and corporate social responsibility*, Nomos, Baden-Baden, 127–145.

Rohwer, A. (2009) 'Measuring corruption: A comparison between the transparency international's corruption perceptions index and the World Bank's worldwide governance indicators' *CESifo DICE Report 3/2009*. Available at: https://www.cesifo-group.de/portal/pls/portal/docs/1/1192926.PDF (Accessed 20 September 2015).

Moss Kanter, R., Stein, B.A., Jick, T.D.(1992) *The challenge of organizational change and how companies experience it and leaders guide it*, New York Free Press.

Roth, M. (2014) 'Compliance – Die ungeteilte Verantwortung', in: Bungenberg, M., Dutzi, A., Krebs, P., and Zimmermann, N. (eds) *Corporate compliance and corporate social responsibility*, Nomos, Baden-Baden, 45–58.

Schein, E, Schein, P. (2016). *Organizational Culture and Leadership* (5th ed.), Hoboken: John Wiley & Sons.

Shover, N., Hochstetler, A. (2002) 'Cultural explanation and organisational crime' *Crime, law and social change*, 37:1-18.

Siemens (2016) *Responsible behaviour* [Online]. Available at https://www.siemens.com/content/dam/internet/siemens-com/global/company/sustainability/downloads/responsible-business-behavior-compliance-at-siemens.pdf (Accessed 22 February 2018).

Siemens (n.d.) *The Siemens Compliance System* [Online]. Available at https://w5.siemens.com/web/ua/en/about/compliance/pages/compliance.aspx?istablet=true (Accessed 7 November 2018).

Simpson, S.S. (2013) White-Collar Crime: A Review of Recent Developments and Promising Directions for Future Research' *Annual Review of Sociology*, 39:309–331.

Simon, H.A. (1947) *Administrative Behavior. A Study of Decision-Making Processes in Administrative Organizations*, New York/London.

Snider, L. (2008) 'Corporate economic crimes', in: Minkes, J., and Minkes L. *Corporate and white collar crime*, Los Angeles [u.a.]: Sage, 39-60.

Sydow, J., & Duschek, S. (2011). Management interorganisationaler Beziehungen: Netzwerke, Cluster, Allianzen edn. *Management, Kohlhammer, Stuttgart Google Scholar*.

Tacke, V. (2015) 'Formalität und Informalität', in: Groddeck, V., and Wilz, M.S., *Formalität und Informalität in Organisationen*, Wiesbaden: Springer Fachmedien Wiesbaden, 37-92.

Transparency International (2017b) *Corruption Perceptions Index* [Online]. Available at https://www.transparency.org/news/feature/corruption_perceptions_index_2017#table (Accessed 14 May 2018).

Umphress, E.E., Bingham J.B.,und Mitchell, M.M. (2010) 'Unethical Behavior in the Name of the Company' *Journal of Applied Psychology*, 95:769–780.

Volkswagen US Media Site (2018) *Volkswagen of America reports December and 2017 year-end sales results* [Online]. Available at https://media.vw.com/releases/966 (Accessed 10 October 2018).

Weick, K.E. (1995) 'Sensemaking in organizations' *Foundations for organizational science*, Thousands Oaks: Sage Publications Inc.

Wittgenstein, L. (1953) *Philosophical Investigations,* Oxford: Basil Blackwell, 1953, 41.

## Interviews top management source co-occurrence analysis

( ) Number of appearance in the entire text
Under the header we list the most important co-occurrences (mentioned in the context with header, by frequency)

| *Employees (206)* | | *Company (71)* | | *Structure (44)* | | *Consulting (30)* | |
|---|---|---|---|---|---|---|---|
| Change | 39 | Change | 16 | Change | 16 | HR | 4 |
| HR | 28 | Employees | 15 | Employees | 9 | Processes | 3 |
| Communication | 23 | Challenge | 8 | Organization | 7 | Strategy | 3 |
| Challenge | 22 | Leadership | 8 | Challenge | 6 | Change | 3 |
| Leadership | 15 | Speed | 8 | Leadership | 5 | | |
| Organization | 15 | Clients | 5 | Speed | 5 | *Growth (30)* | |
| Company | 15 | | | | | China | 7 |
| | | *Speed (70)* | | *Competition (42)* | | Competition | 6 |
| *Change (190)* | | Change | 15 | Change | 8 | Dezentralization | 3 |
| Employees | 36 | Challenge | 12 | Growth | 6 | Speed | 3 |
| Challenge | 18 | Employee | 11 | Challenge | 5 | Crisis | 3 |
| Company | 16 | Company | 8 | China | 4 | Employees | 3 |
| Leadership | 15 | Decentralization | 7 | Speed | 4 | | |
| Speed | 15 | Leadership | 6 | | | *Market (29)* | |
| Structure | 15 | Clients | 6 | *IT (38)* | | Clients | 7 |
| Clients | 14 | | | Change | 8 | Change | 7 |
| Digitalization | 10 | *Challenges (67)* | | Employees | 7 | Employees | 6 |
| | | Employees | 24 | Digitalization | 6 | Internationality | 3 |
| *Leadership (102)* | | Change | 20 | HR | 6 | Competition | 3 |
| Employees | 17 | Leadership | 14 | Software | 6 | | |
| Change | 16 | Speed | 12 | Processes | 5 | *Processes (29)* | |
| Management | 15 | Company | 8 | | | IT | 5 |
| Challenge | 15 | Management | 7 | *Strategy (38)* | | Employees | 5 |
| HR | 11 | Structure | 6 | Employees | 13 | Consulting | 3 |
| Communication | 10 | Digitalization | 5 | Organization | 6 | Connectness | 3 |
| | | Complexity | 5 | Leadership | 5 | Change | 3 |
| *Clients (n.a.)* | | Competition | 5 | Management | 5 | | |
| Change | 16 | | | Board | 5 | *Innovation (27)* | |
| Employees | 12 | *Communication (64)* | | Strategy process | 4 | Change | 8 |
| Complexity | 8 | Employees | 25 | Consulting | 3 | Digitalization | 4 |
| Market | 7 | Leadership | 10 | Speed | 3 | Speed | 4 |
| Speed | 6 | Board | 7 | | | Startup | 4 |
| Decentralization | 5 | Hierarchy | 6 | *Complexity (36)* | | | |
| Globalization | 5 | Management | 5 | Clients | 8 | *Dezentralization (26)* | |
| communication | 5 | Clients | 5 | Connected | 7 | Centralization | 15 |
| Sales | 5 | Meetings | 5 | Leadership | 6 | Speed | 7 |
| | | Team | 5 | Speed | 5 | Clients | 5 |
| *Management (76)* | | Change | 5 | Challenge | 5 | Change | 4 |
| Leadership | 16 | | | Change | 5 | | |
| Employees | 14 | *Organization (55)* | | Business Model | 4 | *Centralization (26)* | |
| Change | 11 | Employees | 14 | | | Dezentralization | 15 |
| Challenge | 7 | Change | 10 | | | Leadership | 4 |
| Communication | 5 | Leadership | 7 | | | Employees | 4 |
| HR | 5 | Structure | 7 | | | Internationality | 3 |
| Training | 5 | Strategy | 6 | | | | |
| Strategy | 5 | | | | | | |
| Role Model | 5 | | | | | | |

| HR (75) | | Digitalization (48) | | China (35) | | Language (22) | |
|---|---|---|---|---|---|---|---|
| Employees | 27 | Change | 11 | Growth | 7 | Terminology | 5 |
| Leadership | 11 | IT | 6 | Boom | 4 | English | 3 |
| HR (Development) | 8 | Interconnection | 6 | Export | 4 | Leadership | 3 |
| Change | 8 | Leadership | 5 | Competition | 4 | Management | 3 |
| IT | 6 | Change | 5 | Acquisitions | 4 | Employees | 3 |
| Speed | 5 | Speed | 4 | Infrastructure | 3 | Terminology | 3 |
| Change | 3 | HR | 4 | Employees | 3 | | |
| Backoffice | 3 | Innovation | 4 | Over Capacities | 3 | *Hierarchy (22)* | |
| IT | 3 | Competition | 4 | | | Employees | 7 |
| Complexity | 3 | | | *Board / CEO (34)* | | Communication | |
| Clients | 3 | *Inter-Connected (26)* | | Communication | 7 | Management | 3 |
| | | Digitalization | 6 | Employees | 7 | Networks | 3 |
| *Business Modell (26)* | | Complexity | 6 | Strategy | 5 | Company | 3 |
| Change | 7 | Change | 4 | Leadership | 4 | | |
| Employees | 5 | | | Management | 4 | *Startups (20)* | |
| Digitalization | 3 | *Success (25)* | | Meetings | 4 | Speed | 4 |
| Challenges | 3 | Change | 7 | Seize of Board | 4 | Innovation | 4 |
| Complexity | 3 | Employees | 4 | | | Company | 4 |
| Competition | 3 | Organization | 3 | *Internationality (25)* | | Employees | 3 |
| Technology | 3 | | | Employees | 7 | | |
| | | *Globalization (24)* | | Clients | 6 | | |
| | | Challenge | 5 | Foreign countries | 5 | | |
| | | Regionality | 5 | Flexibility | 3 | | |
| | | | | Market | 3 | | |
| | | | | Regionality | 3 | | |
| | | | | *Flexibility (24)* | | | |
| | | | | Employees | 7 | | |
| | | | | Leadership | 4 | | |
| | | | | Challenge | 4 | | |
| | | | | Organization | 4 | | |

# Overcoming the current system of corporate criminal law – sanctioning corporate citizens. Crime prevention within the limits of the rule of law[1]

*Gerhard Dannecker and Thomas Schröder*

1     Corporate crime: A danger foreseen is half avoided? The example of corruption

*Thesis 1: Current surveys indicate that while corruption is recognized as a major problem around the world, corporate personnel—and especially current young professionals—are still willing to engage in bribery to support business interests.*

Corporate crime exists in many forms. This treatise shall commence with an example which assesses one of the most notorious manifestations of corporate crime: The problem of corruption seems to be known world-wide in terms of its consequences and extent. In particular, this applies to the upcoming generation of young people entering the professional world:

In 2017, the World Economic Forum conducted its annual survey in 186 countries, questioning around 25,000 18 to 35 year-olds, the so-called Millennials, on how they perceive the world and what changes they want to bring about. A central question to the respondents concerned the biggest social issues in their respective home country. As might be expected, the answers varied from state to state: While over-aging of society was perceived as the greatest problem in Switzerland, it was poverty in Benin and inequality due to income disparities and discrimination in the USA. Overall, however, and just as the year before, the Millennials held the opinion that lack of accountability and transparency of governments as well as corruption were the most pressing problems in their home country (Global Shapers Community, 2017, p. 15) And those who had

---

[1] This paper is based on two lectures given by the authors at the Herrenhausen Symposium. The lecture form was largely retained.

© Springer Fachmedien Wiesbaden GmbH, part of Springer Nature 2020
M. Pohlmann et al. (eds.), *Bribery, Fraud, Cheating*, Organization, Management and Crime – Organisation, Management und Kriminalität,
https://doi.org/10.1007/978-3-658-29062-7_16

decided against working in civil service did not quote bad pay or the possible monotony of work as their main reason, but above all they were worried about corruption in this sector (Global Shapers Community, 2016, p. 43).

In the private sector, however, awareness of the corruption problem does not go hand in hand with changes in business conduct. Of 500 board members questioned worldwide by the law-firm Eversheds Sutherland in 2016, 80 % admitted to discover bribery or corruption in their organization on a regular basis (Eversheds Sutherland, 2016, p. 9). In 2017, the auditing firm Ernst & Young surveyed over 4,000 company members from 41 countries for a study on white-collar crime (Ernst & Young, 2017a, p. 9 et seq.; Ernst & Young, 2017b, p. 14). One-third of the managerial staff believed they were entitled to pay bribes to win or maintain business. Only 20% of the non-managerial staff shared this opinion. In this study, too, the younger generation's—in that case the 25 to 35 year-olds—views are worrying. While 25% of them consider business-enabling bribes to be justified, only 10% of the staff aged 45 or more share this view. And while 80% of the older respondents believe their colleagues are not willing to behave unethically in favor of their career, half of the "Generation Y" see it differently. Regarding their own top management, 70% of the younger interviewees held the opinion that the managerial staff would violate rules to sustain business.

Therefore, young professionals not only predominantly share a pessimistic view of corporate compliance but also predominantly share a lack of initiative to resist corruptive structures if they are exposed to them.

In any case, these surveys also reveal that the interviewees seem to be able to comprehend the concept of corruption almost intuitively. Corruption appears to be a global phenomenon, seemingly timeless and cross-cultural (accurate assessment by Sowada, 2009, margin no. 41). However, the exact meaning of the term "corruption" varies significantly according to the respective scientific discipline, interest group, epoch and society, and from our current Western perspective on states and state law, the concept is still only restrictedly applicable to some cultures in other parts of the world (Engels, 2006, p. 315; Weilert, 2015, p. 220 et seq.). But then, it does not seem particularly surprising or worrisome that an interdisciplinary corruption term cannot be achieved, since the conceptual (research) interests are too heterogeneous. For instance, a western non-governmental organization that aims at combatting non-transparency and bribery will tend to outline its area of competence fairly generous while governments and societies shaped by dynastic elements and family ties will take a strong stance against the presumed disparagement and criminalization of their traditional political and economic system.

From a criminal law or criminological perspective, rather elaborate descriptions of corruption are common. They are certainly more elaborate than the descriptions preferred for example by some non-governmental organizations.[2] However, this is due to—at least indirectly—the fact that burdensome legal consequences can be attached to the favored term: If the legitimation of punishment is based on the assumption that a specific and particularly socially harmful form of attack on institutions has taken place (i.e., corruption), then a corresponding obligation for the lawmaker arises not to intermingle the diagnoses of corruption with other phenomena that are only closely related to corruption, but that are not congruent with it (such as breaches of competition law or violations of fiduciary duties). Building on past research, the following definition of corruption may be proposed: The essential characteristic of corruption is "a contradiction between the interests which the agent has to observe on account of his particular set of duties and the interest to which he has bound himself to by the acceptance of the advantage" (Dannecker and Schröder, 2016, p. 43). Therefore, corruptibility is a "form of attack" which "always demands a conflict of interests within the internal relationship between principal and agent" (Kindhäuser, 2011, p. 463).

## 2    On the severe effects of corruption

*Thesis 2: The grave consequences of corruption for economy and other essential institutions of the public and private sector justify the collateral damage caused by the counter-measures against it.*

Taking legal action against corruption involves detrimental effects. This is obvious with regard to the personal freedom to act that is cut back by statutory

---

[2] For example, see Transparency International (2017): Corruption is "the abuse of entrusted power for private gain".

prohibitions banning previous business practices. Especially new penal laws combatting economic corruption are sometimes viewed as overblown and as a moralization of law (see Bernsmann et al., 2014 margin nos. 558 et seq.; Dann, 2016, p. 204; Gaede, 2014, p. 284) . In addition, preventive and repressive actions against corruption do have indirect disadvantages for "social capital".[3] The rigorism practiced in some cases of anti-corruption measures damages informal structures and relationship networks, which are quite functional in the Western world as well as in other societies.[4] Further, poorly structured and executed compliance management creates its own risks of criminal liability.[5]

Nonetheless, the direct disadvantages of corruption—grand and petty corruption—clearly prevail. Corruption in the public and private sector causes substantial material and non-material damage to individuals and the general public (European Commission, 2014, p. 2).[6]

Regarding the importance of combating corruption in the public as well as in the private sector, the following shall be remarked briefly: If vital institutions of an orderly community life are increasingly privatized in the framework of global competition (the general economic order, anyway, but also with regard to healthcare, water supply, telecommunications, the penitentiary system and so

---

[3] For the concept of social capital see Petermann (2015, p. 19 et seq.)

[4] Contemporary Compliance tends to develop into a rather bureaucratic and very principled concept—thus hampering or even destroying informal communication and relationships. This outcome is dysfunctional for the communication and workflows within large organizations for they rely on a certain amount of tolerance towards informal approaches and solutions. Succumbing to compliance as a management task, supposedly without alternative, impairs the efforts to search for alternative concepts for law abidance see Armbruster (2013, p. 9); Bergmann (2015, p. 346) et seq.; Kropf and Newbury-Smith (2016, p. 3) et seq.; Schröder (forthcoming) part 3.

[5] Especially, ambitious and out-of-proportion compliance schemes create new legal risks due to supplementary promises made to customers, the adoption of foreign law standards (especially U.S. and arab states' law requirements), a malevolent interpretation of internal target shortfalls and the intermixture of state and soft law for didactic reasons see Hugger (2012, p. 67); Dannecker and Schröder (2016) margin nos. 138, 159; Kuhlen (2009, p. 22) et seq.; Rotsch (2015) para. 2 margin no. 5; Schröder (2017, p. 284) et seq., Zimmermann (2014, p. 82, 2014, p. 92, 2014, p. 247, 2014, p. 275) et seq.

[6] For a discussion of the negative effects of corruption on business organizations (i.e., corporate fines, confiscations, exclusion from public tenders, reputational damage etc.) out of which corruption offenses occurred see Greeve (2016 margin nos. 97 et seq).

forth), it should not be doubted that—in addition to the certainly more important corruption prevention measures—anti-corruption criminal law should not only protect the initial reference object of the corruption law (i.e., the national public service and its integrity), but also these private institutions—domestically and abroad.[7]

Irrespective of its concrete coverage by criminal law, corruption is rightly assessed negatively because of its detrimental effects (Graeff, 2002, p. 291f; Schröder, 2016, p. 123 et seq.) In economic terms, corruption leads to overpriced services (including the bribes already incorporated in the tender, see Bannenberg, 2014 margin no. 26) due to the displacement of more efficient competitors and, thus, often inadequate quality, subsequently leading to increased spending in households of both the public and private sector (which, in turn, results in general tax and price increases).

Corruption alone is supposed to cost the economy of the EU member states approximately 120 billion euros each year—hardly less than the annual budget of the EU (European Commission, 2014, p. 3). The EU itself protects its financial interests also by means of criminal law. While it is disputed whether Art. 325 Treaty on the Functioning of the European Union (TFEU) provides for area specific legislative powers of the EU itself in the field of criminal law, it is incontrovertible that Art. 325 AEUV demands the EU member states to provide efficient (not necessarily criminal) sanctions to counter fraud and any other illegal activities affecting the financial interests of the EU. According to Art. 4 Directive (EU) 2017/1371, these "other illegal activities" not only comprise money laundering and misappropriation, but also passive and active corruption that involve public officials (see Dannecker and Dannecker, 2016, p. 163 et seq.; Hauck, 2017, p. 460; Rosenau, 2017 margin no. 17). Further, Art. 4 Regulation (EU) 2017/1939 stipulates that the newly established European Public Prosecutor's Office (EPPO) shall be responsible for investigating, prosecuting and bringing to judgment the perpetrators of and accomplices to criminal offenses

---

[7] For the debate on the legitimacy of new penal legislation to combat corruption in the private sector (focusing on the example of the German health care sector) see Dannecker and Schröder (2017 margin no. 52 et seq.) with further references.

affecting the financial interests of the Union (see Brodowski, 2017, p. 684). Therefore, the EU has emphasized the importance it gives to anti-corruption measures by fathering its own institution to combat and chase down on—often tender-related and, therefore, corporate—corruption.

Corruption hits poorer countries disproportionately hard because it prompts the redirection of funding that was supposed to contribute to the improvement of education, infrastructure and other instruments of future economic growth—instead it cements inequality and social injustice for the benefit of a few. Corruption also deters (foreign) investors.

It is therefore a major obstacle to growth, especially for underdeveloped countries (Annan, 2004; Lambsdorff and Beck, 2009, p. 22 et seq.; Lambsdorff and Beck, 2009, p. 19). Thus, corruption is also one of the most evident manifestations of our western "externalization society" (Lessenich, 2016, p. 77 et seq.).

No less damaging is the macrosocial damage caused by corruption. It undermines institutions—and public confidence in them—that are essential for a successful civil society. Or—following the vocabulary of the latest financial crisis—institutions that are "systematically relevant" (Dölling, 2007, p. 27; Graeff, 2002, p. 298 et seq.; Graeff, 2002, p. 291). If the citizens' confidence in the incorruptibility of the actors in the respective subsystem decreases, the willingness to "accept" their offers, recommendations and decisions will be diminished and thus a condition for the functionality of important subsystems as a whole (Loos, 1974, p. 889 et seq.).[8] With regard to further white-collar crime, corruption can also have a "suction and spiral" effect (Bannenberg, 2014 margin no. 28; Schmitt-Leonardy, 2013, p. 58 et seq.; Tiedemann, 1980, p. 37, 1980, p. 1) because it is often related to additional penal offenses, e. g., money laundering, tax evasion, fraud and so forth (Dölling, 2007, p. 28). Generally speaking—and the current surveys unfortunately just mentioned account for the following statement—the overall general public tends to put aside the interests of third

---

[8] With regard to bribery involving public officials pursuant to sections 331 et seq. German Criminal Code.

parties and the community and to recklessly enforce its personal interests in the wake of corruption (Dölling, 1996, p. 28).

The detection of bribery and corruption is made difficult by a certain features of these offenses. It may be true that in the face of the negative implications outlined above, it seems to be an inadequately heuphemistic description to label corruption offenses as "victimless crimes" (see Bannenberg, 2014 margin no. 27; Korte, 2014 margin no. 12).[9] Third persons and the general public are severely harmed by bribery offenses. However, this frequently mentioned catchphrase does correctly point to the fact that the offenders on both sides of an illicit arrangement expect the deal to be beneficial to them (Graeff, 2002, p. 298 et seq.; Schmidt, 2003, p. 87 et seq.). For this reason, neither the donor nor the beneficiary has a natural interest in the revelation of the offense. Confessions are rarely to be expected at the outset of criminal investigations due to the frequent difficulties proving an intentional connection between the benefit on the one hand and the possible professional decision-making in this context on the other hand (Dannecker and Schröder, 2017 margin no. 134). Therefore, the ratio of unreported corruption cases is very high. Estimates for Germany go as far as to assess that approximately 95 % of corruption in the public sector remains undetected (Bannenberg and Schaupensteiner, 2007, p. 40).

In addition, the high professional qualifications often required to be able to dispose of the necessary resources (on the donor side) or to take the desired decision (on the receiving side) regularly point to the fact that the intelligence and cunning of corruption perpetrators is at least not below average.

If bribery within an organization is endemic, that is to say, it is arising cumulatively from or within a particular company, then it is often accompanied by certain symptoms—such as the existence of slush funds or fictitious consultancy agreements. These measures are designed to circumvent internal and external control mechanisms. Such elaborate schemes can point to a cooperative and systematic network of deviance that is supported by a group of employees which is insufficiently committed to law abidance. Even though the transactions ena-

---

[9] On the limited explanatory power of the phrase "victimless crime" Wolf (2014, p. 30).

bled by corruption themselves are regularly not voided by law, the unlawful fashion in which these deals are facilitated makes it adequate to regard endemic corruption as second-degree-organized-crime—and in any cases as corporate crime.[10]

## 3 Moving beyond detailed dogmatic discussions

*Thesis 3: The current German discussion on corporate crime initially needs to step back from detailed dogmatic and technical issues and needs to strengthen its focus on the criminology of deviance by corporations and their staff.*

Inevitably, the question arises how the grave legal violations committed by corporate entities can be explained.

Not least, one explanation could lead to the inadequate design of current commercial criminal law regimes, especially their insufficient balancing of the responsibility of corporations on one side and the responsibility of individuals on the other. This issue is a current point of discussion for example in the USA and this paper will return to this debate further on (see below, 10).

However, the same also applies to the German corporate sanctions regime. According to an increasingly endorsed viewpoint, this regime is suffering from various shortcomings, such as the absence of the mandatory prosecution principle, its unequal application by insufficiently sensitized law enforcement agencies, inadequate sanctions—all in all also resulting in an insufficient symbolic impact.[11]

---

[10] For a discussion of the – controversial – features linked to the term of organized crime, see Kirkpatrick (2016, p. 378) for further references. For further descriptions of the term "organized crime" see also Art. 2a United Nations Convention against Transnational Organized Crime of 15 Nov. 2000 and Section 2.1 of Attachment E of the German Guidelines for criminal and administrative fine proceedings of 1 Sep. 2016 ("Richtlinien für das Strafverfahren und das Bußgeldverfahren").

[11] To counter this criticism, the German Federal Ministry of Justice and Consumer Protection presented a draft bill for a new Corporate Sanctions Act in August 2019. For an overview of the preceding discussion see the papers gathered in the conference proceedings by Henssler et al. (2017); Jahn et al. (2016); Kempf et al. (2012). Further contributions to the legal controversy include Böse (2014); Dannecker (2001); Ehrhardt (1994); Freier (2009); Frisch (2013); Greco (2015); Heine (1995); Hirsch (1995); Hoven (2014); Kirch-Heim (2010); Kubiciel (2014); Mitsch

Further, the German corporate crime proceedings of the recent past cannot serve to falsify this assertion. Firstly, they were predominantly directed against individual persons and secondly, most of the accusations related to the embezzlement of funds and therefore to internal affairs (cf. the criminal proceedings with regard to Mannesmann, Sal. Oppenheim, HSH-Nordbank and even the Siemens case). Thus, offenses against third parties or the general public committed by companies were at least not in the limelight of these trials.

Notwithstanding these possible shortcomings, however, this paper shall not focus on a detailed analysis of the current law, but rather on preliminary considerations to reorganize commercial criminal law and in particular corporate criminal law. Although existing law is an important starting point, it seems at least to be equally important to include all other criminological factors as well in order to substantiate a "constructive and rational vote" against the current law regime.

The sociologist Erving Goffman (1974; 1997, p. 221 et seq.) has paid a lot of attention to the holistic method of observing and possibly evaluating all actual circumstances. His "frame analysis" requires not only taking into account the social role of other social actors—but also the protagonist's own prejudices, values and reflections. With his concept of observing and describing everyday phenomena, it becomes easier to determine the perspectives of the respective actors and, above all, their respective limitations. Especially, the legal actor's "framing" of a situation or problem becomes visible. Then, the legislator can and should also explain the objectives of his legislation, the assessments and value conceptions he builds on, his understanding of companies and market rules, and the responsibilities he assigns to companies on the one hand and individuals on the other in the case of commercial criminal law and so forth.

This seemingly tedious task of gathering all sorts of information, judgements and prejudices is firstly of added value to legislative procedure because the mere conduct of this task already reveals the complexity of legislative decisions. Secondly, and even more importantly, it also makes transparent the necessity for a

---

(2014); Mittelsdorf (2007); Ortmann (2017); Ransiek (1996); Rogall (2015); Rönnau and Wegner (2014); Rotsch (1998); Sachoulidou (forthcoming); Schmitt-Leonardy (2013); Schroth (1993); Schünemann (2014); Zieschang (2014).

reduction of complexity and, in order to do so, forces the legislator to disclose his instruments, preferences and priorities applied in order to reach a well-considered decision.

As a prerequisite for detailed dogmatic discussions on the design of a future corporate criminal law, it seems particularly useful to continue the efforts made in commercial criminology (Krüger, 2013, p. 403; Mittelsdorf, 2007; Sachoulidou, 2019; Schmitt-Leonardy, 2013; Trunk, 2013, p. 421) to better understand the situation and motivation of white-collar offenders acting in the context of business enterprises. According to this understanding, a comprehensive legal approach—which also includes criminal law—that has a chance to lead to better norm acceptance in and by companies, can be deployed.

In the context of company-related criminal charges this implies taking into consideration both the realities of corporations and of individual members of these organizations.

## 4  Realities of corporate activities in the modern world[12]

*Thesis 4: Corporations are key protagonists of the 21st century and need to take responsibility for the diffusion of individual accountability in the modern working world.*

Today's working landscape—not only in transnational corporations, but especially there—is shaped by the differentiation of tasks and responsibilities. Partly because and partly in spite of the advent of new technologies, it is widely accepted that a new wave of division of labor is inevitable. Further, the current period of globalization tends to increasingly promote work segmentation for, as Adam Smith (1976, p. 31) famously phrased it: "[…] the division of labor […] must always be limited by the extent […] of the market".

Therefore, corporations and their bodies need to delegate the tasks und duties arising. Or, more precisely from a legal point of view: A delegation of duties in terms of a unilateral discharge from legal duties is inconceivable. Rather, assign-

---

[12] This section (4.) derives from Schröder (2019, parts 1.1 and 2.1.2).

ing tasks and duties to lower-level staff results in a modification of their own original obligations: They then become control und surveillance duties for the top management.

However, these duties are not designed to hold managerial staff criminally responsible for each and every violation of law committed by the organization. Further, in many cases, regulations on surveillance duties will only—if at all—serve as a deficient substitute for the absent possibility of attributing the primary violation of law within an organization to an individual. For the division of labor correlates with a diffusion of responsibility (Schmitt-Leonardy, 2013, p. 260 et seq.). In particular (but not exclusively) with regard to negligence offenses, mere causal contributions of an individual within a complex workflow are not sufficient to constitute charges of negligent behavior. The combined occurrence of "aimless contributions" by individuals and the "systemic collective responsibility" (Mittelsdorf, 2007, p. 61) of the organizational body have already led several lawmakers (e.g., Germany, Switzerland, USA) to lower the requirements regarding the proof of individual law violations as a prerequisite of corporate criminal responsibility.

Organizations can be characterized as key protagonists of the 21st century due to their sheer size and the plenitude of power that is associated with them. Their ontological status as "corporate actors" (Luhmann, 1964, p. 185; Schmitt-Leonardy, 2013, p. 384, 2013, p. 154 et seq., p. 456) can no longer be disputed at least in terms of institutional facts.[13] As the German business economist Günther Ortmann (2010, p. 9) phrased it, business corporations greatly enlarge the possibilities and potentials to act responsibly but also to act irresponsibly. Today, internal dynamics and the rise of organizations' autonomous intentions may lead to corporate behavior that is very different from the intentions of the individuals who make up these organizations. For them, a corporation was a means to their ends and according to Ortmann, it was not foreseeable then and is presently no longer avoidable that organizations became mighty corporate protagonists which have—on a large scale—severed the ties that had closely linked them to the objectives of their supposed leaders.

---

[13] For a general theory of institutional facts see Searle (1995, p. 31, p. 79, p. 113) et seq.

## 5 Attitudes of individuals acting for and within corporations

*Thesis 5: People that are sufficiently law-abiding in their private environment develop a "tactical relationship" towards law when acting in their role as employees.*

If company members commit criminal offenses, their situation and motivation deserves special attention. It seems particularly interesting to investigate which values, preferences and attitudes generally characterize these persons—and this is precisely what was being done at the Herrenhausen Symposium and by the members of the research group "The Fight against Manipulation and Corruption"[14] over the last years.

In grossly simplified terms, there seem to be two conversed assumptions regarding corporate perpetrators: On the one hand, white-collar offenders within corporations could be assessed as persons with a general willingness to deviate that also characterizes them in their private lives. On the other hand, these persons may be "averagely compliant people" that predominantly become offenders due to the various pressures exerted upon them in business enterprises, namely due to a deviant corporate culture, a corresponding esprit de corps and a lack of lawful conduct by the company leadership. To put it pointedly: Do law-abiding citizens become criminal when entering the office and do they cast off the compliant part of their personality in order to slip into their suit and tie (Schmitt-Leonardy, 2013, p. 60 et seq.)? At least the surveys presented at the outset of this paper (see above, 1.) suggest that actors in the field of economic life perceive law as a "tactical factor" (Luhmann, 1964, p. 307).

This attitude is the factual manifestation of a legal debate, particularly in the USA, on the limits of permissible behavior in the market, which can be characterized by the contrasting slogans "law-as-price" vs. "law-as-limit" (Fleischer, 2005, p. 147 taking up terminology coined by Williams 1998, 1280 et seq.).

For the "law-as-price" concept, questions of efficiency and expediency are the crucial factor. To each possible action plan there are attached legal "price tags"

---

[14] For the online presence of the project see the website of the Heidelberg Research Group.

of different sizes. According to these preferences for decision-making, only significant detection risks, draconian punishments and severe risks of reputational damage motivate company personnel to prefer the less efficient but compliant business decision.

From a sociological perspective, this criminal behavior may further be interpreted as "useful illegality", a term coined by the sociologist Niklas Luhmann. According to a current interpretation of this concept, white-collar crime is not motivated by personal gains but rather by the notion of responsible staff that the infringement of formal expectations is helpful for the overall performance of the organization (Bull and Mehde, 2015, p. 76 et seq.; question left open by Hank and Meck, 2015; Kühl, 2007, p. 273; Kühl and Billerbeck, 2016; Pohlmann and Markova, 2011, p. 170 et seq.).

However, it seems doubtful whether this concept can be applied to violations of state law in a way that illegality was in fact functional for the corporation: Law will always aim at raising the costs of illegality to a non-useful level (Schröder, 2019, parts 2.5.3 and 3). Hence, it seems that useful illegality is merely a matter of the accounting period[15]: In the long term, state law will always push not only to even out but also to retaliate against illegal behavior—therefore leaving the mere and reckless hope of remaining undetected as the only aspect that sustains the concept of useful illegality. Otherwise, illegality with regard to state laws is regularly dysfunctional.

Still, the term of "useful illegality" may provide some explanatory power as firstly, it serves to highlight a contemptuous attitude within corporations towards law that is calling for new answers and legal concepts. Secondly, the widespread recourse to "useful illegality" indicates that the legal regime in place to counteract this manner of conducting business is insufficient and therefore itself dysfunctional.

---

[15] For a similar assessment see Ortmann (2003, p. 255): "It is a painful insight that the recourse to 'system requirements' is by no means able to control the dimensions of rule abidance and rule infringements. Rather, the concept of 'system requirements' turns out to be far too ambiguous and itself depending on the relative perspectives, situations and contexts that it could be capable of establishing a clear and generally valid dividing line. On the contrary, often enough it only transpires ex post facto which action is [or would have been] of use for the system requirements."

## 6 The ungrateful task of compliance in corporations taking a dubious stance towards law

*Thesis 6: The current sub-system of compliance and its staff are overstrained in an overall system governed by the notion of "useful illegality".*

Compliance as a sub-system is dependent on the main decision-makers and the corporate culture to be in accordance with the key messages of the compliance unit. If "useful illegality" is part of corporate culture, it contradicts compliance efforts and ridicules its aims and methods while at the same time placing compliance staff at high legal risks (see Schröder, 2019, part 2.5.2). Increasing this tendency, the current German corporate crime system tends to allow for "double standards" of compliance and law enforcement by vigorously pursuing individual intentional law infringements while leaving a generous amount of leeway for managerial staff and the organization itself. It is not exceptional that compliance is tailored to mainly exonerate the board of directors and therefore aims at combining "knowledge management" with strict guidelines for lower level staff (Schröder, 2017, p. 295, 299, 301). If compliance is designed in such a manner, a criminal corporate culture may persist while at the same time cauterizing efficient informal structures at lower levels that are, comparatively speaking, rather innocuous.

## 7 Restriction on the punishment of individuals

*Thesis 7: In Germany, the focus of prevention in the field of white-collar crime is on "natural persons" who are obligated to rules, monitored and sanctioned. Corporate compliances systems are also focused on obligating and monitoring individuals. However, there are clear auspices for a paradigm shift.*

Speaking in the terms of Goffman's natural frameworks, the dictum "societas delinquere non potest" (a legal entity cannot be sanctioned) seems questionable. The Catholic Church made this statement in the 13th century to avoid being sanctioned by Holy Roman Emperor Frederick II (Tiedemann, 2014 margin nos. 375 et seq.). In a secularised law, an appeal to this thesis of the Middle Ages is at least dubious and probably impermissible.

Law has to be functional: If companies are granted freedom and privileges, they may also be subject to obligations. These obligations also have to be enforceable. To that end, sanctions by means of administrative, civil and criminal law are essential.

Corruption and other white-collar crime is traditionally and primarily threatened by punishment. This is reflected in the national legal systems[16] as well as in the guidelines of international organizations (see Dannecker, 2017b, p. 132 et seq.; Dannecker and Dannecker, 2016, p. 163 et seq.) In this area, the application of criminal law is indispensable (Dannecker, 2017b, p. 155 et seq.).

In all European states, corruption in the public as well as the private sector is forbidden and punishable (Vogel and Eisele, 2017 margin no. 60). Criminal sanctions reach up to long term imprisonments and all states also provide for the confiscation of gross profits. Compliance management systems advise on specific behavior of individuals and monitor them accordingly. Nonetheless, we cannot argue that, by this means, effective prevention has already been achieved. Therefore, it seems necessary to seek new approaches to organize an effective system leading to better prevention.

The Anglo-American system traditionally knows the criminal responsibility of companies (in detail Partsch, 2012, p. 55 et seq.; Rogall, 2018 margin nos. 267, 276). There has also been a development towards a criminal responsibility of corporations in the European Union over the past 25 years (see Dannecker, 2017b, p. 129 et seq.). In some special areas (such as the sanctions under antitrust law) German legislation has made a clear turn towards a responsibility of companies as well (Dannecker and Müller, 2014 margin nos. 141 et seq.). With regard to a future corporate criminal law in general it is important to note: Legislation is not bound by traditional concepts of criminal law. Rather, the lawmaker is free to seek for new models of sanctioning and is only limited by the constitution (Dannecker and Dannecker, 2016, p. 171 et seq.). In this context, it seems noteworthy that the draft coalition agreement for a new German federal govern-

---

[16] For a comparative law overview see see Bundesjustizministerium (2002, p. 259)et seq; Rogall (2018 margin nos. 263 et seq).

ment provides for the introduction of a new set of rules to sanction corporate wrongdoing (see CDU et al., 2018) which by now (as of: August 2019) has been followed up by a first draft bill by the German Federal Ministry of Justice and Consumer Protection.

## 8 The legal responsibility of corporations for corruption

*Thesis 8: In addition to the responsibility of "natural persons", companies should be held responsible as actors (see Thesis 4). This requires a corporate criminal law that supplements criminal law against individuals and triggers liability for damages ("private enforcement"). In addition, companies should be obliged to take recourse against their criminal employees.*

Corruption has two faces: individual and organizational corruption (Zimmermann, 1999, p. 858). The current fight against corruption aiming at individual behaviour is insufficient. Rather, an organizational approach is necessary that places companies as independent actors, as responsible subjects apart from individual responsibility. Appropriate prevention of corruption therefore requires both: individual responsibility and corporate responsibility.[17]

According to current German law, legal entities—and not enterprises—can only be subject to an administrative fine, not to criminal sanctions. The current German situation thus differs from the extensive conception of the European Union, which refers to the enterprise as a commercial economic unit (Dannecker and Dannecker, 2016, p. 166; Dannecker and Müller, 2014 margin no. 206). This is the acknowledgement of an actual criminal liability for enterprises already long practiced in the Anglo-American sphere.

As of today, it is consensus that civil liability law should also be included to supplement the effectiveness of penal sanctions through private enforcement (see also Sarhan, 2006, p. 21 et seq. with further references; Schmitt-Leonardy, 2016, p. 294). It has to be made easier for the damaged parties to assert their damage

---

[17] In Switzerland, where the legal responsibility of corporations is in principle only applied if the punishment of a natural person is not possible, corporations are punished in addition to the responsibility of natural persons in the field of corruption; see Rogall (2018 margin no. 274).

claims against the individual and corporate perpetrators (Schmitt-Leonardy, 2013 margin nos. 875 et seq.). The fact that this is quite easily possible has already been proven in the field of antitrust law. There, the enforcement of damages is facilitated by the circumstance that a final criminal guilty verdict is legally binding for the civil courts.[18] Therefore, the civil courts have to assess only the amount of damages.

Further, the companies should be obliged to take recourse against the individual perpetrators to reduce the corporate damage suffered.[19]

## 9 Priority of special prevention and measures to improve compliance in the company

*Thesis 9: The punishment of companies should not be based on deterrence by means of draconian penalties, but on moderate penalties supplemented by compliance measures.*

Administrative sanctions can only be imposed if they are proportionate (Dannecker, 2017b, p. 149, 2017c, p. 22; Lüderssen, 2012, p. 387 et seq.). This means that they have to be suitable, necessary and adequate. This has the disadvantage that administrative fines, as they have to pass the suitability test, are regularly extremely high (Dannecker, 2017c, p. 21; Papakiriakou, 2002, p. 157). Criminal sanctions, on the other hand, only have to be appropriate to the defendant's guilt (Miebach and Maier, 2016 margin nos. 32 et seq.).

But what goals should be pursued when criminal sanctions are imposed on corporations? In the United States, but also in the antitrust law of the European Union, extremely high fines are imposed to achieve deterrence. Crime should not pay off. However, the experience in antitrust cases shows that even extremely high fines do not prevent subsequent offenses.[20]

---

[18] See section 33b para. 4 s. 2 of the Act against Restraints of Competition ("GWB").
[19] This, however, cannot be extended to a recourse regarding corporate fines (see below, 10.).
[20] See with regard to Europe: Nowak (2016 margin no. 4); with regard to the USA: United States Sentencing Commission (2016, p. 323 et seq.).

On the other hand, Austria aims at special prevention through criminal sanctions against enterprises. In particular, comparatively low fines are imposed especially in cases of tax evasion. These sanctions can be suspended for probation partially or completely under the condition that a compliance system is introduced or improved.[21]

Prevention of corruption should begin with the socialisation of the staff and aim at their integrity (Bussmann, 2016, p. 54 et seq.). Therefore, as we all know by now, an integrative corporate culture is indispensable (Bussmann, 2016, p. 52).

Therefore, socialisation within the enterprise plays a vital role (Bussmann, 2016, p. 52). In addition, modern morality research discovered a fragmentation of norm validity (Nunner-Winkler, 2000, p. 332 with further references). Although offenses are generally condemned, the validity of norms is made dependent on the current corporate situation. Depending on situation and context, rules are applied differently as it has already been mentioned in this paper (see above, Thesis 5): Honest people believe that they are allowed to act unlawful in their roles as agents of the enterprise. Still, they seem to conceive themselves as honorable citizens. It is therefore necessary to take up further insights of ethical research: It is increasingly observed that phenomena of "voluntary self-commitment to insight", including insight into the common good, are also possible within corporate working conditions if they are fostered and incentivized—which is first and foremost the task of a top echelon committing itself to these principles as well (Bussmann, 2016, p. 52; Nunner-Winkler, 1997, p. 381 et seq.).

This assumption calls for the enterprise and its managerial staff to promote "integrity". Firstly, it is obvious that practices that are legally and socially highly questionable are not conducted. But also, opening communication channels on ethically difficult business decisions in advance is paramount (Bussmann, 2016, p. 57). Retributions against staff that is seeking help from the compliance department or their superiors regarding difficult legal or ethical issues have to remain an exception.

---

[21] A similar rule is introduced in sections 7 para. 1 no. 2, 8 para. 2 no. 3 VerbStrG-E NRW (Draft Corporate Criminal Law Code, published by the Ministry of Justice of North Rhine-Westphalia in 2014); see Hein (2014, p. 78 et seq.).

Therefore, compliance programs, and, much more important, the DNA of the umbrella organization, has to include a "surplus" of corporate responsibility and should discontinue standard corporate actions on the verge of the acceptable (Rotsch, 2015 para 1 margin no. 7; Schorn, 2016 margin no. 25).

This leads to the question of how detailed a compliance system should be. Or, to put it more pointedly: How much bureaucratization is permissible? Compliance measures must not lead to over-protection and over-socialization, to the constraint or even termination of creativity and innovation (Bussmann, 2016, p. 50 et seq.; Hölters, 2017 margin no. 99). Progress based on new ideas and developments are indispensable if an enterprise is to succeed on the market. Furthermore, a climate of distrust must not arise. Otherwise, circumvention strategies are imminent and compliance becomes counterproductive (Bussmann, 2016, p. 50 et seq.). Thus, a balance between trust and control is required, that is not detrimental to enterprises. Therefore, we should dare to trust in principles instead of drafting rule after rule (Bussmann, 2016, p. 53 et seq.; Schröder, 2019, part 3).

## 10 Parallel sanctioning of employees and the company

*Thesis 10: The punishment of employees and the enterprise should not be applied alternatively, but cumulatively. The possibility of the company taking recourse against its employees for a penalty imposed on the company itself has to be ruled out.*

The principle of culpability (see Miebach and Maier, 2016 margin nos. 28 et seq.; Streng, 2017 margin nos. 19 et seq.) is one of the fundamental pillars on which contemporary German criminal law is based ("Lissabon Ruling" of the Federal Constitutional Court, BVerfGE 123, 267, margin no. 364). Culpability is invariably related to wrongfulness. Criminal liability is always a legal liability and therefore has to be aligned with the responsibility of the culprit in question.

Everyone is responsible for the injustice they have committed. It is also possible for several persons to be individually responsible for a particular damage in different ways (Joecks, 2017 margin nos. 300 et seq.). This has to include the responsibility of the enterprise itself.

Therefore, one of the great assignments still lying ahead for the design of a convincing structure of corporate criminal responsibility is to balance organizational and individual contributions to a criminal offense—as well as to spread and balance the sanctions between corporate persons and natural entities acting within the sphere of influence of these persons (see Mittelsdorf, 2007, p. 175 et seq.; Rönnau and Wegner, 2014, p. 159 et seq.; Sachoulidou, 2019, part 3, A II.; Schmitt-Leonardy, 2013, p. 494 et seq.; Schröder, 2016, p. 462 et seq.; Trüg, 2016, p. 315 et seq.).

The issue of assessing and balancing corporate and individual responsibility is not only important for the sentencing structures within a future commercial criminal law regime. Rather, an adequate balance is already essential for the design of behavioral norms, including the design of purely preventive, non-retributive elements of legal behavioral control within the economic realm.

However, a side glance at the situation in the United States shows that, despite parallel responsibility, the main focus of a corporate criminal law regime can be problematic. While in the U.S. the criminal prosecution of companies was at the center of attention of many law enforcement agencies for a long time, this seems to have changed recently by means of the "Yates Memorandum" of 2015 (see Deputy Attorney General Yates, S.Q., of the United States Department of Justice, 2015, p. 1, 4; discussed by Kelly and Mandelbaum, 2016; Luttermann, 2016; Mayer, 2016; Pant, 2015). The interest in maintaining an efficient and deterring criminal law system in cases of corporate misconduct has prompted the U.S. Department of Justice to shift the focus of its criminal law enforcement from corporate criminal responsibility towards seeking accountability from the individuals who perpetrated the wrongdoing. This was "one of the most effective ways to combat corporate misconduct" (Deputy Attorney General Yates, S.Q., of the United States Department of Justice, 2015, p. 1). For this reason, the "Yates Memorandum" requires corporate defendants to pass on all available detrimental information regarding the investigated conduct of its managerial staff as a prerequisite of a settlement. The quintessence of the so-called "Yates Memorandum" therefore lies in an uncompromising pursuit of individuals as responsible persons. At least it can be said that a future structure of corporate criminal law in Europe should have its reservations regarding this concept due to the rule of law (Dannecker, 2017c, p. 41).

A corporation is to be understood as a holder of primary obligations, which encompass the business as a whole. The obligations of the individual members of the corporation derive from these obligations (Dannecker, 2015 margin nos. 14 et seq.).

A sole responsibility of individual staff members may arise if the individual commits an offense that may be connected to their function as a member of staff, but still has to be deemed an excess offense because it is committed on their own initiative and against the interests of the company. In addition, a sole responsibility of the individual should be considered if the law infringement in question was unavoidable for the corporation or if the corporation did everything possible to prevent that violation of law.[22]

A sole responsibility of the corporation comes into play if the individual cannot be identified. From the perspective of criminal law, this is especially relevant in view of failures to act with regard to duties of staff selection and supervision (Hoven et al., 2014, p. 162 et seq.; Kubiciel and Hoven, 2016, p. 170 et seq.).

On the other hand, corporations and their staff are jointly responsible if a body of the corporation commits a criminal offense, if a duty is violated that originally addressed the corporation or if supervisory obligations regarding staff members are violated (Kubiciel, 2014, p. 136). If one is to assume an original responsibility of corporations, it—on the one hand—includes its internal organization (the structuring of hierarchies, the arrangement of the division of labor and safeguarding of adequate supervision and control mechanisms) and—on the other hand—exerting influence on the behavior of the employees in order for them to respect the legal rights of third parties and to ward off the specific systemic risks stemming from a certain corporation (especially shaping a corporate culture that complies with legal obligations). Nowadays, the necessity of anti-corruption compliance is out of question (see Bannenberg, 2014 margin nos. 36 et seq.; Greeve, 2016 margin nos. 177 et seq.) However, and as just mentioned, compliance cannot prevent every kind of corruption. Therefore, one needs to clarify the

---

[22] Example for an excess offense, BGHSt 52, 323; Kubiciel and Hoven (2016 margin nos. 170 et seq.)

wrongfulness enterprises are accountable for. These should be the risks exclusively stemming from the corporate system (Dannecker, 2017c, p. 63 et seq.). If an individual wrongdoing could have been prevented by corporate supervision, a corporate criminal responsibility has to be considered. Not least, this seems appropriate as institutions possess a stronger potential to act rationally than individuals.

The discussion in the USA provides at least ample warning that an often very profitable corporate fines system may distract the legislator and law enforcement agencies from the fact that criminal law proceedings against high level individuals responsible remain a vital component for combatting corporate crime. Therefore, regular reviews and possible adjustments in the overall strategy will always be necessary at regular intervals.

If an individual commits a legal infringement that affects third parties and/or the general public, the corporation is only responsible for internal procedures. If the corporation was not able to foresee and prevent law infringements committed by an individual, the former cannot be held responsible (Kubiciel and Hoven, 2016, p. 170 et seq.). One could argue that it seems at any rate appropriate to establish statutory grounds for mitigation of the penalty in favor of an individual accused should it become apparent that the organization ordered him or her to perform tasks that could hardly be achieved by lawful means, only. For instance, one may recall the performance targets for bank employees in the United States (see Ortmann, 2017, p. 248) that may even have contributed to the subprime mortgage crisis in 2007.

If the original corporate guilt within a system of corporate criminal responsibility can be defined as either wrongdoing by its managerial bodies or as a lack of surveillance with regard to law infringements committed by lower-level staff, then the possibility of the company to take recourse against its employees for a penalty imposed on the company itself has to be ruled out. Regarding the parallel discussion taking place in the field of corporate law, more and more scholars also agree that the raison d'être of penalties against corporations does not allow for any recourse of the legal entity against its employees for the amount it was fined (Fleischer, 2014; Grunewald, 2016; Lotze and Smolinski, 2015; Thomas, 2015; see also LAG Düsseldorf, ZIP 2015, p. 829).

The parallel sanctioning of employees and the company does not violate the prohibition of double jeopardy under the German constitution (Art. 103 para. 3 Basic Law) because the penalties are directed at separate addressees. Further, the possible collateral effects on employees that may be caused by sanctions against their employer are not relevant to this case as the individual staff member is not the target of the corporate fine. However, an overall system of corporate criminal law allowing for parallel sanctioning still has to be in line with the principle of proportionality which also has constitutional status in Germany. In this regard, it is of special importance that the principle of proportionality has also got to be observed regarding any preventive measures that may be administered and any compensations awarded as a result of corporate wrongdoing (Poelzig and Bauermeister, 2017, p. 568).

## 11    Promoting the detection and termination of corruptive behaviour

*Thesis 11: Due to the lack of visible victims and of damages caused by corruption and due to the regular involvement of a group of persons in corporate corruptive structures, the introduction of a leniency system is recommendable.*

As already addressed, corruption is characterized by its invisibility. Thus, whistleblowers may be of some importance (Dannecker, 2017a margin no. 67a). However, a leniency program may be far more important in view of the mentioned difficulties. This concept has already been introduced in an area of similar structure and discretion where it is very successful—anti-trust law:[23] In order to reward support in antitrust-investigations, a leniency program was introduced at the European level. This regulation was introduced by the European Commission in 1996 (European Commission, 1996, p. 4) and was revised in 2006 (European Commission, 2006, p. 17). It has been the cornerstone of cartel prosecution for over 20 years now. All antitrust proceedings in which fines are imposed are nowadays initiated on the basis of leniency statements. If a corporation discloses its participation in a cartel, the Commission waives the fine which otherwise

---

[23] Half of the antitrust cases conducted by the German Federal Antitrust Office ("Bundeskartellamt") originate from the leniency program, which was established in the year 2000; see Bundeskartellamt (2017).

would have been imposed, provided that the business is the first to give information and pieces of evidence which enable the Commission to carry out specific investigations related to the infringement.[24] The Commission only waives the fine if it does not already possess sufficient evidence to carry out an investigation in connection with the cartel at the time of the disclosure and if the Commission has not discovered an infringement on its own. Corporations that disclose their participation in a cartel and do not meet the conditions for a waiver of the fine may at least benefit from a reduction of the fine which would have been imposed otherwise (European Commission, 2006, p. 17 margin nos. 23 et seq.). Such a reduction requires the corporation to provide the Commission with pieces of evidence regarding the law infringement. Further, these pieces of evidence have to be of considerable added value compared to the evidence the Commission is already possessing.

A leniency program would facilitate the exposure of corruption and would allow the termination of criminal behavior without criminal proceedings in cases of self-incrimination.

---

[24] Concerning the requirements in detail see European Commission (2006, p. 17 margin nos. 8 et seq.)

## 12 Conclusion: Comprehensive responsibility of corporations while recognizing them as corporate citizens

*Thesis 12: If companies are comprehensively committed to the law and made responsible under criminal law, they must be provided with the legal guarantees traditionally associated with criminal law. Corporations must receive the status of corporate citizens.*

Finally, another thought on a lawful and civilized corporate criminal law shall be briefly introduced. For this purpose, it seems useful to return to the perspective presented by Goffman's method: It had been outlined that the consideration of all possible circumstances of the outside world broadens the horizon and helps to achieve a corporate criminal law regime that is hopefully consistent with social reality.

However, the necessary reduction of complexity in the course of drafting such laws has to respect the boundaries set by the constitutional and European law—even at the expense of efficiency. The case law of the European Court of Human Rights provides guidelines (see Esser, 2018 para. 9 margin no. 132; Gaede, 2013, p. 58 et seq.; Gaede, 2013 margin nos. 13 et seq.; Satzger, 2016 para. 11 margin nos. 105 et seq.), which could be transferred to enterprises in order to establish such a system of guarantees.

If enterprises are responsible as corporate citizens, they have to be granted the rights of citizens. Therefore, especially the right to remain silent has to be granted to corporations, too (Dannecker and Dannecker, 2016, p. 177).

# References

Annan, K. A. (2004) 'Foreword', in *United Nations Office on drugs and crime United Nations convention against corruption* [Online], New York. Available at http://www.unodc.org/documents/treaties/UNCAC/Publications/Convention/08-50026_E.pdf.

Armbruster, B. (2013) 'Damit alles schön ordentlich abläuft', *duz - Deutsche Universitätszeitung*, 2013, p. 9 [Online]. Available at http://www.duz.de/duz-magazin/2013/03/damit-alles-schoen-ordentlich-ablaeuft/156 (Accessed 13 August 2018).

Bannenberg, B. (2014) '12. Kapitel Korruption', in Wabnitz, H.-B., Janovsky, T. and Bannenberg, B. (eds) *Handbuch des Wirtschafts- und Steuerstrafrechts* [Online], 4th edn, München, Beck. Available at https://beck-online.beck.de/?vpath=bibdata/komm/HdbWirtschSteuerstrafR_4/cont/HdbWirtschSteuerstrafR%2Ehtm.

Bannenberg, B. and Schaupensteiner, W. (2007) *Korruption in Deutschland: Portrait einer Wachstumsbranche*, 3rd edn, München, Beck.

Bergmann, J. (2015) 'Scheiternde Rechtsnormbildung im Rahmen von Compliance-Kontrolle', *Neue Kriminalpolitik*, vol. 16, no. 4, pp. 346–358.

Bernsmann, K., Rausch, K. and Gatzweiler, N. (2014) *Verteidigung bei Korruptionsfällen* [Online], 2nd edn, Heidelberg, München, Landsberg, Frechen, Hamburg, Müller. Available at https://www.juris.de/perma?d=samson-SHJRhjrh-vkorrT0000.

Böse, M. (2014) 'Strafbarkeit juristischer Personen – Selbstverständlichkeit oder Paradigmenwechsel im Strafrecht', *Zeitschrift für die gesamte Strafrechtswissenschaft*, vol. 126, no. 1.

Brodowski, D. (2017) 'Die europäische Staatsanwaltschaft – eine Einführung', *StV – Strafverteidiger*, vol. 37, no. 10, p. 684.

Bull, H. P. and Mehde, V. (2015) *Allgemeines Verwaltungsrecht mit Verwaltungslehre*, 9th edn, Heidelberg, C.F. Müller.

Bundesjustizministerium (2002) 'Referat II A 1', in Hettinger, M. (ed) *Verbandsstrafe: Bericht der Arbeitsgruppe "Strafbarkeit juristischer Personen" an die Kommission nebst Gutachten sowie Auszug aus dem Abschlußbericht der Kommission zur Reform des strafrechtlichen Sanktionenrechts*, Baden-Baden, Nomos-Verl.-Ges.

Bundeskartellamt (2017) *Bonusregelung* [Online]. Available at http://www.bundeskartellamt.de/DE/Kartellverbot/Bonusregelung/bonusregelung_node.html (Accessed 12 August 2018).

Bussmann, K.-D. (2016) 'Integrität durch nachhaltiges Compliance Management über Risiken, Werte und Unternehmenskultur', *CCZ – Corporate-Compliance-Zeitschrift*, vol. 9, no. 2, p. 50.

CDU, CSU and SPD (2018) *Ein neuer Aufbruch für Europa. Eine neue Dynamik für Deutschland. Ein neuer Zusammenhalt für unser Land: Koalitionsvertrag zwischen CDU, CSU und SPD* [Online]. Available at http://www.zeit.de/politik/deutschland/2018-02/koalitionsvertrag.pdf (Accessed 13 August 2018).

Dann, M. (2016) 'Und immer ein Stück weiter – Die Reform des deutschen Korruptionsstrafrechts', *NJW – Neue Juristische Wochenschrift*, vol. 69, no. 4, pp. 203–206.

Dannecker, C. and Schröder, T. (2017) '§ 299a StGB Bestechlichkeit im Gesundheitswesen', in Kindhäuser, U., Neumann, U., Paeffgen, H.-U. and Albrecht, H.-J. (eds) *Strafgesetzbuch* [Online], 5th edn, Baden-Baden, Nomos.

Dannecker, G. (2001) 'Zur Notwendigkeit der Einführung kriminalrechtlicher Sanktionen gegen Verbände', *GA – Goltdammer's Archiv für Strafrecht*, vol. 148, pp. 101–130.

Dannecker, G. (2015) '§ 5 Strafrechtliche Verantwortung nach Delegation', in Beckemper, K. and Rotsch, T. (eds) *Criminal Compliance: Handbuch*, Baden-Baden, Nomos-Verl.-Ges.

Dannecker, G. (2017a) '§ 203 StGB Verletzung von Privatgeheimnissen', in Graf, J. P., Jäger, M., Wittig, P. and Allgayer, P. (eds) *Wirtschafts- und Steuerstrafrecht* [Online], 2nd edn.

Dannecker, G. (2017b) 'Verbandsverantwortlichkeit: Strafe oder bloße Ordnungswidrigkeit – europäische Vorgaben und Entwicklungen', in Leitner, R. and Brandl, R. (eds) *Finanzstrafrecht 2016: Bilanzstrafrecht neu - interdisziplinäre Analyse (Strafecht, Gesellschafts- und Bilanzrecht, Praxis der Wirtschaftsprüfung) ; Verbandsverantwortlichkeit (europäische Vorgaben und Entwicklungen, Verfassungskonformität, Umfang und Grenzen des Opportunitätsprinzips, sachgerechte tax-compliance zur Abwendung der Verbandsverantwortlichkeit für Finanzvergehen ; mit neuester Rechtsprechung und Literatur zum Finanzstrafrecht*.

Dannecker, G. (2017c) 'Zur Ausgestaltung der Verbandsverantwortlichkeit als straf- oder verwaltungsrechtliches Sanktionssystem', in Henssler, M., Hoven, E., Kubiciel, M. and Weigend, T. (eds) *Grundfragen eines modernen Verbandsstrafrechts*, Nomos Verlagsgesellschaft mbH & Co. KG, pp. 15–70.

Dannecker, G. and Dannecker, C. (2016) 'Europäische und verfassungsrechtliche Vorgaben für das materielle und formelle Unternehmensstrafrecht', *NZWiSt – Neue Zeitschrift für Wirtschafts-, Steuer- und Unternehmensstrafrecht*, vol. 5, p. 162.

Dannecker, G. and Müller, N. (2014) '18. Kapitel Kartellstraf- und -ordnungswidrigkeitenrecht', in Wabnitz, H.-B., Janovsky, T. and Bannenberg, B. (eds) *Handbuch des Wirtschafts- und Steuerstrafrechts* [Online], 4th edn, München, Beck.

Dannecker, G. and Schröder, T. (2016) 'Zu den neuen §§ 299a, 299b StGB - auch zu ihren Risiken und Nebenwirkungen', in Hoven, E. and Kubiciel, M. (eds) *Korruption im Gesundheitswesen: Tagungen und Kolloquien* [Online], Baden-Baden, Nomos Verlagsgesellschaft mbH & Co. KG. Available at https://doi.org/10.5771/9783845280080.

Deputy Attorney General Yates, S.Q., of the United States Department of Justice (2015) *Individual Accountability for Corporate Wrongdoing ("Yates-Memorandum")* [Online], United States Department of Justice. Available at https://www.justice.gov/archives/dag/file/769036/download (Accessed 13 August 2018).

Dölling, D. (1996) 'Empfehlen sich Änderungen des Straf- und Strafprozeßrechts, um der Gefahr von Korruption in Staat, Wirtschaft und Gesellschaft wirksam zu begegnen?', in Ständige Deputation des Deutschen Juristentages (ed) *Verhandlungen des Einundsechzigsten Deutschen Juristentages,* München, Beck.

Dölling, D., ed. (2007) *Handbuch der Korruptionsprävention: Für Wirtschaftsunternehmen und öffentliche Verwaltung,* München, Beck.

Ehrhardt, A. (1994) *Unternehmensdelinquenz und Unternehmensstrafe: Sanktionen gegen juristische Personen nach deutschem und US-amerikanischem Recht* (Zugl.: Köln, Univ., Diss., 1993), Berlin, Duncker & Humblot.

Engels, J. I. (2006) 'Politische Korruption in der Moderne: Debatten und Praktiken in Großbritannien und Deutschland im 19. Jahrhundert', *Historische Zeitschrift*, vol. 282, pp. 313–350.

Ernst & Young (2017a) *EMEIA Fraud Survey: Ergebnisse für Deutschland* [Online]. Available at http://www.ey.com/Publication/vwLUAssets/EY_-_EMEIA_Fraud_Survey_%E2%80%93_Ergebnisse_f%C3%BCr_Deutschland_April_2017/$FILE/ey-emeia-fraud-survey-ergebnisse-fuer-deutschland-april-2017.pdf (Accessed 13 August 2018).

Ernst & Young (2017b) *Europe, Middle East, India and Africa (EMEIA) Fraud Study 2017* [Online]. Available at http://www.ey.com/Publication/vwLUAssets/EY_-_EMEIA_Fraud_Survey_2017/$FILE/ey-emeia-fraud-survey-2017.pdf (Accessed 13 August 2018).

Esser, R. (2018) *Europäisches und Internationales Strafrecht,* 2nd edn, München, C.H. Beck.

European Commission (1996) *Notice on the non-imposition or reduction of fines in cartel cases* [Online]. Available at http://eur-lex.europa.eu/legal-content/EN/TXT/HTML/?uri=CELEX:31996Y0718(01)&from=EN (Accessed 13 August 2018).

European Commission (2006) *Notice on Immunity from fines and reduction of fines in cartel cases* [Online]. Available at http://eur-lex.europa.eu/legal-content/EN/TXT/HTML/?uri=CELEX:52006XC1208(04)&from=EN (Accessed 13 August 2018).

European Commission (2014) *Report from the Commission to the Council and the European Parliament: EU Anti-Corruption Report/\*COM/2014/038 final\*/* [Online]. Available at http://eur-lex.europa.eu/legal-content/EN/TXT/HTML/?uri=CELEX:52014DC0038&from=EN (Accessed 13 August 2018).

Eversheds Sutherland (2016) *„Beneath the Surface" – bribery and corruption report 2016* [Online]. Available at http://www.eversheds-sutherland.com/global/en/what/practices/

white-collar-and-investigations/publications/bribery-report/bribery-corruption-report-zmag.page (Accessed 13 August 2018).

Fleischer, H. (2005) 'Aktienrechtliche Legalitätspflicht und „nützliche" Pflichtverletzungen von Vorstandsmitgliedern', *ZIP – Zeitschrift für Wirtschaftsrecht und Insolvenzpraxis*, vol. 25, p. 141.

Fleischer, H. (2014) 'Regresshaftung von Geschäftsleitern wegen Verbandsgeldbußen', *DB – Der Betrieb*, vol. 67, p. 345.

Freier, F. v. (2009) 'Zurück hinter die Aufklärung: Zur Wiedereinführung von Verbandsstrafen', *GA – Goltdammer's Archiv für Strafrecht*, vol. 156, p. 98.

Frisch, W. (2013) 'Strafbarkeit juristischer Personen und Zurechnung', in Zöller, M. A., Hilger, H., Küper, W. and Roxin, C. (eds) *Gesamte Strafrechtswissenschaft in internationaler Dimension. Festschrift für Jürgen Wolter zum 70. Geburtstag am 7. September 2013*, Duncker & Humblot.

Gaede, K. (2013) '§ 3 Grund- und Verfahrensrechte im europäischen Strafverfahren', in Böse, M. (ed) *Europäisches Strafrecht: Mit polizeilicher Zusammenarbeit* [Online], Baden-Baden, Nomos. Available at http://dx.doi.org/10.5771/9783845258393.

Gaede, K. (2014) 'Die Zukunft der europäisierten Wirtschaftskorruption gemäß § 299 StGB: Eine Evaluation des Referentenentwurfs des BMJV vom 13.6.2014', *NZWiSt – Neue Zeitschrift für Wirtschafts-, Steuer- und Unternehmensstrafrecht*, vol. 3, p. 281.

Global Shapers Community (2016) *Annual Survey 2016* [Online]. Available at http://bhbcucusa.org/wp-content/uploads/2016/12/report.pdf (Accessed 13 August 2018).

Global Shapers Community (2017) *Annual Survey 2017* [Online]. Available at http://shaperssurvey2017.org/static/data/WEF_GSC_Annual_Survey_2017.pdf (Accessed 13 August 2018).

Goffman, E. (1974) *Frame analysis: An essay on the organization of experience*, New York, Harper & Row.

Goffman, E. (1997) 'Introduction to Frame Analysis', in Alexander, J. C. (ed) *The classical tradition in sociology: The American tradition*, London, SAGE.

Graeff, P. (2002) 'Positive und negative Aspekte von Korruption', *SUB – Sozialwissenschaften und Berufspraxis*, vol. 25, p. 291.

Greco, L. (2015) 'Steht das Schuldprinzip der Einführung einer Strafbarkeit juristischer Personen entgegen?', *GA – Goltdammer's Archiv für Strafrecht*, vol. 162, p. 503.

Greeve, G. (2016) '§ 25 Korruptionsbekämpfung', in Hauschka, C. E., Moosmayer, K. and Lösler, T. (eds) *Corporate Compliance: Handbuch der Haftungsvermeidung im Unternehmen* [Online], 3rd edn, München, C.H. Beck. Available at https://beck-online.beck.de/?vpath=bibdata/komm/HauschkaHdbCC_3/cont/HauschkaHdbCC.htm.

Grunewald, B. (2016) 'Die Abwälzung von Bußgeldern, Verbands- und Vertragsstrafen im Wege des Regresses', *NZG – Neue Zeitschrift für Gesellschaftsrecht*, vol. 19, p. 1121.

Hank, R. and Meck, G. (2015) 'Was geschah bei VW? Nützliche Kriminalität', *FAZ - Frankfurter Allgemeine Zeitung*, 2015 [Online]. Available at http://www.faz.net/aktuell/wirtschaft/diesel-affaere/was-geschah-bei-vw-nuetzliche-kriminalitaet-13837008.html (Accessed 13 August 2018).

Hauck, P. (2017) 'Der Betrugstatbestand des § 263 StGB an den Klippen der Internationalisierung: USA, UK, EU', *wistra – Zeitschrift für Wirtschafts- und Steuerstrafrecht*, vol. 36, p. 457.

Heidelberg Research Group *The Fight against Manipulation and Corruption* [Online]. Available at https://www.soz.uni-heidelberg.de/the-fight-against-manipulation-and-corruption/ (Accessed 13 August 2018).

Hein, O. (2014) 'Verbandsstrafgesetzbuch (VerbStrG-E) – Bietet der Entwurf Anreize zur Vermeidung von Wirtschaftskriminalität in Unternehmen?', *CCZ – Corporate-Compliance-Zeitschrift*, vol. 7, p. 75.

Heine, G. (1995) *Die strafrechtliche Verantwortlichkeit von Unternehmen: Von individuellem Fehlverhalten zu kollektiven Fehlentwicklungen, insbesondere bei Großrisiken* (Zugl.: Basel, Univ., Habil.-Schr., 1994), Baden-Baden, Nomos Verl.-Ges.

Henssler, M., Hoven, E., Kubiciel, M. and Weigend, T., eds. (2017) *Grundfragen eines modernen Verbandsstrafrechts: Tagungen und Kolloquien* [Online], Baden-Baden, Nomos Verlagsgesellschaft mbH & Co. KG. Available at https://doi.org/10.5771/9783845285351.

Hirsch, H. J. (1995) 'Strafrechtliche Verantwortlichkeit von Unternehmen', *ZStW – Zeitschrift für die gesamte Strafrechtswissenschaft*, vol. 107, p. 285.

Hölters, W. (2017) '§ 93 Sorgfaltspflicht und Verantwortlichkeit der Vorstandmitglieder', in Hölters, W. (ed) *Aktiengesetz: Kommentar*, 3rd edn, München, München, C.H. Beck; Verlag Vahlen.

Hoven, E. (2014) 'Der nordrhein-westfälische Entwurf eines Verbandsstrafgesetzbuchs – Eine kritische Betrachtung von Begründungsmodell und Voraussetzungen der Straftatbestände', *ZIS – Zeitschrift für Internationale Strafrechtsdogmatik*, vol. 9, p. 19.

Hoven, E., Wimmer, R., Schwarz, T. and Schumann, S. (2014) 'Der nordrhein-westfälische Entwurf eines Verbandsstrafgesetzes: Kritische Anmerkungen aus Wissenschaft und Praxis Teil 1', *NZWiSt – Neue Zeitschrift für Wirtschafts-, Steuer- und Unternehmensstrafrecht*, vol. 3, p. 161.

Hugger, H. (2012) 'S20-Leitfaden „Hospitality und Strafrecht"', *CCZ – Corporate-Compliance-Zeitschrift*, vol. 5, p. 65.

Jahn, M., Schmitt-Leonardy, C. and Schoop, C., eds. (2016) *Das Unternehmensstrafrecht und seine Alternativen* [Online], Baden-Baden, Nomos Verlagsgesellschaft mbH & Co. KG. Available at http://dx.doi.org/10.5771/9783845257563.

Joecks, W. (2017) '§ 25 StGB Täterschaft', Heintschel-Heinegg, B. v. (ed) *Münchener Kommentar zum Strafgesetzbuch,* 3rd edn, München, C.H. Beck.

Kelly, M. P. and Mandelbaum, R. (2016) 'Are the Yates Memorandum and the Federal Judiciary's Concerns About Over-Criminalization Destined to Collide?', *American Law Review,* vol. 53, p. 899.

Kempf, E., Lüderssen, K. and Volk, K., eds. (2012) *Unternehmensstrafrecht* [Online], Berlin, de Gruyter. Available at http://www.degruyter.com/doi/book/10.1515/9783110285840.

Kindhäuser, U. (2011) 'Voraussetzungen strafbarer Korruption in Staat, Wirtschaft und Gesellschaft', *ZIS – Zeitschrift für Internationale Strafrechtsdogmatik,* vol. 6, p. 461.

Kirch-Heim, C. (2010) *Sanktionen gegen Unternehmen: Rechtsinstrumente zur Bekämpfung unternehmensbezogener Straftaten* [Online], Berlin, Duncker & Humblot. Available at http://gbv.eblib.com/patron/FullRecord.aspx?p=1116608.

Kirkpatrick, D. R. (2016) 'Organisierte Kriminalität - Wirtschaftskriminalität', *wistra – Zeitschrift für Wirtschafts- und Steuerstrafrecht,* vol. 35, p. 375.

Korte, M. (2014) '§ 331 StGB Vorteilsannahme', in Joecks, W., Miebach, K. and Sander, G. M. (eds) *Münchener Kommentar zum Strafgesetzbuch: Paragraphen 263-358 StGB,* 2nd edn, München, Beck; Vahlen.

Kropf, A. and Newbury-Smith, T. C. (2016) 'Wasta as a Form of Social Capital? An Institutional Perspective', in Ramady, M. A. (ed) *The Political Economy of Wasta: Use and Abuse of Social Capital Networking* [Online], Cham, s.l., Springer International Publishing. Available at http://dx.doi.org/10.1007/978-3-319-22201-1.

Krüger, C. (2013) 'Motivation und Situation – Der Wirtschaftsstraftäter im Blickpunkt der Kriminologie', in Dölling, D. and Baier, D. (eds) *Täter, Taten, Opfer: Grundlagenfragen und aktuelle Probleme der Kriminalität und ihrer Kontrolle* [Online], Mönchengladbach, Forum-Verl. Godesberg.

Kubiciel, M. (2014) 'Verbandsstrafe – Verfassungskonformität und Systemkompatibilität', *ZRP – Zeitschrift für Rechtspolitik,* vol. 47, p. 133.

Kubiciel, M. and Hoven, E. (2016) 'Der Entwurf eines Verbandsstrafgesetzes aus Sicht der Rechtswissenschaft', in Jahn, M., Schmitt-Leonardy, C. and Schoop, C. (eds) *Das Unternehmensstrafrecht und seine Alternativen* [Online], Baden-Baden, Nomos Verlagsgesellschaft mbH & Co. KG. Available at http://dx.doi.org/10.5771/9783845257563.

Kühl, S. (2007) 'Formalität, Informalität und Illegalität in der Organisationsberatung: Systemtheoretische Analyse eines Beratungsprozesses', *Soziale Welt,* vol. 58, no. 3, pp. 271–293.

Kühl, S. and Billerbeck, L. v. (2016) *WM Vergabe. Das gekaufte Sommermärchen? Deutschlandfunk Kultur* [Online]. Available at http://www.deutschlandfunkkultur.de/wm-vergabe-das-gekaufte-sommermaerchen.1008.de.html?dram:article_id=347421 (Accessed 13 August 2018).

Kuhlen, L. (2009) 'Strafrechtliche Haftung von Führungskräften', in Maschmann, F. (ed) *Corporate Compliance und Arbeitsrecht: Mannheimer Arbeitsrechtstag 2009* [Online], Baden-Baden, Nomos. Available at https://doi.org/10.5771/9783845218816.

Lambsdorff, J. G. and Beck, L. (2009) 'Korruption als Wachstumsbremse', *APuZ – Aus Politik und Zeitgeschichte*, vol. 59, p. 19.

Lessenich, S. (2016) *Neben uns die Sintflut: Die Externalisierungsgesellschaft und ihr Preis*, München, Carl Hanser Verlag München.

Loos, F. (1974) 'Zum „Rechtsgut" der Bestechungsdelikte', in Stratenwerth, G. (ed) *Festschrift für Hans Welzel zum 70. Geburtstag am 25. März 1974*, Berlin, de Gruyter.

Lotze, A. and Smolinski, S. (2015) 'Entschärfung der Organhaftung für kartellrechtliche Unternehmensgeldbußen', *NZKart – Neue Zeitschrift für Kartellrecht*, vol. 3, pp. 254–258.

Lüderssen, K. (2012) 'The aggregative Model: Jenseits von Fiktionen und Surrogaten', in Kempf, E., Lüderssen, K. and Volk, K. (eds) *Unternehmensstrafrecht* [Online], Berlin, de Gruyter. Available at http://www.degruyter.com/doi/book/10.1515/9783110285840.

Luhmann, N. (1964) *Funktionen und Folgen formaler Organisation*, Berlin, Duncker & Humblot.

Luttermann, C. (2016) 'Persönliche prozessuale Haftungsverschärfung bei „Corporate Misconduct" (U.S. Yates Memorandum): Regulierungsmaß und Schutzstrategie', *DB – Der Betrieb*, vol. 60, no. 18, pp. 1059–1063.

Mayer, B. R. (2016) 'Die Auswirkungen des „Yates Memorandums" in den USA und die Diskussion um ein Unternehmensstrafrecht in Deutschland', *ZWH – Zeitschrift für Wirtschaftsrecht und Haftung im Unternehmen*, vol. 7, no. 10, pp. 301–304.

Miebach, K. and Maier, S. (2016) '§ 46 StGB Grundsätze der Strafzumessung', Heintschel-Heinegg, B. v. (ed) *Münchener Kommentar zum Strafgesetzbuch,* 3rd edn, München, C.H. Beck.

Mitsch, W. (2014) 'Täterschaft und Teilnahme bei der „Verbandsstraftat"', *NZWiSt – Neue Zeitschrift für Wirtschafts-, Steuer- und Unternehmensstrafrecht*, vol. 3, p. 1.

Mittelsdorf, K. (2007) *Unternehmensstrafrecht im Kontext* (Zugl.: Jena, Univ., Diss., 2006-2007), Heidelberg, Müller.

Nowak, C. (2016) 'Art. 23 VerfVO Geldbußen', Loewenheim, U., Meessen, K. M., Riesenkampff, A., Kersting, C. and Meyer-Lindemann, H. J. (eds) *Kartellrecht: Kommentar*, 3rd edn, München, C.H. Beck.

Nunner-Winkler, G. (1997) 'Zurück zu Durkheim? Geteilte Werte als Basis gesellschaftlichen Zusammenhalts', in Heitmeyer, W. (ed) *Was hält die Gesellschaft zusammen?*, Frankfurt am Main, Suhrkamp.

Nunner-Winkler, G. (2000) 'Wandel in den Moralvorstellungen. Ein Generationenvergleich', in Edelstein, W. and Nunner-Winkler, G. (eds) *Moral im sozialen Kontext*, Frankfurt am Main, Suhrkamp.

Ortmann, G. (2003) *Regel und Ausnahme: Paradoxien sozialer Ordnung*, Frankfurt am Main, Suhrkamp.

Ortmann, G. (2010) *Organisation und Moral: Die dunkle Seite*, Weilerswist, Velbrück Wissenschaft.

Ortmann, G. (2017) 'Für ein Unternehmensstrafrecht Sechs Thesen, sieben Fragen, eine Nachbemerkung', *NZWiSt – Neue Zeitschrift für Wirtschafts-, Steuer- und Unternehmensstrafrecht*, vol. 6, p. 241.

Pant, M. (2015) '„…so mag alßdann peinlich frag gebraucht werden". Zum sog. „Yates-Memorandum": Das U.S.-Justizministerium gewährt künftig Strafrabatt nur noch gegen Auslieferung von Managern', *CCZ – Corporate-Compliance-Zeitschrift*, vol. 6, p. 242.

Papakiriakou, T. (2002) *Das Griechische Verwaltungsstrafrecht in Kartellsachen: Zugleich ein Beitrag zur Lehre vom Verwaltungs- und Unternehmensstrafrecht* [Online], Herbolzheim, s.l., Centaurus Verlag & Media. Available at http://dx.doi.org/10.1007/978-3-86226-320-2.

Partsch, C. (2012) 'Hundert Jahre Erfahrung mit einem Unternehmensstrafrecht in den USA', in Kempf, E., Lüderssen, K. and Volk, K. (eds) *Unternehmensstrafrecht* [Online], Berlin, de Gruyter. Available at http://www.degruyter.com/doi/book/10.1515/9783110285840.

Petermann, S. (2015) *Persönliches soziales Kapital in Stadtgesellschaften* (Zugl.: Halle-Wittenberg, Martin-Luther-Univ., Habil., 2012) [Online], Wiesbaden, Springer VS. Available at http://dx.doi.org/10.1007/978-3-658-05418-2.

Poelzig, D. and Bauermeister, T. (2017) 'Kartellrechtsdurchsetzung, ne bis in idem und Verhältnismäßigkeit (Teil 1) – Die kartellrechtlichen Sanktionen und ne bis in idem', *NZKart – Neue Zeitschrift für Kartellrecht*, vol. 5, no. 10, p. 491.

Pohlmann, M. and Markova, H. (2011) *Soziologie der Organisation: Eine Einführung* [Online], Konstanz, Stuttgart, UVK-Verl.-Ges; UTB. Available at http://www.utb-studi-e-book.de/9783838535739.

Ransiek, A. (1996) *Unternehmensstrafrecht: Strafrecht, Verfassungsrecht, Regelungsalternativen* (Zugl.: Bielefeld, Univ., Habil.-Schr., 1994), Heidelberg, Müller.

Rogall, K. (2015) 'Kriminalstrafe gegen juristische Personen?', *GA – Goltdammer's Archiv für Strafrecht*, vol. 162, p. 260.

Rogall, K. (2018) '§ 30 OWiG Geldbuße gegen juristische Personenvereinigungen', Mitsch, W. (ed) *Karlsruher Kommentar zum Gesetz über Ordnungswidrigkeiten*, 5th edn, München, C.H. Beck.

Rönnau, T. and Wegner, K. (2014) 'Reform des Rechts der Verbandssanktionen – europäische und internationale Vorgaben', *ZRP – Zeitschrift für Rechtspolitik*, vol. 47, pp. 158–163.

Rosenau, H. (2017) 'Artikel 325 AEUV [Schutz der finanziellen Interessen der Union]', in Leitner, W., Rosenau, H., Ahlbrecht, H. and Burchard, C. (eds) *Wirtschafts- und Steuerstrafrecht*, Baden-Baden, Nomos.

Rotsch, T. (1998) *Individuelle Haftung in Großunternehmen: Plädoyer für den Rückzug des Umweltstrafrechts* (Zugl.: Kiel, Univ., Diss., 1997), Baden-Baden, Nomos-Verl.-Ges.

Rotsch, T. (2015) '§ 1 Criminal Compliance – Begriff, Abgrenzung, Entwicklung; § 2 Grundfragen der Criminal Compliance', in Beckemper, K. and Rotsch, T. (eds) *Criminal Compliance: Handbuch*, Baden-Baden, Nomos-Verl.-Ges.

Sachoulidou, A. (2019) *Unternehmensverantwortung und -sanktionierung* (Zugl. Heidelberg, Uni. Diss., 2005), Tübingen, Mohr Siebeck.

Sarhan, A. (2006) *Wiedergutmachung zugunsten des Opfers im Lichte strafrechtlicher Trennungsdogmatik: Plädoyer für eine opferorientierte Neuausrichtung des Strafgrundes* (Zugl.: Bonn, Univ., Diss., 2005), Berlin, BWV Berliner Wiss.-Verl.

Satzger, H. (2016) *Internationales und Europäisches Strafrecht: Strafanwendungsrecht, europäisches Straf- und Strafverfahrensrecht, Völkerstrafrecht* [Online], 7th edn, Baden-Baden, Nomos. Available at https://doi.org/10.5771/9783845261508.

Schmidt, K. (2003) 'Korruption aus (vorwiegend) ökonomischer Sicht', in Nell, V., Schwitzgebel, G. and Vollet, M. (eds) *Korruption: Interdisziplinäre Zugänge zu einem komplexen Phänomen* [Online], Wiesbaden, Deutscher Universitätsverlag. Available at http://dx.doi.org/10.1007/978-3-322-81310-7.

Schmitt-Leonardy, C. (2013) *Unternehmenskriminalität ohne Strafrecht?* (Zugl.: Saarbrücken, Univ., Diss., 2009-2010), Heidelberg, Hamburg, Müller Verl.-Gruppe Hüthig Jehle Rehm.

Schmitt-Leonardy, C. (2016) 'Eine Alternative zum Unternehmensstrafrecht: der Folgenverantwortungsdialog', in Jahn, M., Schmitt-Leonardy, C. and Schoop, C. (eds) *Das Unternehmensstrafrecht und seine Alternativen* [Online], Baden-Baden, Nomos Verlagsgesellschaft mbH & Co. KG. Available at http://dx.doi.org/10.5771/9783845257563.

Schorn, R. (2016) '§ 13 Compliance-Ziele', in Hauschka, C. E., Moosmayer, K. and Lösler, T. (eds) *Corporate Compliance: Handbuch der Haftungsvermeidung im Unternehmen* [Online], 3rd edn, München, C.H. Beck. Available at https://beck-online.beck.de/?vpath=bibdata/komm/HauschkaHdbCC_3/cont/HauschkaHdbCC.htm.

Schröder, T. (2019) 'Corporate Crime, the Lawmaker's Options for Corporate Criminal Laws and *Luhmann's* Concept of "Useful Illegality"', *IJLCJ – International Journal of Law, Crime and Justice*, vol 57, p. 13.

Schröder, T. (2016) 'Die neue Strafgesetzgebung gegen Korruption im Gesundheitswesen – Vertrauens- durch Wettbewerbsschutz?', in Frewer, A., Bergemann, L. and Jäger, C. (eds) *Interessen und Gewissen: Moralische Zielkonflikte in der Medizin*, Würzburg, Königshausen & Neumann.

Schröder, T. (2017) 'Compliance an Universitäten – ein Albtraum oder überfälliges Strukturelement?', *ZIS – Zeitschrift für Internationale Strafrechtsdogmatik*, vol. 12, p. 279.

Schroth, H.-J. (1993) *Unternehmen als Normadressaten und Sanktionssubjekte: Eine Studie zum Unternehmensstrafrecht* (Zugl.: Gießen, Univ., Habil.-Schr., 1992), Gießen, Brühl.

Schünemann, B. (2014) 'Die aktuelle Forderung eines Verbandsstrafrechts – Ein kriminalpolitischer Zombie', *ZIS – Zeitschrift für Internationale Strafrechtsdogmatik*, vol. 9, p. 1.

Searle, J. R. (1995) *The construction of social reality*, New York, Free Press.

Smith, A. (1976 [1776]) 'An Inquiry into the Nature and Causes of the Wealth of Nations', in Todd, W. B. (ed) *The Glasgow Edition of the Works and Correspondence of Adam Smith*, Oxford.

Sowada, C. (2009 [2009]) 'Vor §§ 331 – Vorbemerkungen', in Sowada, C., Hilgendorf, E. and Lilie, H. (eds) *331-358* [Online], 12th edn, Munchen, de Gruyter. Available at http://gbv.eblib.com/patron/FullRecord.aspx?p=3040955.

Streng, F. (2017) '§ 46 StGB Grundsätze der Strafzumessung', in Kindhäuser, U., Neumann, U., Paeffgen, H.-U. and Albrecht, H.-J. (eds) *Strafgesetzbuch* [Online], 5th edn, Baden-Baden, Nomos. Available at https://beck-online.beck.de/?vpath=bibdata/komm/KinNeuPaeKoStGB_5/cont/KinNeuPaeKoStGB.htm

Thomas, S. (2015) 'Bußgeldregress, Übelszufügung und D&O-Versicherung', *NZG – Neue Zeitschrift für Gesellschaftsrecht*, vol. 18, p. 1409.

Tiedemann, K. (1980) 'Delinquenzverhalten und Machtmißbrauch multinationaler Unternehmen', in Tiedemann, K. and Bacigalupo, E. (eds) *Multinationale Unternehmen und Strafrecht: Beiträge zum Problem der Kriminalität im grenzüberschreitenden Geschäftsverkehr*, Köln, Heymanns.

Tiedemann, K. (2014) *Wirtschaftsstrafrecht: Einführung und Allgemeiner Teil ; mit wichtigen Rechtstexten*, 4th edn, München, Verlag Franz Vahlen.

Transparency International (2017) *FAQs on corruption* [Online]. Available at https://www.transparency.org/whoweare/organisation/faqs_on_corruption/9/ (Accessed 13 August 2018).

Trüg, G. (2016) 'Was kann und soll ein Unternehmensstrafrecht bei der Sanktion leisten?', in Jahn, M., Schmitt-Leonardy, C. and Schoop, C. (eds) *Das Unternehmensstrafrecht und seine Alternativen* [Online], Baden-Baden, Nomos Verlagsgesellschaft mbH & Co. KG. Available at http://dx.doi.org/10.5771/9783845257563.

Trunk, D. (2013) 'Der Wirtschaftsstraftäter im organisationalen Kontext. Kriminalpräventive Wirkung von Antikorruptionsprogrammen', in Dölling, D. and Baier, D. (eds) *Täter, Taten, Opfer: Grundlagenfragen und aktuelle Probleme der Kriminalität und ihrer Kontrolle* [Online], Mönchengladbach, Forum-Verl. Godesberg. Available at http://www.krimg.de/drupal/files/9783942865111.pdf.

United States Sentencing Commission (2016) *Guidelines Manual 2016* [Online]. Available at https://www.ussc.gov/sites/default/files/pdf/guidelines-manual/2016/GLMFull.pdf (Accessed 13 August 2018).

Vogel, J. and Eisele, J. (2017) 'Art. 86 AEUV Europäische Staatsanwaltschaft', in Grabitz, E., Hilf, M. and Nettesheim, M. (eds) *Das Recht der Europäischen Union*, 62nd edn, München, Beck.

Weilert, A. K. (2015) 'United Nations Convention against Corruption (UNCAC) – After Ten Years of Being in Force', in Lachenmann, F., Röder, T. and Wolfrum, R. (eds) *Max Planck Yearbook of United Nations Law. Vol. 19 (2015)*, Leiden, Brill / Martinus Nijhoff.

Williams, C. A. (1998) 'Corporate compliance with the law in the era of efficiency', *N.C.L. Rev. – North Carolina Law Review*, vol. 76, no. 4, p. 1265.

Wolf, S. (2014) *Korruption, Antikorruptionspolitik und öffentliche Verwaltung: Einführung und europapolitische Bezüge*, Wiesbaden, Springer VS.

Zieschang, F. (2014) 'Das Verbandsstrafgesetzbuch', *GA – Goltdammer's Archiv für Strafrecht*, vol. 161, p. 91.

Zimmermann, B. (1999) 'Die Bekämpfung der Korruption', *Kriminalistik*, vol. 53, p. 585.

Zimmermann, S. A. (2014) *Strafbarkeitsrisiken durch Compliance: Auswirkungen von Compliance-Regelungen auf das Wirtschaftsstrafrecht* (Zugl.: Universität Bayreuth, Diss., 2014) [Online], Berlin, Duncker & Humblot. Available at http://elibrary.duncker-humblot.de/9783428544332/U1.

# Does illegality become natural? Systemic and preventive effects of the market economy

*Kai-D. Bussmann*

## 1 Introduction

Generally speaking, criminological literature views the market economy as a driving force behind profit-driven crime with titles such as *Crime as an American Way of Life* (Bell, 1953) and *Crime and the American Dream* (Messner and Rosenfeld, 2007). Basically, US-American capitalism is taken as a critical example of a culture of rigid competition conveying the values of social Darwinism in which solidarity and consideration for others are alien concepts (Currie, 1997; Hagan et al., 2000). Although there is much justification for this criticism of the dominance of the economic system, particularly by the institutional anomie theory of Messner and Rosenfeld (2007), it fails to differentiate between not only driving but also preventive effects of the market economy. Therefore, this paper introduces the concept of systemic crime and directs attention towards the way in which the market economy makes positive contributions to socialization that surprisingly support many of the values of our civilization.

## 2 Systemic crime

Over the last two decades, there has been a notable stagnation or even a decline in the number of cases of robbery and theft in Germany, whereas that of reported cases of fraud has almost doubled (Oberwittler, 2012).

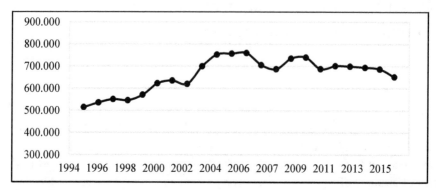

**Figure 1: Reported cases of fraud**
Source: BKA PKS, 2016

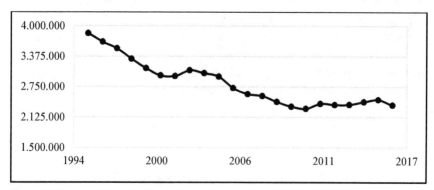

**Figure 2: Reported cases of theft**
Source: BKA PKS, 2016

In general, other industrial nations such as the United States and the United Kingdom have also experienced a shift from theft to fraud (Karstedt, 2015, 2016), as seen in the FBI statistics:

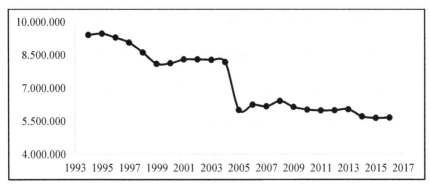

**Figure 3: Reported cases of larceny theft and motor vehicle theft**
Source: FBI Uniform Crime Reporting, o.J.

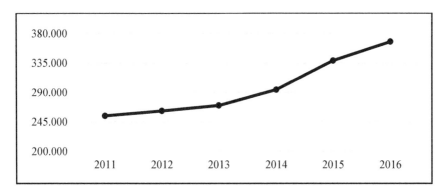

**Figure 4: Reported cases of fraud**
Source: FBI National Incident-Based Reporting System, o.J.

Some authors even go so far as to view fraud as the characteristic offense of our century (Albanese, 2005). What is certain, nonetheless, is that dark field studies indicate that citizens are harmed more frequently by fraud than by other types of crimes such as burglary, theft, or robbery (Shover and Hochstetler, 2006).

Part of the increase in fraud is attributed to a change in opportunity structures. There can be no doubt that just like the spread of self-service stores encouraged shoplifting, the internet has now created new opportunities for fraud. Nonetheless, it is questionable whether this increase in fraud can be traced back primarily to the growing importance of online sales (Karstedt, 2015). Although it is possible that fewer goods are being purchased in shops, all goods are still physically present in the world and therefore could potentially be stolen. Opportunities for theft and robbery have not decreased.

The initial premise here is far more that the market economy has a particular affinity for not only fraud (Gerschlager, 2001a, 2005) but also corruption and related offenses such as competition law infringements or industrial espionage. Other offenses such as theft and robbery, in contrast, are alien to it (see Section 3 below.).

Systemic offenses are not just *normal* in the way that every form of crime has been assumed to be since Emile Durkheim (1982).They are crimes that are *inseparable* from the operation of the functional system known as the economy, and they are encouraged permanently by this system. This is particularly the case for the following reasons:

1. *Competing promises*: Even Adam Smith (1978) could not conceive of exchange or trade taking place without illusions and fraud, for which he was criticized strongly by his contemporaries (Gerschlager, 2001a). The reasons are to be found in the rationale of free-market competition. For example, it is not just the two sides of the market—the seller and the buyer—who observe each other. Producers also monitor how their competitors' sales develop, because the way customers form their preferences is relatively hard to fathom (Luhmann, 1989; White, 1981). Hence, driven by competition, sellers apply every incentive they can that will encourage their customers to buy. In addition, through the logic of competition, the profits of all providers are always being pushed down towards zero (Boyes, 2011; Cable and Mueller, 2008). Competitors maintain their profit margins only through technological innovations, good marketing, establishing a brand, or providing a special service. But according to the supporters of dynamic economic theory—especially since Schumpeter (Hayek, 1968; Schumpeter, 1942)—all competitive advantages are only temporary. Hence, the market sets incentives to gain customers not only by making promises to them but also through raising false expectations. Fraud and trade are inseparably entangled.

2. *Information asymmetry:* Misleading promises and advertising may be limited by a company's interest in functioning as a repeat player: in winning customer loyalty, building up a reputation, or establishing a brand name. However, this limitation is only partial, and generally does not function without a legal regulatory framework. *George Akerlof* uses the example of the used car market to show the need for a regulatory framework (Akerlof, 1970). The starting point is the problem of resolving asymmetries in information, because customers cannot be as well-informed as the seller about any potential problems a used car may cause. This is why the prices for these riskier vehicles are below those of brand new ones. Because the latter cannot compete with the former in terms of prices, they leave the market. This results in a 'market of lemons' with cheap, defective vehicles and the risk of poorer economic development or even a collapse of the market, because customers are hesitant about buying from it due to their lack of trust. Proponents of the *New Institutionalism* (North, 1990) use this analysis as an example of the inability of markets to heal by themselves because of the continuous information asymmetry between buyer and seller.
3. *Emotional reasons:* Emotions accompany all forms of crime. However, in contrast to robbery and theft, it is easier for an offender committing fraud and corruption to avoid a guilty conscience, because it is harder to perceive any injury. With theft, something is really lost; with robbery, there may also be physical injury. With fraud, in contrast, not only does the injury make far less of an impression on the offender, but the victim has also played a part, even if only by being deceived. Neither the damage caused nor the responsibility of the offender are particularly obvious, as popular national activities such as insurance fraud and tax evasion clearly illustrate. As for corruption, scientists were long uncertain about the harmfulness of this offense, asking themselves whether it could also deliver many economic advantages (Lambsdorff, 2007).
4. *Low risk of detection and prosecution*: Victims of fraud are less aware of the fact that they have paid too much or not received enough due to the information asymmetry—just as it is difficult for the tax office to be aware of an incorrect tax return. All fraud offenses, but also corruption, offer major advantages in terms of a low risk of detection and

prosecution. Payments are usually made in cash or credit. Monetary advantages are gained not only through the element of surprise but also through deception. As for corruption, companies or administrations find it very hard to detect; and, in particular, it is hard to ascertain the economic advantages to the offender due to the information asymmetry that is also found in every organization. This offense is not an offense with no victim either, but one with many invisible victims: society and the market economy along with the people's trust in politics, administration, and democracy.

In addition, a *prosecution* requires proof of the deception and the misapprehension of the (purported) injured party. Fraud and corruption offenses also involve more difficult legal definition issues than robbery and theft. With fraud, for example, it is necessary to distinguish between misapprehensions on the side of the customer who has a right to be protected, and permissible advertising practices of the seller. Tax evasion also raises legal questions more frequently than any property offense. Hence, with both fraud and corruption, advantages for offenders accumulate mostly factually and legally. All these factors decrease the risk of being detected and prosecuted, and thereby increase opportunity.

From a phenomenological perspective, *shoplifting* takes an intermediate position between theft and fraud. In a normal business scenario, the shoplifter behaves in a completely inconspicuous way. Shop owners have a limited ability to determine whether goods already 'disappeared' before delivery, had been taken by staff, or stolen by a customer. Like confidence tricksters, a shoplifter commits a similar crime to fraud, because an element of deception is involved. Hence, shoplifting should be less affected by the decline of theft and robbery.

5. *Self-deception:* Fraud is also determined systemically on the side of the deceived. From research in psychology, we know that people tend to underestimate risks in general and attribute above-average abilities to themselves. Surveys on car drivers reveal that the majority consider themselves to be above-average drivers (Gosselin et al., 2010). Similarly, people also tend to overestimate their ability to notice fraud (Croson, 2005). The subtlety of fraud is also revealed by the way in which victims generally feel they have made a good deal; they feel enriched. From an

economic perspective, however, they may be richer in terms of goods or services, but poorer in terms of value for money.

In addition, customers often have exaggerated expectations regarding their purchases: they may be disappointed, but have they been deceived? Fraud can attain the level of self-deception (Gerschlager, 2001b). For *Adam Smith*, and later for the economic sociologist *Max Weber* as well, people's wishes, desires, and self-interest form a particularly important driving force for the market economy. Without them, it would not function properly. Hence, we should not just focus on the greed of the fraudsters. Many times, it is the *greed of the victims* that first makes fraud possible; and in everyday consumer behaviour, it is the search for the lowest price.

6. *Deception as a negative market learning experience:* The structural proximity of fraud to normal market activity offers more opportunity to learn from experience. Fraud retains the form of a market transaction. Through the business practices of companies, customers also learn that they can, at least in fact, assert their own financial interests by applying unfair business methods. *'Consumers do not riot today, but neither are they inclined to dismiss unfair practices in the marketplace as a mere inconvenience. [...] They react with strong intentions to hit back whenever the opportunity arises'* as Susanne Karstedt and Steven Farrell phrase succinctly (Karstedt and Farrall, 2006, p. 1026). One is allowed to be cunning up to a punishable 'pain threshold'. Not every deception is punishable—such as the small print in insurance company contracts or subtle advertising that constantly skirts the borders of criminal deception. Fraud also always maintains the exterior form of an orderly business relationship and transaction. Corruption proceeds in the form of an additional exchange—an 'underhand' business.

7. *Influence of illegal markets:* There are also economic reasons that favour fraud and serve to disadvantage theft and robbery. Thanks to increasing prosperity and technological progress, all households in the industrialized wealthy nations actually have more valuable consumer goods than ever before, and this leads to a drop in their market prices. Hence, economic crime is influenced not only by an increase or decrease in crime opportunities but also by the market price for illegal goods, and this drops

in line with the falling prices for legal goods. As a result, burglary and robbery are becoming increasingly less attractive.

Moreover, stealing things has the disadvantage of having to sell them on the black market to obtain the universal means of exchange in which the thieves are interested: money. The transaction costs of stealing are higher when one is not interested (unlike perhaps a shoplifter) in the stolen property itself. Moreover, in general, market prices for stolen goods will be lower in wealthy industrial nations than in developing countries as evidenced by the way that stolen luxury motor vehicles are smuggled to Eastern Europe. The strong demand for stolen high-value art supports this premise. Its market value corresponds to that on the legal art market. Hence, the attractiveness of theft and robbery are influenced by markets, and in this case, illegal markets.

8. *Change in payment transactions:* Payment transactions have also changed for economic reasons. Industrial nations have long replaced the pay packet with a salary account just as paper money previously reduced the importance of coins. With increasing technological innovations, the practical significance of cash will continue to decline in payment transactions due to the cost factor. Nowadays, private persons keep hardly any cash in their homes: less than 3 per cent of households keep between 1,000 and 5,000 Euros in cash and only 0.5 per cent keep more than 5,000 Euros in cash (ECB, 2011). Although cash continues to be a very important means of payment in smaller transactions, it is of only marginal significance for larger sums. In the United States, two-thirds of transactions up to 10 dollars but less than 10 per cent of payments over 100 dollars are made in cash (Bennett et al., 2014; Rogoff, 2016). The same applies to Europe, where sums up to 10 Euros are generally paid in cash. Indeed, 91 per cent of Germans report always or frequently paying these small sums in cash. Even though Germany is a rather cash-focused country, few people pay four-digit sums in cash. When making purchases over 10,000 Euros, for example, for a motor vehicle, only 4 per cent pay in cash (ECB, 2011).

This change in payment transactions makes all forms of theft increasingly less attractive. Opportunities evaporate through being uneconomic. Nowadays, cash continues to be highly important only on the black market. Studies in both the United States and Europe show that only a fraction of the total cash volume is held by private persons and companies. In the Eurozone, private persons keep only approximately 100 billion out of a total cash count of 750 billion in worldwide circulation (ECB, 2011; Rogoff, 2016). Rogoff (2016) concludes that, '[a]s a result, just as with the US dollar, a large portion of Euro cash cannot be traced back to domestic legal possession' (translated).

## 3 Systemic effects: Exclusion of violence, robbery, and theft

The term systemic crime introduces a distinction that can also be used to analyse the other group of behaviours that society defines as crime. This includes the entire spectrum from libel over assault up to espionage. What these offenses have in common is that they are not generated by the mechanism of the market economy itself but are even pushed back by it.

Historically speaking, robbery is one of those economic crimes that have undergone a major change in terms of its evaluation by society over the years: from what was presented at the time as an 'honourable' ambush to what is now a serious crime sanctioned much more heavily than theft and fraud. From the early Middle Ages until today, our society has never been so free of violence (Elias, 1978; Hagan, 1994; Pinker, 2011). In this context, it is only necessary to think of the times of the *robber barons*. In an age in which there was no state monopoly on power and no constitutional state as we know it today, the line between legal and illegal violence was blurred. There was no authoritative position yet to distinguish robbery from 'legal feuds' (Andermann, 1997): For the nobility as well as for the common people of the Middle Ages up until the 16th century, violence was a widespread means of asserting their economic interests. This is why there was no free market economy as we know it today.

1. *Condemnation of violence:* The renunciation of the use of violence to assert economic interests was made possible and ensured through the establishment of the *state monopoly* on the use of violence and a judicial system. Through a range of commercial 'rules of the game', the use of violence to assert economic interests became 'clothed in legal terms' so that it appeared to take the form of legal and economic constraints while

being broadly pushed back in its directly physical form. If necessary, those who are in the right can assert their economic interests through the use of violence by the state. The rise of the judicial system as a consequence of the development of national states thereby created the preconditions for more profitable non-violent business models. Robbery no longer served as a stable business idea. In modern industrial nations, robbery emerges more intermittently as the activity of individual offenders or gangs of robbers who generally lack any stable cohesion. Attempts to use robbery to set up a sustainable business model generally fail.

2. *Shortage of goods:* The change in values additionally encouraged all non-violent forms of crime. Robbery also always threatens the personal good of life and limb, and this is also a good that can in no way be increased by a flourishing economy. In the rationale of economics, health remains a scarce and irreplaceable good for every person. Hence, thieves and fraudsters benefit from the prosperity of a modern society whereas robbers do not. Robbers attack even when they only threaten a non-increasable personal good such as life and limb, and they are therefore clearly the 'losers' in our civilizational and economic progress. This is certainly nothing to complain about.

3. *Non-corporal offense*: The growing devaluation of *physicality* in a world of trade and service and, most recently, digitalization has led to a change in the types of enrichment that reveals certain social parallels to the world of work: burglaries, robberies, and all types requiring the use of a certain degree of physical force evolve towards more subtle forms of crime such as fraud and fraud-like offenses such as shoplifting or corruption—hence, offenses based on deception and falsity rather than on violence and physical dexterity. The criminal preferences of offenders when committing crimes are changing, just as work is becoming increasingly technologized and the share of physical work and particularly of heavy physical work is in continuous decline.

4. *Development of a universal means of payment*: In addition, the development of money was accompanied not only by the inestimable advantage of no longer having to trade by exchanging natural products, but also by money having made exchange easier. Money regulates the

problem of scarcity of goods in a non-violent way. This aspect is hardly ever acknowledged anymore today because of the dominance of money: *"Money prevents violence in the area in which it can provide order"* (Luhmann, 1989, p. 253 translated). Hence, the availability of money increases the probability of economic transactions. Price incentives arise from supply and demand. Those who can pay the price do not need to use violence.

However, in the history of the monetary economy, the problem of scarcity shifts to the availability of money and thereby to issues regarding the discrepancy between wealth and poverty in a country (see section 5). Viewed from this perspective, it is not the market economy that is responsible for robberies—these business models have simply survived in a modern market economy and in a modern constitutional state. It is unresolved issues of distribution in a society that lead to such assaults.

5. *Rationale of the market economy*: From the perspective of *Adam Smith's* classical work on economics, the market economy promotes *non-violence* because violence permanently destroys the exchange of goods and thereby of all trade (Clark and Lee, 2011). How little robbery and theft are reconcilable with the rationale of exchange can be seen in the way these offenses specifically prevent the exchange of goods. Theft makes a market economy temporarily impossible; and it only becomes possible again after a temporal break while thieves convert their booty into cash through a dealer in stolen goods or, alternatively, when they go shopping themselves with the cash they have stolen. Fraud, in contrast, may initially allow an exchange as part of the market economy. It is only subsequently that it destroys *trust* in the market. The same is true for corruption in which nothing is taken away, but something is given, frequently disguised as a present.

Hence, the example of robbery shows how two closely entangled aspects—the taboo of violence as a social value on the one side and the changes in both the working world and the rationality of the market on the other—form a synthesis. Compared to theft, robbery undergoes a categorical rejection, also due to a general civilizational development in modern society towards a rejection of any kind of violence—physical but also psychological. The premise is that there is an interaction between the tabooing of violence and an economy that socializes non-violence. The world society is going through a centuries-long civilizational process that may well be advancing at very different speeds on a regional level but has led to the tabooing of violence.

## 4    Functionality of self-interest in the market economy

When considering the criticism of a rigid economy as presented in the introduction, we should not overlook the fact that our current prosperity is based on the success of a modern market economy that draws its strength specifically from *self-interest*. The greed of economic criminals is not the cause of their criminality, because it cannot be distinguished from the unrestrained pursuit of profit by others. The self-interest of criminals is condemned only because it takes illegal forms. There is no upper limit for prosperity; no condemnation of wealth. It is ironic that precisely Martin Luther had little sympathy for business and the short-term profit motive, but that the Reformation unintentionally reformed more than just faith. Viewed historically, it was Protestantism and Calvinism that first permitted changes that promoted the radicalization of capitalist ideas with their moral upgrading of the pursuit of profit (Heller, 2011).

For the moral philosopher Adam Smith, the theoretical founder of modern economics at the end of the 18th century (Smith, 1978), it was only the self-interest of, in his example, the baker that led to better supply and more prosperity, freedom, and also to justice for large parts of the society. Only a free market economy could replace the early capitalist forms of feudalism characterized by far greater poverty and inequality than anything we know today (Katz, 1993). For Max Weber as well, traditional capitalism was shaped by moderate profits, less competition, and a resistance to innovation (Weber 1985). Changes led to a radical breakdown of social power structures. This becomes evident when we look at the fact that it was only the dominance of the market economy combined with the growing prosperity of many social classes that led to the declining economic, social, and political significance of the nobility: *"The reform lies not in the increasing dependence of the nobility on money but on the increasing independence of money from the nobility"* (Luhmann, 1997, p. 724 translated).

Nonetheless, a current shift towards a new form of *financial feudalism* cannot be denied. According to (Piketty, 2014) and Stiglitz (2012), the chances of accumulating capital through income from work are declining increasingly compared to the chances of accumulating capital through income from capital assets. Despite growing global prosperity, there has also been a dramatic increase in the unequal distribution of wealth in modern industrial nations. Prosperity does not come naturally from the market economy. One cannot let the fire of the market economy carry on raging without subjecting it to the control of a socio-political regulatory framework. Otherwise, it will clearly have destructive social consequences. Nonetheless, an approach to criminology that places the market economy at the centre of its analysis will not just uncover values such as greed or egoism.

## 5 Values, socialization, and integration through the market

The market economy is a *socialization agency* in which one may learn economic and social ruthlessness, but not the choice of violence or the theft of goods to assert one's interests. Although economic desperation, severe social disruptions, particularly in nations on the way to democracy, can lead to an increase in violence and theft, this has not been learned through the market economy. These are historically rooted behaviours that can be found in every society as a means to secure a livelihood.

Even for *Georg Simmel* in 1907, *exchange* did not simply lead to socialization, but *"it is far more a socialization of those relationships whose existence transforms a sum of individuals into a social group, because 'society' is identical to the sum of these relationships"* (Simmel, 1989 <1907>, p. 210 translated).

In his study on *Wirtschaft und Gesellschaft* [Economy and Society] published in 1922, *Max Weber* included a short but nonetheless separate chapter with the succinct title of *Die Marketvergesellschaftung* [The Societalization of Market]. This referred notably to the use of money:

> "Every exchange based on money (purchase) is also a communal activity due to the use of money that is granted its function only through its relation to the potential actions of others ... Societalization through the use of money is the

characteristic opposite pole to societalization through rationally contracted or imposed order" (Weber, 1985 <1968>, p. 382 translated).

*Max Weber* takes the premise of the self-interested *homo oeconomicus* and adds the premise that on the market, no actor acts in isolation from others but always in the view of those who are potentially interested in buying or selling. All actors follow the same logic of action—exchange—and since the emergence of the monetary economy, they do this using the same medium—money. The everyday use of *money* generates a habituation to the acquisition of goods without violence or theft. Trade and consumption acknowledge no limits apart from the scarcity of money, but also no use of violence to assert economic interests. The customer is courted, perhaps also duped into buying, but not robbed. All participants in the market economy develop the natural expectation of a non-violent business situation that is free of violence and the theft of goods or money. This unites all actors, although they might otherwise have little in common.

Of course, the market economy can lead to extreme differences in income that come threateningly close to exclusion. However, and this is what is decisive, the market economy does *not* live from discrimination; that is not its rationale. It is at best a consequence when a socio-political regulatory framework is lacking. It only resembles exclusion if a lack of financial means emerges. One does not have to believe in the market economy in order to belong to it.

The impersonality of market relationships that may initially seem so unpleasant is not really disturbing at all. In contrast, market actors are socialized towards tolerance and equality as the values of coexistence in the market economy. As Max Weber emphasizes in the aforementioned chapter on market societalization:

> "Where the market is left to follow its own laws, it recognizes only the appearance of things, not the appearance of the person, no obligations to fraternity or piety, none of the elemental human relationships born by personal communities. ... Rational interests and rational legality determine the market processes to a particularly high degree ...." (Weber, 1985 <1968>, p. 383 translated).

The basic idea of the market is to bridge cultural, ethnic, social, and also religious differences in order to enable trade. Individual actors may discriminate against others, but this is not a part of the logic of the much criticized rational benefit maximizer who is acting as a buyer or seller (Clark and Lee, 2011,

p. 17ff.). One would have to put one's religious, xenophobic, or other discriminatory interests before one's economic interests—which is known to have been a general practice even in the stronghold of capitalism, the USA—particularly in relation to African Americans.

The rationality of economics, which is precisely the reason why it is criticized, is completely indifferent to the morals and lifestyle of others. The market economy does not recognize membership (Luhmann, 1989, p. 317). This makes it fundamentally different from religions that deliver solidarity and peacefulness among believers, but contain major risks ranging from intolerance to excesses of violence towards non-believers. At least from a historical perspective, no religion seems to be an exception when it comes to moral crusades. The market, in contrast, prefers peace, as *Max Weber* emphasizes: "The *intensive expansion of relations of exchange runs parallel to a relative pacification everywhere*" (Weber, 1985 <1968>, p. 358 translated).

Of course, by engaging in lots of arms trafficking, the market economy can share responsibility for wars and thereby for a great deal of violence, hardship, and repression. Nonetheless, one can see how little robbery and theft are compatible with the rationale of the market economy when even dictators and mafia bosses show an interest in establishing a profitable market economy and in suppressing the criminality of others (Olson, 2000, pp. 1–24). Crime disturbs business and scares away customers—a phenomenon gang leaders in red-light districts are only too aware of. It is not a moral conscience that ensures these customers' security, but market economy rationality.

The history of many nations shows that wars can break out over resources, markets, and trade routes. However, this is not the market economy. Areas such as North America became more prosperous than Latin America by no longer focusing primarily on plundering but on trade and developing their economies. Studies confirm the significance of a value culture for the prosperity of a society that favours entrepreneurship and self-interest (Swedberg, 2003). *Seymour Lipset* attributes the market economy difference between North and Latin America to the values of the original Spanish and Portuguese elites in Latin America who attached particularly little value to physical labour, profit making, and trade while valuing soldiery and priesthood (Swedberg, 2003). Evidently, the change in values due to Protestantism and Calvinism made a decisive contribution here (see section 5 above).

However, the premise is not that the economy and its sub-system the market economy can flourish without a legal regulatory framework as illustrated by *George Akerlof* for the 'lemon market' (Akerlof, 1970). Even the founder of modern economics *Adam Smith* cannot serve as the leading advocate of unrestrained market liberalism. Smith adopted positions in moral philosophy, did not conceive the actors in the market as amoral beings, and continued to emphasize the need for a state regulatory framework while turning against the misery and injustice of the feudalism of his time by proposing the idea of a free market that would promise prosperity for broader social classes (Clark and Lee, 2011, p. 6ff.).

Instead, the premise is that the market socializes civilizational values through trade and barter. In this sense, *Adam Smith's* frequently cited image of the *'invisible hand'* of the market illustrates, on the one side, the subtlety of this effect and, on the other side, that socialization is not part of the program of the market. It does not have to be intended by anyone. In the depth and quality of its effect, the market comes barely second to familial socialization and in some ways may even be more powerful. Compared with the way children are brought up in many families, one can also see that wanting to be good does not always result in being good:

1. *Values*: As they grow up to be adults, all people become familiar with the rationale of everyday barter trade. And this also includes values that exert an integrative influence such as *freedom, non-violence, equality,* and *tolerance*—values that do not necessarily belong to every child's socialization. There is no denying that the family shoulders the main burden of socialization, because this task already starts in childhood. However, the crime-inhibiting socialization achievements of the market will be underestimated if one complains only about its negative effects such as crimes typical of the affluent society, extreme gaps between poverty and wealth, or the arms trade and the like.
2. *Integration*: The market possesses *no discrimination of its own*; it acknowledges no exclusion, but has a permanent interest in inclusion, and

in having the highest possible number of prospective buyers. It does not focus on 'market believers'; nobody has to be converted in order to participate. Discrimination or even racism is a luxury that the market economy can do without. It is something that a society has to be able to afford and to want to afford. Economically, however, it will scarcely bring any benefits. Global competition will act to discipline it. And this is not something to complain about.

3. *Socialization*: In contrast to familial socialization, the influence of the market goes beyond childhood and adolescence. Its strongest adult critics can avoid it only with difficulty. Even a 'dropout' can hardly survive without any contact with the market. There are many things one can do without, but to fundamentally reject money as a means of barter is a difficult endeavour. Hence, any withdrawal from the socializing power of the use of money and exchange can only be limited.

4. *Medium of trade*: The market socializes through trade, through learning its techniques of exchange and its different forms of payment in cash or credit, through getting to know the right temporal succession, the buying conditions that guarantee provision, and so forth. All actors therefore have to acquire a range of competencies for dealing with the everyday market. This may include deception, but there is one thing they do not learn here: to assert their economic interests in the form of robbery or theft.

5. *Integration through innovation*: Through the market economy, new forms of societalization are developing continuously through the creation of new spaces and products in the market economy. In modern big cities, in shopping centres, supermarkets, discotheques, all types of theme parks, and now on the internet, meeting places with integrative effects are being created for people of all beliefs and ethnicities. One becomes accustomed to *diversity*. The modern consumer and entertainment industry also creates media communalities. The market economy brings together people from different regions, cultures, ethnicities, and beliefs because this is the rationality of exchange and not that of consumption. And, in part, this proceeds in very subtle ways.

The success of Facebook is certainly the most recent example of this: users would never see themselves as customers, although they actually are. The fact is that the product brings together people who would otherwise have found hardly any way to interact with each other. Although the newly emerging risks and, in our context, the new opportunities for crime cannot be disputed, this masks all too strongly the integrative power of the market that tends to inhibit rather than promote violent forms of crime.

The socialization achievement of the market is one reason, although certainly not the only reason, why robbery and theft tend to be carried out by younger offenders. With increasing market experience, such offenses start to be viewed as primitive and become increasingly less attractive. With increasing age, other ways of self-enrichment become available that are not excluded by the market but even intrinsic to it.

## 6    Prevention in the market through globalization

Fraud, corruption, and other economic crimes are generated by the market economy itself. They are not alien to it like theft or robbery. The premise is that we can expect a dominance of theft and robbery in developing countries, whereas fraud becomes increasingly dominant in more advanced industrial nations.

However, the premise is not that all industrial nations are inevitably exposed to an unstoppable increase in *systemic crime*. The following will briefly analyse the opposing forces in the market economy that also impose constraints on systemic offenses.

First, all offenders act within the economic context and therefore also think within this logic of maximizing profit. Although shaped by this, they are simultaneously embedded in a social context and act as '*embedded egoists*' (Granovetter, 1985, p. 487). And this is what grants relevance to normative and also moral preferences. Products that are traded or produced ecologically or under fair trade conditions find buyers—despite higher prices at times—precisely because of the moral considerations or even the preferences of many consumers. The same is true for the stock exchange. Companies are rated by special equity funds and rating agencies according to criteria of social and ecological sustainability (e.g., Dow Jones Sustainability Index).

In all eras, the market has been accompanied by morals and ethics backed up by criminal law. There is no time in the history of the civilized world when the economy has not been regulated. There has always been a *moral economy* (Karstedt, 2015). Not everything with which one could trade profitably has been considered to be legally permissible and acceptable to the majority of citizens. Examples are organ trafficking, drug trafficking, and child prostitution. A modern society uses a number of ways to domesticate the economic system and its medium, money. These indubitably tend to shoot past the target and view everything as being for sale and tradeable. People do not allow their idea of a community worth living in to be taken away: They wish for and live in a moral economy.

Regarding fraud, there are further preventive effects of the market economy:

*Fraud*: Trade does not thrive on stealing goods but on exchanging them. However, the risk of deception is inherent, and sometimes reveals a more or less intentional slip into punishable actions. Nonetheless, costs for fraudulent behaviour emerge on the market: these are not only the threat of prosecution but also the loss of trust, reputation, and eventually the loss of customers. The market also creates prevention mechanisms through the work of professional testers and an increase in customer evaluations that have now become far easier to perform and to access through the internet. Although markets do not possess self-healing powers for systemic offenses, as we know since the work of Akerlof (1970) and new institutionalism (North, 1990), states develop market mechanisms that make legal behaviour more attractive and thereby encourage it by working together within a legal regulatory framework, promoting education, and emphasizing important elements of a strong democracy.

Although the market generates systemically determined fraud risks, the competition between national economies also provides strong incentives to suppress each and every form of crime. For example, the condemnation of violence encourages the development of a successful market economy, so that in evolutionary terms, it is the less violent national economies that assert themselves in international and increasingly global trade (Elias, 1978). It was only by securing lengthy transport routes that large-scale trade across national borders became in any way possible. The success of economic alliances among cities as in the *Hanseatic League* came from establishing legal certainty and thereby a trust that was also based on guaranteeing non-violence between partners trading over great distances (e.g., Lloyd, 1991). Other ethnic or religiously based communities such as the Greeks living in the Ottoman Empire, the Amish people, or Jews were able to enjoy similar trading advantages. Their social exclusion encouraged an internal cohesion that established the necessary trust for their trade to flourish (Diekmann, 2007).

Not only violent crime but also fraud undermines the development of the generalized trust that contributes decisively to the prosperity of nations:

> "if widespread levels of citizen trust exists in society, this serves to reduce transaction costs in the market economy, it helps to minimize the deadweight burdens of enforcing and policing agreements, and holds down the diseconomies of fraud and theft. Thus, it can be argued that trust greatly facilitates economic and social relationships" (Whiteley, 2000, p. 443).

Hence, in the international competition between national economies, advantages accrue to all who concentrate on abolishing not only fraud but also violent crime. The resulting 'high-trust societies' are considered to be more open to innovation and more venturesome (Bussmann, 2016a; Whiteley, 2000). Although illegal markets also prosper through world trade and through the internationalization of markets in general (United Nations Office on Drugs and Crime, 2010), globalization is certainly an ally in the fight against crime. Countries with high crime rates have serious developmental problems, and globalization only increases their level of crime, whereas all countries with lower crime rates prosper more swiftly.

*Corruption*: This is also a systemic offense, because a company offering bribes gains a competitive advantage. The market itself creates an incentive for corruption. Nonetheless, bribing public or private customers is only a backup plan: a business model that is neither based on a convincing price–performance ratio nor on quality. This is why paying bribes generates additional costs and is advantageous only in the short-term. As with fraud, this shows that the interest of companies in corruption is also ambivalent.

From both an economic and a social perspective, the outcome of corruption is clearly negative. It undermines all structures of the state and destroys the independent rationality of such individual functional systems as the judiciary, politics, or the media. The economic growth of a national economy suffers compared to one that is less corrupt (Lambsdorff, 2007, p. 71f.). In contrast, a prosperous economy creates wealth that not only provides but also demands educational opportunities to address global competition. Better education introduces intergenerational cultural change (Inglehart and Welzel, 2005, p. 25) that makes people more aware of the causes of corruption and the damage it causes.

Moreover, the market economy supports a change in values. Although the market economy's values such as freedom, non-violence, equality, and tolerance in no way enforce a verdict on corruption, the market economy attacks the weak spots of corruption by providing a basis to promote the value of equality. Individualistic value orientations prevail and suppress those collectivistic orientations that favour nepotism, clientelism, and corruption. The idea of a free market economy is in latent conflict with high power distances and hierarchically structured societal formations. In developing countries, it is particularly the middle class that experiences this emancipatory effect of socio-economic development and revolts against corruption (Inglehart and Welzel, 2005, p. 25).

Although corruption is a systemic offense that is specifically promoted by competition, *globalization* paradoxically has an inhibiting effect on it: the lower the level of corruption in a national economy, the better it can assert itself on the world market. Globalization also generates losers and winners in the fight against corruption—even with the risk that economically underdeveloped countries may hardly be able to free themselves from corruption through their own efforts.

However, when combined with effective criminal prosecution, further market economy incentives for the implementation of a corresponding compliance system can develop. Major international companies, motivated particularly by the strict US FCPA, have begun to implement anti-corruption policies in their supply chains as well (Bussmann, 2015). On the whole, corruption will probably be pushed back much more quickly than fraud throughout the world.

## 7 Conclusion

This article could only sketch the significance of the market economy for trends in the types of crime. The market includes not only exchange but also deception. This deception is intrinsic to the system. Fraud and comparable systemic offenses are embedded inseparably in the way the functional system of the economy operates, and they are generated permanently by this system. There can be no doubt that the greed of criminals feeds on its rationality. However, our prosperity is based inseparably on self-interest. The market economy also does not condemn great wealth, so the greed of criminals cannot be distinguished from the unchecked striving for profit of others. It is only the path of illegality that separates the two.

Compared to theft and robbery, fraud is not an alien element in the market economy and the economy in general. The market economy possesses both supportive and preventive effects. It promotes the discrimination of certain offenses that do not retain the appearance of a legal business. In addition, its effect in imparting values is in no way negative: the rationale of the market socializes many of the values of our civilization such as freedom, non-violence, equality, and tolerance. In all, the market possesses an integrative power; its rationale and its mechanisms are themselves a socialization agency, and in no way just in a negative sense.

Although the self-healing powers of the market are too low for it to free itself particularly from its systemic criminality, it is once again market economy constraints that emerge when the focus shifts to the competition between nations. Together with a legal regulatory framework, the promotion of education, and an emphasis on major elements of a strong democracy, systemic offenses can also be repressed. Remarkably, it is globalization that is their enemy. The wealth of nations can unfold not only through a free market economy but also and primarily through the creation of generalized trust. This premise can already be found in *Adam Smith's* works. As important as it is to conceive the law as society's immune system in order to create trust, it would be wrong to underestimate the preventive and integrative mechanisms of the market economy. As foreign to each other as the rationalities of the functional systems of law and economics may be, they can complement each other to achieve effective crime prevention that neither system would have been capable of producing alone.

# References

Akerlof, George A. (1970) 'The market for "Lemons". Quality uncertainty and the market mechanism', in *The Quarterly Journal of Economics* 84 (3), p. 488.

Albanese, Jay S. (2005) 'Fraud. The characteristic crime of the twenty-first century', in *Trends Organ Crim* 8 (4), pp. 6–14.

Andermann, Kurt (Ed.) (1997) *"Raubritter" oder "Rechtschaffene vom Adel"? Aspekte von Politik, Friede und Recht im späten Mittelalter*, Sigmaringen, Thorbecke (Oberrheinische Studien, 14).

Bell, Daniel (1953) 'Crime as an American way of life', in *The Antioch Review* 13 (2), p. 131.

Bennett, Barbara; Conover, Douglas; O'Brian, Shaun; Advincula, Ross (2014) *Cash continues to play a key role in consumer spending: Evidence from the diary of consumer payment choice*, Federal Reserve Bank of San Francisco.

BKA PKS (2016) *Polizeiliche Kriminalstatistik 2016, Zeitreihen Übersicht Falltabellen*, Grundtabelle ab 1987.

Boyes, William J. (2011) *Managerial economics. Markets and the firm*, 2nd ed. Mason, Ohio, South-Western/Cengage Learning.

Bussmann, Kai-Detlef (2015) 'The impact of personality and company culture on company anti-corruption programmes', in Judith Gabriël van Erp, Wim Huisman, Gudrun Vande Walle (eds.) *The Routledge Handbook of white-collar and corporate crime in Europe*, with assistance of Joep Beckers, Abingdon, New York, Routledge Taylor & Francis Group, pp. 435–452.

Bussmann, Kai-Detlef (2016) *Grundlagen - Markt- und Alltagskriminalität*, München, Verlag Franz Vahlen (Wirtschaftskriminologie, / von Kai-D. Bussmann ; I).

Cable, John R.; Mueller, Dennis C. (2008) 'Testing for persistence of profits' differences across firms', in *International Journal of the Economics of Business* 15 (2).

Clark, J. R.; Lee, Dwight R. (2011) 'Markets and morality', in *CATO Journal* 31 (1), pp. 1–25.

Croson, R.T.A. (2005) 'Deception in economics experiments', in Caroline Gerschlager (ed.): *Deception in markets. An economic analysis*, Basingstoke, Palgrave Macmillan, pp. 113–130.

Currie, Elliott (1997) 'Market, crime and community', in *Theoretical Criminology* 1 (2), pp. 147–172.

Diekmann, Andreas (2007) 'Dimensionen des Sozialkapitals', in *Kölner Zeitschrift für Soziologie und Sozialpsychologie* Sonderheft 47, pp. 47–65.

Durkheim, Émile (1982) *The rules of sociological method and selected texts on sociology and its method*, New York, The Free Press (Theoretical traditions in the social sciences).

ECB (2011) *The use of euro banknotes – Results of two surveys among households and firms*, European Central Bank Monthly Bulletin.

Elias, Norbert (1978) *The civilizing process*, Oxford, Blackwell.

FBI National Incident-Based Reporting System (o.J.) 'UCR Publications. National Incident-Based Reporting System', *Federal Bureau of Investigations*.

FBI Uniform Crime Reporting (o.J.) 'Crime in the U.S. Crime Index Offenses Reported', *Federal Bureau of Investigations*.

Gerschlager, Caroline (Ed.) (2001a) *Expanding the economic concept of exchange. Deception, self-deception and illusions*, Boston, MA, s.l., Springer US.

Gerschlager, Caroline (2001b) 'Is (self)deception an indispensible quality of exchange. A new approach to Adams Smith's concept', in Caroline Gerschlager (ed.) *Expanding the economic concept of exchange. Deception, self-deception and illusions*, Boston, MA, s.l., Springer US, pp. 27–51.

Gerschlager, Caroline (Ed.) (2005) *Deception in markets. An economic analysis*, Basingstoke, Palgrave Macmillan.

Gosselin, Dominique; Gagnon, Sylvain; Stinchcombe, Arne; Joanisse, Mélanie (2010) 'Comparative optimism among drivers. An intergenerational portrait', in *Accident; analysis and prevention* 42 (2), pp. 734–740.

Granovetter, Mark (1985) 'Economic action and social structure. The problem of embeddedness', in *American Journal of Sociology* 91 (3), pp. 481–510.

Hagan, John (1994) *Crime and disrepute*, Thousand Oaks, Sage Publications (Sociology for a New Century Series).

Hagan, John; Hefler, Gerd; Classen, Gabriele; Boehnke, Klaus; Merkens, Hans (2000) 'Subterranean sources of subcultural delinquency, beyond the American dream', in Kai-D. Bussmann, Susanne Karstedt (eds.) *Social dynamics of crime and control. New theories for a world in transition*, Oxford, Portland, Or, Hart Pub (Oñati international series in law and society), pp. 27–52.

Hayek, Friedrich (1968) 'Competition as a discovery procedure', in *Quarterly Journal of Austrian Economics* 5 (3), pp. 9–23.

Heller, Henry (2011) *The birth of capitalism*, Pluto Press.

Inglehart, Ronald; Welzel, Christian (2005) *Modernization, cultural change, and democracy. The human development sequence*, Cambridge, Cambridge Univ. Press.

Karstedt, Susanne (2015) 'Charting Europe's moral economies', in Judith Gabriël van Erp, Wim Huisman, Gudrun Vande Walle (eds.) *The Routledge Handbook of white-collar and corporate crime in Europe*, with assistance of Joep Beckers, Abingdon, New York, Routledge Taylor & Francis Group, pp. 57–88.

Karstedt, Susanne (2016) 'Middle class crime: Moral economies between crime in the streets and crime in the suits', in Shanna R. van Slyke, Michael L. Benson, Francis T. Cullen (eds.) *The Oxford handbook of white-collar crime*, first edition, New York, Oxford University Press (The Oxford handbooks in criminology and criminal justice), pp. 168–200.

Karstedt, Susanne; Farrall, Stephen (2006) 'The moral economy of everyday crime', in *The British Journal of Criminology* 46 (6), pp. 1011–1036.

Katz, Claudio J. (1993) 'Karl Marx on the transition from feudalism to capitalism', in *Theor Soc* 22 (3), pp. 363–389.

Lambsdorff, Johann (2007) *The institutional economics of corruption and reform. Theory, evidence and policy*, Cambridge, Cambridge Univ. Press.

Lloyd, Terrence Henry (1991) *England and the German Hanse, 1157-1611. A study of their trade and commercial diplomacy*, Cambridge, Cambridge University Press.

Luhmann, Niklas (1989) *Die Wirtschaft der Gesellschaft*, 2. Aufl., Frankfurt/M., Suhrkamp.

Luhmann, Niklas (1997) *Die Gesellschaft der Gesellschaft*, 1. Aufl., Frankfurt am Main, Suhrkamp.

Messner, Steven F.; Rosenfeld, Richard (2007) *Crime and the American dream*, 4th ed. Belmont, CA, Wadsworth Cengage Learning.

North, Douglass Cecil (1990) *Institutions, institutional change and economic performance*, Cambridge, Cambridge Univ. Press (Political economy of institutions and decisions).

Oberwittler, Dietrich (2012) 'Delinquenz und Kriminalität als soziales in Problem', in Günter Albrecht, Axel Groenemeyer (eds.) *Handbuch soziale Probleme*. 2. überarb. Aufl., Wiesbaden, Springer VS, pp. 772–860.

Olson, Mancur (2000) *Power and prosperity. Outgrowing communist and capitalist dictatorships*, New York, Basic Books.

Piketty, Thomas (2014) *Capital in the twenty-first century*, Cambridge Massachusetts, The Belknap Press of Harvard University Press.

Pinker, Steven (2011) *The better angels of our nature. A history of violence and humanity*, London, Penguin.

Rogoff, Kenneth S. (2016) *The curse of cash*, Princeton, Princeton University Press.

Schumpeter, Joseph A. (1942) *Capitalism, socialism and democracy*, New York, Harper & Brothers.

Shover, Neal; Hochstetler, Andrew (2006) *Choosing white-collar crime*, Cambridge, Cambridge University Press (Cambridge studies in criminology).

Simmel, Georg (1989 <1907>) *Philosophie des Geldes* [The Philosophy of money], New York, Routledge.

Smith, Adam (1978) *The Wealth of Nations*, London, Wordsworth.

Stiglitz, Joseph E. (2012) *The price of inequality. How today's divided society endangers our future*, New York, Norton & Company.

Swedberg, Richard (2003) *Principles of economic sociology*, Princeton, Princeton Univ. Press.

United Nations Office on Drugs and Crime (2010) *The globalization of crime. A transnational organized crime threat assesment*, UN.

Weber, Max (1985 <1968>) *Wirtschaft und Gesellschaft* [Economy and society: an outline of interpretive sociology], vol. 3. New York, Bedminster Press.

White, Harrison C. (1981) 'Where do markets come from?', in *American Journal of Sociology* 87 (3), pp. 517–547.

Whiteley, Paul F. (2000) 'Economic growth and social capital', in *Political Studies* 48 (3), pp. 443–466.

# About the authors

### ASNER, MARCUS
Partner at Arnold & Porter Kaye Scholer LLP, USA. Trial lawyer and Co-Chair of the firm's Anti-Corruption practice. He has extensive experience with investigations and prosecutions involving alleged violations of the Foreign Corrupt Practices Act (FCPA), and cases involving public corruption, healthcare fraud, financial fraud and money laundering, cyber crime, corporate espionage, data breaches, tax fraud, scientific misconduct, and environmental and natural resources crime. Mr. Asner served on the President's Advisory Council on Wildlife Trafficking.

### BUSSMANN, KAI-D.
Professor of Penal Law and Criminology at the Martin Luther University of Halle-Wittenberg. He is a member of the Advisory Board of the Business Law Association (WISTEV). His research interests lie in the field of economic crime (e.g., corruption, fraud, industrial espionage, cartel law infringements and money laundering). Professor Bussmann conducted surveys on the evaluation of compliance programmes with a particular focus on company cultures and national cultures. On behalf of the German Ministry of Finance (BMF) he conducted two surveys on the prevalence and risks of money laundering in Germany.

### DANNECKER, GERHARD
Professor of Criminal Law and Law of Criminal Procedures and former Director of the Institute for German, European and International Criminal Law and Law of Criminal Procedures of Heidelberg University, Germany. He is a member of the Presidium of the Association of European Criminal Law and of the Editorial Board at the journals: NZWiSt (Neue Zeitschrift für Wirtschafts-, Steuer- und Unternehmensstrafrecht), „Rivista Trimestrale di Diritto Penale dell'Economica", „Revista de Concorrência e Regulação" and „ELTE Law Journal". Professor Dannecker is also a member of the Main Editorial Advisory Board of the "European Financial Services Law" in London and of the scientific committee of the internetportal disCRIME.

© Springer Fachmedien Wiesbaden GmbH, part of Springer Nature 2020
M. Pohlmann et al. (eds.), *Bribery, Fraud, Cheating*, Organization, Management and Crime – Organisation, Management und Kriminalität,
https://doi.org/10.1007/978-3-658-29062-7

## DE SANCTIS, FAUSTO

Federal Appellate Judge at Brazil's Federal Court for the 3th region with jurisdiction over the states of São Paulo and Mato Grosso do Sul. He holds a doctorate in Criminal Law from Sao Paulo's School of Law University (USP). He was selected to handle a specialized federal court created in Brazil for complex cases involving financial crimes and money laundering offenses. He has also been an Advisory Council member at the American University Washington College of Law on its program for Judicial and Legal Studies Brazil – United States.

## GEBRAN NETO, JOÃO PEDRO

Federal Judge at the Federal Regional Court of Appeals for the fourth region. He has a master's degree in Constitutional Law and and a post graduation in Penal and Penal Procedural Sciences from the Federal University of Paraná (UFPR). He is also a law professor teaching post-graduation courses at the Brazilian universities EMESCAM and UniCuritiba. He was awarded with the title of *doctor honoris causa* in Heath Law from the Faculty EMESCAM.

## GEBHARDT, CHRISTIANE

Vice President and Head Global Initiatives at the Malik Institute in Switzerland – an internationally renowned organization for industry, university and government studies as well as for consulting projects that foster an integrated management approach. She obtained her doctorate at Giessen University (Political Sciences) and carried out research at Chicago University and the MIT in the USA. She teaches master courses in management and innovation studies at Heidelberg University.

## GRAEFF, PETER

Professor of Sociology and Empirical Social Sciences at Kiel University and a Fellow of the International Sociological Association, where he serves on the committee on "Logic and Methodology in Sociology". He is also a member of the American Sociological Association (ASA), the International Institute of Sociology (ISS), and the German Sociological Association (GSA). He also runs the scientific working group of Transparency International in Germany, which has published on the corruption case of Siemens (2009) and on disciplinary perspectives on corruption (2012). His research interests include positive and negative aspects of social capital, deviance and social networks (corruption, trust, and volunteering). Currently, he and his research team examine the governmental capabilities for fighting corruption.

HUSTUS, LUDMILA

Research Associate at the Institute of Criminology (Prof. Dr. Dieter Dölling) and at the Institute for German, European and International Criminal Law and Law of Criminal Procedure (Prof. Dr. Gerhard Dannecker) at Heidelberg University, Germany. After completing her education as a piano teacher, accompanist and chamber musician in the Ukraine she studied law in Germany at Heidelberg University (Magistra of Law) and at Goethe University Frankfurt (Magistra Legum of European and International Business Law). She earned her degree in administrative sciences at Speyer University, majoring in Public Management and State and Economy (Magistra rerum publicarum). Furthermore, she is a graduate of the Academy of Food Law of the Research Centre for German and European Food and Feed Law at Philipps University of Marburg and has completed additional training in Journalism and Law. She is a Fellow of the European Law Institute, Belgium.

YANG, JIANYUAN

Partner at Fangda Partners, China. She specializes in regulatory compliance, government enforcement, cybersecurity, and data privacy. She has extensive experience in complex investigations that involve legal issues in a broad range of areas of law and concurrent proceedings before different authorities. Furthermore, she has a lot of experience assisting the establishment, enhancement, and implementation of anti-corruption compliance policies for various types of companies.

## KIRKPATRICK, DAVID

Head of Department for Economic Crimes at the Public Prosecutor's Office Darmstadt, Germany. He served as Head of the Central Office for the Fight against Organized Crime at the Attorney Generalship Frankfurt for many years, before he became the Head of Department for Economic Crimes at the Public Prosecutor's Office Darmstadt. Moreover, he has served as a lecturer at the University of Applied Sciences in Wiesbaden, as well as in twinning projects with Serbia and Albania on criminal procedural issues in the fight against organized crime and on the enforcement of laws against money laundering.

## KLEINEWIESE, JULIA

Researcher and lecturer at the Department of Social Sciences, Kiel University. She is currently completing her Ph.D. in sociology and holds a double-master's degree in international sociology and British/American studies. Her research focuses on social cohesion, including its positive (e.g., work efficiency) and negative (e.g., corruption) effects, quantitative sociology and volunteering.

## KLEINHEMPEL, MATTHIAS

Professor at IAE Business School and its Center for Governance and Transparency, where he currently teaches MBA and Executive Education courses. His research focuses on corporate governance, anti-corruption, compliance, and the organization of international companies in Latin America. He also served in a number of positions at Siemens: He was President and CEO of Siemens Venezuela and, simultaneously, CFO for Siemens in the Andean Region; CEO of the Power Cables Division with responsibility for the worldwide business; and CEO and President of Siemens in Argentina, simultaneously serving as CFO in the Mercosur Region. In Argentina, he is part of the UN-PRME Working Group on Anti-Corruption: "Developing Anti-Corruption Guidelines for Curriculum Change".

## KLINKHAMMER, JULIAN

Research Associate at Heidelberg University's Max Weber Institute of Sociology. Having studied sociology, political science and psychology at Heidelberg University, he completed his doctorate with a dissertation on the careers and mindsets of top managers in Switzerland. His research interests cover comparative capitalism research, economic and corporate crime, as well as career and labor market research. Since 2013, he has been member of the European working group on Organizational Crime (EUROC).

## MANCUSO, WAGNER PRALON

Professor of Political Science at the School of Arts, Sciences and Humanities of the University of Sao Paulo (USP). His main field of interest is the interaction between business people and the state in Brazil and other countries. He is particularly interested in two kinds of interaction that are extremely common in Brazil: lobbying (through companies and/or business associations) and legal and illegal campaign financing.

## POHLMANN, MARKUS

Professor of Sociology at Max-Weber-Institute of Heidelberg University and currently Fellow of the Marsilius Center for Advanced Studies. Prior to his current position, he was Professor at the Friedrich-Alexander-University in Erlangen, and Research Director of the ISO-Institute in Saarbrucken, Germany. His research areas span organizational sociology, the sociology of management, and economic sociology. Currently, he leads the research groups for Organizational Deviance Studies and International Management Studies.

## RESKI, PETRA

Journalist and writer. Since 1989, she writes about Italy and about the mafia. She published numerous novels and books, among them three books on the mafia, one of which was blackened at the behest of German courts. After being exposed to considerable objections to her publications on the business of the mafia in Germany, she now transfers her knowledge into fiction. She has received several awards for her reports and books, most recently as *Reporter of the Year* in Germany. In Italy, she received the *Premio Civitas* and the *Amalfi Coast Media Award* for her continuous anti-mafia commitment.

## SCARPINATO, ROBERTO

Prosecutor General in Palermo. Since 1989 he has been involved in investigations into mafia criminality, corruption, and other economic crimes. He has been part of the Antimafia Pool, collaborating with Giovanni Falcone and Paolo Borsellino, the magistrates assassinated by the mafia in 1992. He dealt with many of the most important legal actions relating to mafia and power relations in post-war Italy. He also conducted investigations into the motives and political backgrounds of the 1992 and 1993 massacres, and on the relationship between the mafia and misguided parts of the freemasonry.

## SCHRÖDER, THOMAS

Postdoctoral Researcher at the chair for Criminal Law and Law of Criminal Procedures with a focus on European and international aspects in Heidelberg, Germany (Prof. Dr. Gerhard Dannecker). His research projects focus on anti-corruption law, constitutional aspects of criminal law, and the law of criminal procedure. He served as a legal research fellow at the Göttingen Institute of Criminal Law and Justice and earned his Ph.D. at Heidelberg University in 2011. He worked also, from 2010 until 2013, as a lawyer with the international law firm Clifford Chance at its Frankfurt office where he was a member of the team focusing on white collar crime and, subsequently, joined Deutsche Bahn Group (2013-2014) as an inhouse lawyer and compliance manager.

## SENZ, ANJA

Professor of contemporary Chinese economy, politics, and society at Heidelberg University. She studied political science, sociology, anthropology, and Chinese language at the University of Trier and the Sun-Yatsen University in Guangzhou. For many years, she was a research fellow at the Institute of East Asia Studies and managing director of the Confucius-Institute Metropolis Ruhr, both at the University of Duisburg-Essen. She gained extensive work experience in Hong Kong, Nepal, India, and Korea. Her research on China focuses on local politics, institutional change, political decision processes, ethnic minorities, and Chinese foreign affairs.

## SHI, XIUYIN

Professor of Sociology at the Chinese Academy of Social Sciences (CASS) in Beijing, China, as well as President of the Chinese Association of Work and Labor. His areas of research are labor relations, civil society, civil rights, labor consciousness, and labor organization.

## SCHULTZE, CHRISTIN

Research Assistant at the Institute for German, European and International Criminal Law and Law of Criminal Procedure at Heidelberg University (Prof. Dr. Gerhard Dannecker) and trainee lawyer at the district court of Heidelberg. She studied law along with a supplementary program in European Law at the Julius-Maximilians-Universität Würzburg.

## VALARINI, ELIZANGELA

Postdoctoral Researcher and Lecturer at Max-Weber-Institute of Heidelberg University. She studied psychology at Universidade Estadual de Maringa, Brazil. At Heidelberg University, she completed her master's degree and her doctorate with a dissertation on career patterns and collective mindsets of Brazilian top managers in the context of globalization. Her current research project focuses on corporate crime and systemic corruption in Brazil.

## VERREL, TORSTEN

Professor of Criminology, Juvenile Criminal Law and the Penal System, and Director of the Institute of Criminology at the University of Bonn. He is member of the Standing Committee on Organ Transplantation and the Supervisory and Control Committee of the German Medical Association since 2006, and of the Ethics Commissions of both the Medical Faculty and the Institute of Psychology of the University of Bonn since 2004 and 2009.